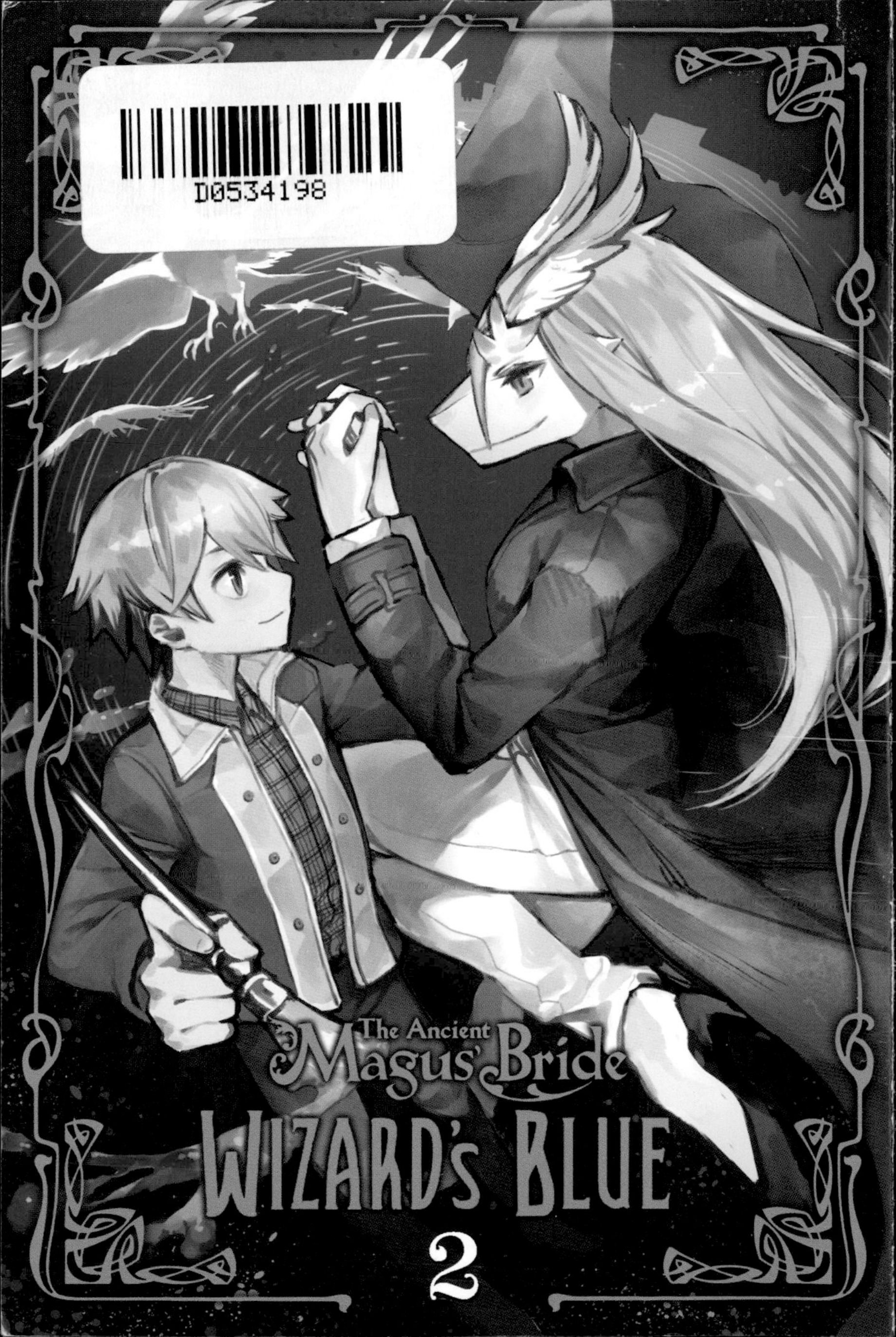

The Ancient
Magus' Bride
WIZARD's BLUE
2

The Ancient Magus' Bride
WIZARD's BLUE
2

Leçon 5
3

Leçon 6
35

Leçon 7
79

Leçon 8
115

Leçon 9
147

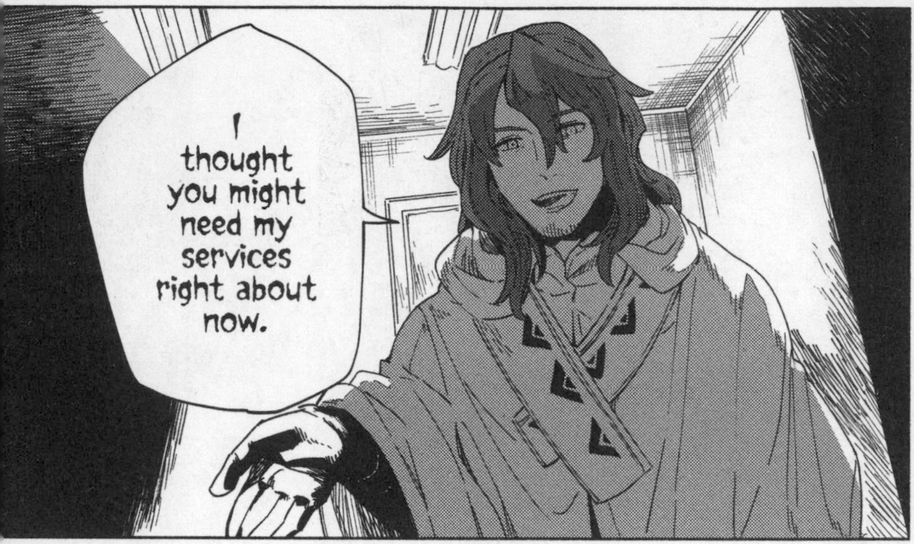
I thought you might need my services right about now.

Leçon 5

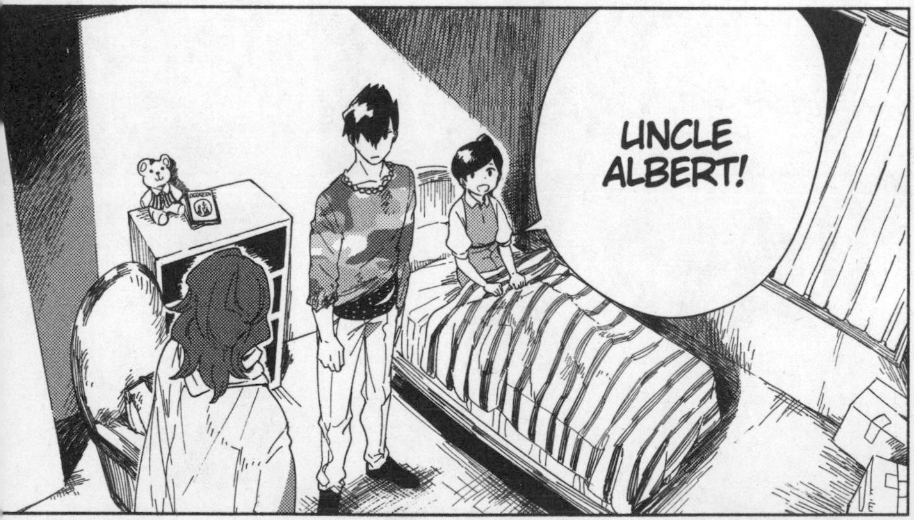
UNCLE ALBERT!

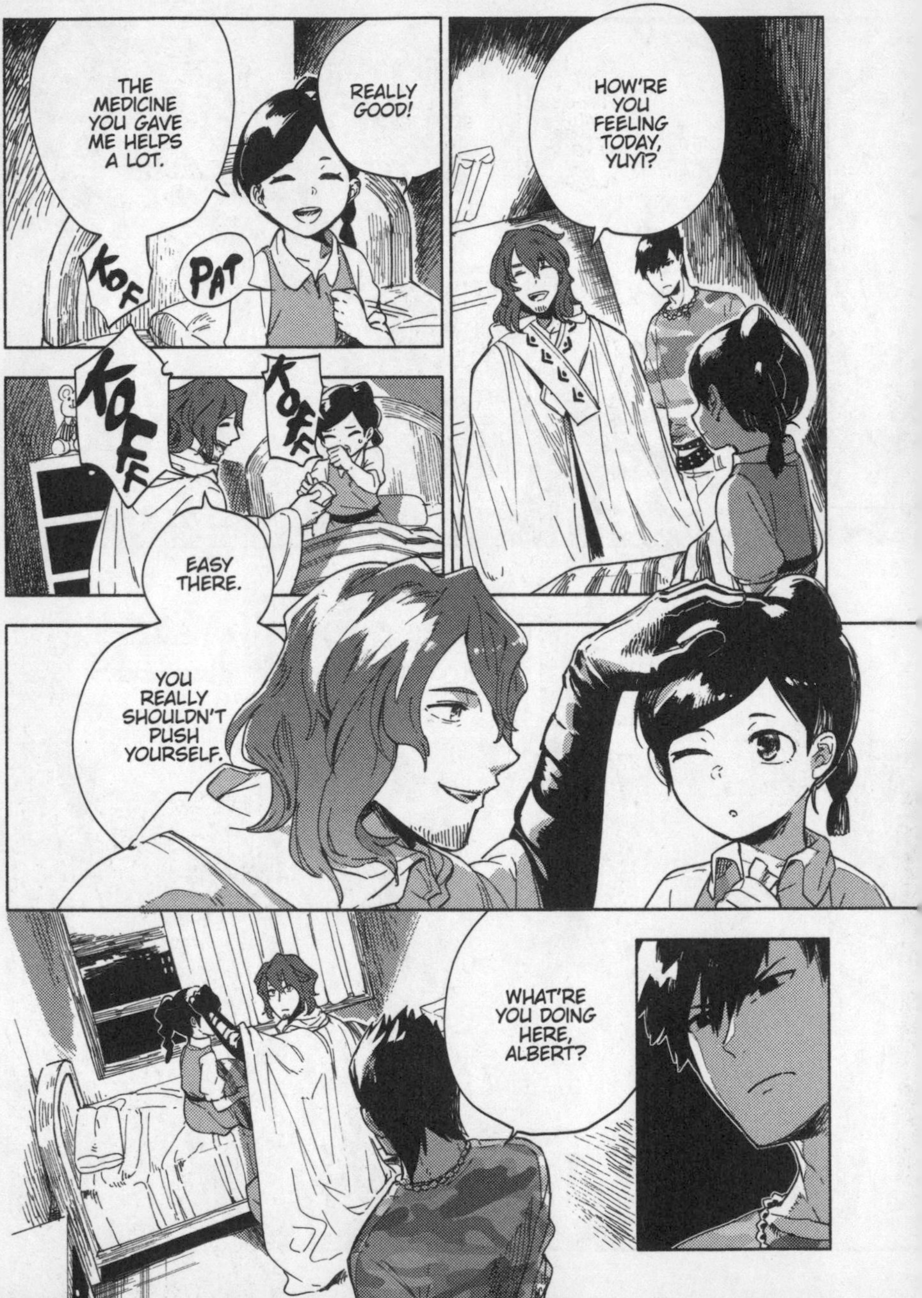
HOW'RE YOU FEELING TODAY, YUYI?
REALLY GOOD!
THE MEDICINE YOU GAVE ME HELPS A LOT.
PAT
KOF
KOFF
KOFF
EASY THERE.
YOU REALLY SHOULDN'T PUSH YOURSELF.
WHAT'RE YOU DOING HERE, ALBERT?

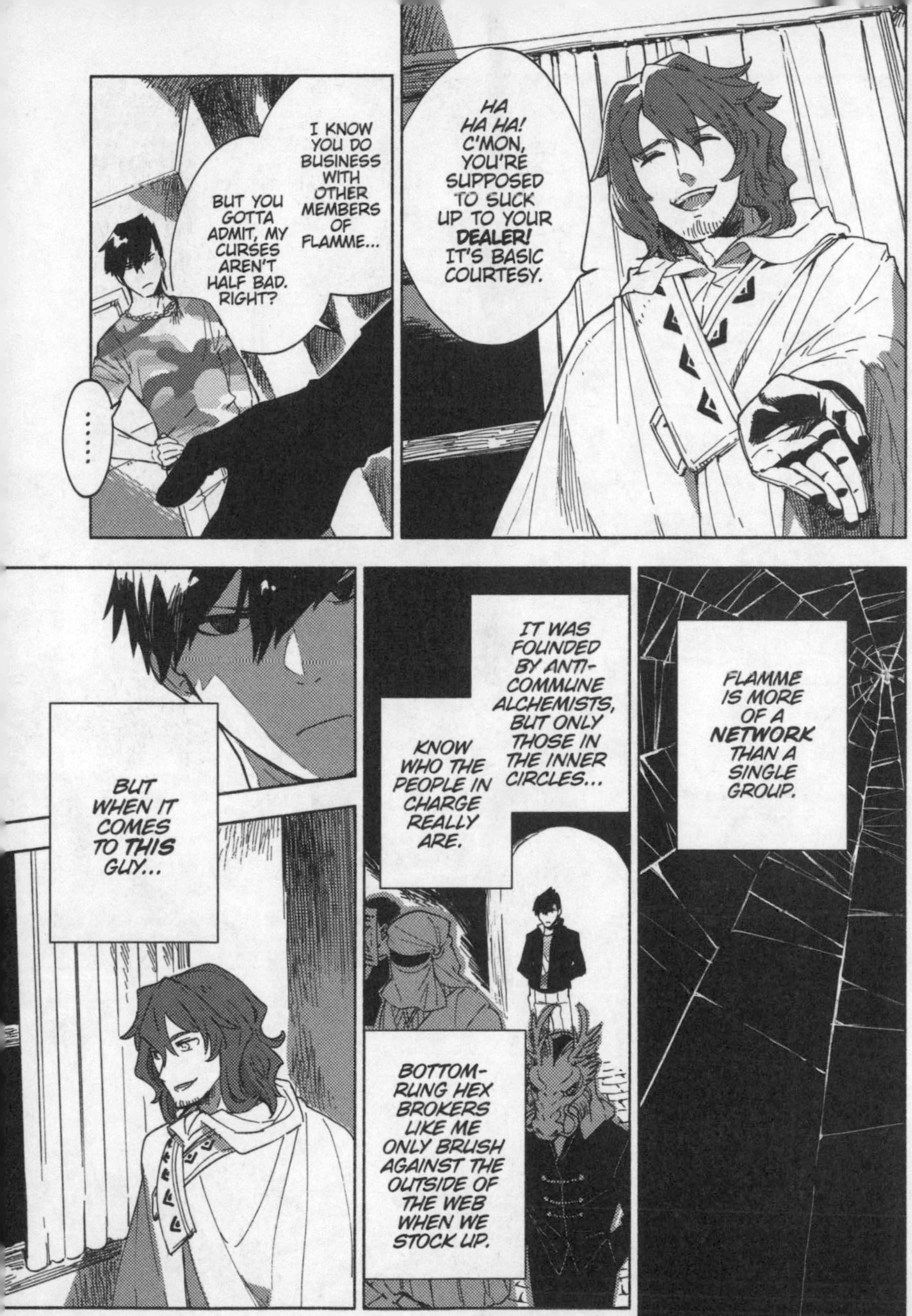
HA HA HA! C'MON, YOU'RE SUPPOSED TO SUCK UP TO YOUR **DEALER!** IT'S BASIC COURTESY.
I KNOW YOU DO BUSINESS WITH OTHER MEMBERS OF FLAMME...
BUT YOU GOTTA ADMIT, MY CURSES AREN'T HALF BAD. RIGHT?
......
FLAMME IS MORE OF A **NETWORK** THAN A SINGLE GROUP.
IT WAS FOUNDED BY ANTI-COMMUNE ALCHEMISTS, BUT ONLY THOSE IN THE INNER CIRCLES...
KNOW WHO THE PEOPLE IN CHARGE REALLY ARE.
BOTTOM-RUNG HEX BROKERS LIKE ME ONLY BRUSH AGAINST THE OUTSIDE OF THE WEB WHEN WE STOCK UP.
BUT WHEN IT COMES TO **THIS** GUY...

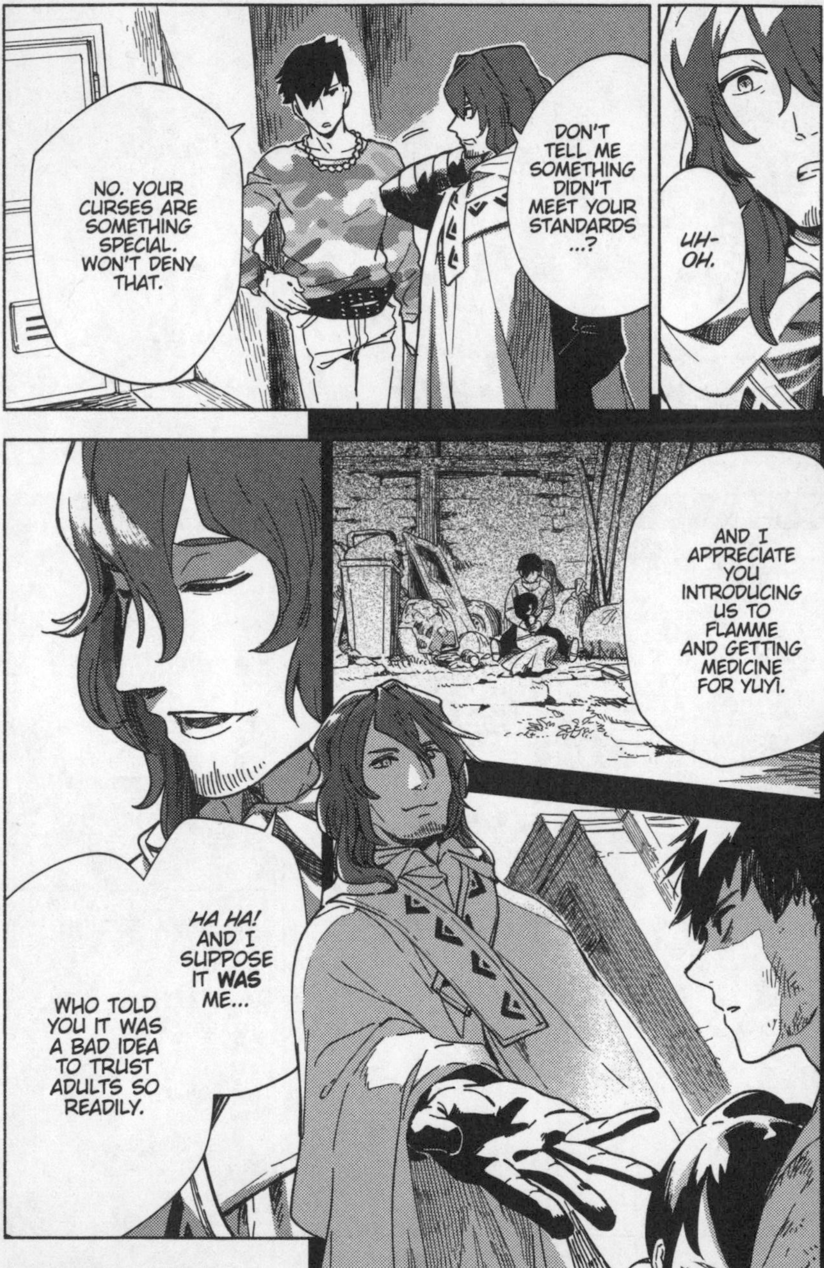
UH-OH.
DON'T TELL ME SOMETHING DIDN'T MEET YOUR STANDARDS ...?
NO. YOUR CURSES ARE SOMETHING SPECIAL. WON'T DENY THAT.
AND I APPRECIATE YOU INTRODUCING US TO FLAMME AND GETTING MEDICINE FOR YUYI.
HA HA! AND I SUPPOSE IT WAS ME...
WHO TOLD YOU IT WAS A BAD IDEA TO TRUST ADULTS SO READILY.

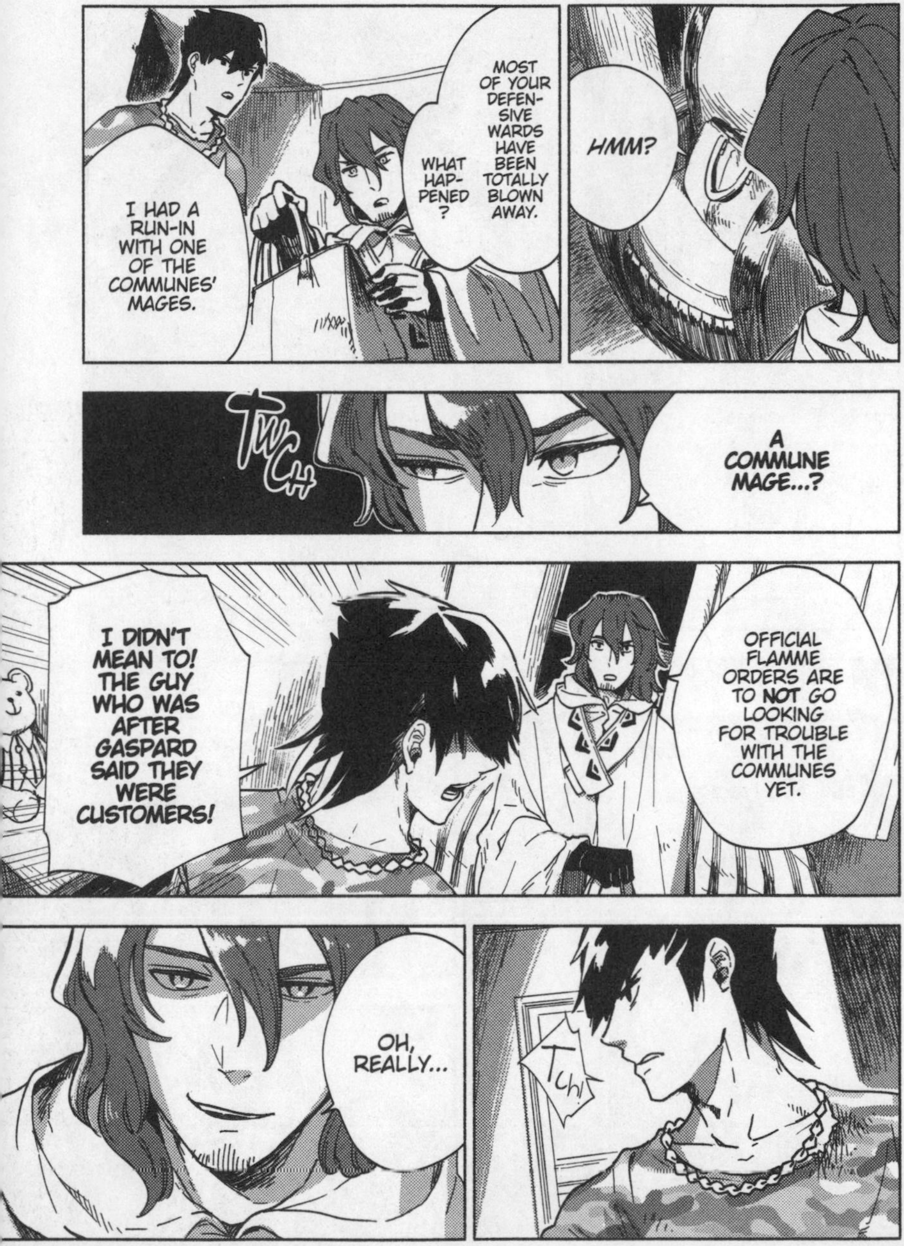
HMM?
MOST OF YOUR DEFEN-SIVE WARDS HAVE BEEN TOTALLY BLOWN AWAY.
WHAT HAP-PENED?
I HAD A RUN-IN WITH ONE OF THE COMMUNES' MAGES.
A COMMUNE MAGE...?
TWITCH
OFFICIAL FLAMME ORDERS ARE TO NOT GO LOOKING FOR TROUBLE WITH THE COMMUNES YET.
I DIDN'T MEAN TO! THE GUY WHO WAS AFTER GASPARD SAID THEY WERE CUSTOMERS!
Tch!
OH, REALLY...

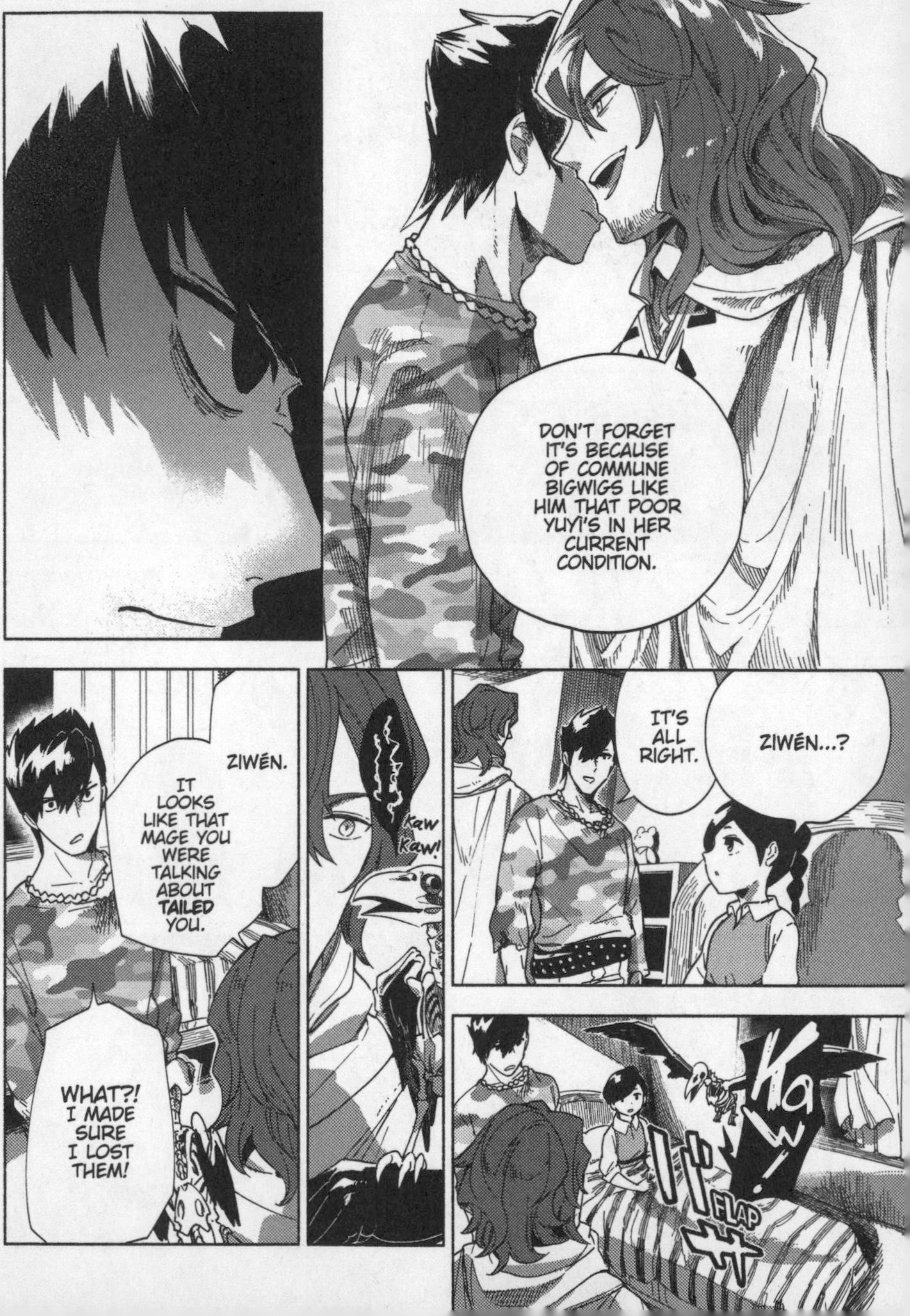
DON'T FORGET IT'S BECAUSE OF COMMUNE BIGWIGS LIKE HIM THAT POOR YUYÍ'S IN HER CURRENT CONDITION.
ZIWÉN...?
IT'S ALL RIGHT.
KAW!
FLAP
Kaw Kaw!
ZIWÉN.
IT LOOKS LIKE THAT MAGE YOU WERE TALKING ABOUT **TAILED** YOU.
WHAT?! I MADE SURE I LOST THEM!

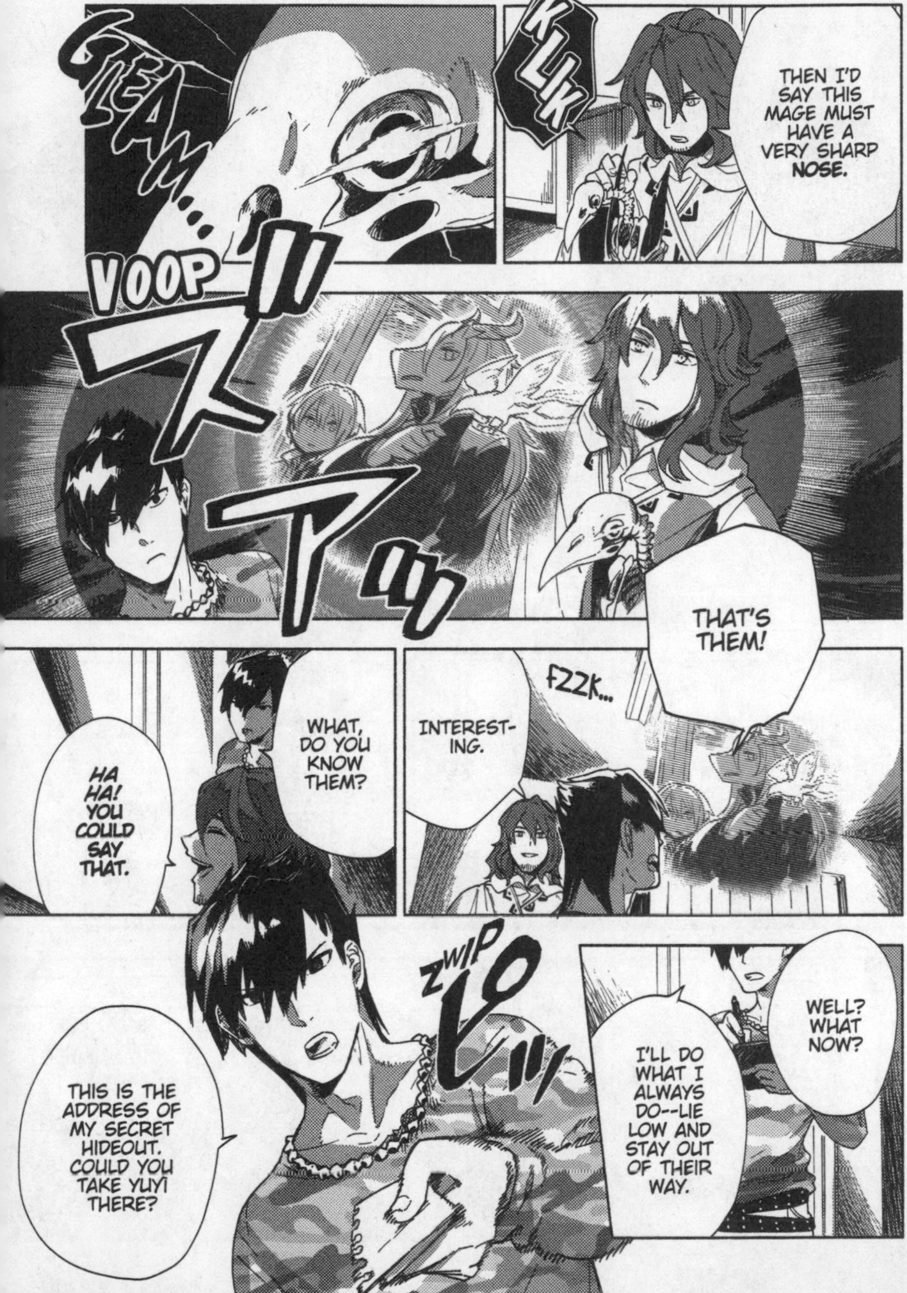
KLIK
THEN I'D SAY THIS MAGE MUST HAVE A VERY SHARP NOSE.
GLEAM...
VOOP
THAT'S THEM!
FZZK...
INTEREST-ING.
WHAT, DO YOU KNOW THEM?
HA HA! YOU COULD SAY THAT.
WELL? WHAT NOW?
I'LL DO WHAT I ALWAYS DO--LIE LOW AND STAY OUT OF THEIR WAY.
ZWIP
THIS IS THE ADDRESS OF MY SECRET HIDEOUT. COULD YOU TAKE YUYI THERE?

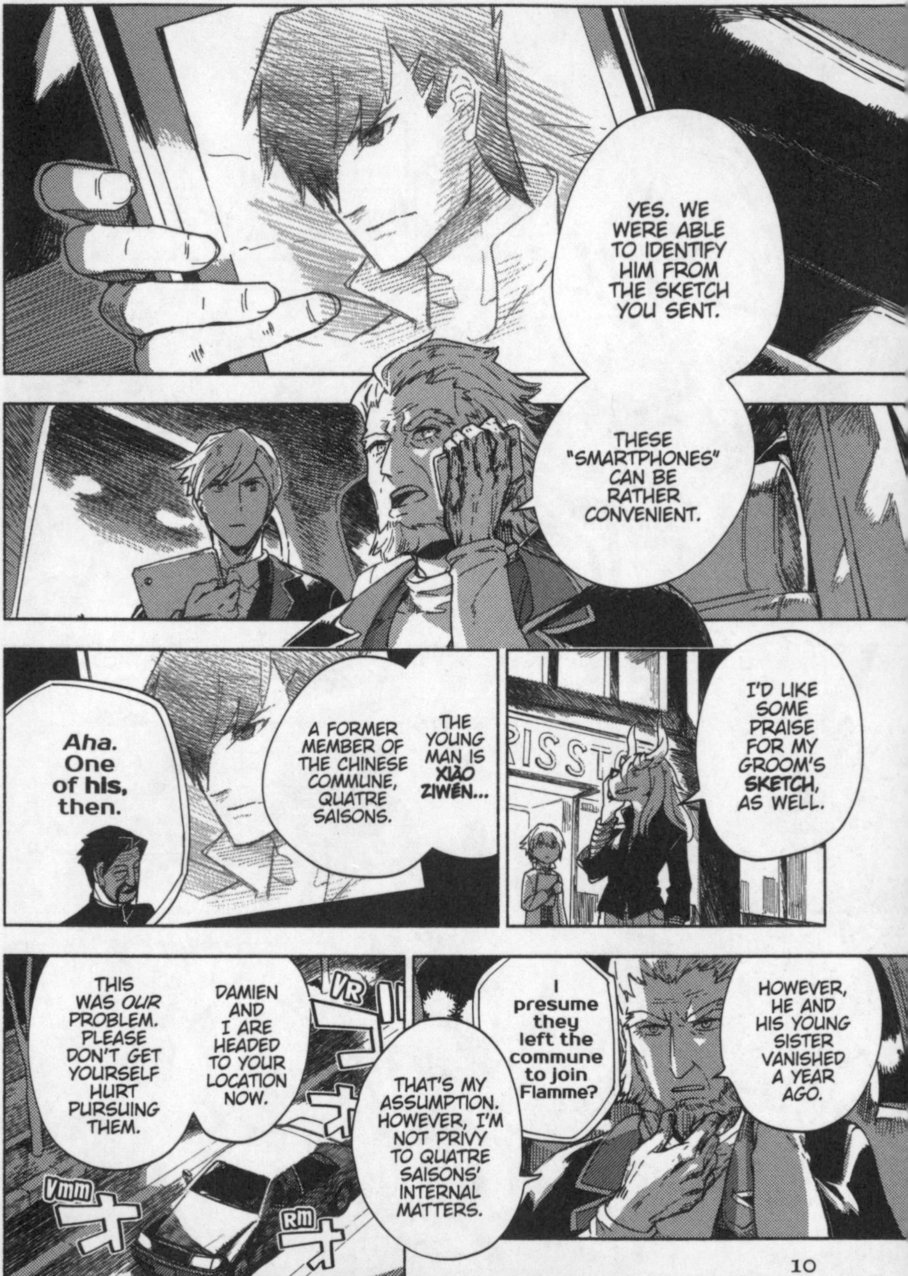
YES. WE WERE ABLE TO IDENTIFY HIM FROM THE SKETCH YOU SENT.
THESE "SMARTPHONES" CAN BE RATHER CONVENIENT.
I'D LIKE SOME PRAISE FOR MY GROOM'S **SKETCH**, AS WELL.
THE YOUNG MAN IS **XIÀO ZIWÉN**...
A FORMER MEMBER OF THE CHINESE COMMUNE, QUATRE SAISONS.
Aha. One of his, then.
HOWEVER, HE AND HIS YOUNG SISTER VANISHED A YEAR AGO.
I presume they left the commune to join Flamme?
THAT'S MY ASSUMPTION. HOWEVER, I'M NOT PRIVY TO QUATRE SAISONS' INTERNAL MATTERS.
DAMIEN AND I ARE HEADED TO YOUR LOCATION NOW.
THIS WAS *OUR* PROBLEM. PLEASE DON'T GET YOURSELF HURT PURSUING THEM.
VR
Vmm
RM

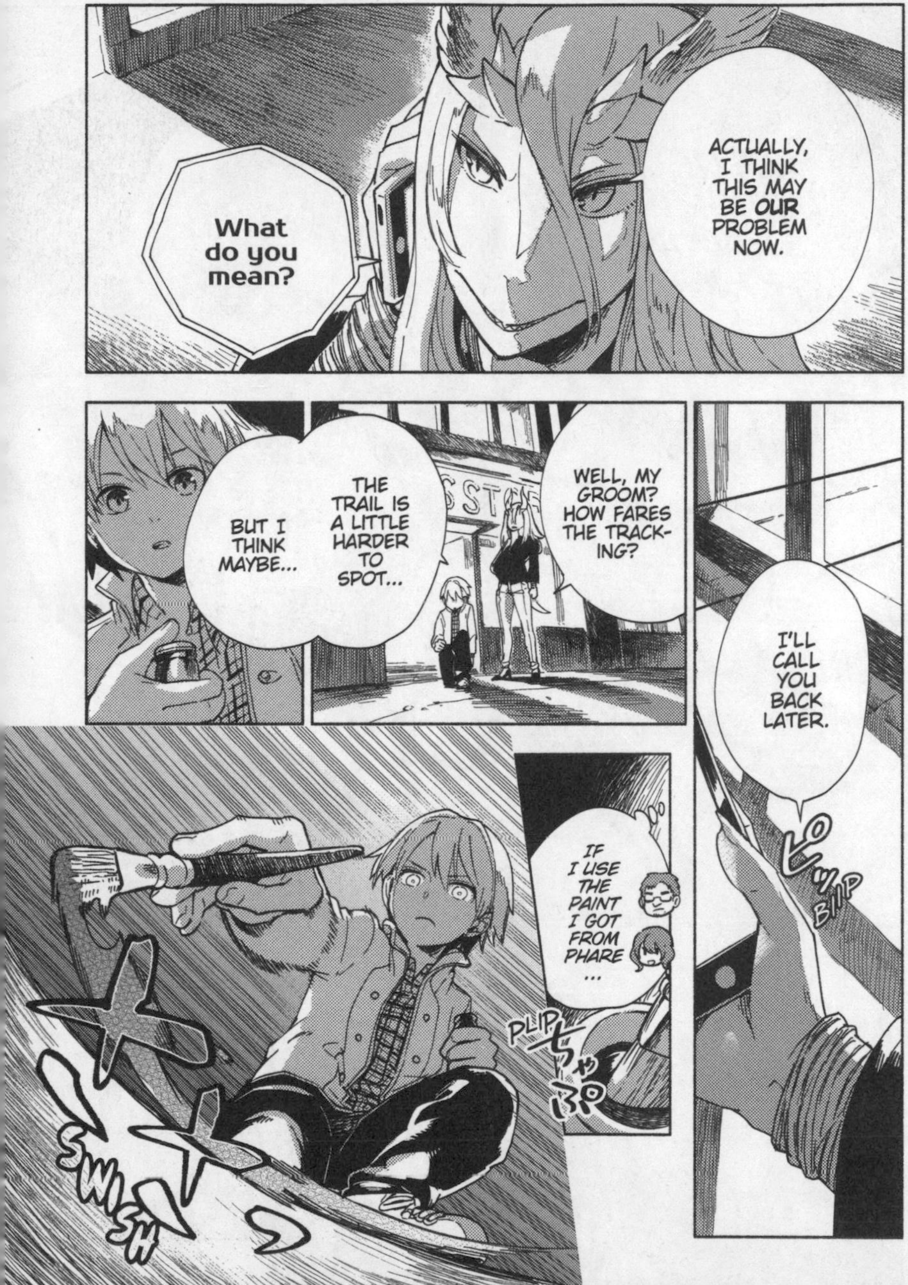
ACTUALLY, I THINK THIS MAY BE **OUR** PROBLEM NOW.
What do you mean?
I'LL CALL YOU BACK LATER.
BIIP
WELL, MY GROOM? HOW FARES THE TRACK-ING?
THE TRAIL IS A LITTLE HARDER TO SPOT...
BUT I THINK MAYBE...
IF I USE THE PAINT I GOT FROM PHARE ...
PLIP
SWISH

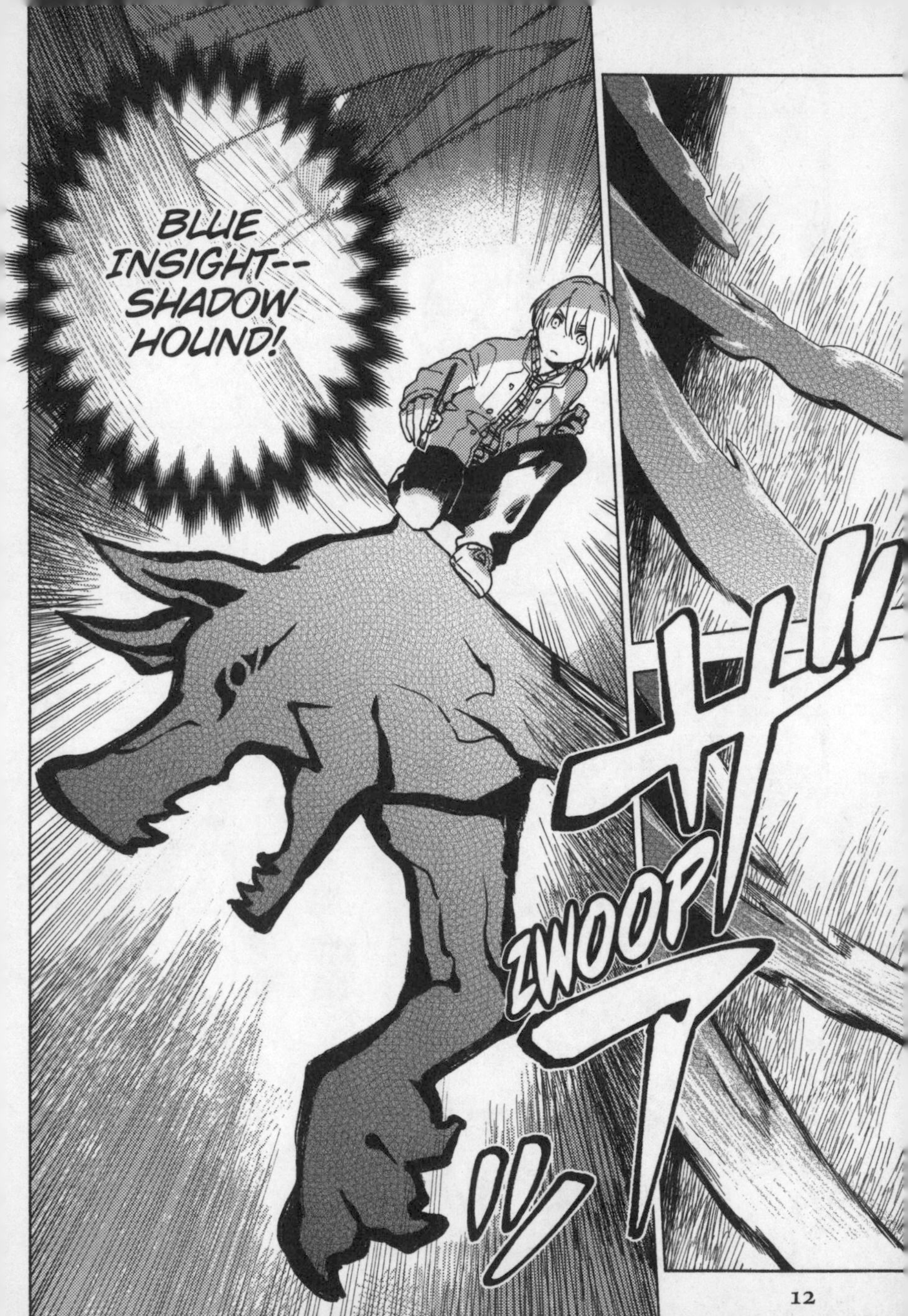
BLUE INSIGHT-- SHADOW HOUND!
ZWOOP

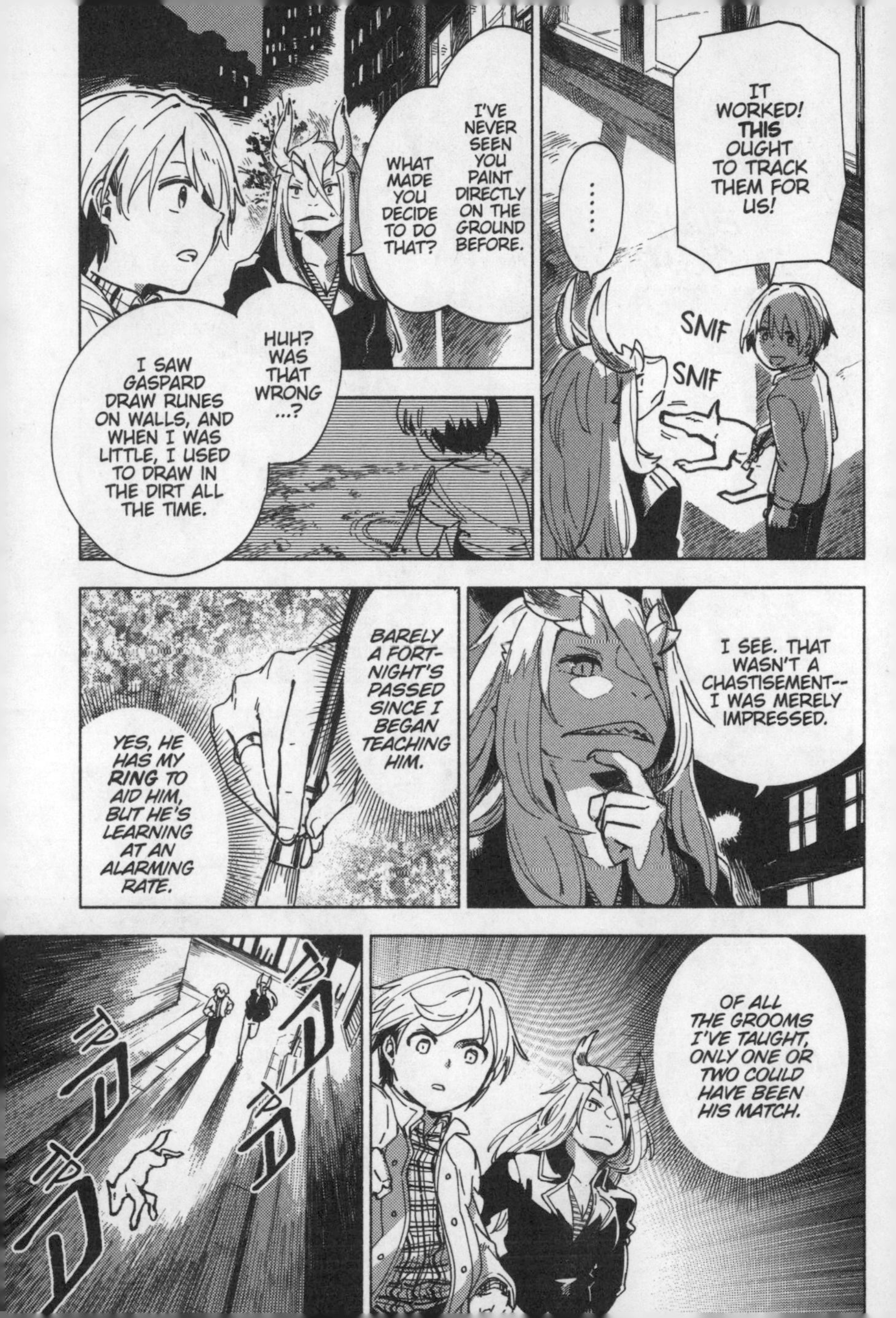
IT WORKED! THIS OUGHT TO TRACK THEM FOR US!
......
SNIF
SNIF
I'VE NEVER SEEN YOU PAINT DIRECTLY ON THE GROUND BEFORE.
WHAT MADE YOU DECIDE TO DO THAT?
HUH? WAS THAT WRONG ...?
I SAW GASPARD DRAW RUNES ON WALLS, AND WHEN I WAS LITTLE, I USED TO DRAW IN THE DIRT ALL THE TIME.
I SEE. THAT WASN'T A CHASTISEMENT-- I WAS MERELY IMPRESSED.
BARELY A FORTNIGHT'S PASSED SINCE I BEGAN TEACHING HIM.
YES, HE HAS MY RING TO AID HIM, BUT HE'S LEARNING AT AN ALARMING RATE.
OF ALL THE GROOMS I'VE TAUGHT, ONLY ONE OR TWO COULD HAVE BEEN HIS MATCH.

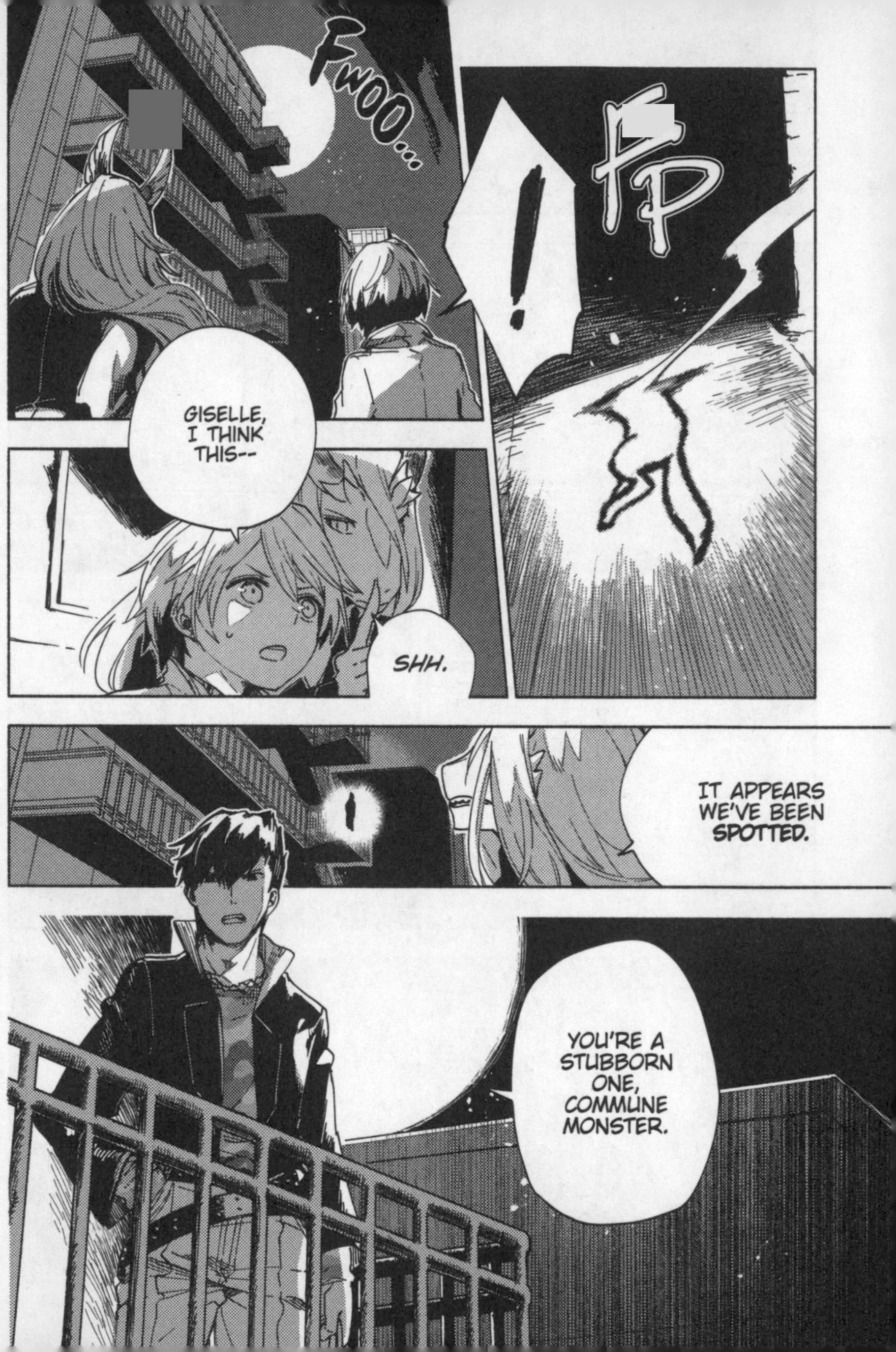
FP
!
FWOO...
GISELLE, I THINK THIS--
SHH.
IT APPEARS WE'VE BEEN SPOTTED.
YOU'RE A STUBBORN ONE, COMMUNE MONSTER.

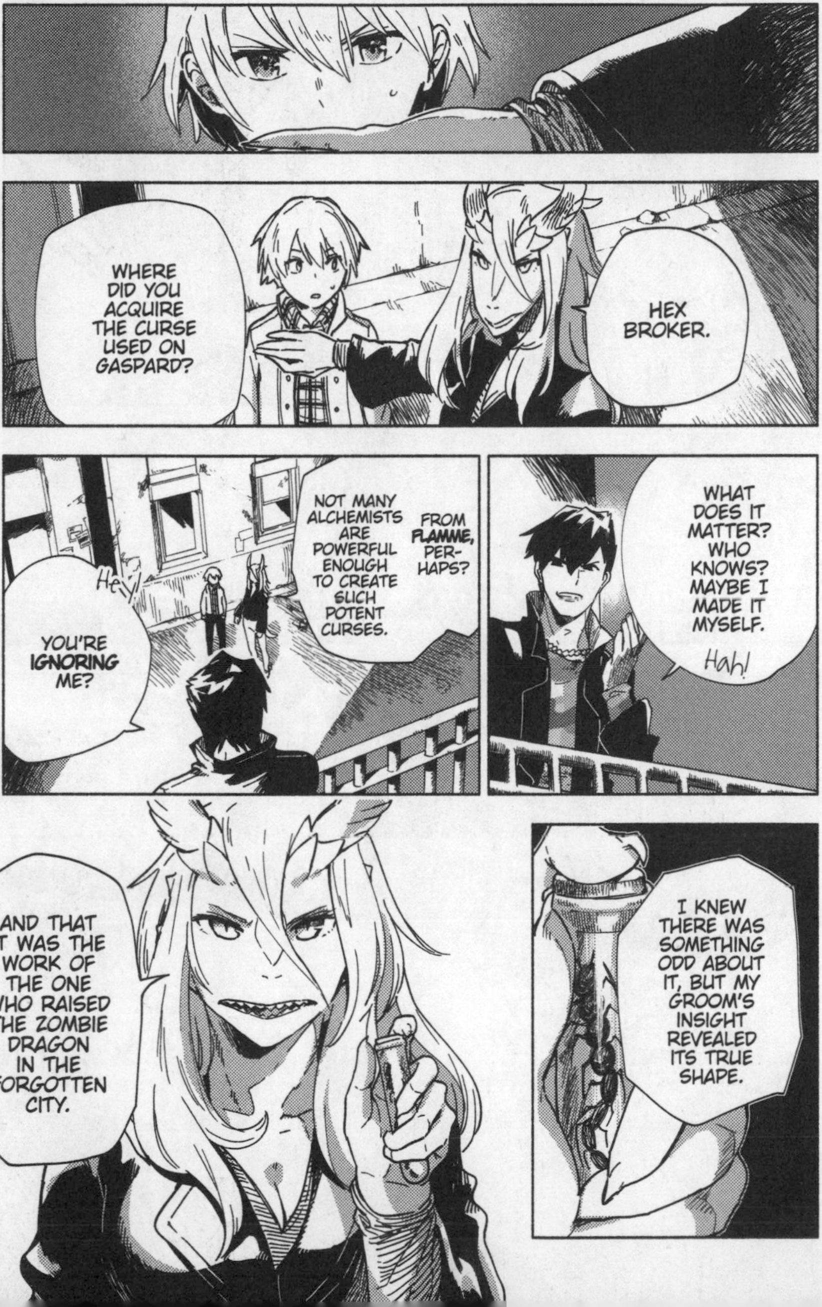
HEX BROKER.
WHERE DID YOU ACQUIRE THE CURSE USED ON GASPARD?
WHAT DOES IT MATTER? WHO KNOWS? MAYBE I MADE IT MYSELF.
Hah!
FROM FLAMME, PER-HAPS?
NOT MANY ALCHEMISTS ARE POWERFUL ENOUGH TO CREATE SUCH POTENT CURSES.
Hey!
YOU'RE IGNORING ME?
I KNEW THERE WAS SOMETHING ODD ABOUT IT, BUT MY GROOM'S INSIGHT REVEALED ITS TRUE SHAPE.
AND THAT IT WAS THE WORK OF THE ONE WHO RAISED THE ZOMBIE DRAGON IN THE FORGOTTEN CITY.

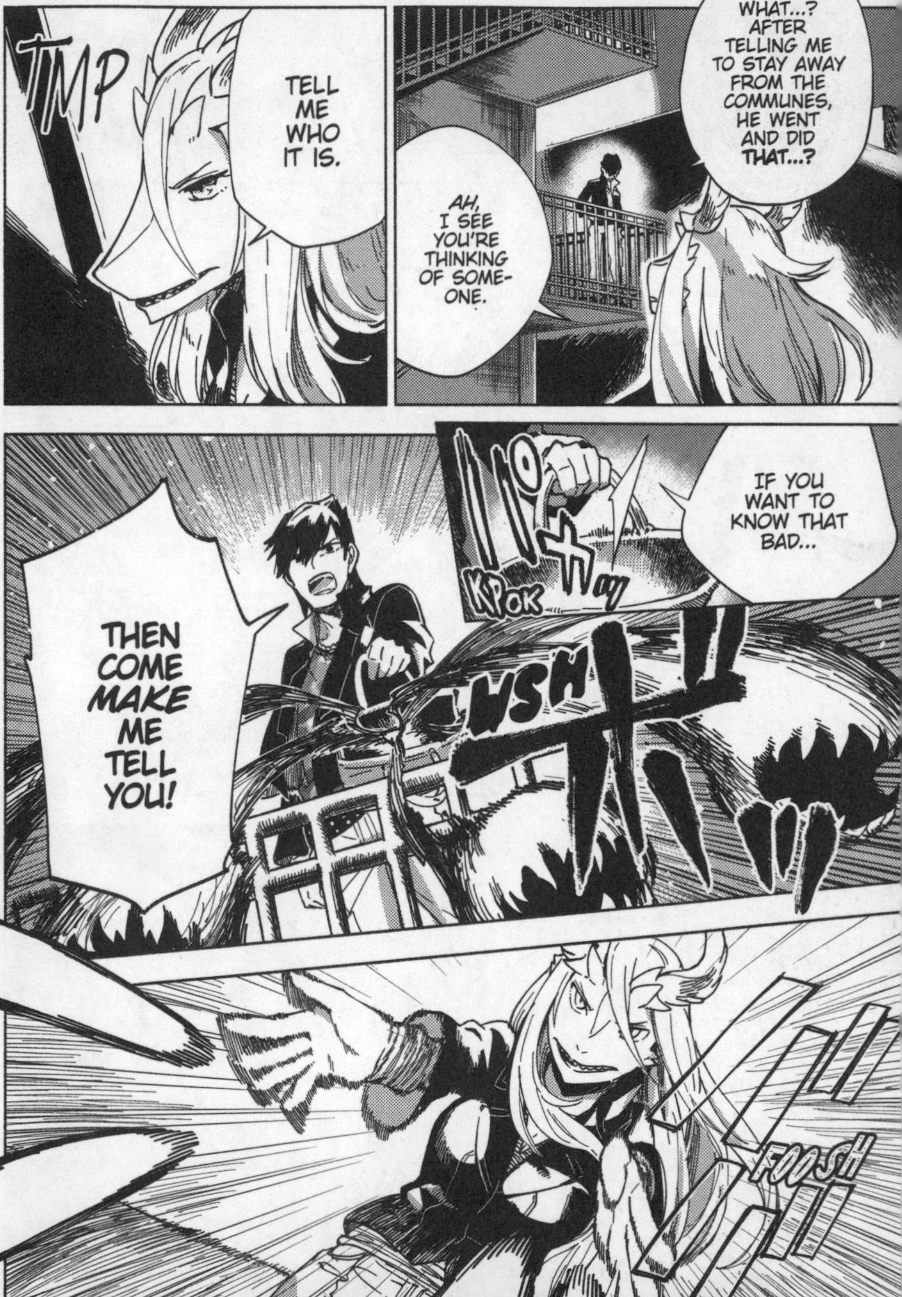
WHAT...? AFTER TELLING ME TO STAY AWAY FROM THE COMMUNES, HE WENT AND DID THAT...?
AH, I SEE YOU'RE THINKING OF SOME-ONE.
TMP
TELL ME WHO IT IS.
IF YOU WANT TO KNOW THAT BAD...
KPOK
THEN COME MAKE ME TELL YOU!
WSH
FOOSH

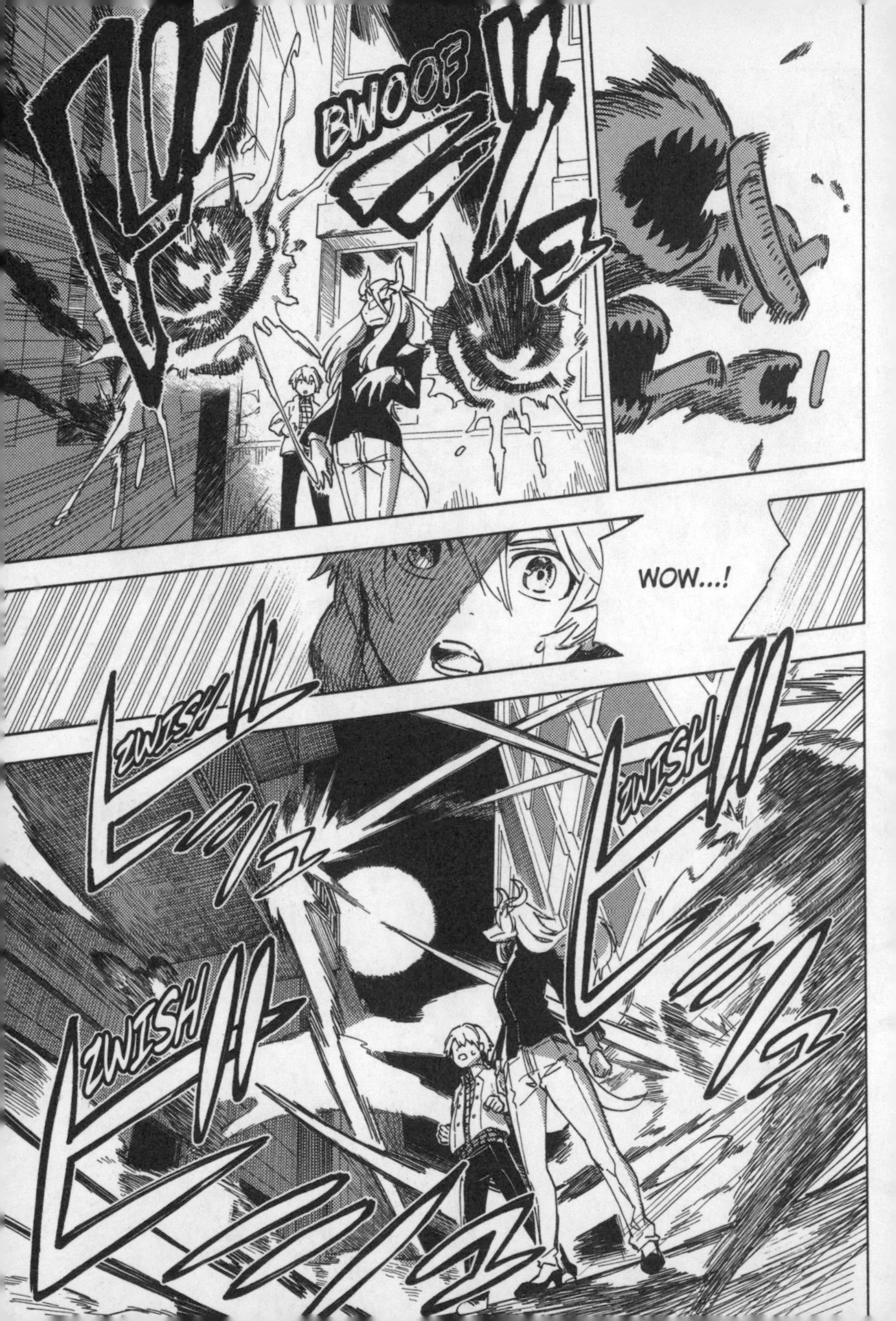
BWOOF
WOW...!
ZWISH
ZWISH
ZWISH

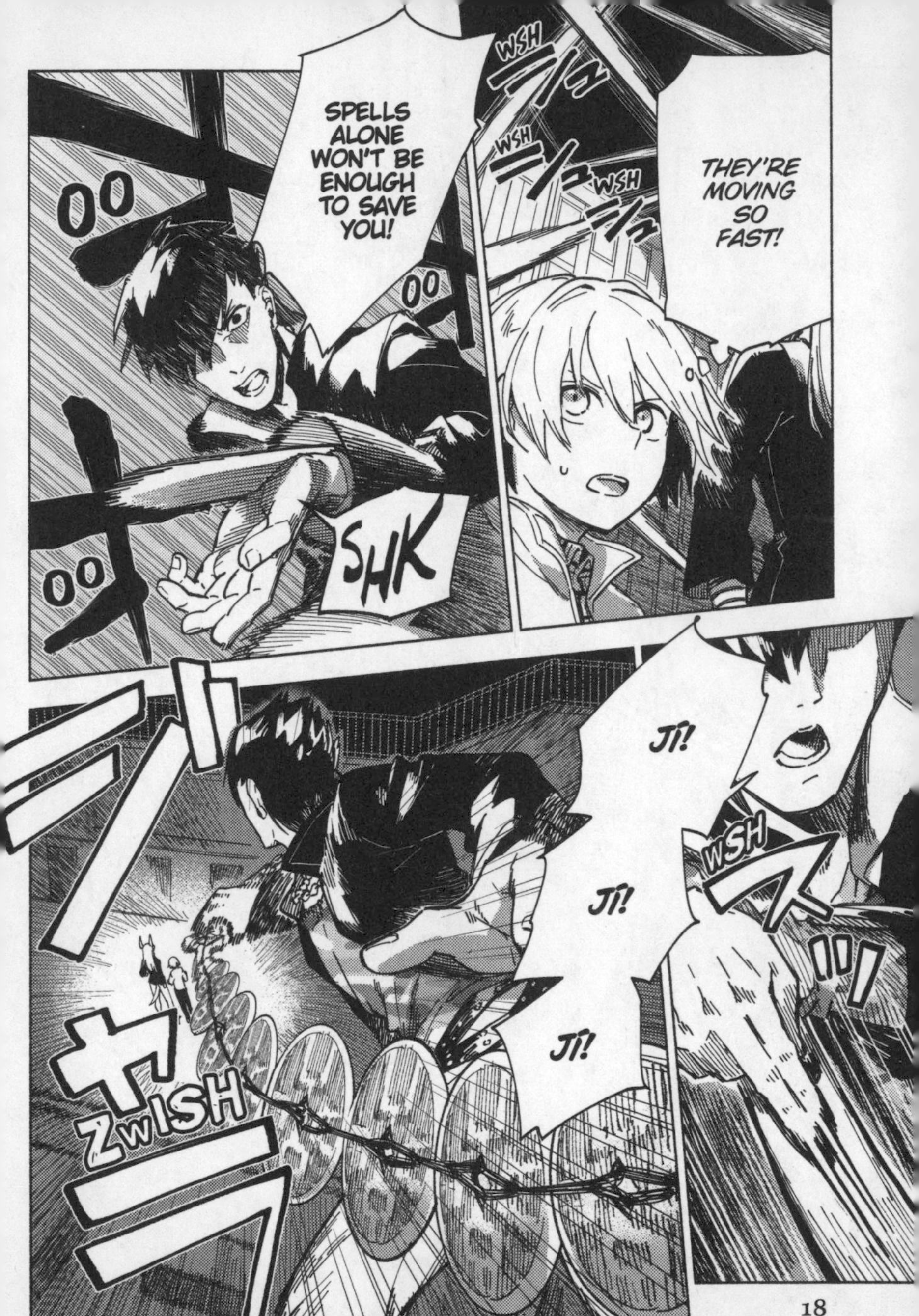
WSH
WSH
WSH
THEY'RE MOVING SO FAST!
SPELLS ALONE WON'T BE ENOUGH TO SAVE YOU!
OO
OO
OO
SHK
WSH
JI!
JI!
JI!
ZWISH

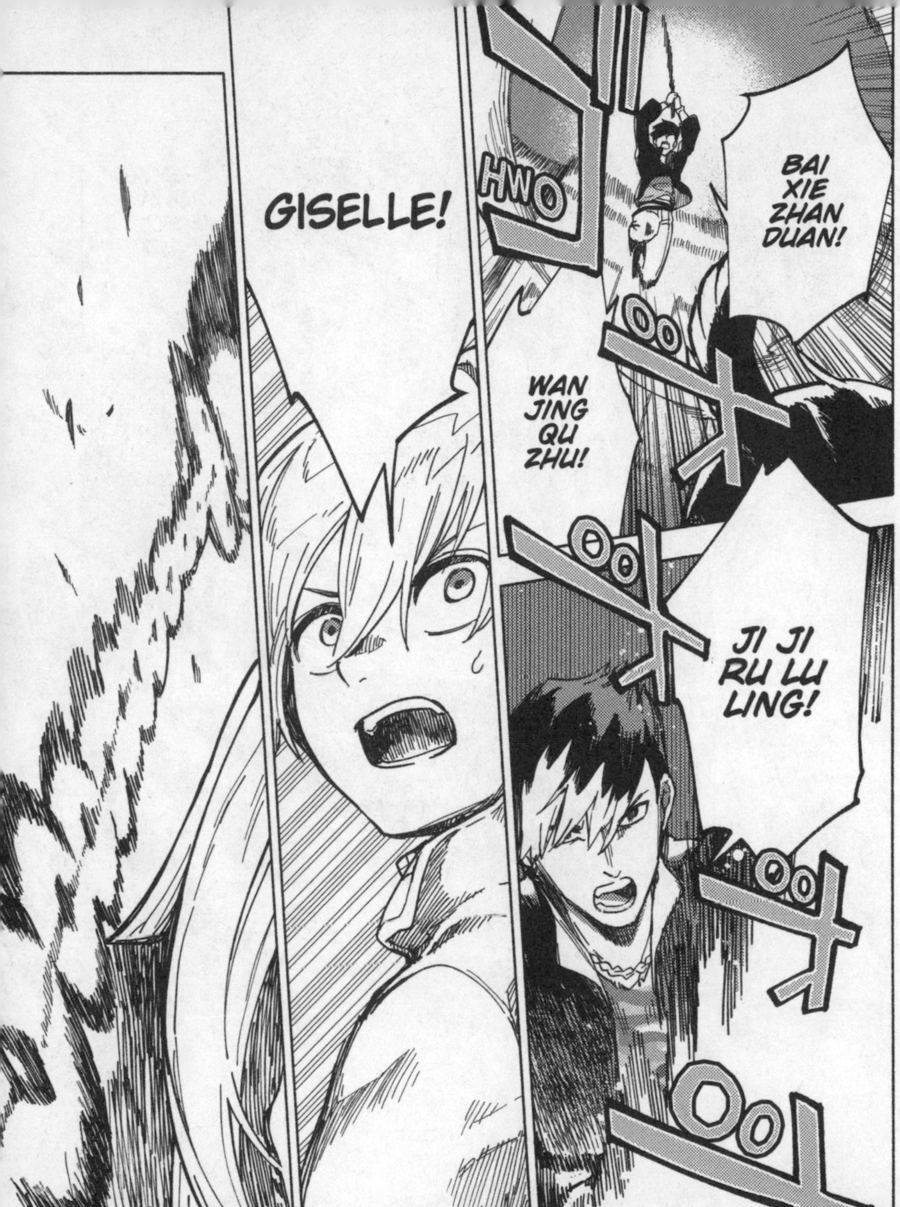
BAI XIE ZHAN DUAN!
HWO
WAN JING QU ZHU!
JI JI RU LU LING!
GISELLE!

*Ziwén is using a real-life Daoist magic chant.

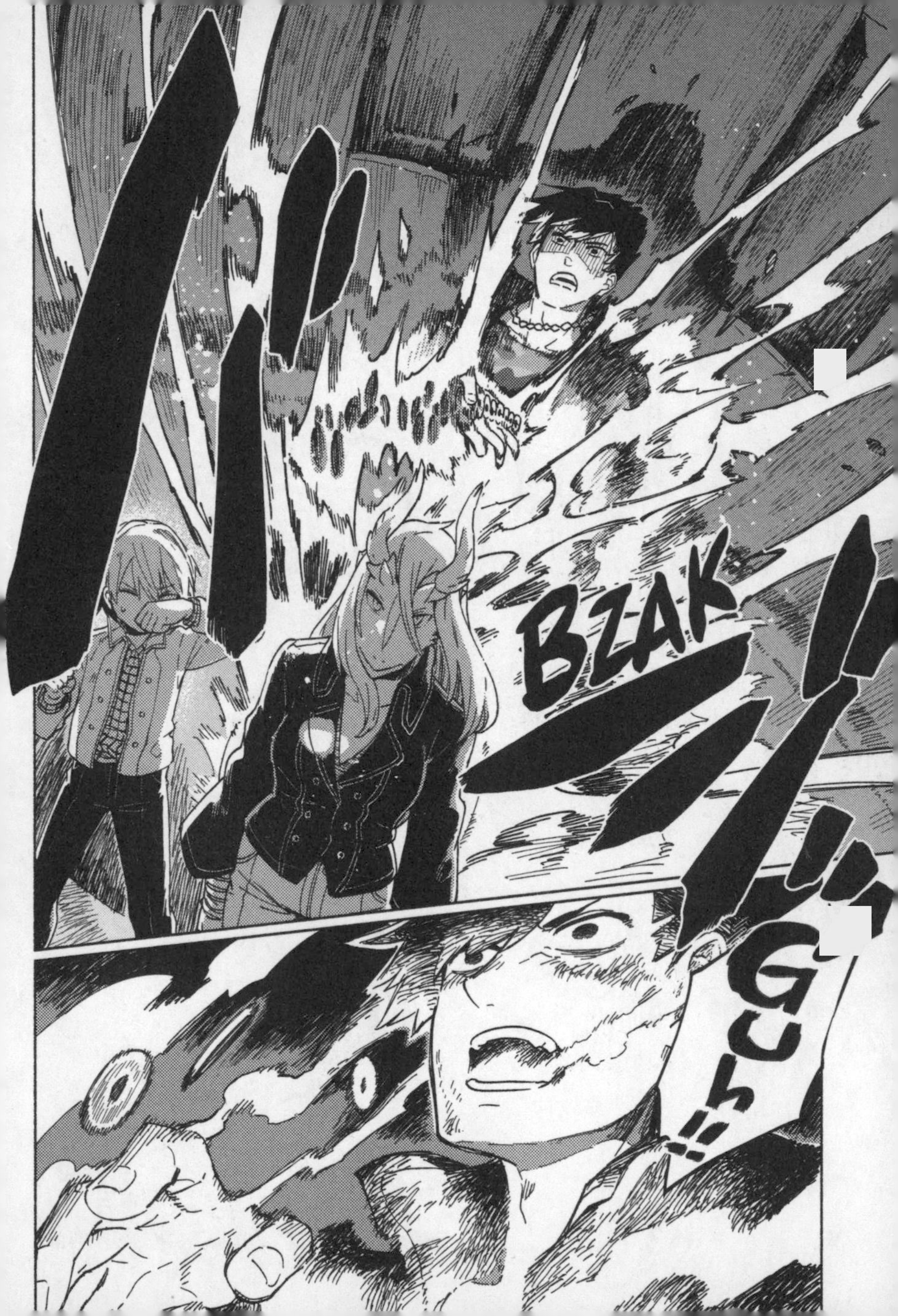
BZAK
GUH!!

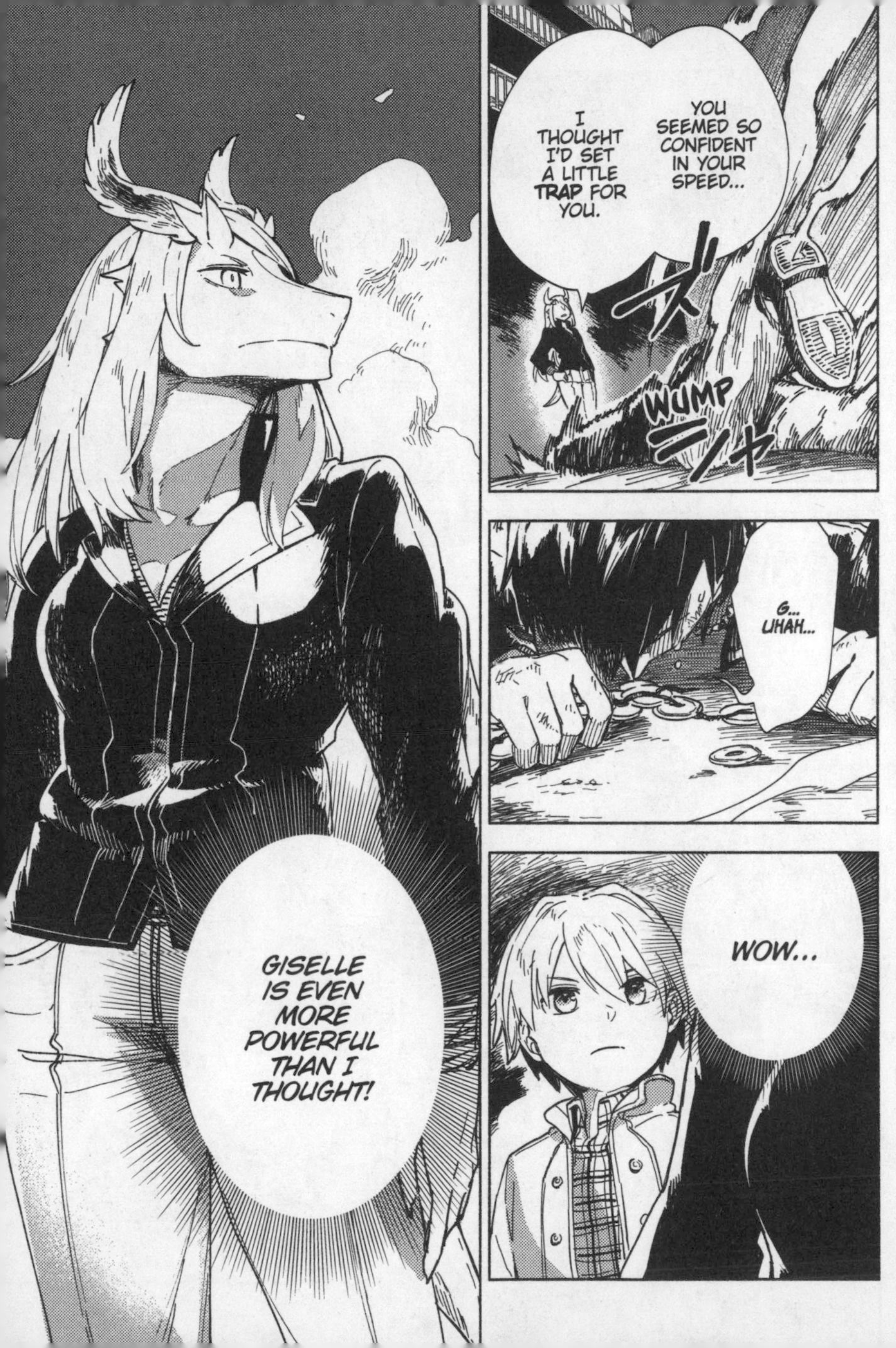
YOU SEEMED SO CONFIDENT IN YOUR SPEED...
I THOUGHT I'D SET A LITTLE TRAP FOR YOU.
WUMP
G... UHAH...
WOW...
GISELLE IS EVEN MORE POWERFUL THAN I THOUGHT!

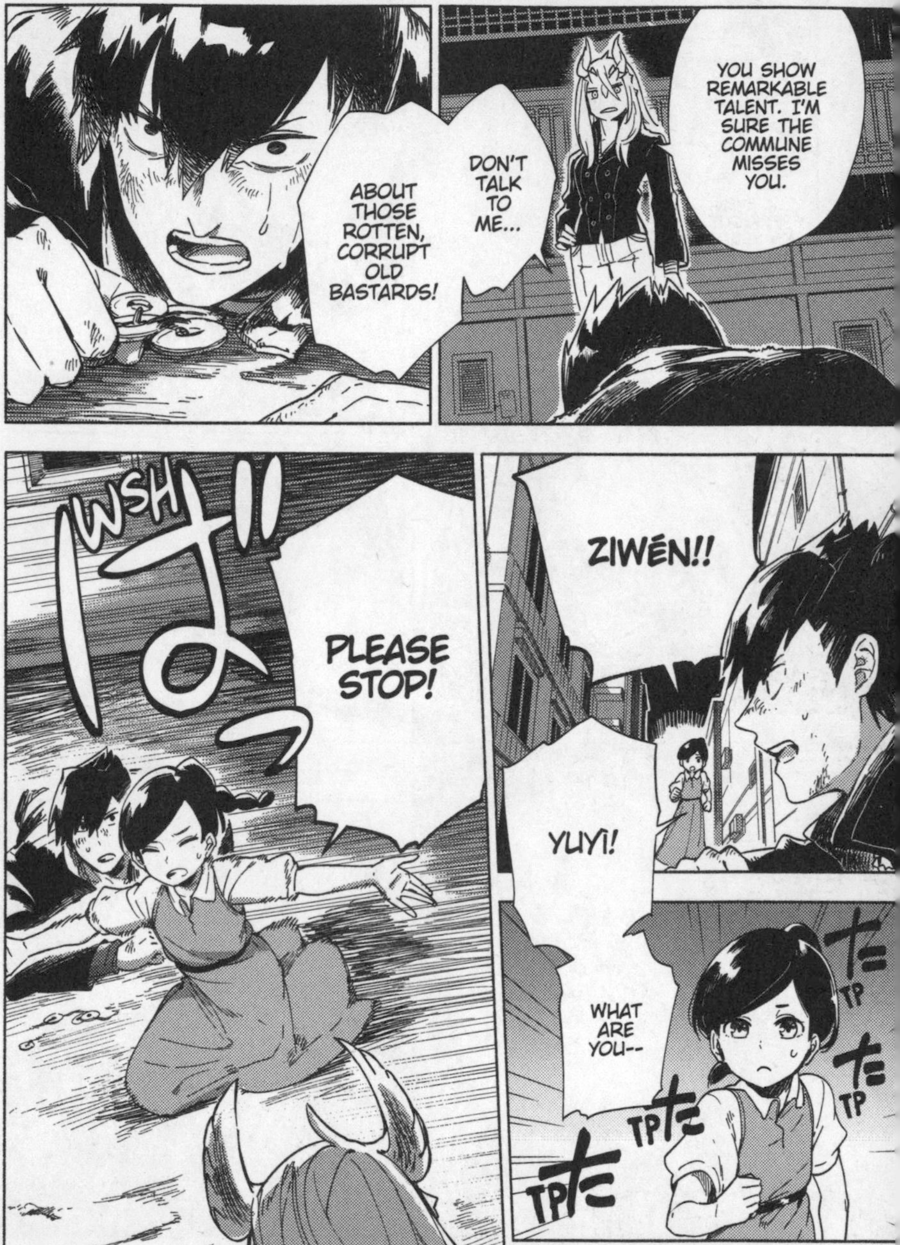
YOU SHOW REMARKABLE TALENT. I'M SURE THE COMMUNE MISSES YOU.
DON'T TALK TO ME...
ABOUT THOSE ROTTEN, CORRUPT OLD BASTARDS!
ZIWÉN!!
YUYÍ!
WHAT ARE YOU--
TP
TP
TP
TP
WSH
PLEASE STOP!

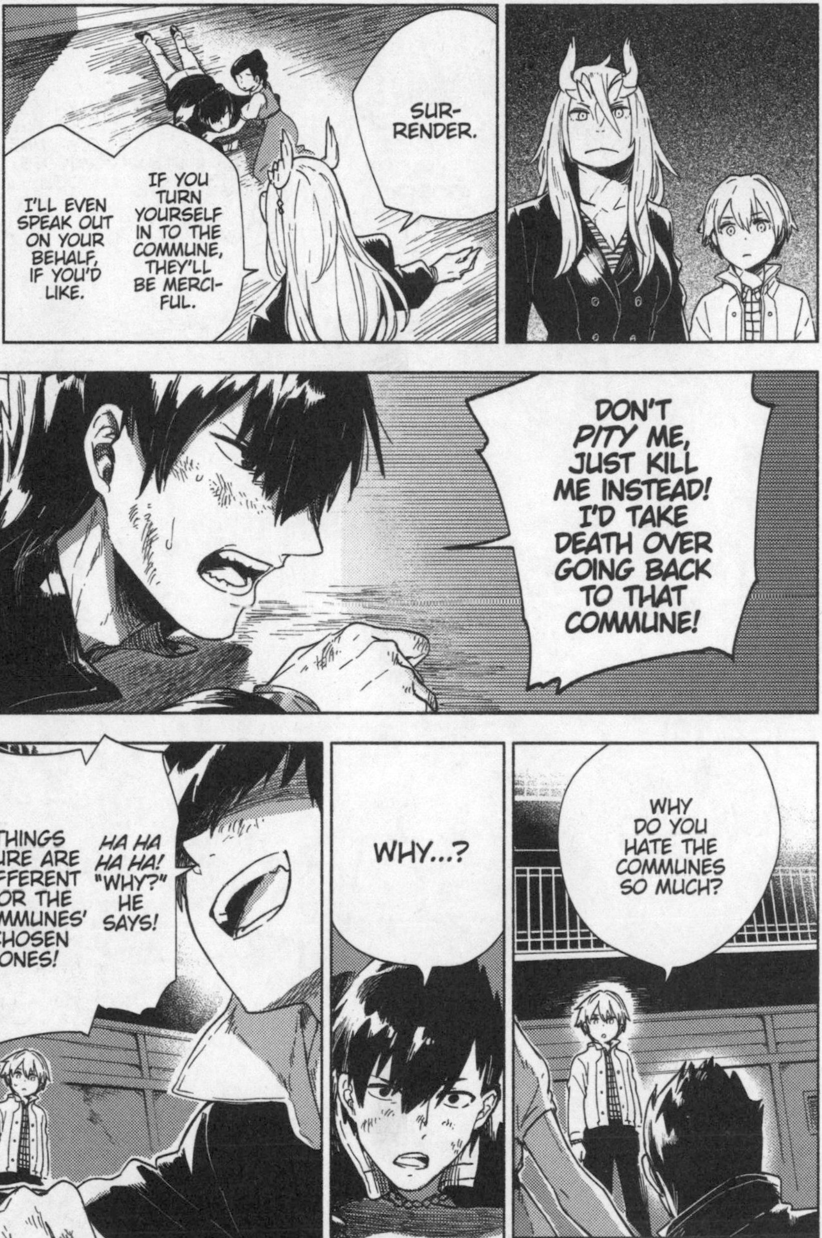
SUR-RENDER.
IF YOU TURN YOURSELF IN TO THE COMMUNE, THEY'LL BE MERCI-FUL.
I'LL EVEN SPEAK OUT ON YOUR BEHALF, IF YOU'D LIKE.
DON'T *PITY* ME, JUST KILL ME INSTEAD! I'D TAKE DEATH OVER GOING BACK TO THAT COMMUNE!
WHY DO YOU HATE THE COMMUNES SO MUCH?
WHY...?
HA HA HA HA! "WHY?" HE SAYS!
THINGS SURE ARE DIFFERENT FOR THE COMMUNES' CHOSEN ONES!

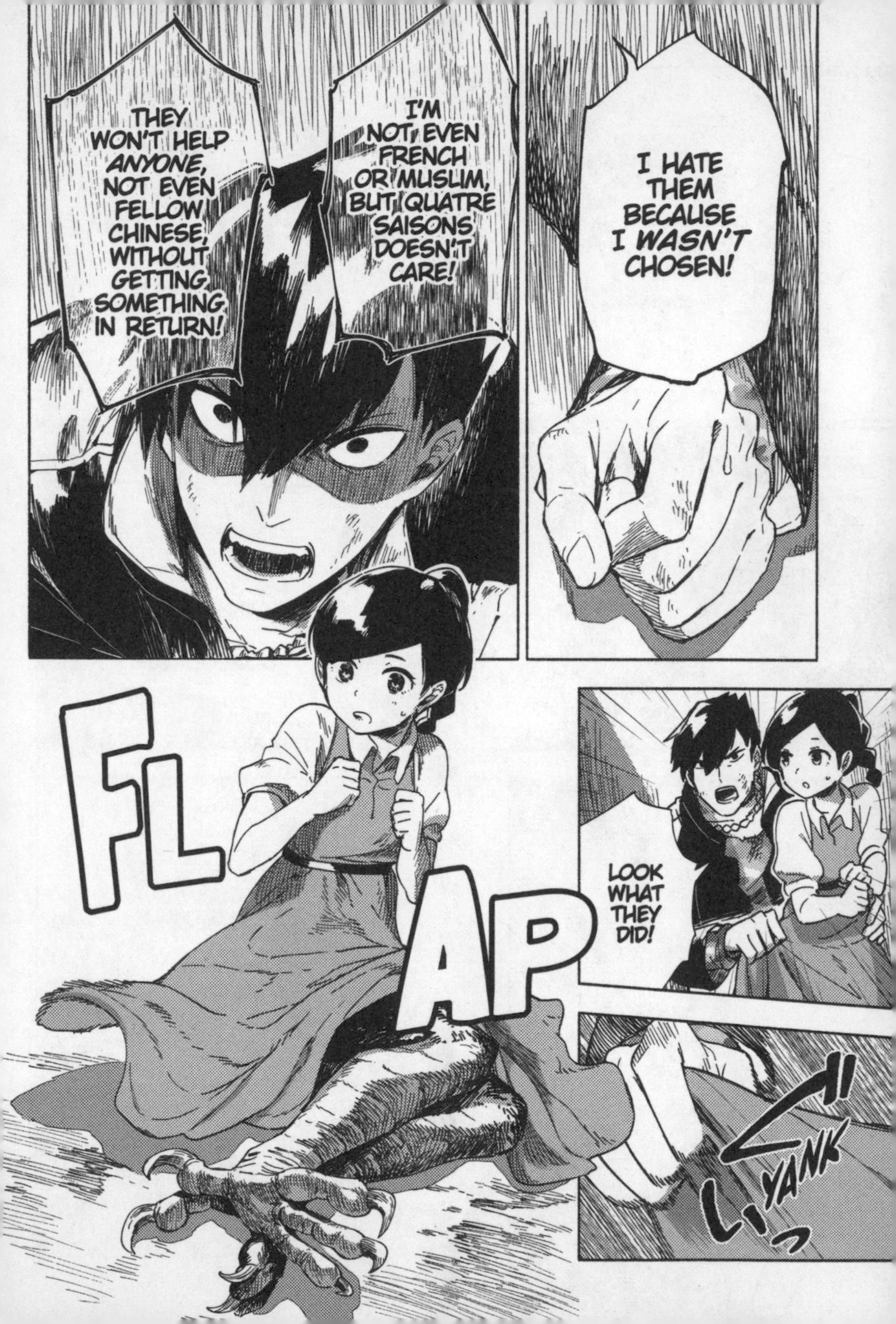

I HATE THEM BECAUSE I *WASN'T* CHOSEN!
I'M NOT EVEN FRENCH OR MUSLIM, BUT QUATRE SAISONS DOESN'T CARE!
THEY WON'T HELP *ANYONE*, NOT EVEN FELLOW CHINESE, WITHOUT GETTING SOMETHING IN RETURN!
LOOK WHAT THEY DID!
YANK
FLAP

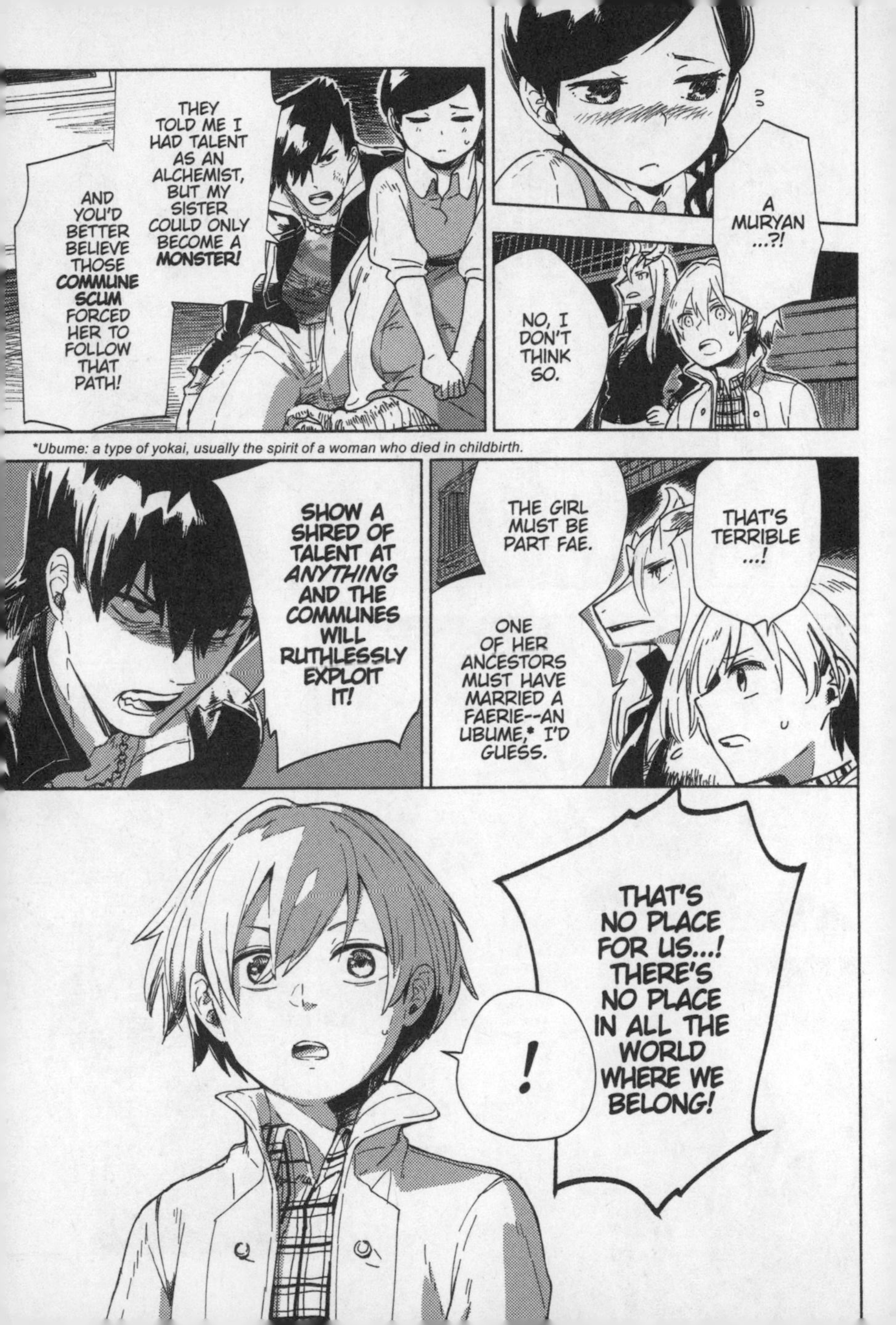
A MURYAN ...?!
NO, I DON'T THINK SO.
THEY TOLD ME I HAD TALENT AS AN ALCHEMIST, BUT MY SISTER COULD ONLY BECOME A **MONSTER!**
AND YOU'D BETTER BELIEVE THOSE **COMMUNE SCUM** FORCED HER TO FOLLOW THAT PATH!
THAT'S TERRIBLE ...!
THE GIRL MUST BE PART FAE.
ONE OF HER ANCESTORS MUST HAVE MARRIED A FAERIE--AN UBUME,* I'D GUESS.
SHOW A SHRED OF TALENT AT *ANYTHING* AND THE COMMUNES WILL RUTHLESSLY EXPLOIT IT!
!
THAT'S NO PLACE FOR US...! THERE'S NO PLACE IN ALL THE WORLD WHERE WE BELONG!

**Ubume: a type of yokai, usually the spirit of a woman who died in childbirth.*

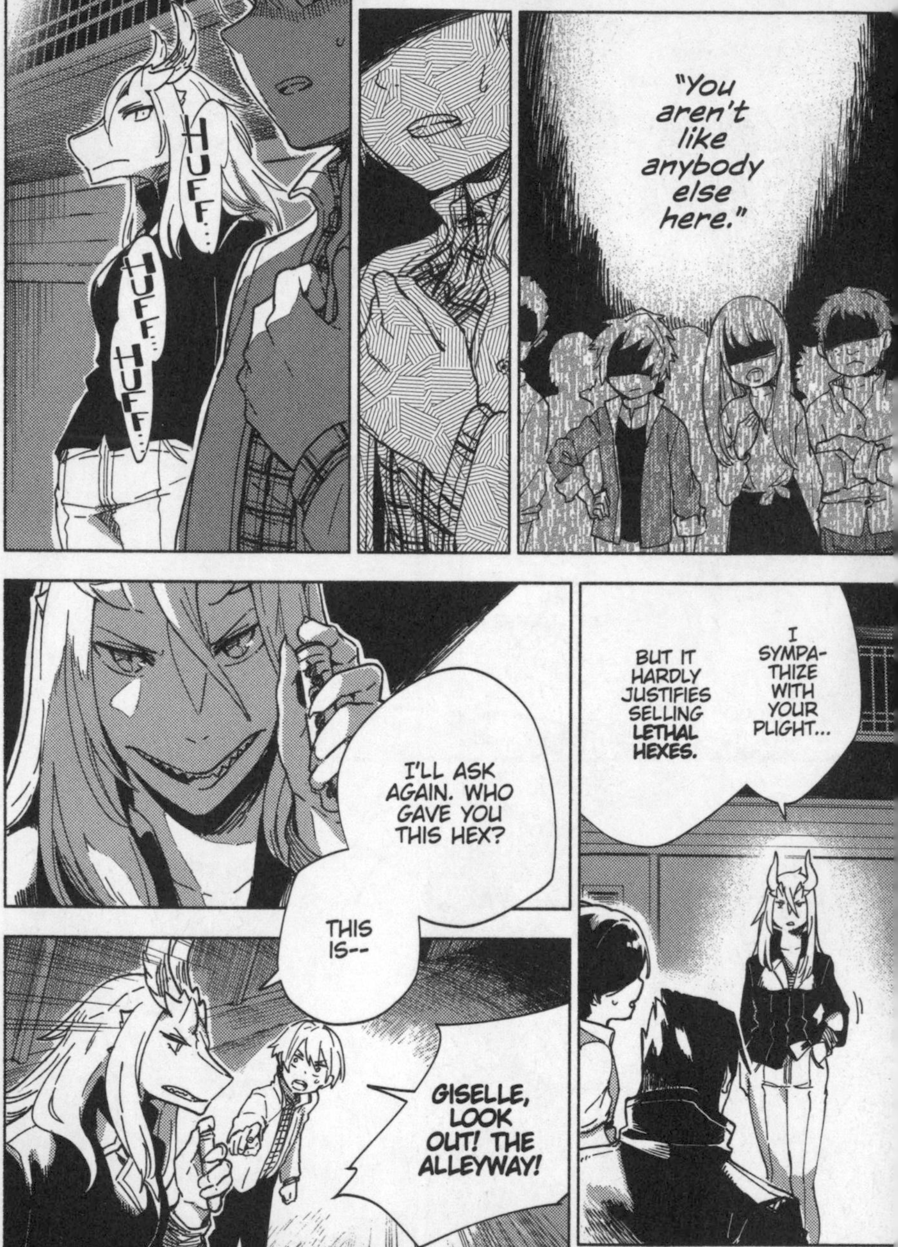
"You aren't like anybody else here."
HUFF...
HUFF...
HUFF...
HUFF...
I SYMPATHIZE WITH YOUR PLIGHT...
BUT IT HARDLY JUSTIFIES SELLING **LETHAL HEXES.**
I'LL ASK AGAIN. WHO GAVE YOU THIS HEX?
THIS IS--
GISELLE, LOOK OUT! THE ALLEYWAY!

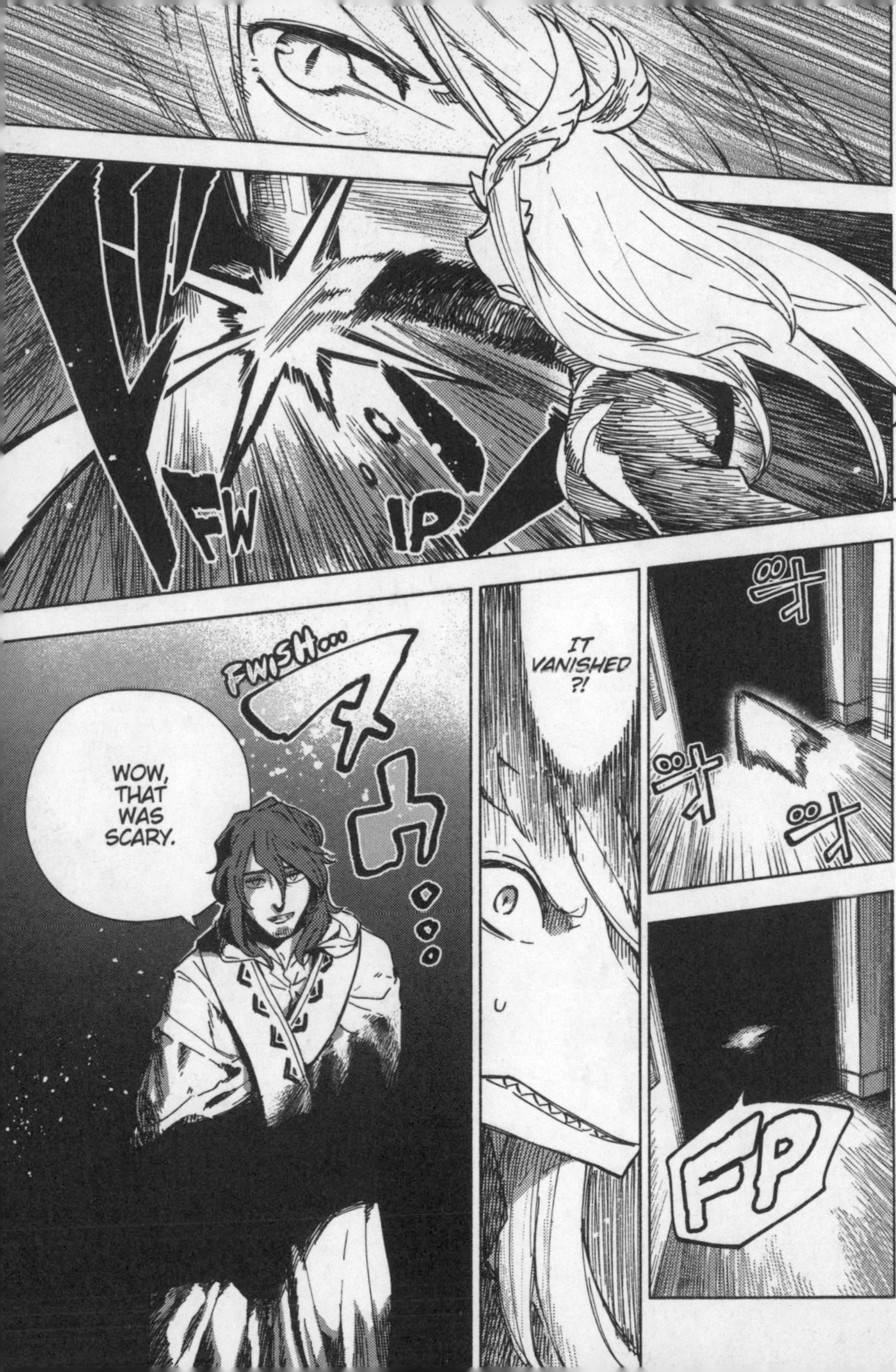
FWIP
FP
IT VANISHED ?!
FWISH...
WOW, THAT WAS SCARY.

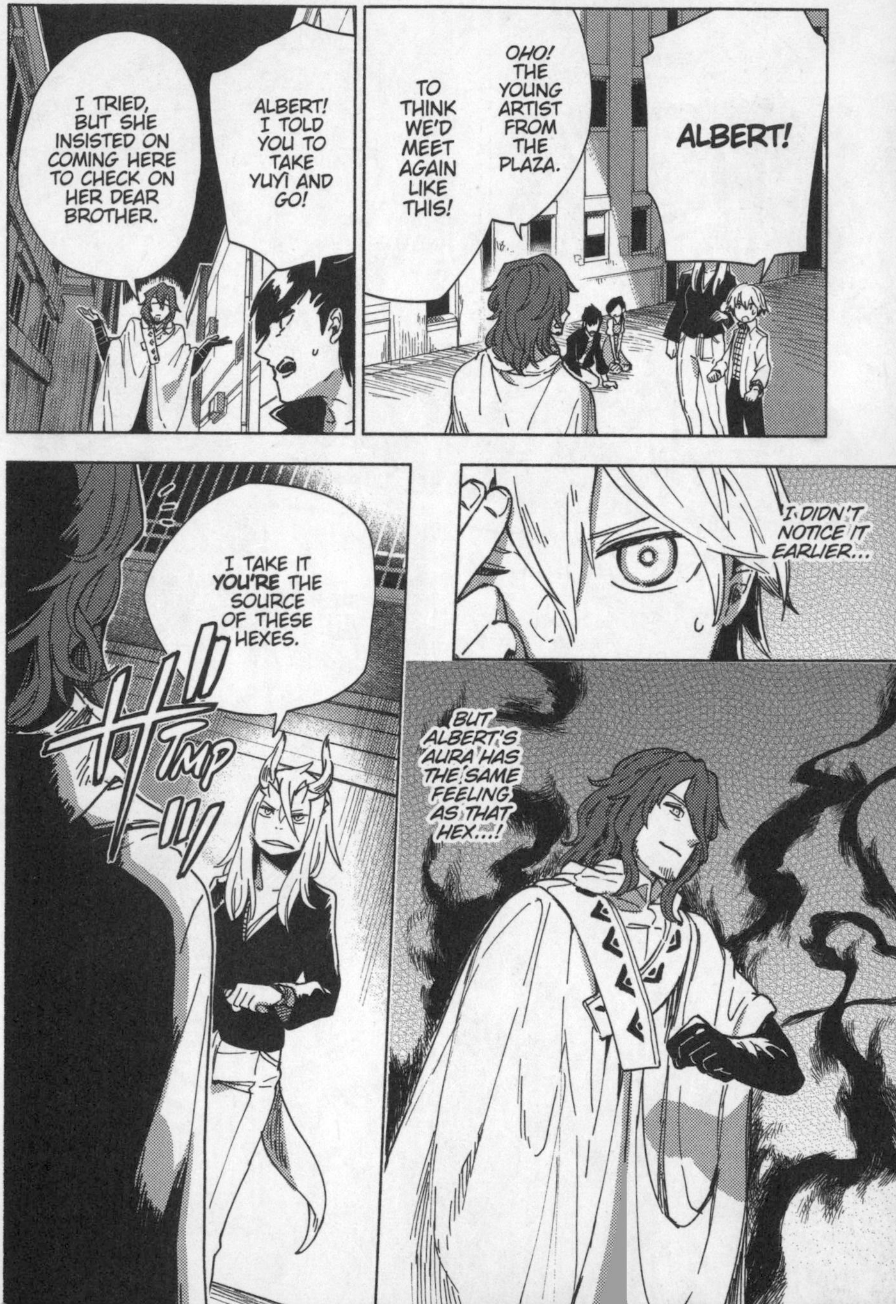
ALBERT!
OHO! THE YOUNG ARTIST FROM THE PLAZA.
TO THINK WE'D MEET AGAIN LIKE THIS!
ALBERT! I TOLD YOU TO TAKE YUYI AND GO!
I TRIED, BUT SHE INSISTED ON COMING HERE TO CHECK ON HER DEAR BROTHER.
I DIDN'T NOTICE IT EARLIER...
BUT ALBERT'S AURA HAS THE SAME FEELING AS THAT HEX...!
I TAKE IT YOU'RE THE SOURCE OF THESE HEXES.
HMP

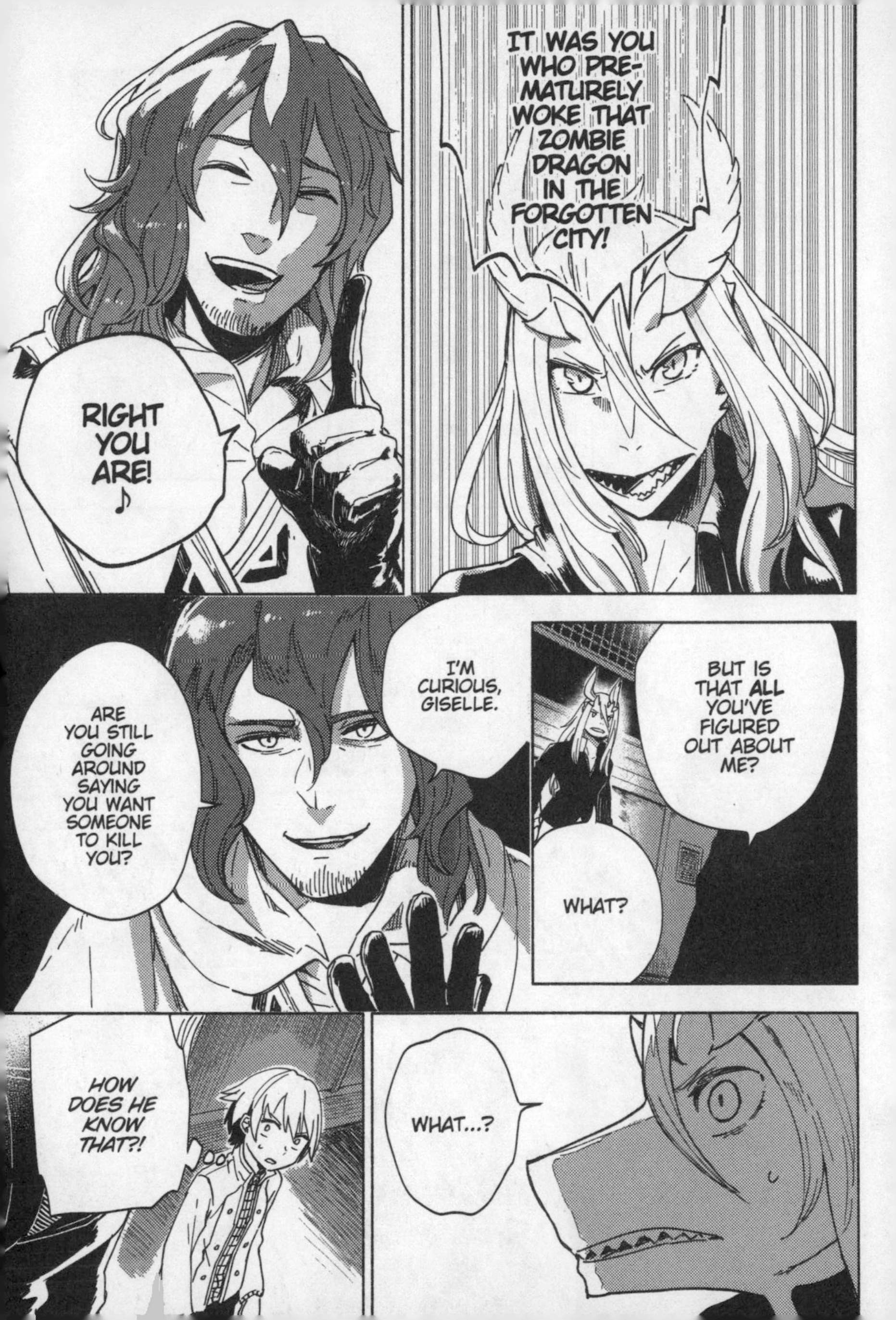
IT WAS YOU WHO PRE-MATURELY WOKE THAT ZOMBIE DRAGON IN THE FORGOTTEN CITY!
RIGHT YOU ARE! ♪
BUT IS THAT ALL YOU'VE FIGURED OUT ABOUT ME?
WHAT?
I'M CURIOUS, GISELLE.
ARE YOU STILL GOING AROUND SAYING YOU WANT SOMEONE TO KILL YOU?
WHAT...?
HOW DOES HE KNOW THAT?!

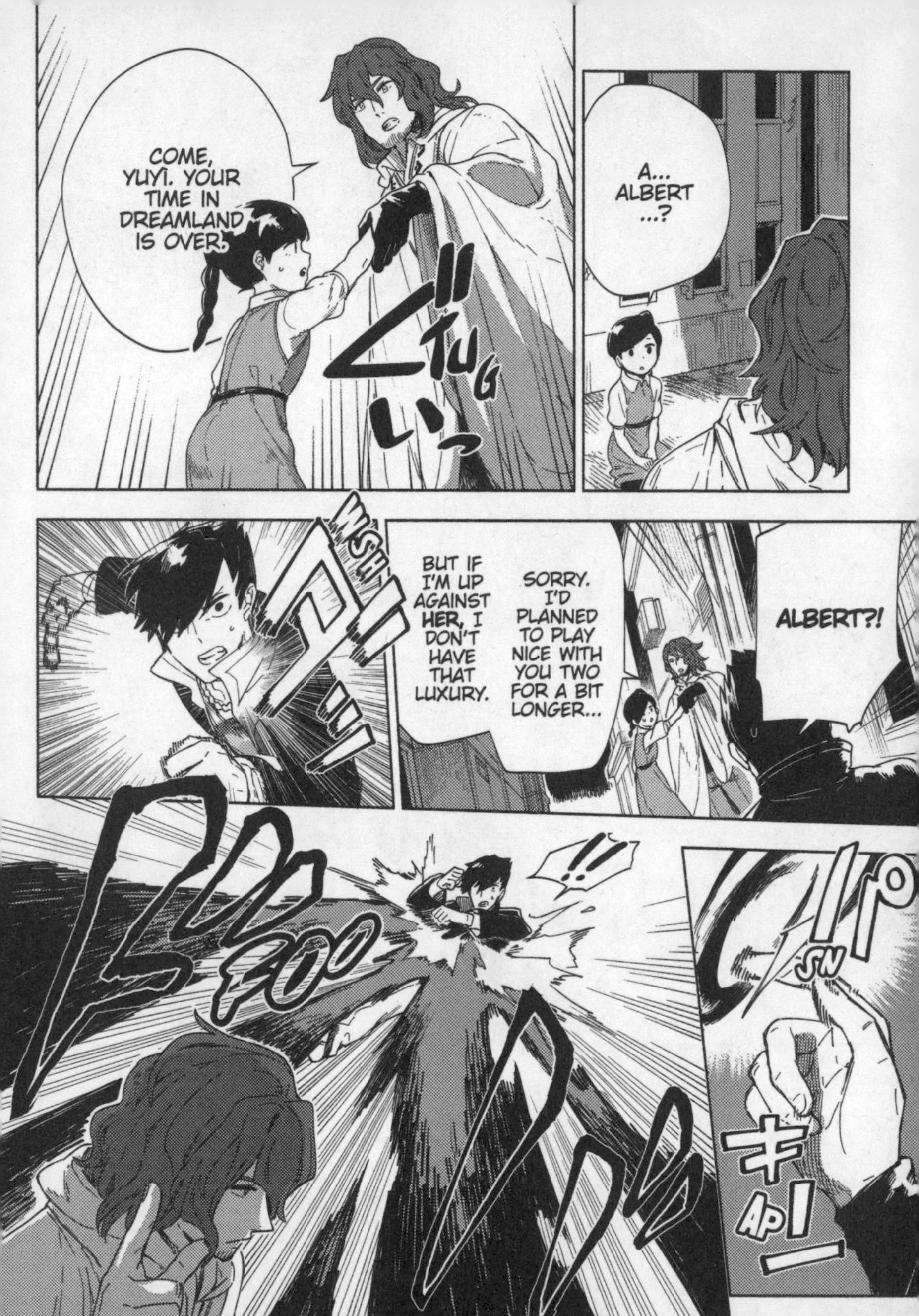
A... ALBERT ...?
COME, YUYI. YOUR TIME IN DREAMLAND IS OVER.
TUG
ALBERT?!
SORRY. I'D PLANNED TO PLAY NICE WITH YOU TWO FOR A BIT LONGER...
BUT IF I'M UP AGAINST HER, I DON'T HAVE THAT LUXURY.
WSH
SN
AP
!!
FOO

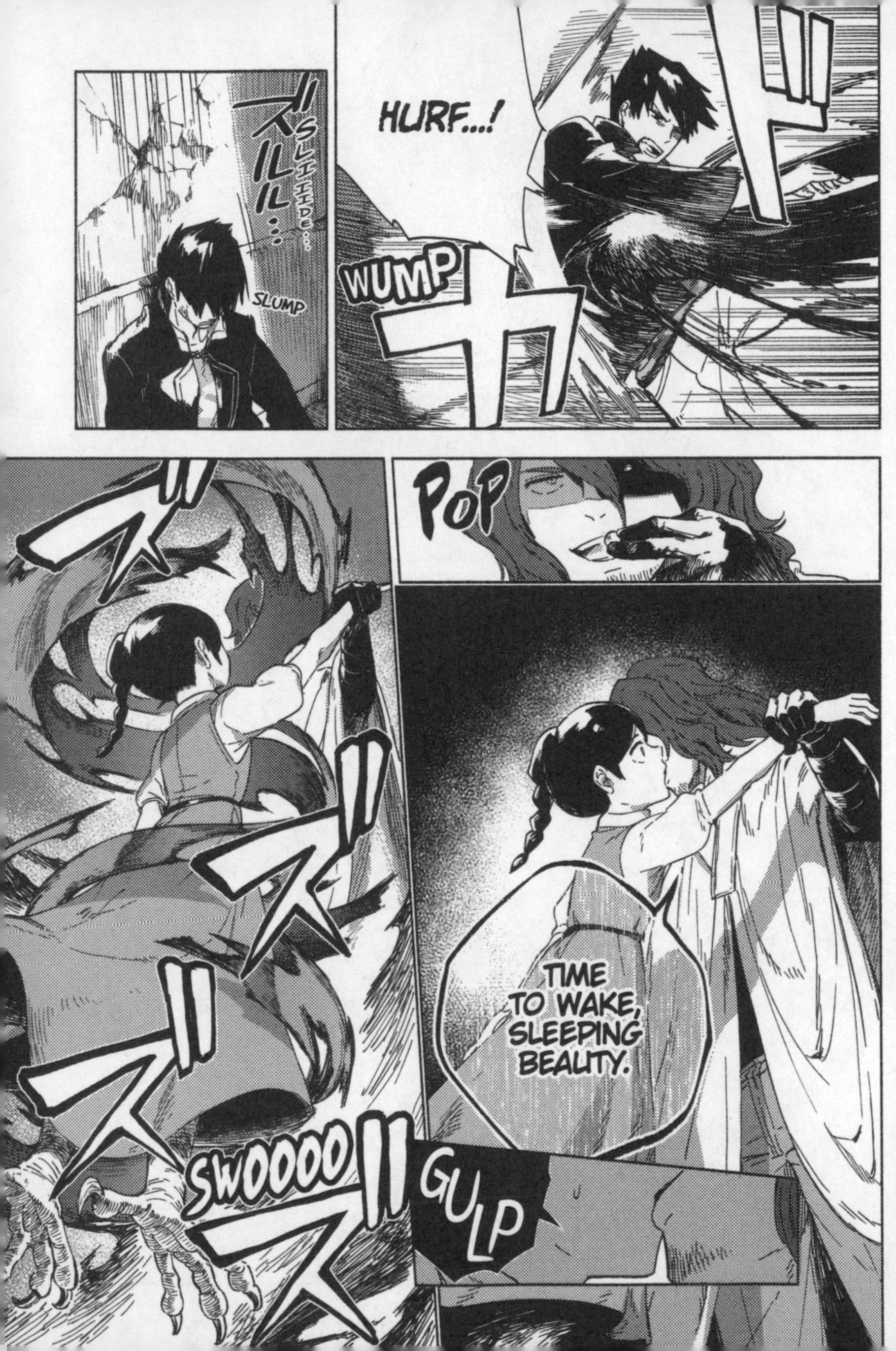
HURF...!
WUMP
SLIIIDE...
SLUMP
POP
TIME TO WAKE, SLEEPING BEAUTY.
GULP
SWOOOO

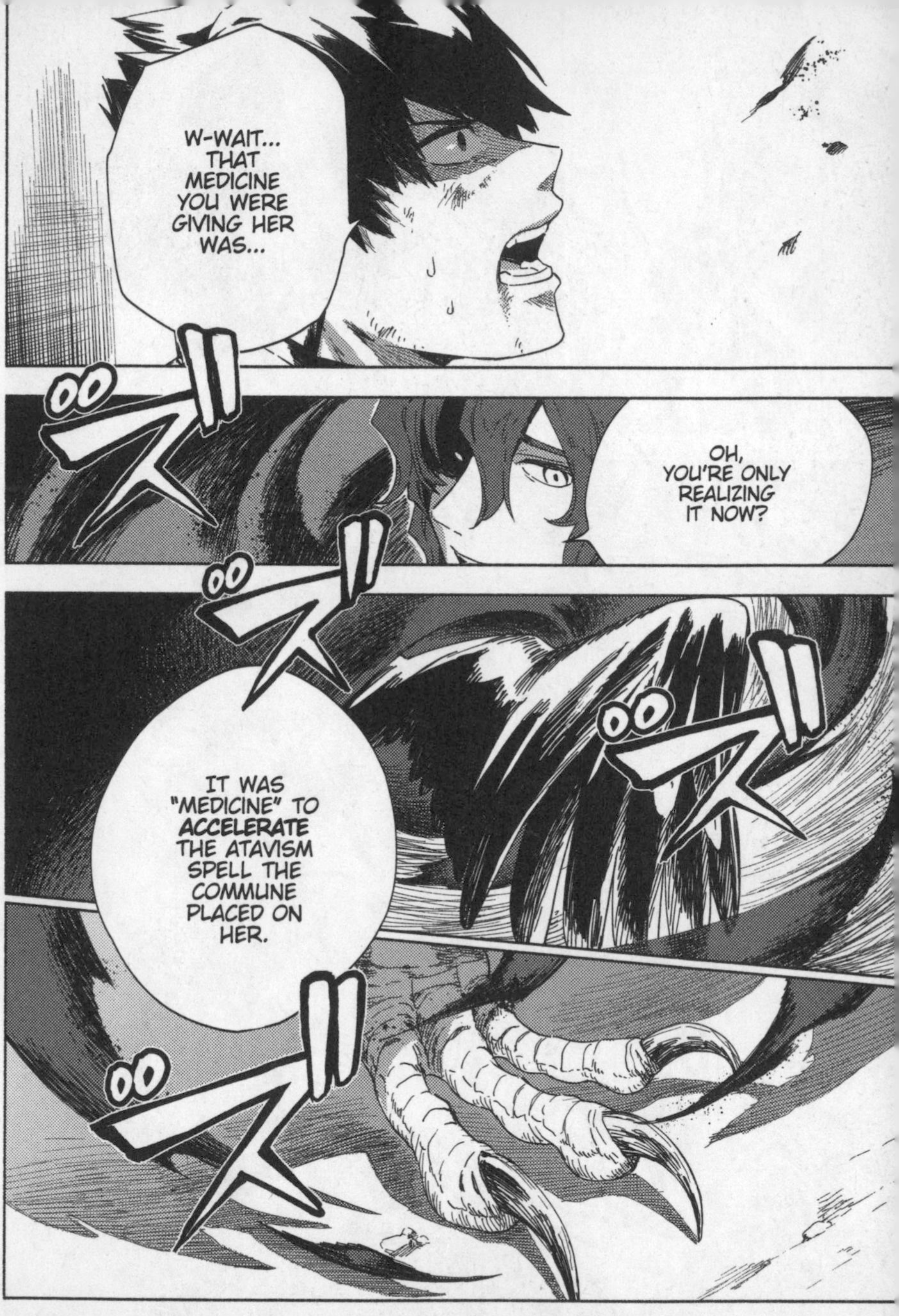
W-WAIT... THAT MEDICINE YOU WERE GIVING HER WAS...
OH, YOU'RE ONLY REALIZING IT NOW?
IT WAS "MEDICINE" TO **ACCELERATE** THE ATAVISM SPELL THE COMMUNE PLACED ON HER.

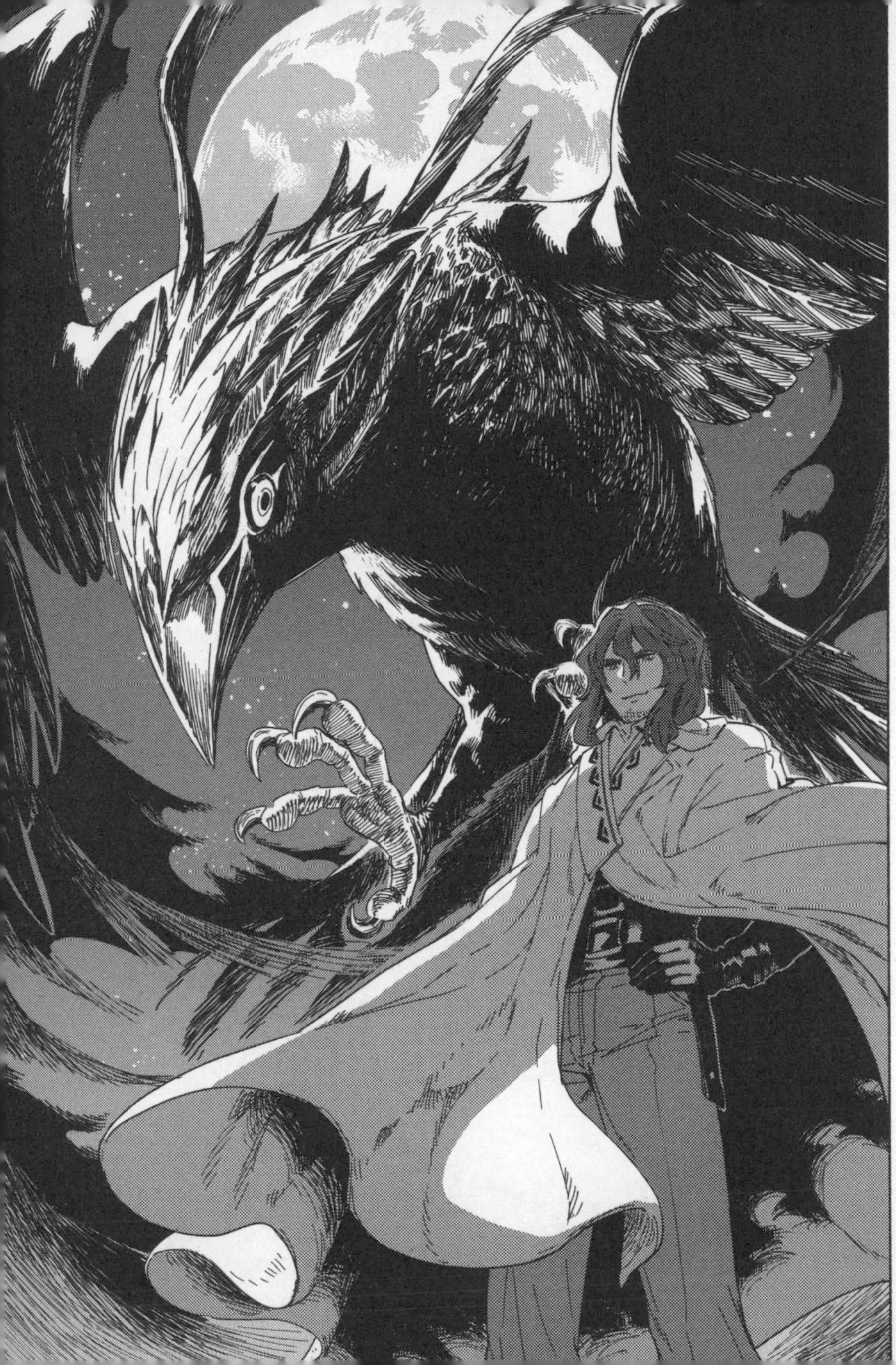

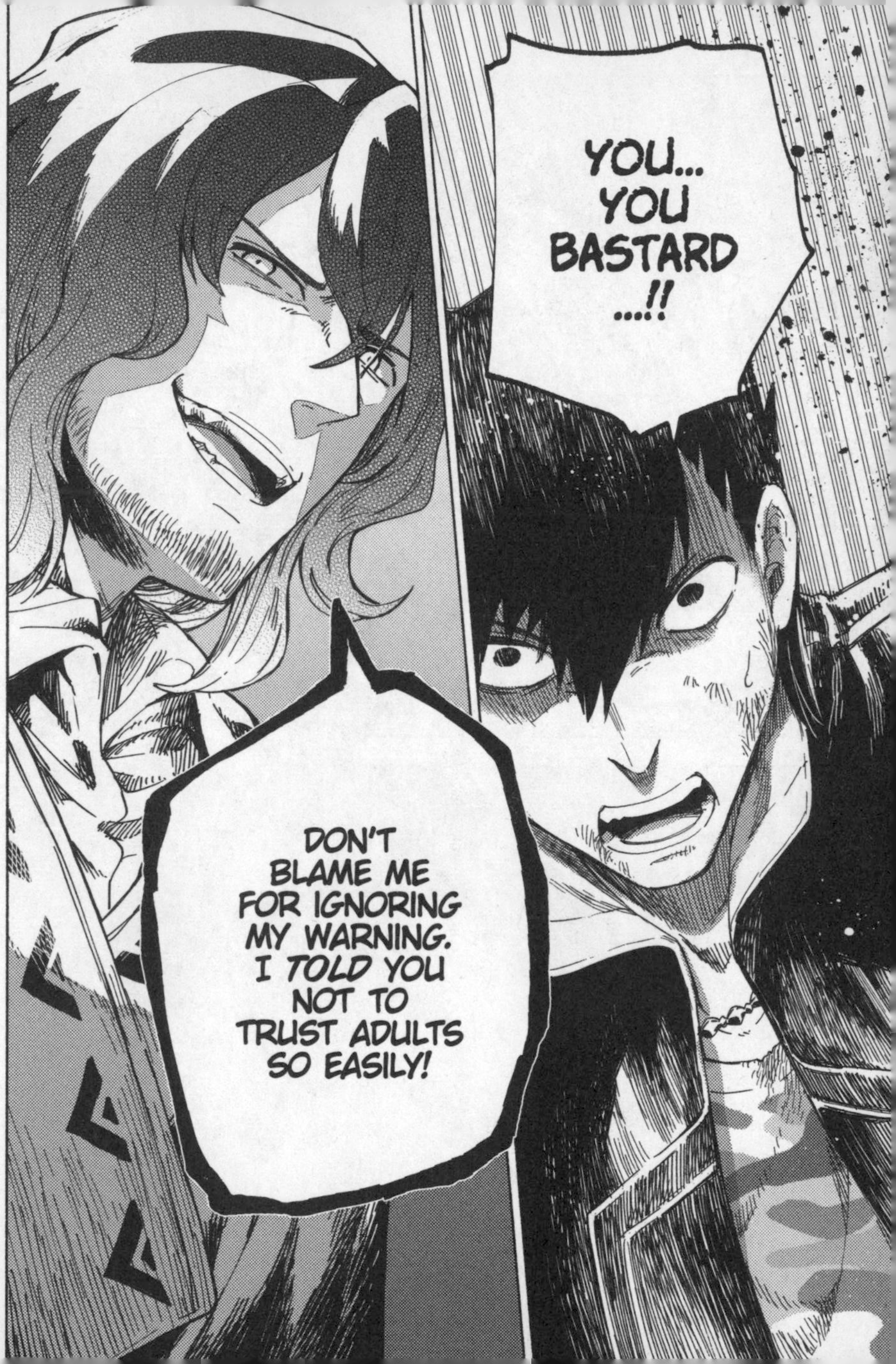
YOU... YOU BASTARD ...!!
DON'T BLAME ME FOR IGNORING MY WARNING. I *TOLD* YOU NOT TO TRUST ADULTS SO EASILY!

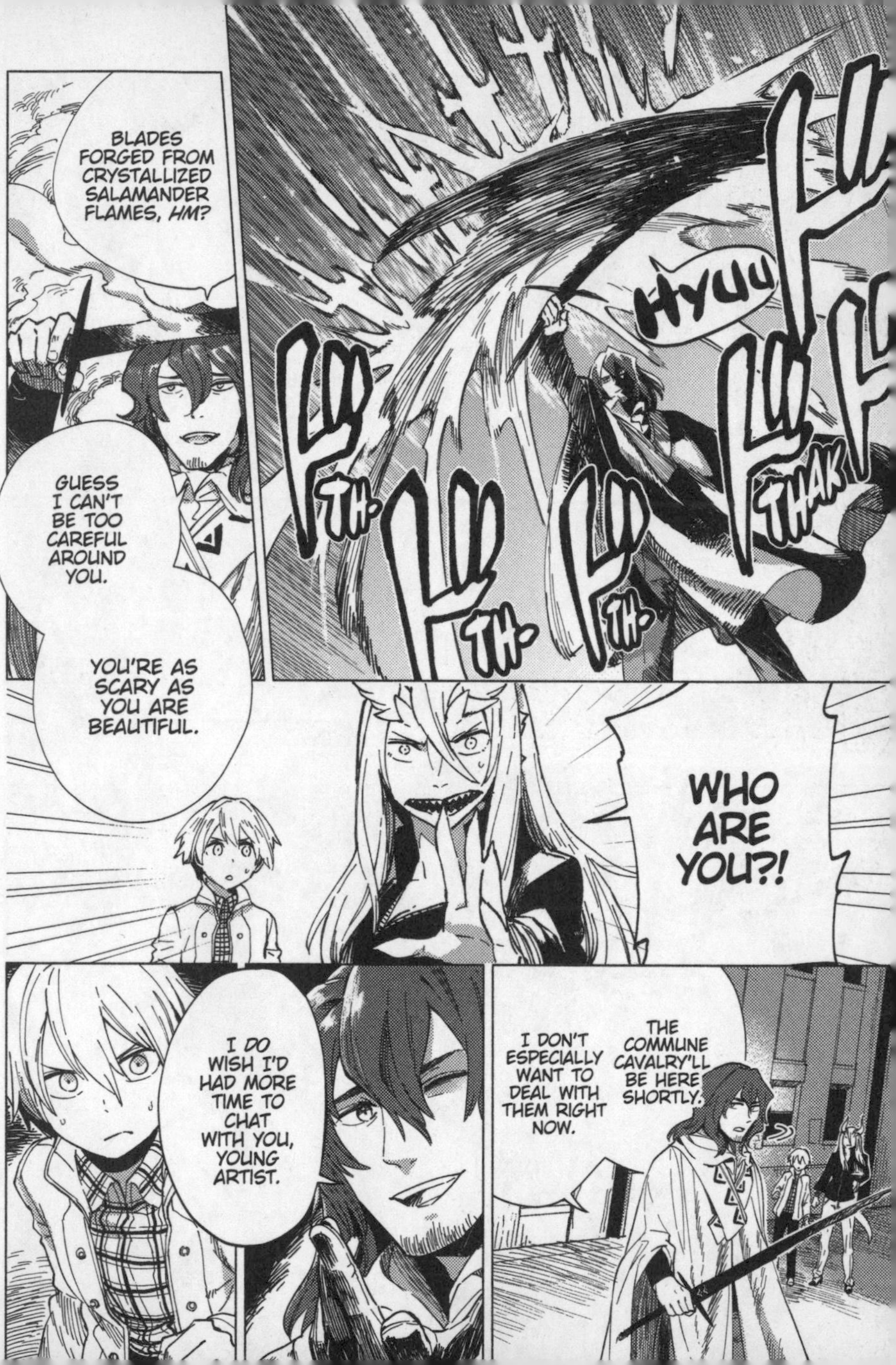
HYUU
THAK
TH-
TH-
TH-
BLADES FORGED FROM CRYSTALLIZED SALAMANDER FLAMES, *HM*?
GUESS I CAN'T BE TOO CAREFUL AROUND YOU.
YOU'RE AS SCARY AS YOU ARE BEAUTIFUL.
WHO ARE YOU?!
THE COMMUNE CAVALRY'LL BE HERE SHORTLY.
I DON'T ESPECIALLY WANT TO DEAL WITH THEM RIGHT NOW.
I *DO* WISH I'D HAD MORE TIME TO CHAT WITH YOU, YOUNG ARTIST.

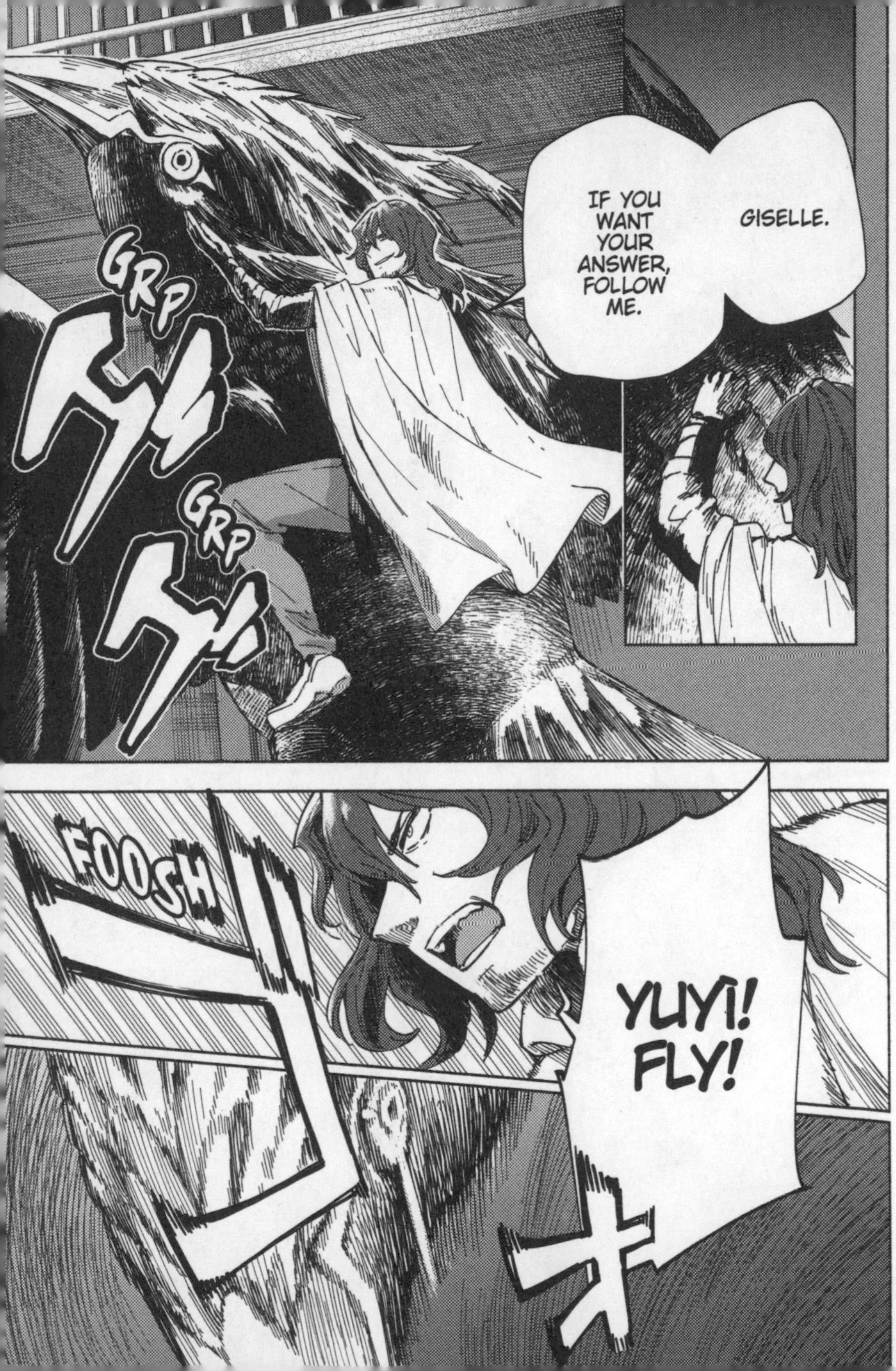
GISELLE.
IF YOU WANT YOUR ANSWER, FOLLOW ME.
GRP
GRP
YUYI! FLY!
FOOSH

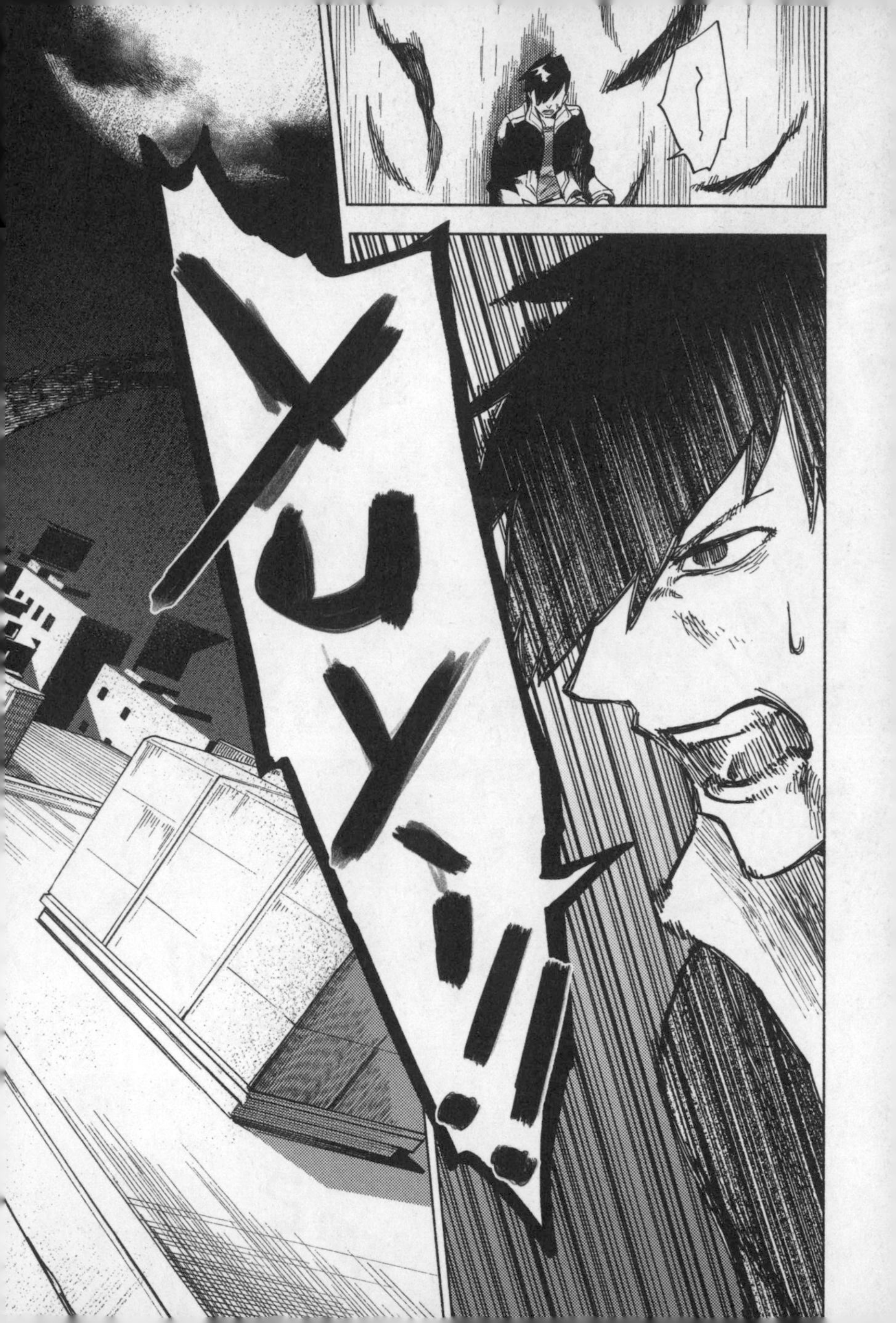

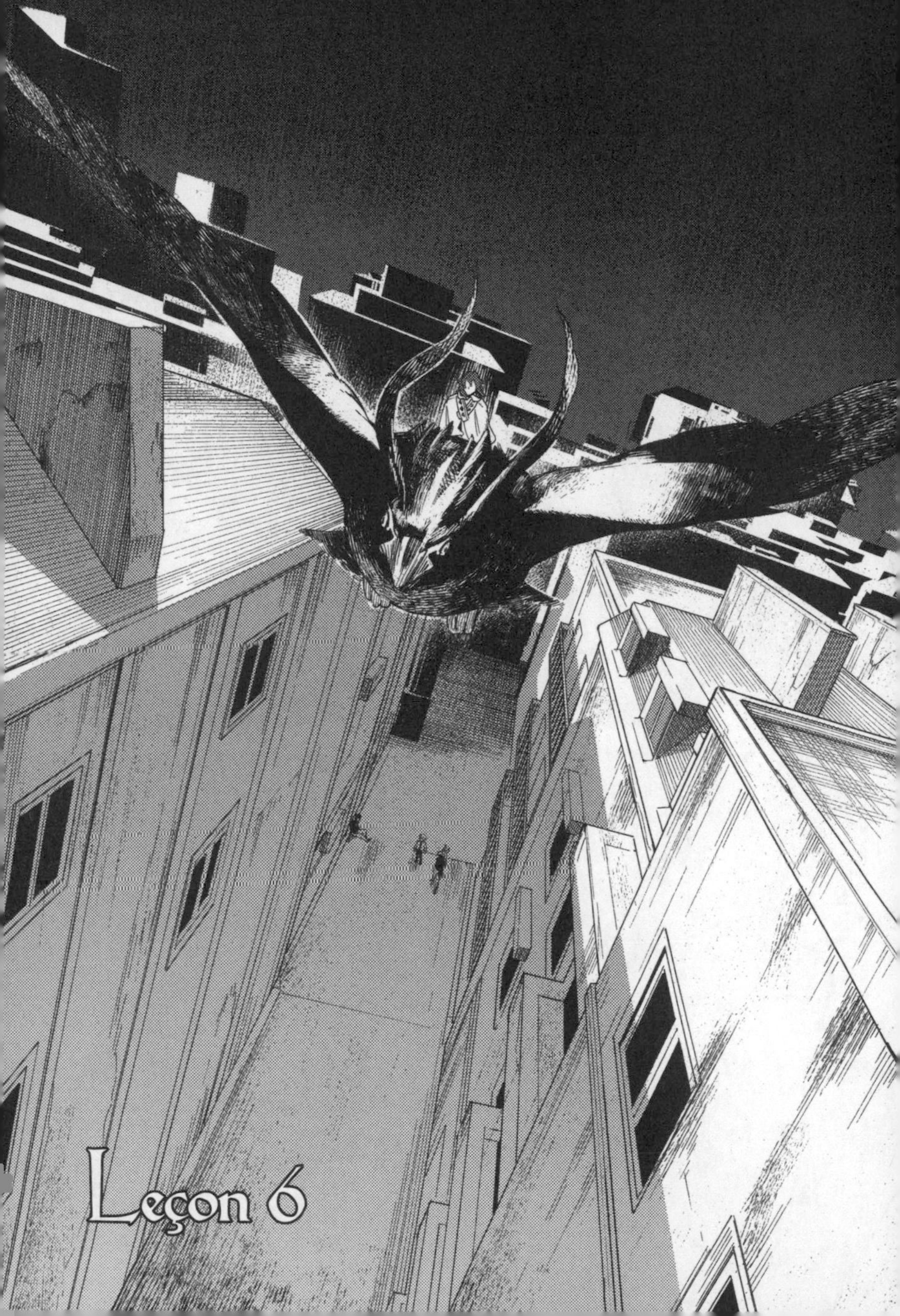
Leçon 6

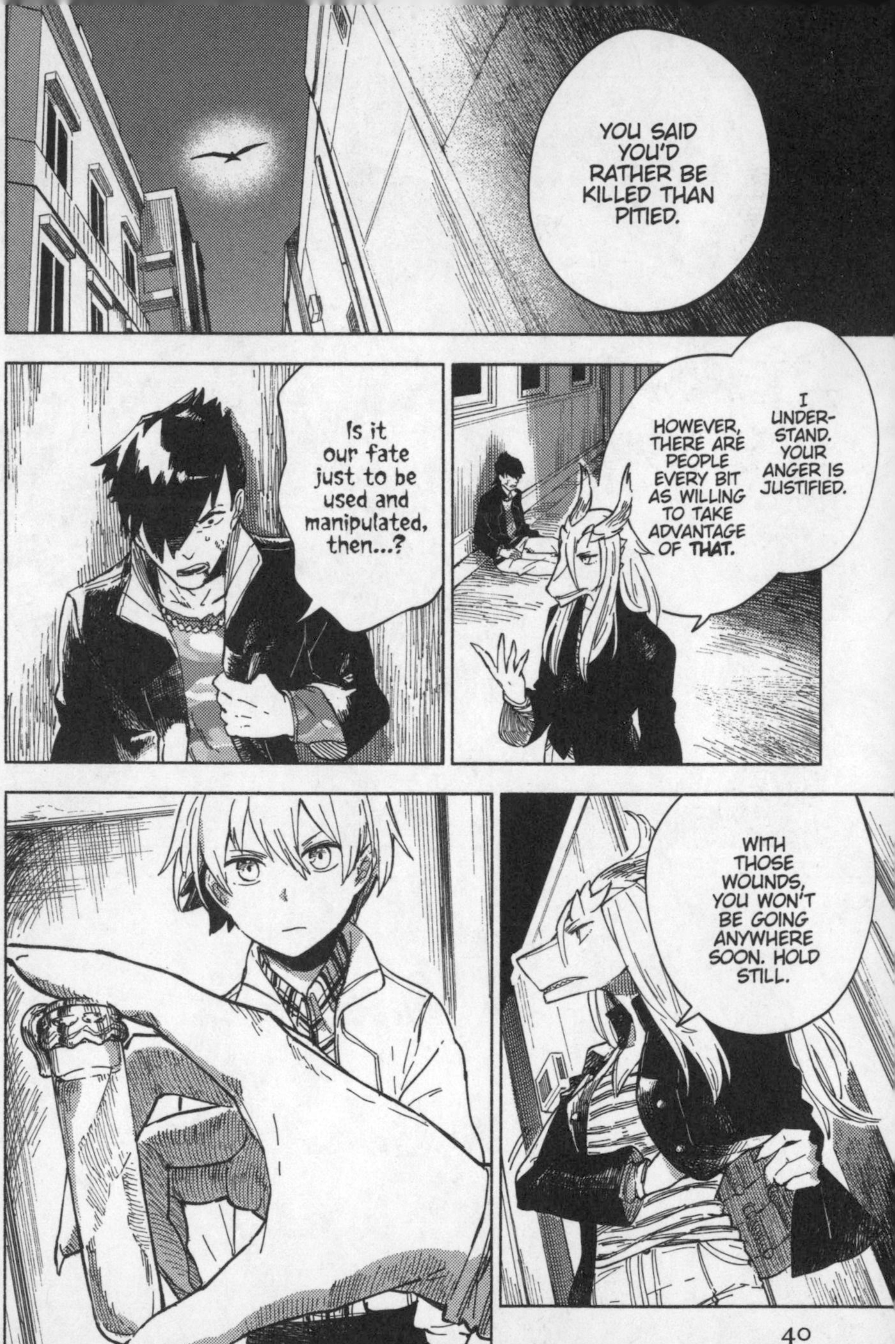
YOU SAID YOU'D RATHER BE KILLED THAN PITIED.
I UNDER-STAND. YOUR ANGER IS JUSTIFIED.
HOWEVER, THERE ARE PEOPLE EVERY BIT AS WILLING TO TAKE ADVANTAGE OF **THAT**.
Is it our fate just to be used and manipulated, then...?
WITH THOSE WOUNDS, YOU WON'T BE GOING ANYWHERE SOON. HOLD STILL.

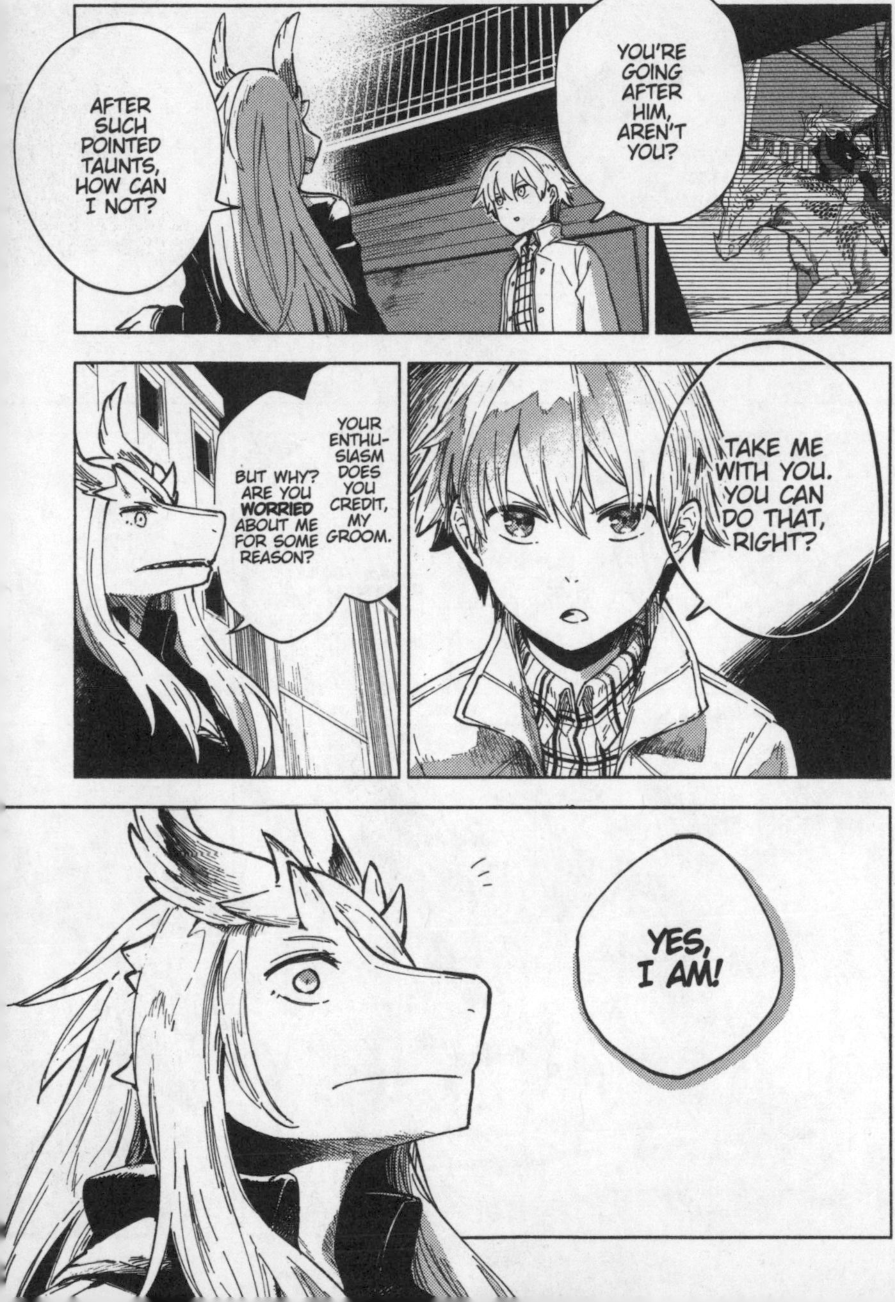
YOU'RE GOING AFTER HIM, AREN'T YOU?
AFTER SUCH POINTED TAUNTS, HOW CAN I NOT?
TAKE ME WITH YOU. YOU CAN DO THAT, RIGHT?
YOUR ENTHUSIASM DOES YOU CREDIT, MY GROOM.
BUT WHY? ARE YOU WORRIED ABOUT ME FOR SOME REASON?
YES, I AM!

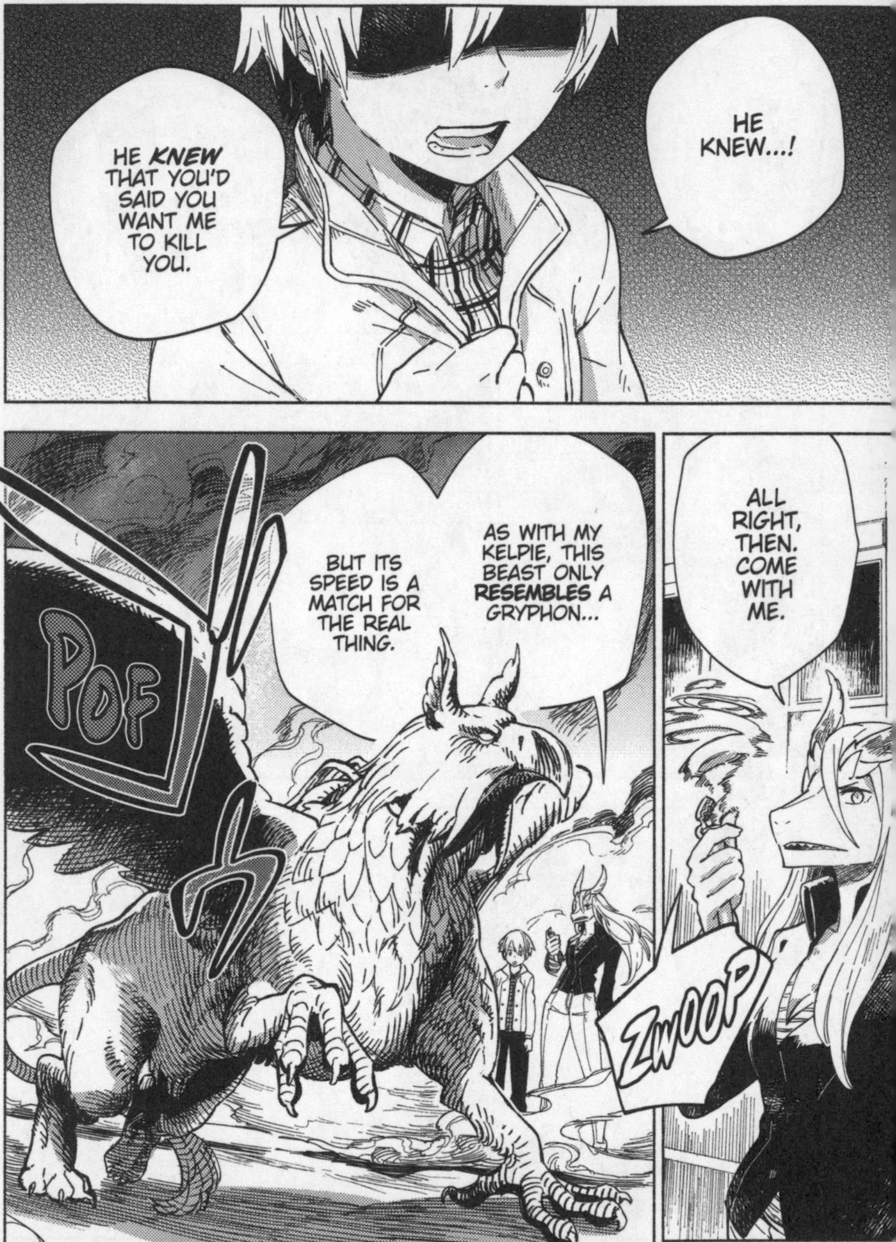
HE KNEW...!
HE *KNEW* THAT YOU'D SAID YOU WANT ME TO KILL YOU.
ALL RIGHT, THEN. COME WITH ME.
ZWOOP
AS WITH MY KELPIE, THIS BEAST ONLY **RESEMBLES** A GRYPHON...
BUT ITS SPEED IS A MATCH FOR THE REAL THING.
POF

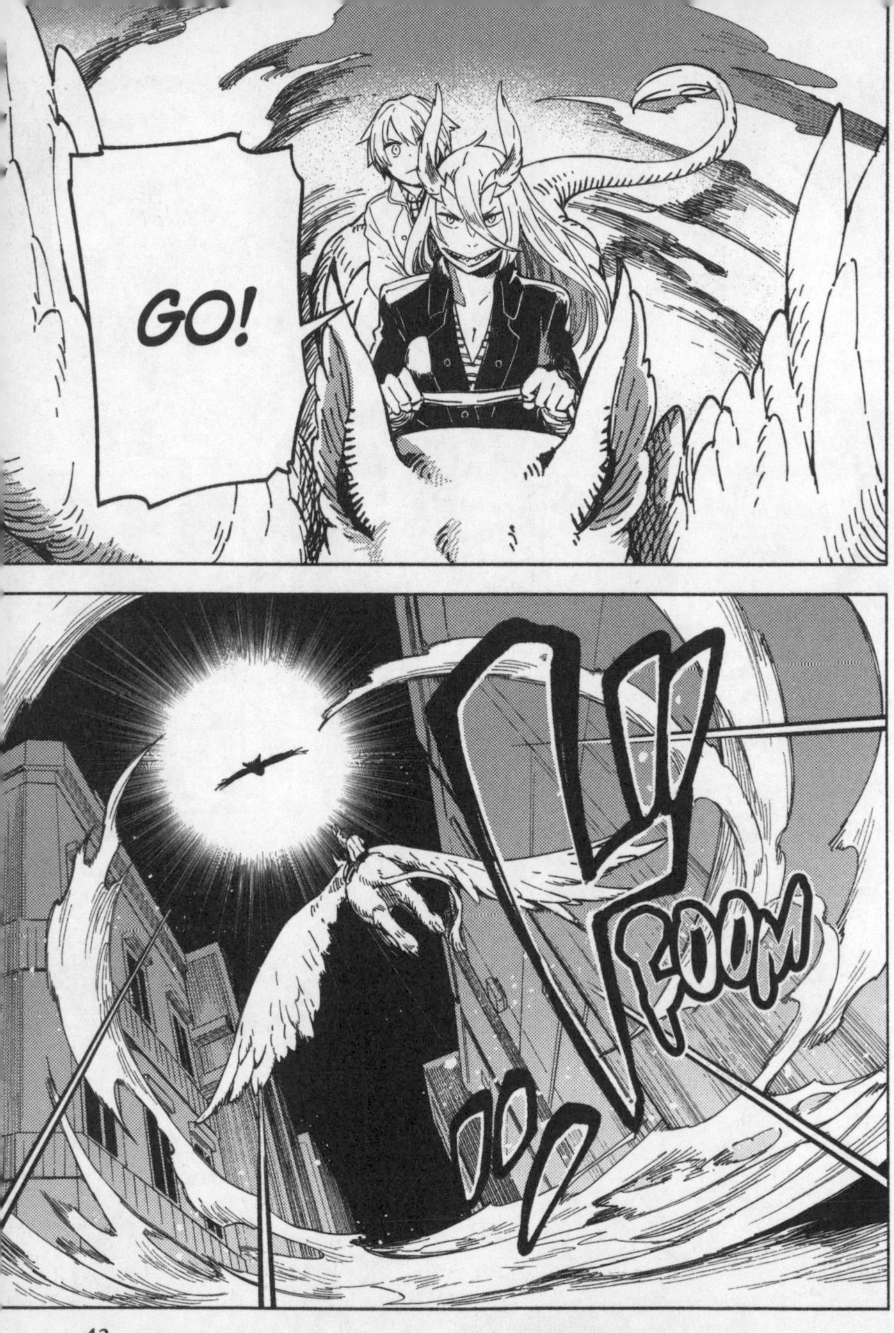
GO!
FOOM

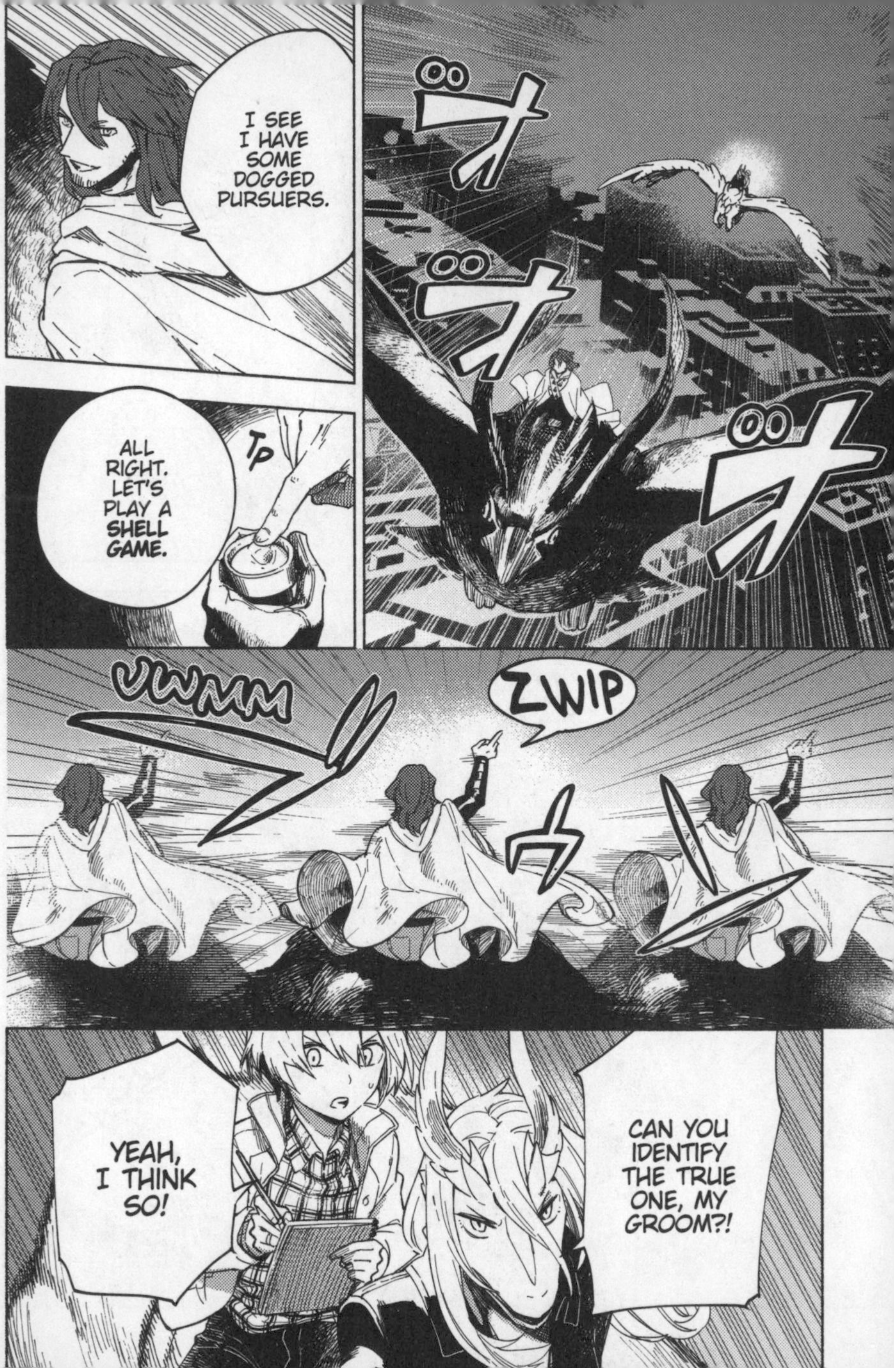
I SEE I HAVE SOME DOGGED PURSUERS.
TP
ALL RIGHT. LET'S PLAY A SHELL GAME.
ZWIP
VWMM
CAN YOU IDENTIFY THE TRUE ONE, MY GROOM?!
YEAH, I THINK SO!

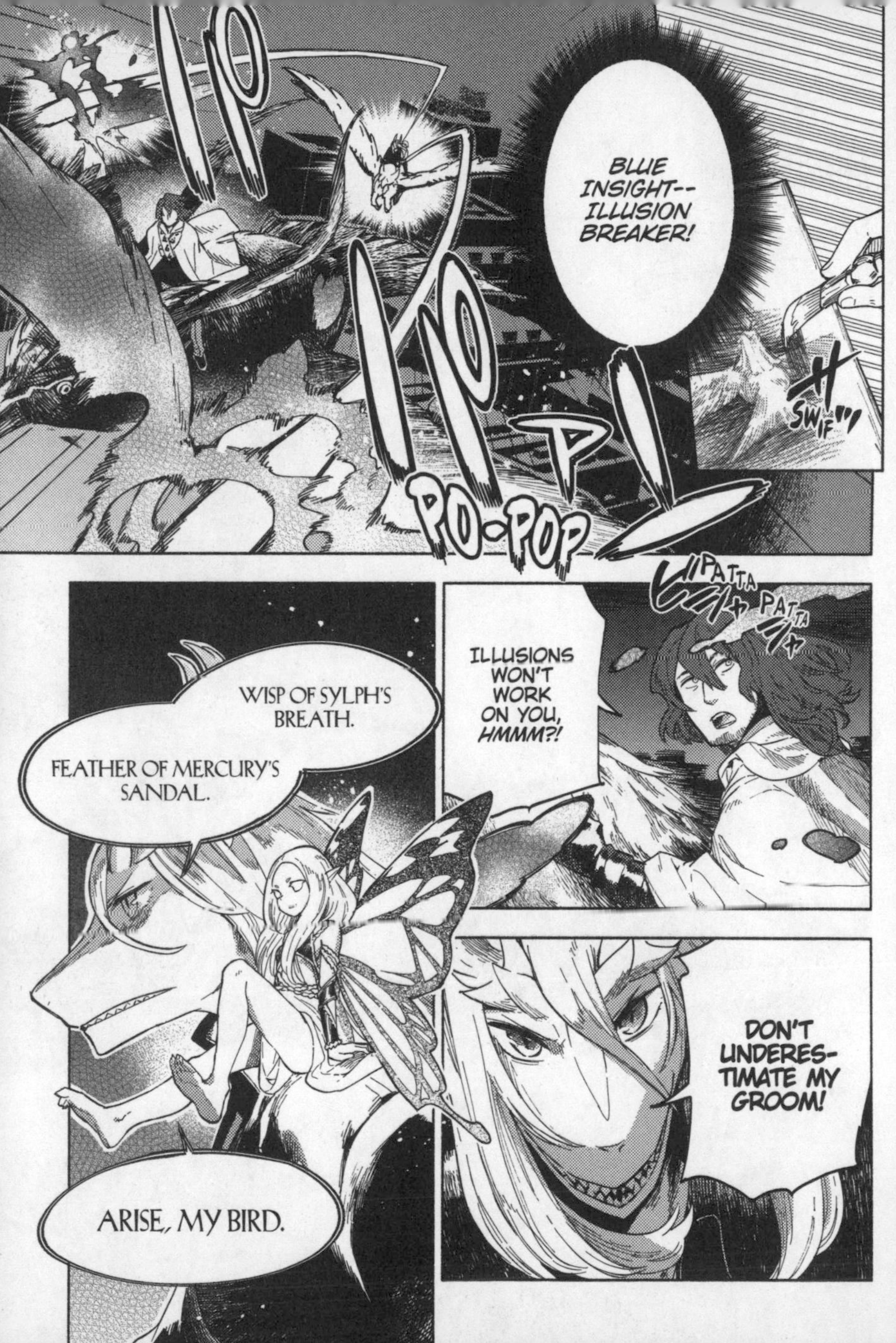
BLUE INSIGHT-- ILLUSION BREAKER!
SWIF
PO-POP
PATTA PATTA
ILLUSIONS WON'T WORK ON YOU, HMMM?!
DON'T UNDERES-TIMATE MY GROOM!
WISP OF SYLPH'S BREATH.
FEATHER OF MERCURY'S SANDAL.
ARISE, MY BIRD.

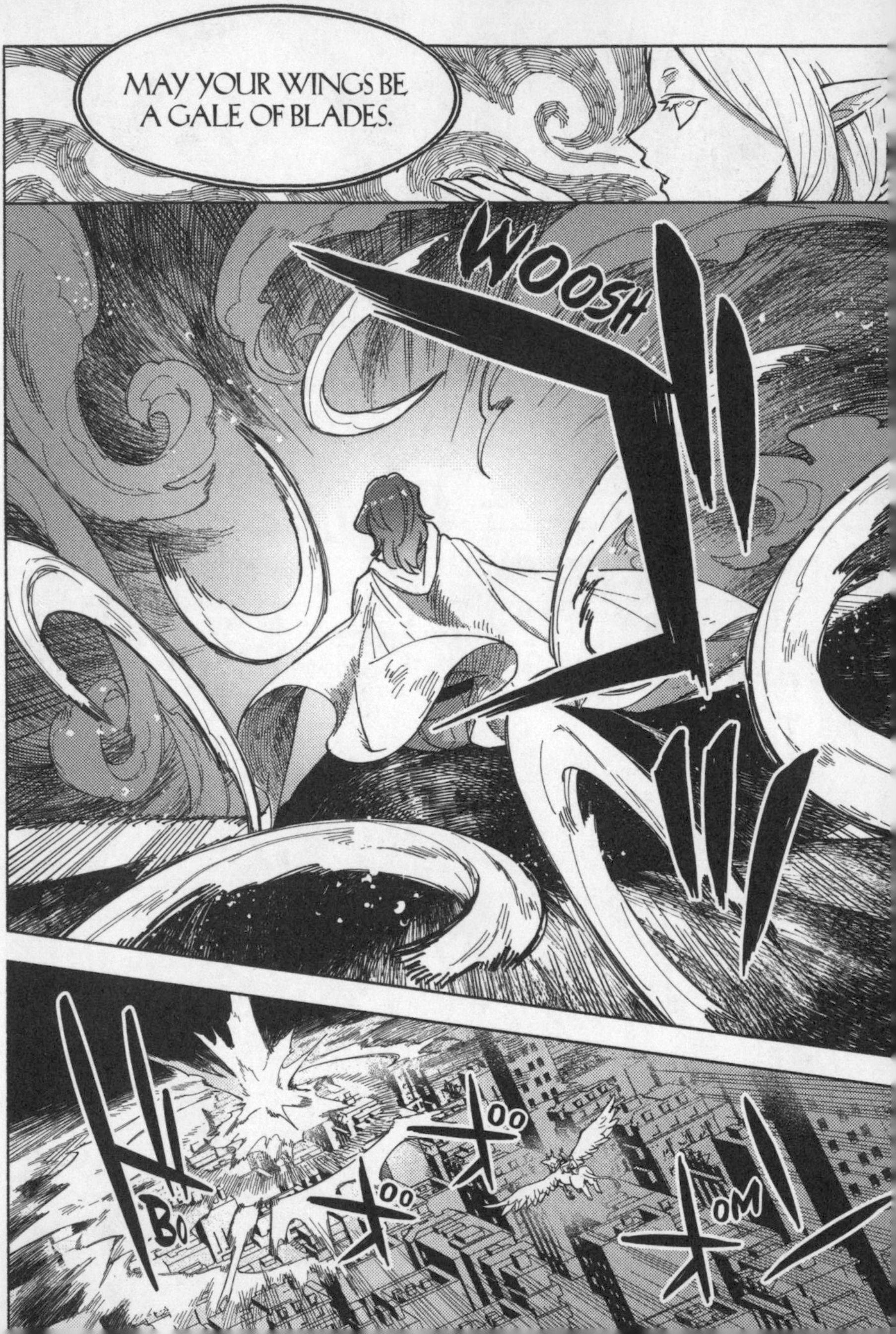
MAY YOUR WINGS BE A GALE OF BLADES.
WOOSH
BOOOOOOM

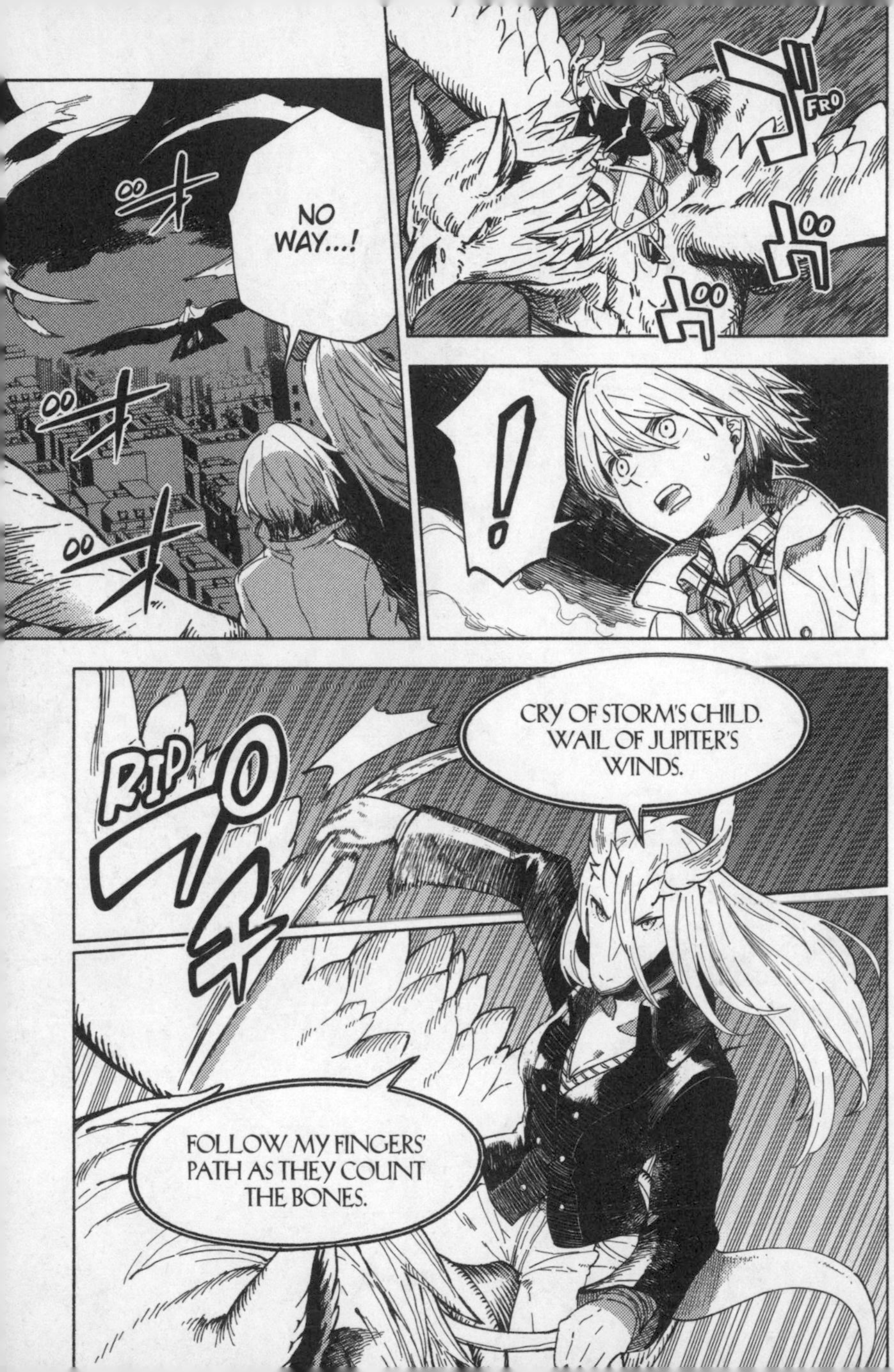
FRO
!
NO WAY...!
CRY OF STORM'S CHILD. WAIL OF JUPITER'S WINDS.
RIP
FOLLOW MY FINGERS' PATH AS THEY COUNT THE BONES.

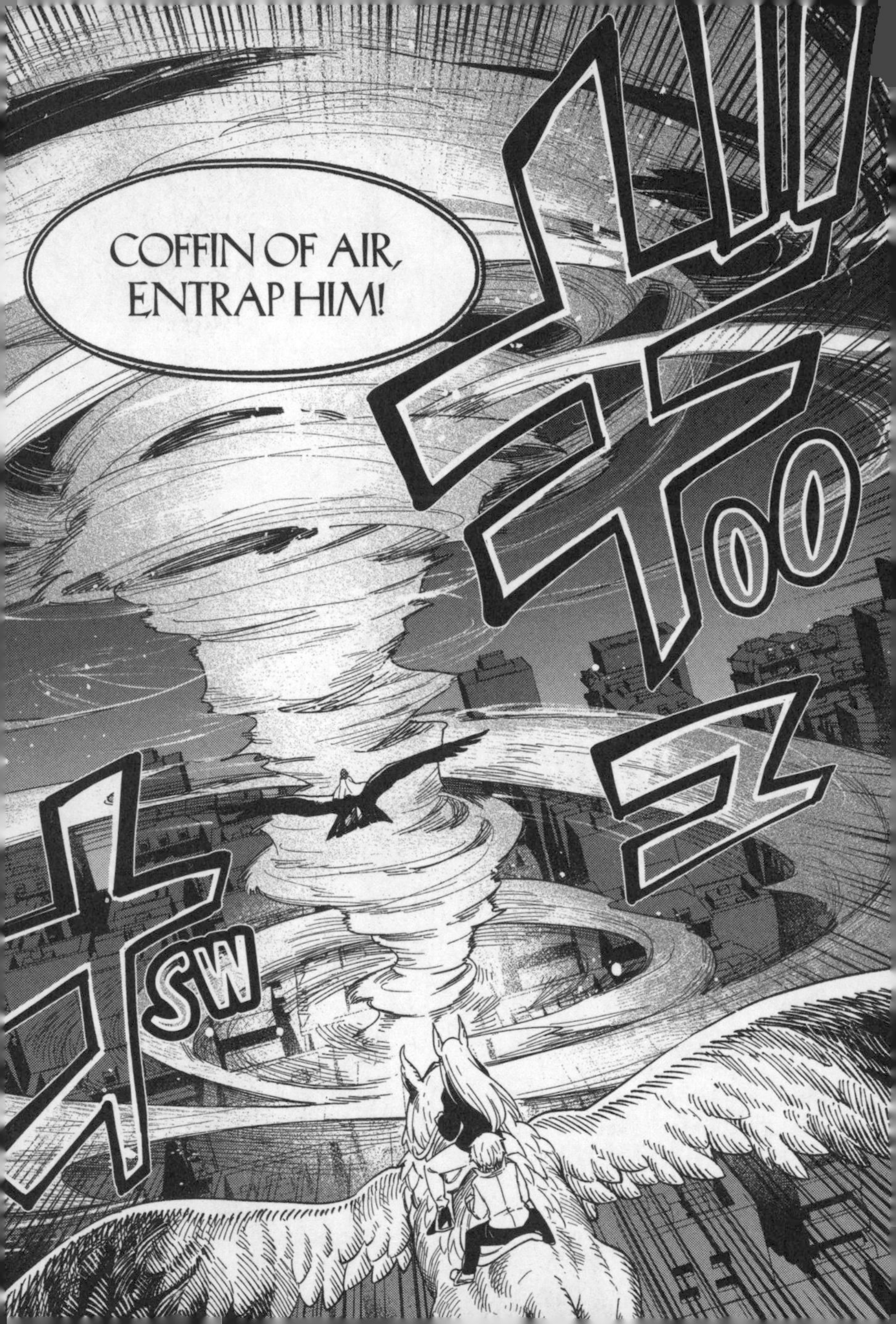
COFFIN OF AIR, ENTRAP HIM!
SW

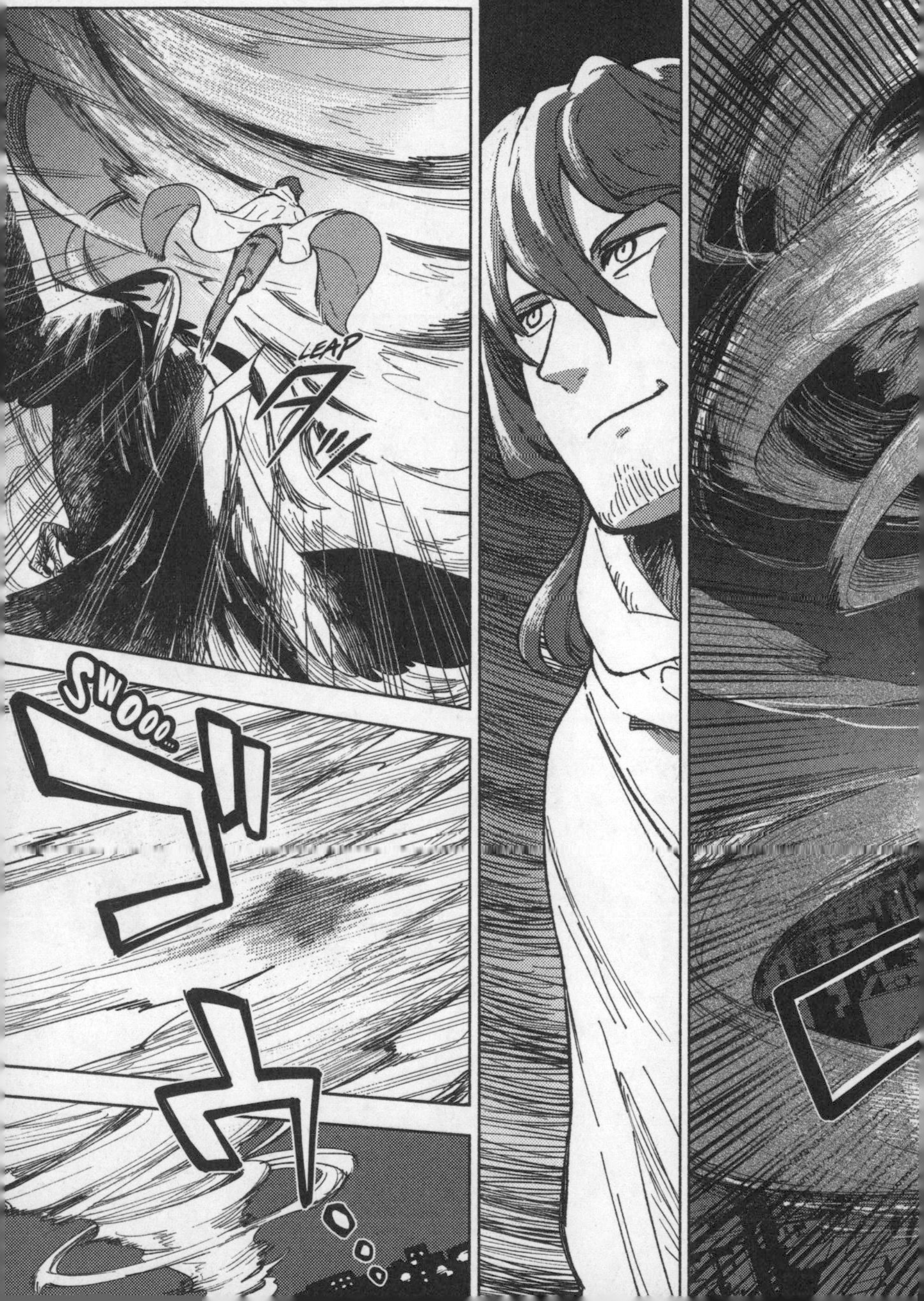
LEAP
SWOOO...

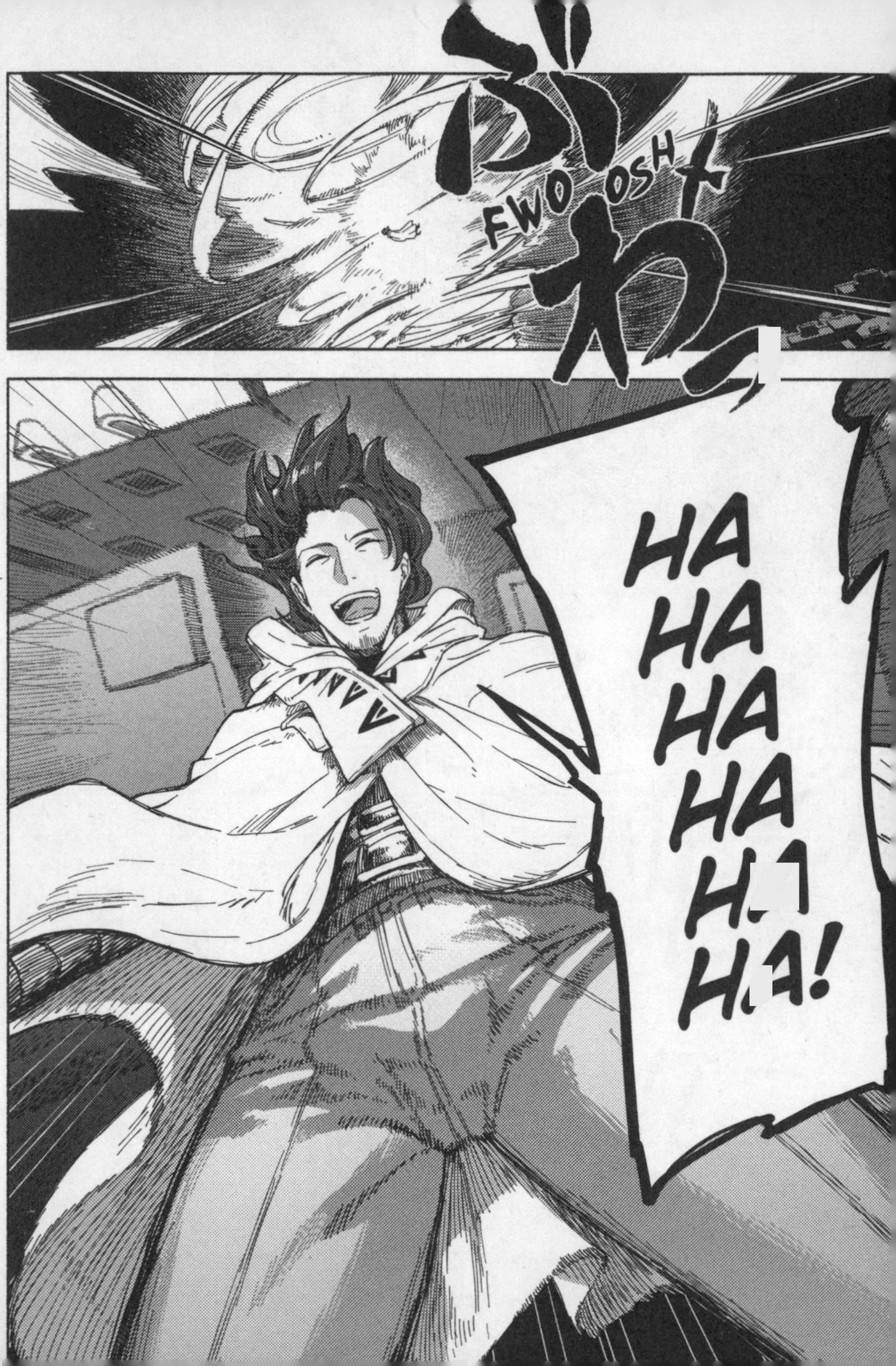
ぶわっ
FWOOSH
HA HA HA HA HA HA HA!

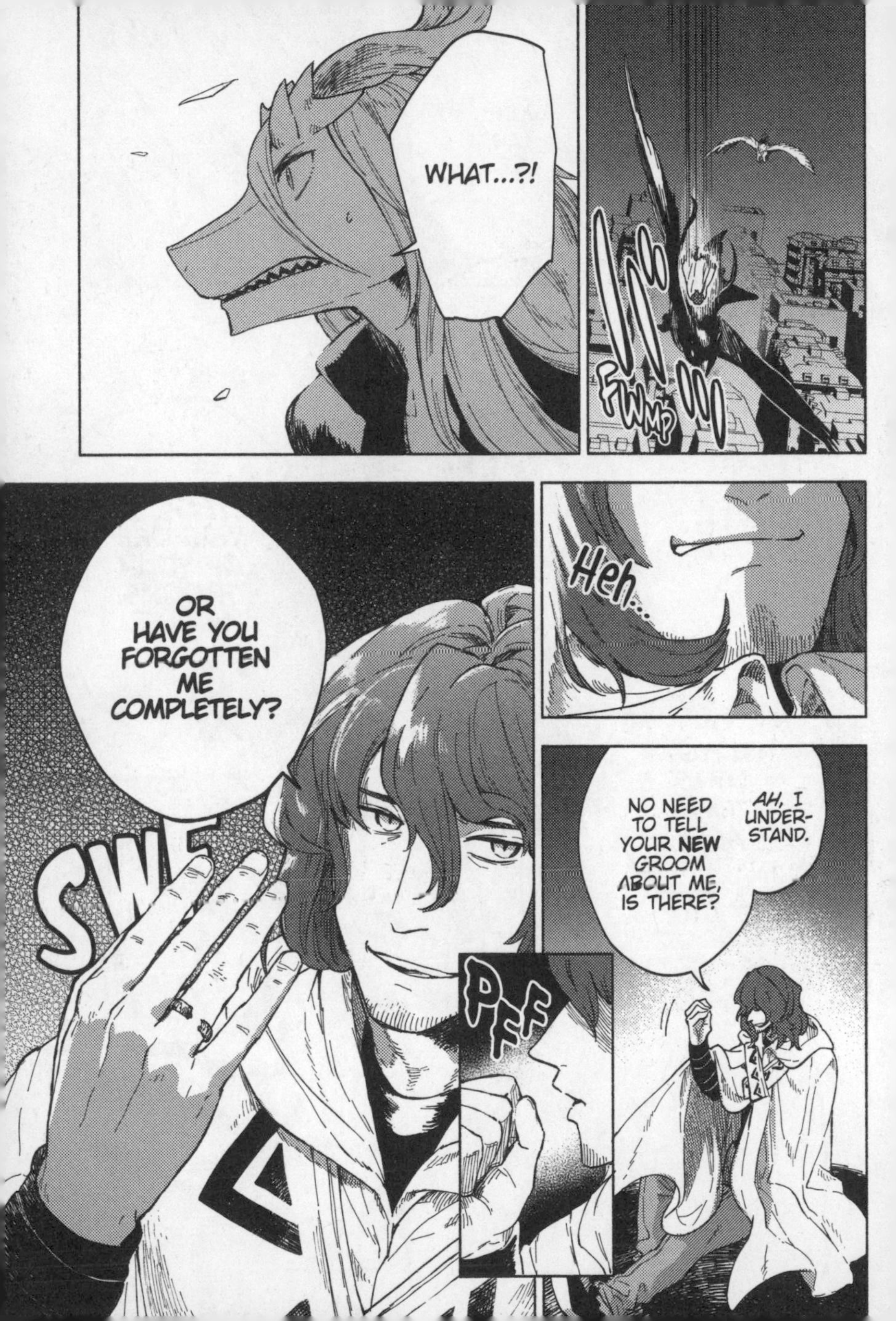
FWMP
WHAT...?!
Heh...
AH, I UNDERSTAND.
NO NEED TO TELL YOUR NEW GROOM ABOUT ME, IS THERE?
PFF
OR HAVE YOU FORGOTTEN ME COMPLETELY?
SWF

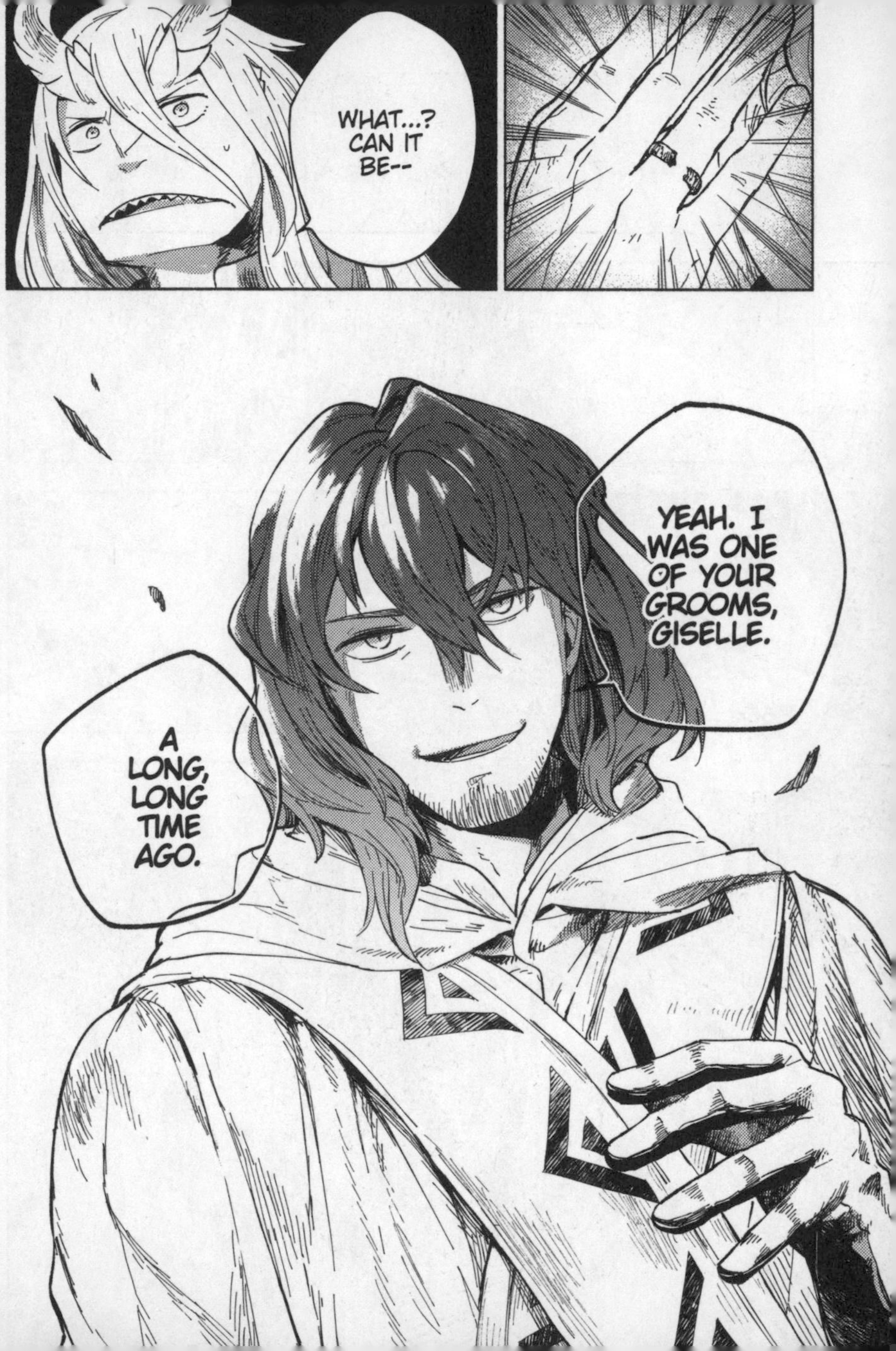
WHAT...? CAN IT BE--
YEAH. I WAS ONE OF YOUR GROOMS, GISELLE.
A LONG, LONG TIME AGO.

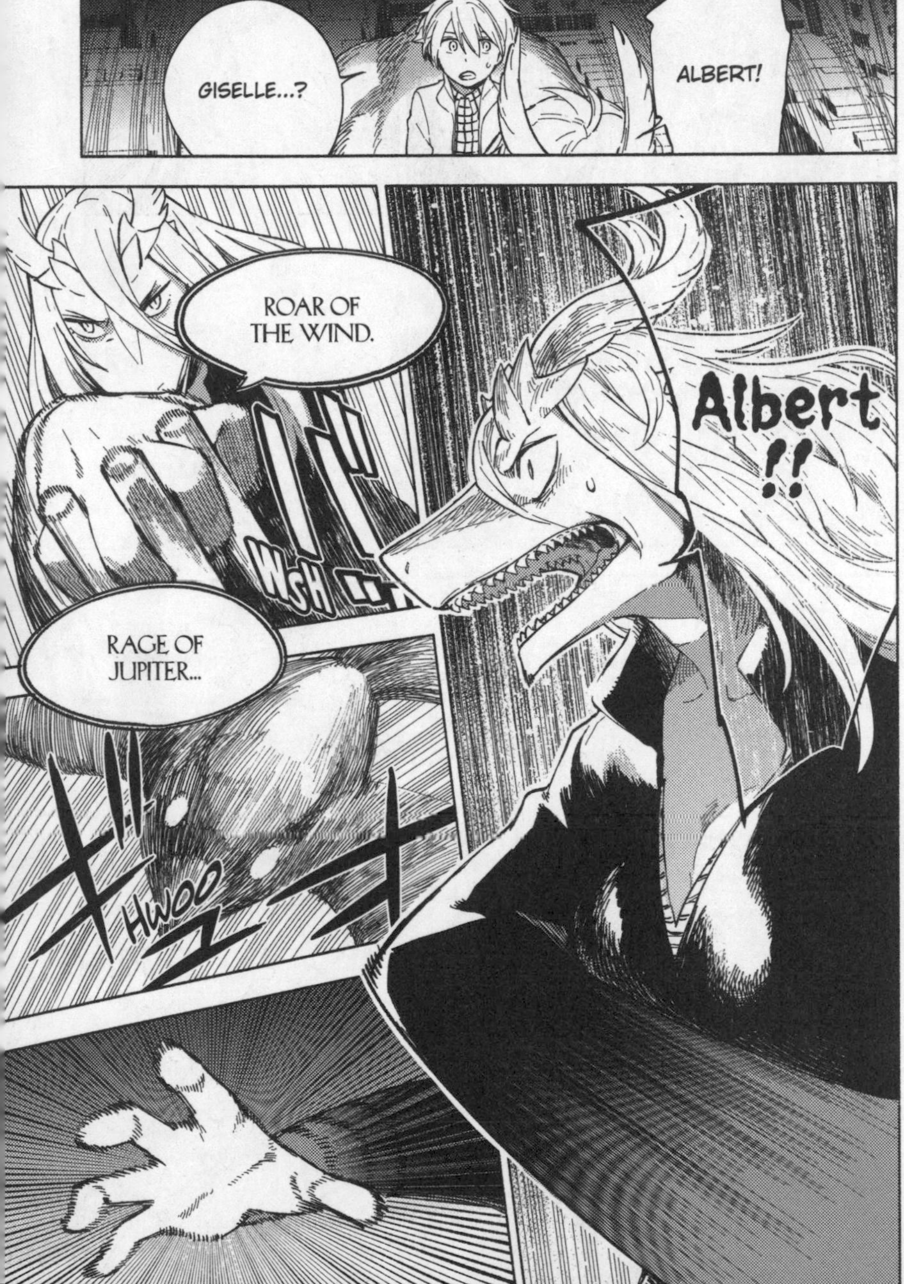
ALBERT!
GISELLE...?
Albert!!
ROAR OF THE WIND.
WSH
RAGE OF JUPITER...
HWOO

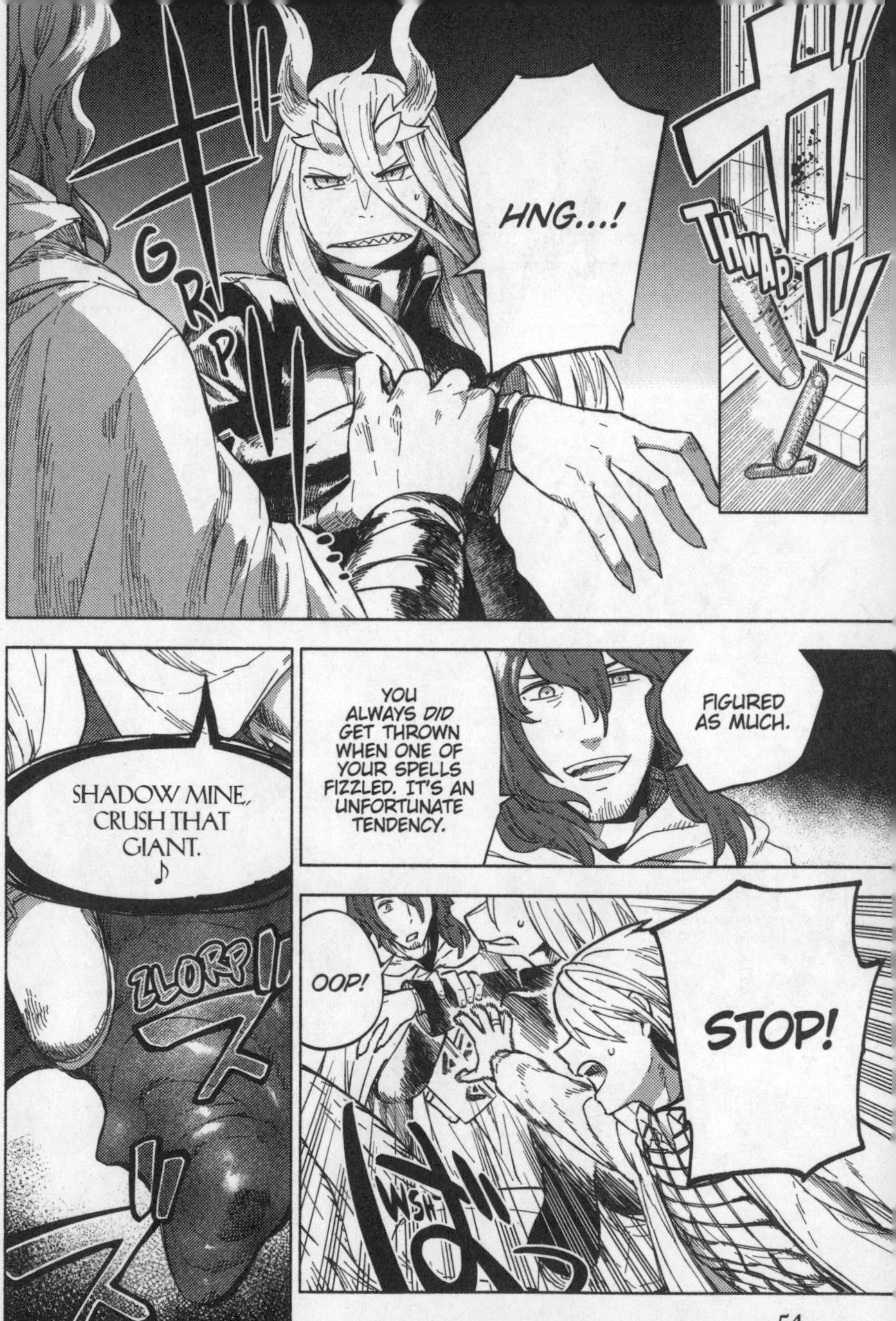
THWAP
HNG...!
GRP
FIGURED AS MUCH.
YOU ALWAYS *DID* GET THROWN WHEN ONE OF YOUR SPELLS FIZZLED. IT'S AN UNFORTUNATE TENDENCY.
STOP!
OOP!
WSH
SHADOW MINE, CRUSH THAT GIANT. ♪
ZLORP

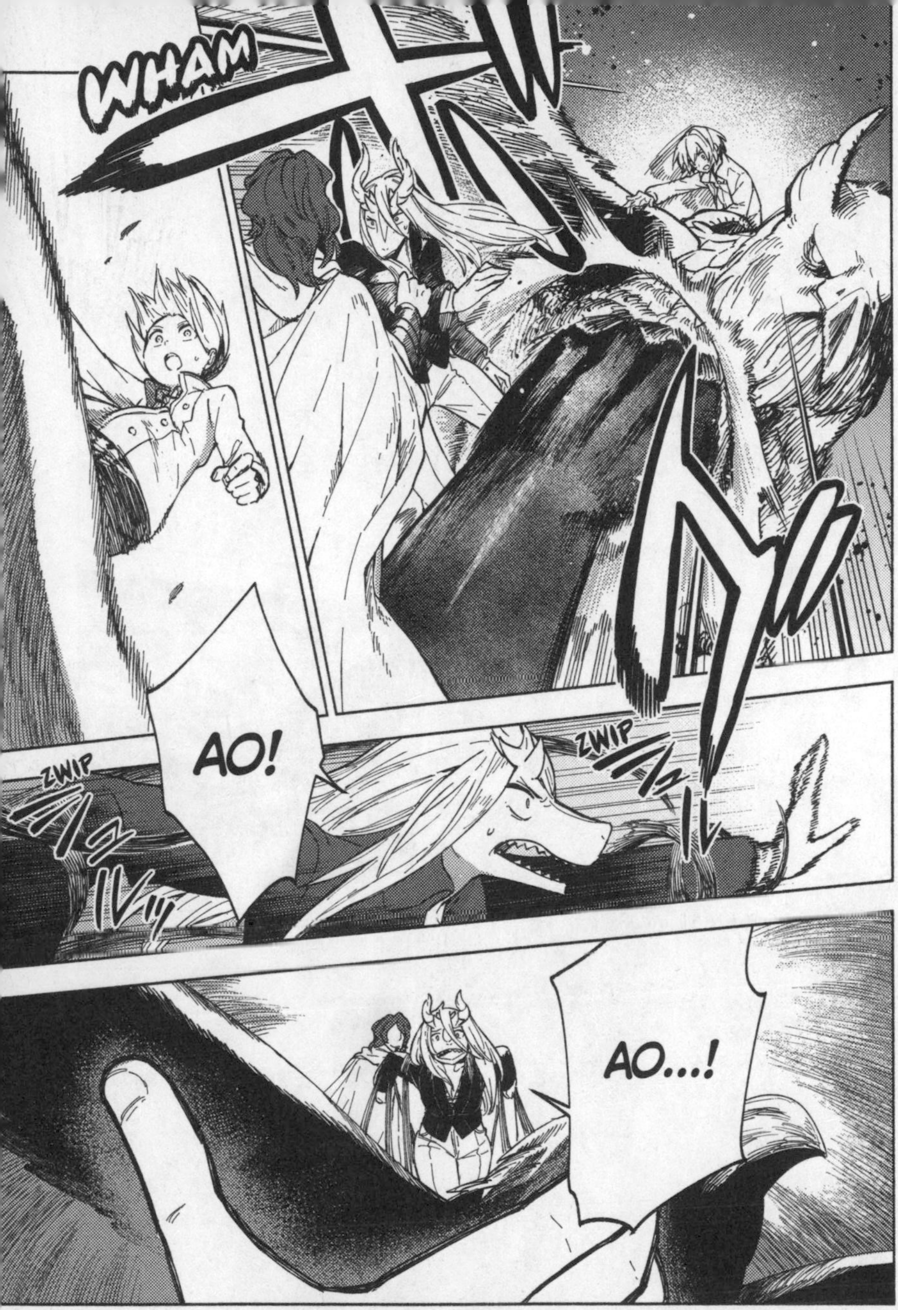
WHAM
ZWIP
AO!
ZWIP
AO...!

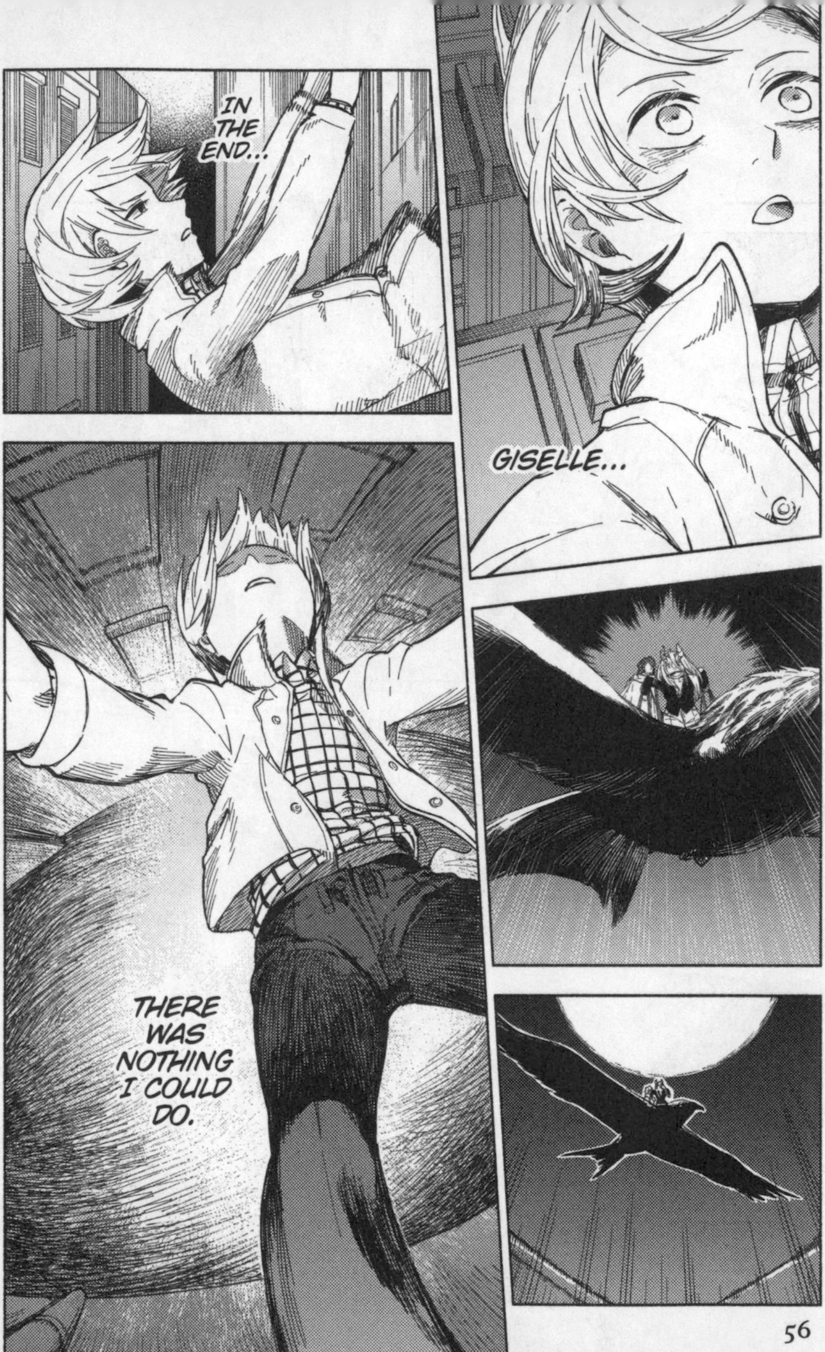
GISELLE...
IN THE END...
THERE WAS NOTHING I COULD DO.

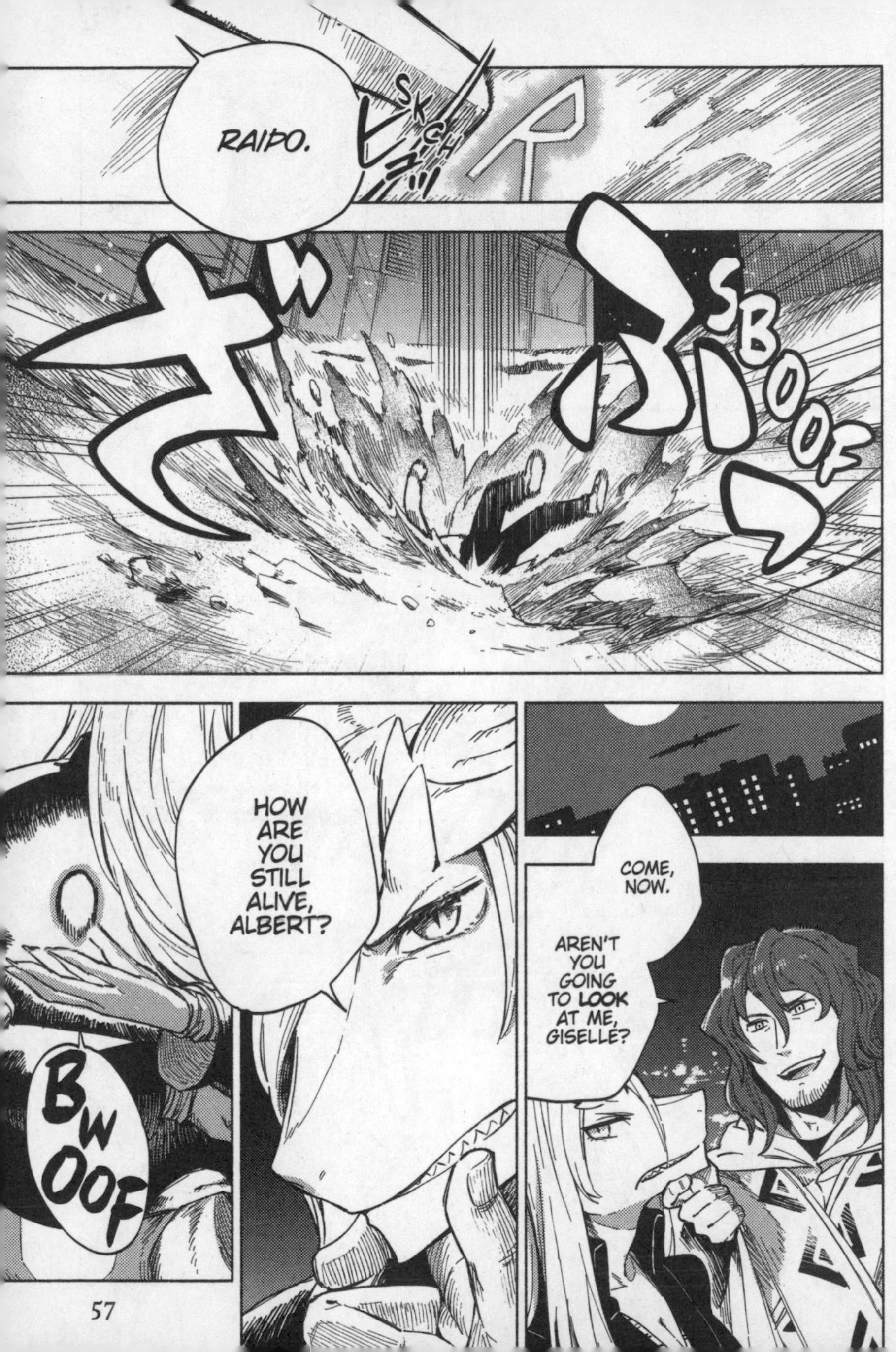
RAIPO.
SKCH
SBOOF
COME, NOW.
AREN'T YOU GOING TO LOOK AT ME, GISELLE?
HOW ARE YOU STILL ALIVE, ALBERT?
BWOOF

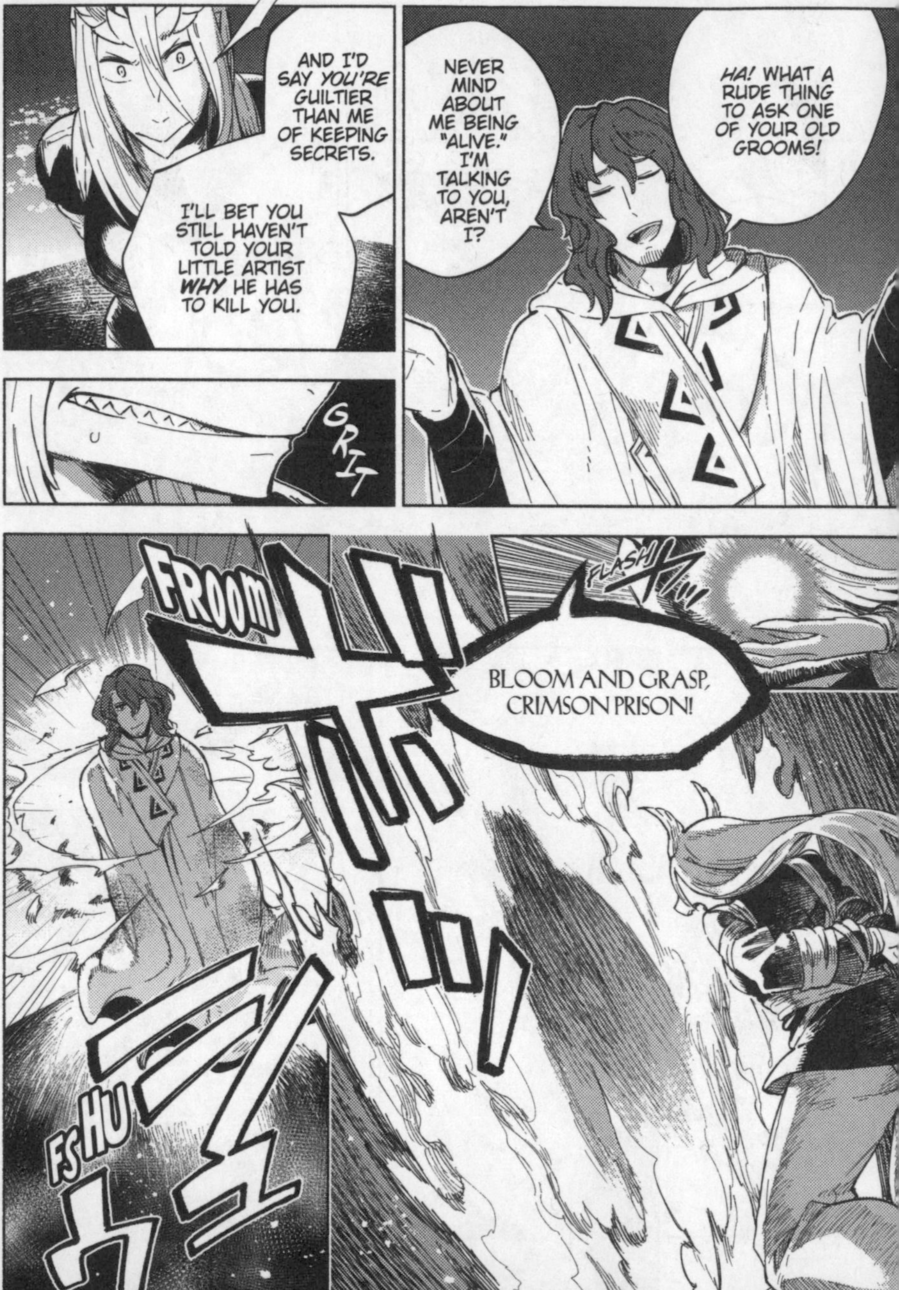
HA! WHAT A RUDE THING TO ASK ONE OF YOUR OLD GROOMS!
NEVER MIND ABOUT ME BEING "ALIVE." I'M TALKING TO YOU, AREN'T I?
AND I'D SAY YOU'RE GUILTIER THAN ME OF KEEPING SECRETS.
I'LL BET YOU STILL HAVEN'T TOLD YOUR LITTLE ARTIST WHY HE HAS TO KILL YOU.
GRIT
FLASH
BLOOM AND GRASP, CRIMSON PRISON!
FROOM
FSHU

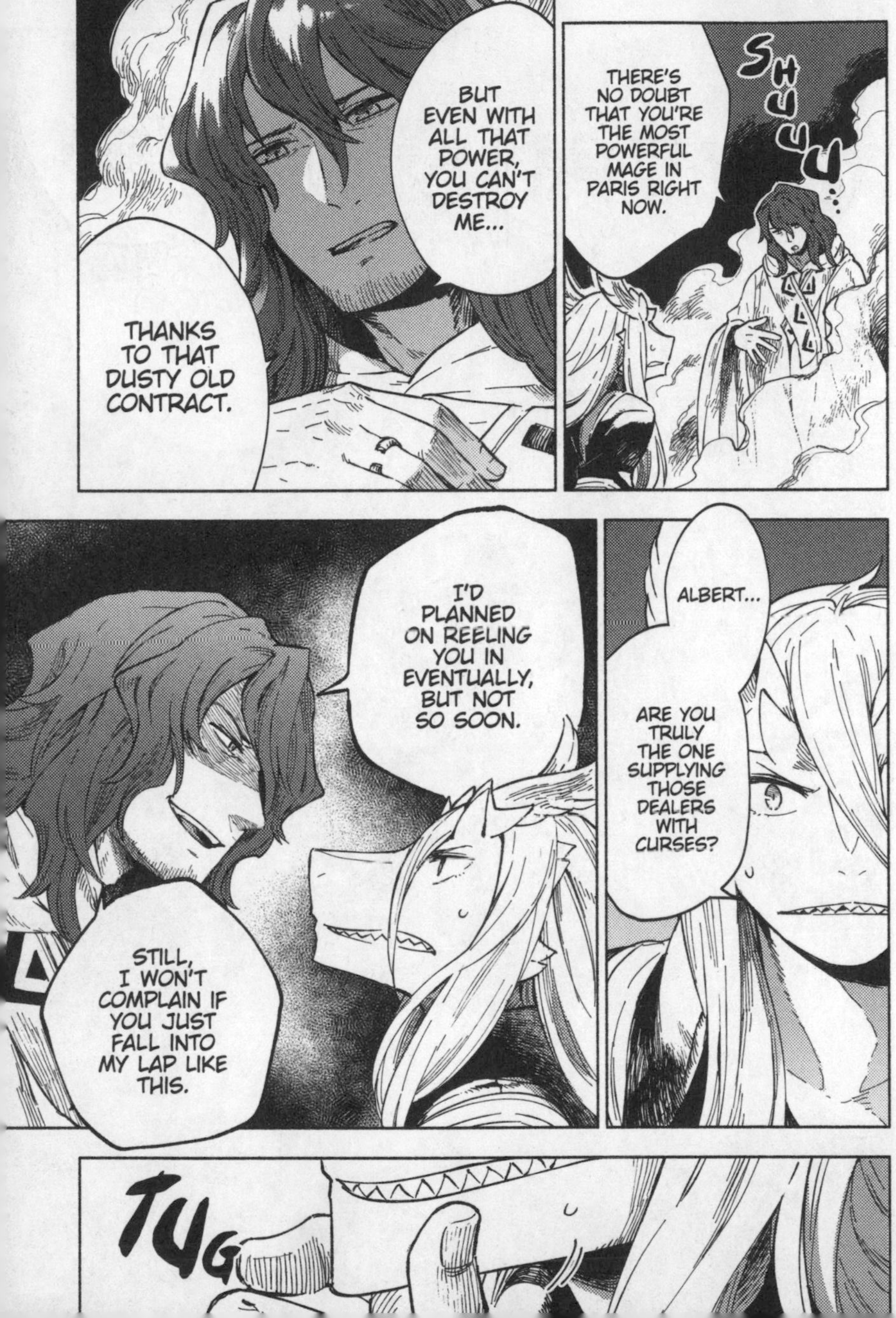
SHUUUU
THERE'S NO DOUBT THAT YOU'RE THE MOST POWERFUL MAGE IN PARIS RIGHT NOW.
BUT EVEN WITH ALL THAT POWER, YOU CAN'T DESTROY ME...
THANKS TO THAT DUSTY OLD CONTRACT.
ALBERT...
ARE YOU TRULY THE ONE SUPPLYING THOSE DEALERS WITH CURSES?
I'D PLANNED ON REELING YOU IN EVENTUALLY, BUT NOT SO SOON.
STILL, I WON'T COMPLAIN IF YOU JUST FALL INTO MY LAP LIKE THIS.
TUG

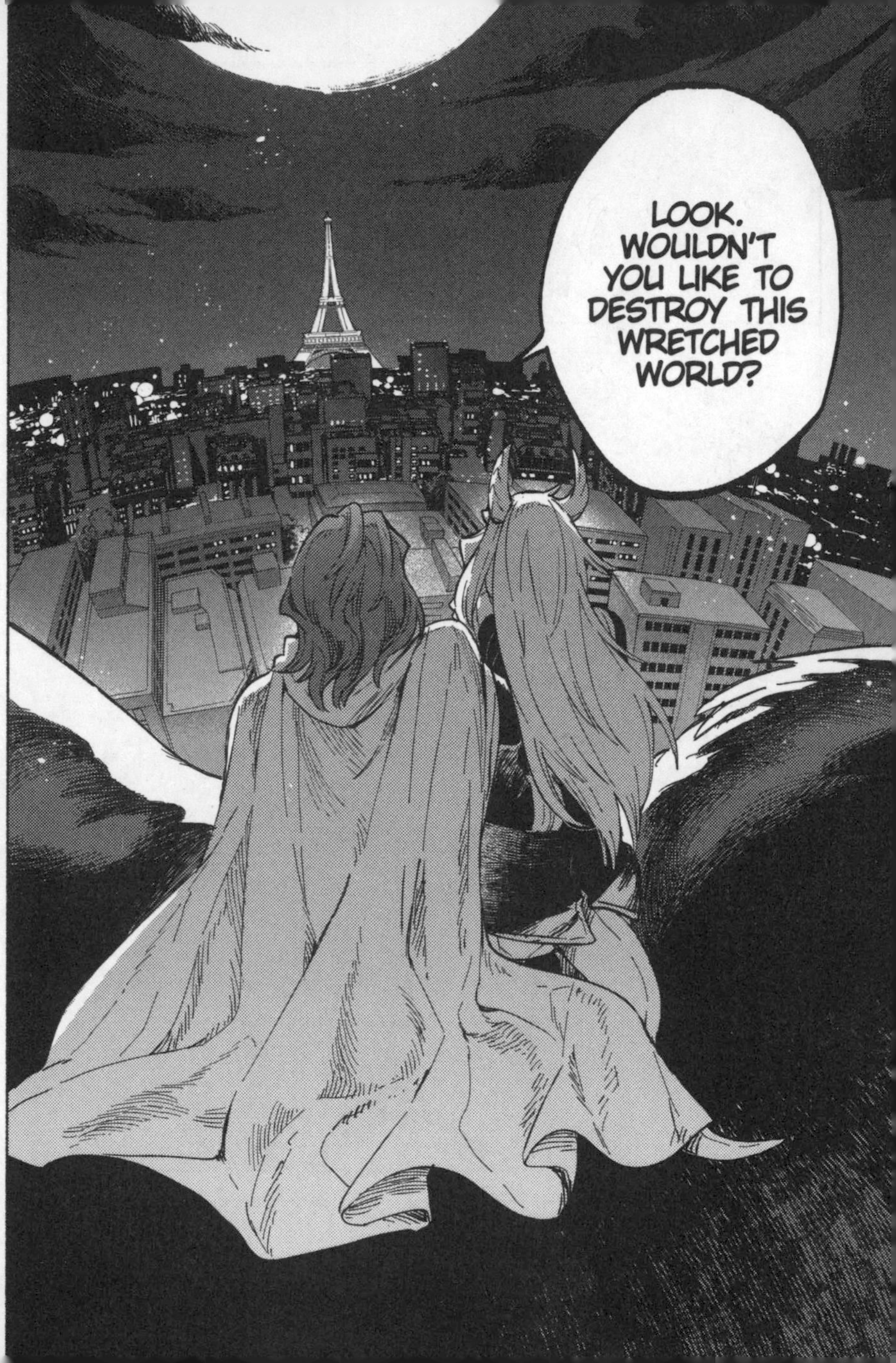
LOOK. WOULDN'T YOU LIKE TO DESTROY THIS WRETCHED WORLD?

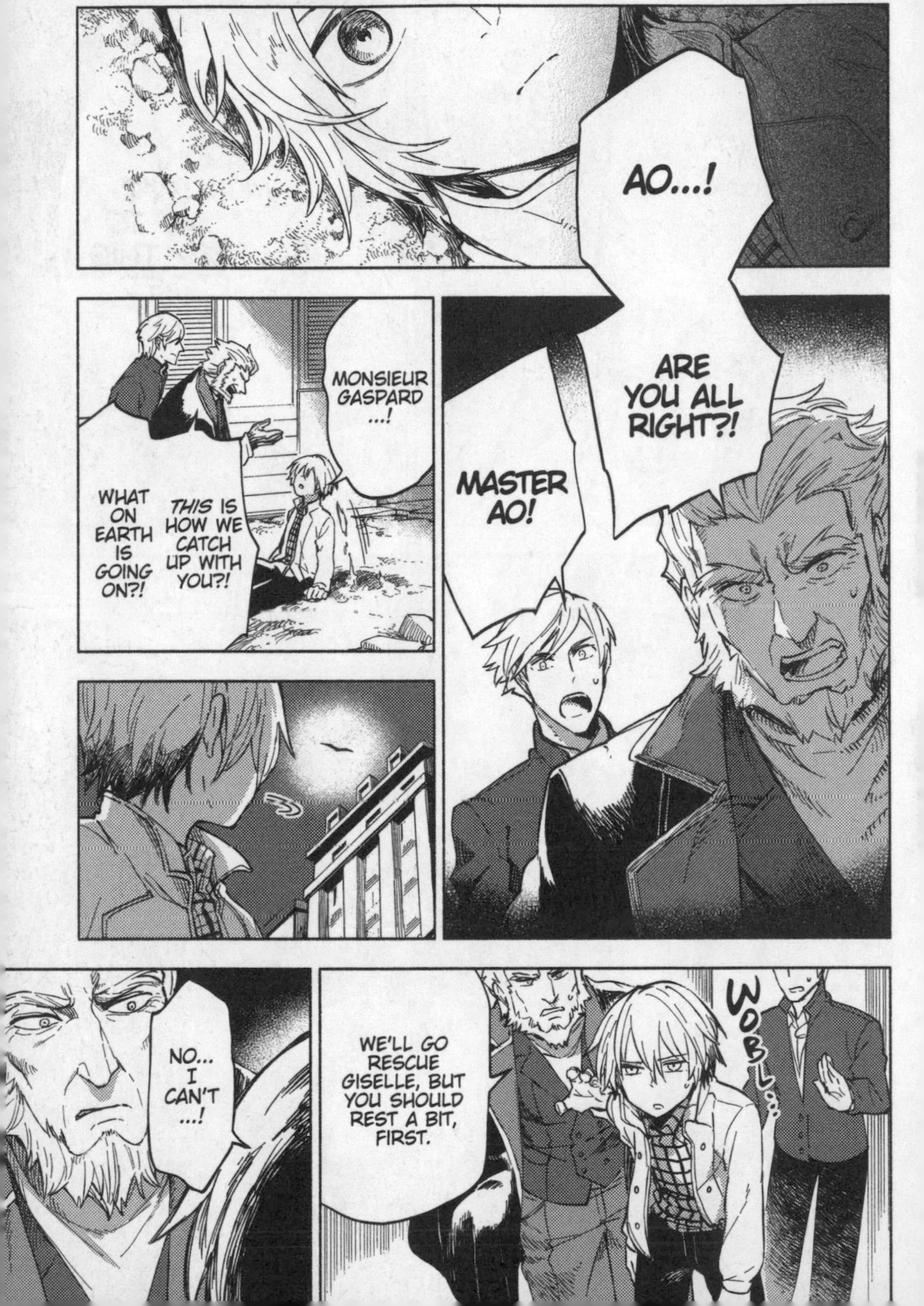
AO...!
ARE YOU ALL RIGHT?!
MASTER AO!
MONSIEUR GASPARD ...!
THIS IS HOW WE CATCH UP WITH YOU?!
WHAT ON EARTH IS GOING ON?!
WOBBL...
WE'LL GO RESCUE GISELLE, BUT YOU SHOULD REST A BIT, FIRST.
NO... I CAN'T ...!

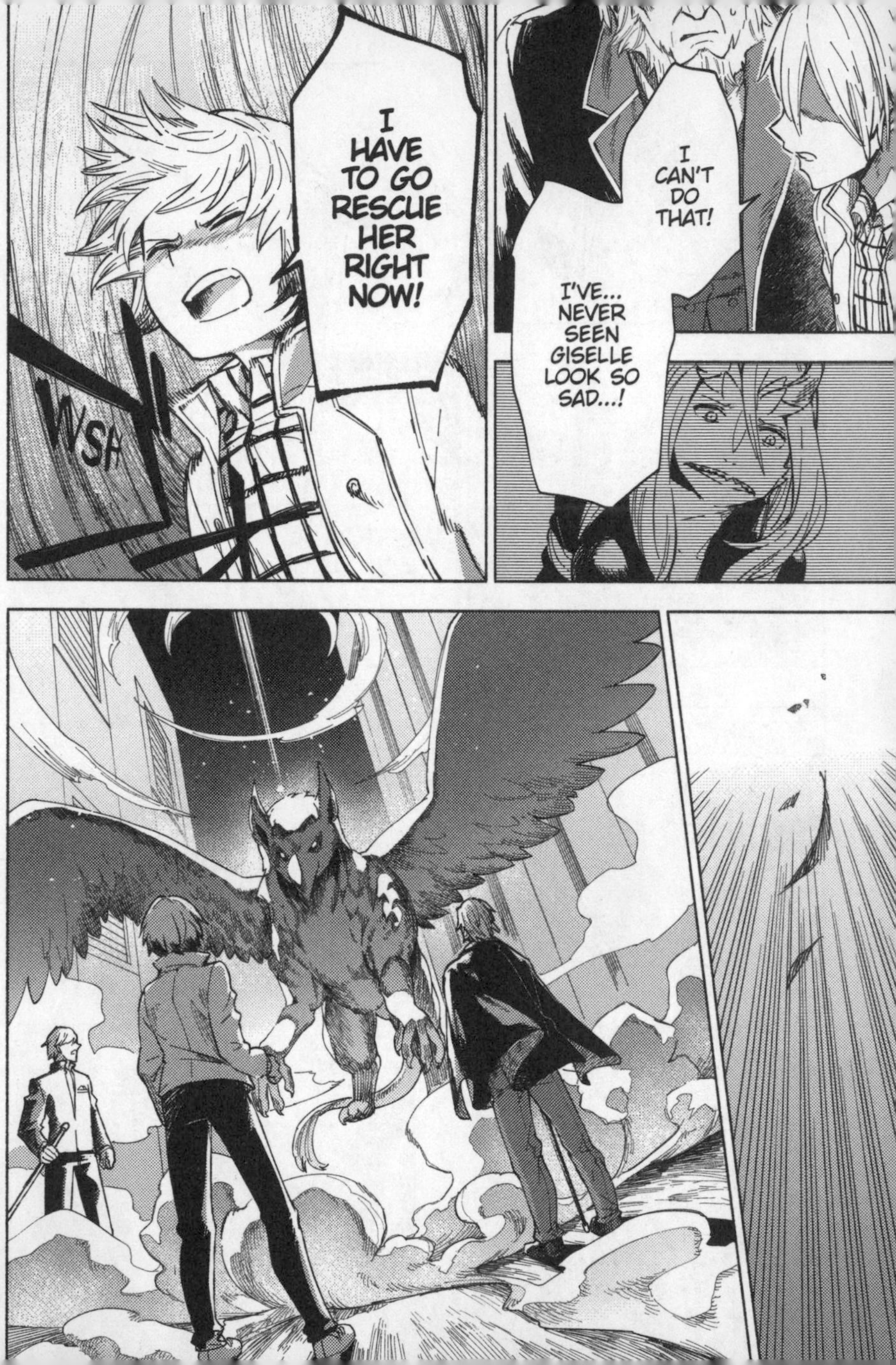
I CAN'T DO THAT!
I'VE... NEVER SEEN GISELLE LOOK SO SAD...!
I HAVE TO GO RESCUE HER RIGHT NOW!
WSH

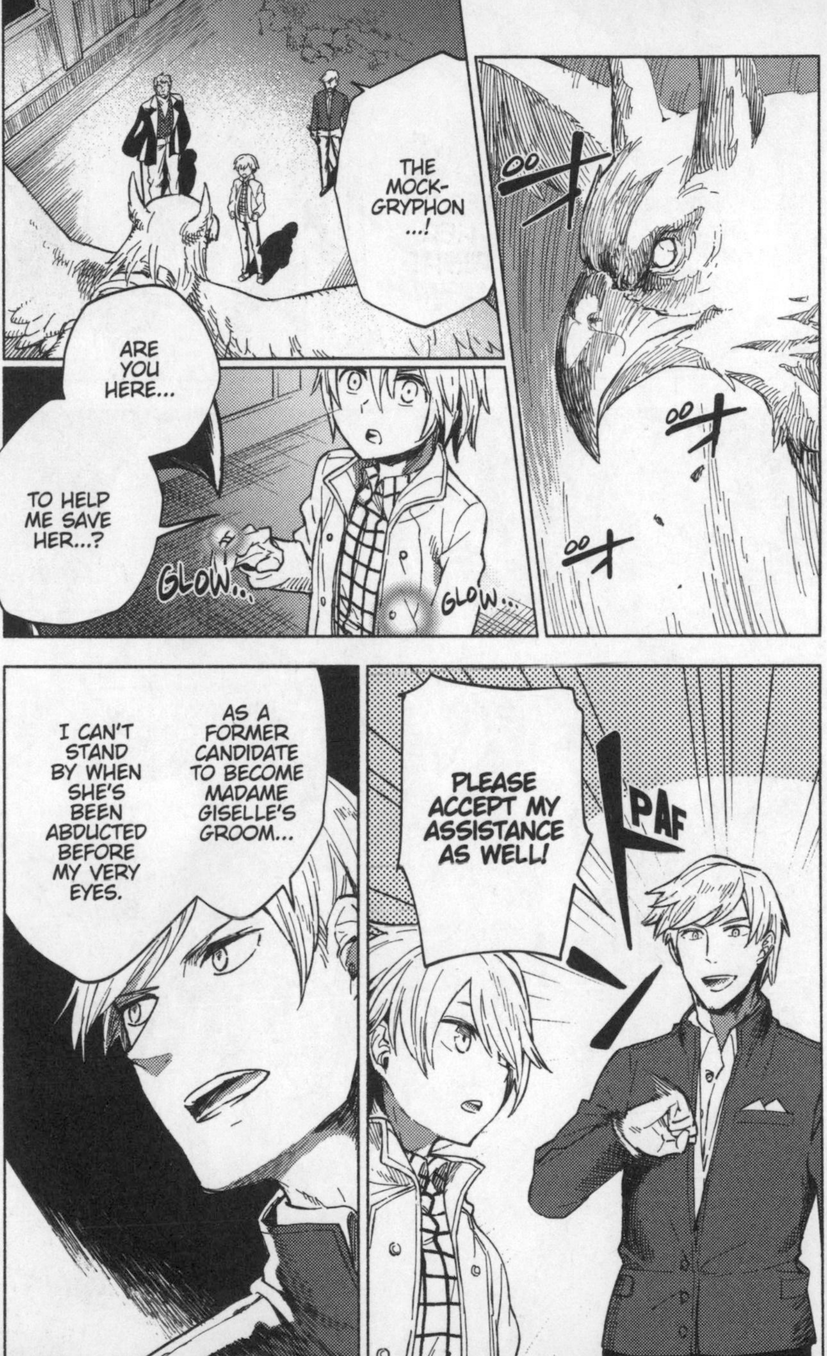
THE MOCK-GRYPHON...!
ARE YOU HERE...
TO HELP ME SAVE HER...?
GLOW...
GLOW...
PLEASE ACCEPT MY ASSISTANCE AS WELL!
PAF
AS A FORMER CANDIDATE TO BECOME MADAME GISELLE'S GROOM...
I CAN'T STAND BY WHEN SHE'S BEEN ABDUCTED BEFORE MY VERY EYES.

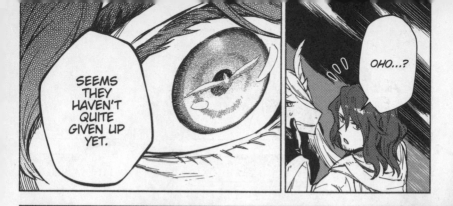

SEEMS THEY HAVEN'T QUITE GIVEN UP YET.

OHO...?

WHA...?!

AO! HOLD THE REINS STEADY!

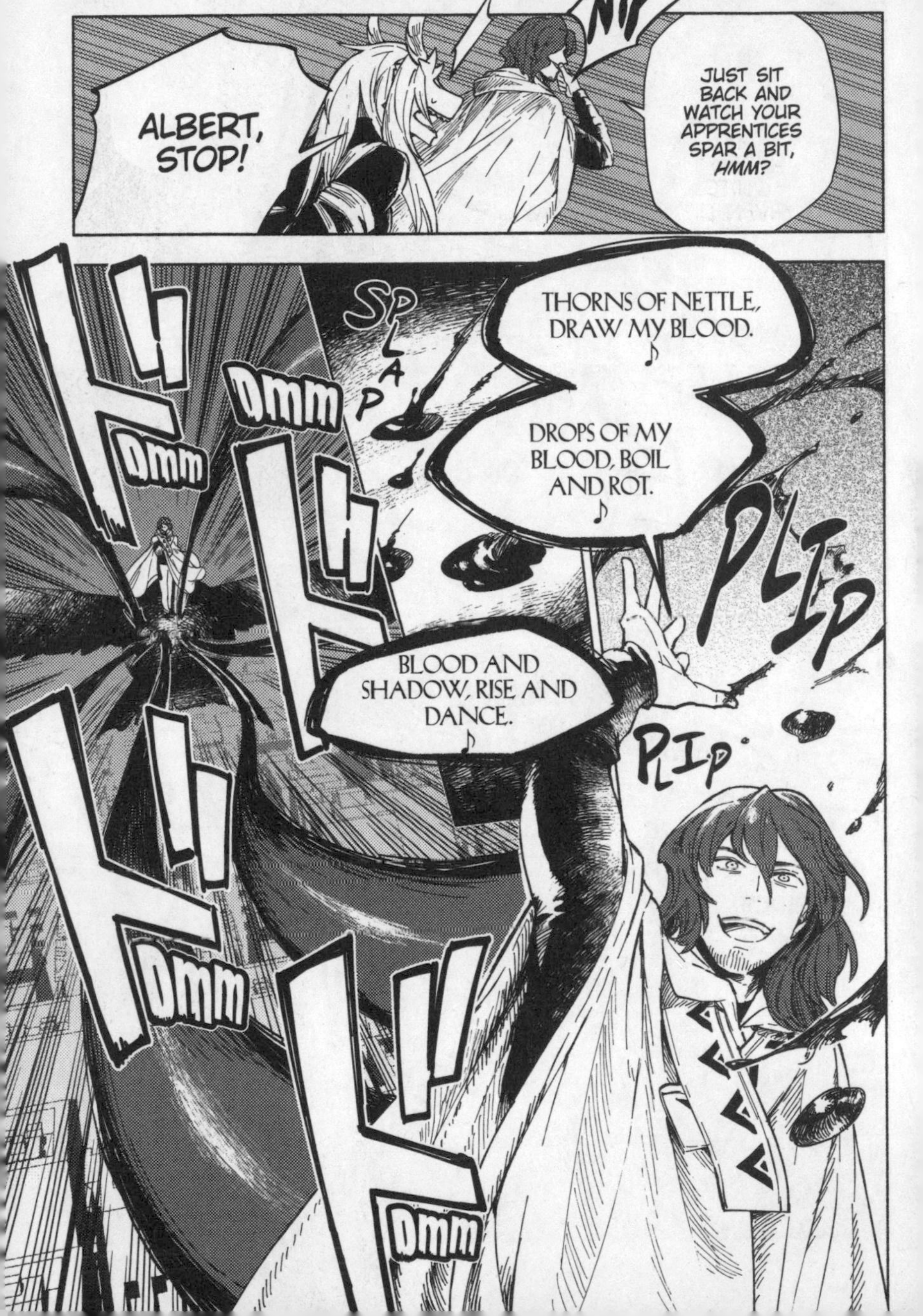
NIP
JUST SIT BACK AND WATCH YOUR APPRENTICES SPAR A BIT, *HMM?*
ALBERT, STOP!
THORNS OF NETTLE, DRAW MY BLOOD. ♪
DROPS OF MY BLOOD, BOIL AND ROT. ♪
PLIP
SPLAP
DOMM
DOMM
BLOOD AND SHADOW, RISE AND DANCE. ♪
PLIP
DOMM
DOMM

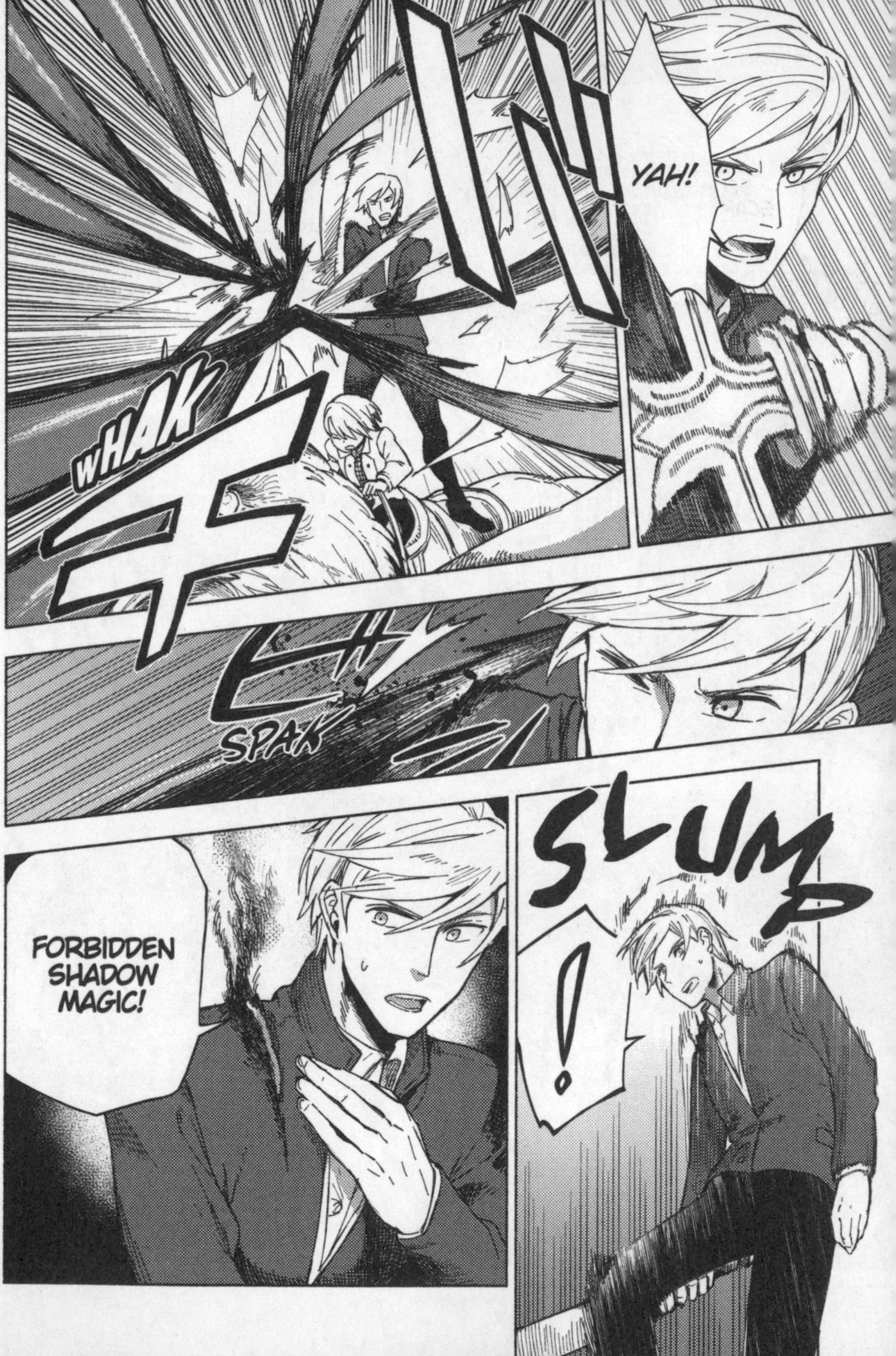
YAH!
WHAK
SPAK
SLUMP
!
FORBIDDEN SHADOW MAGIC!

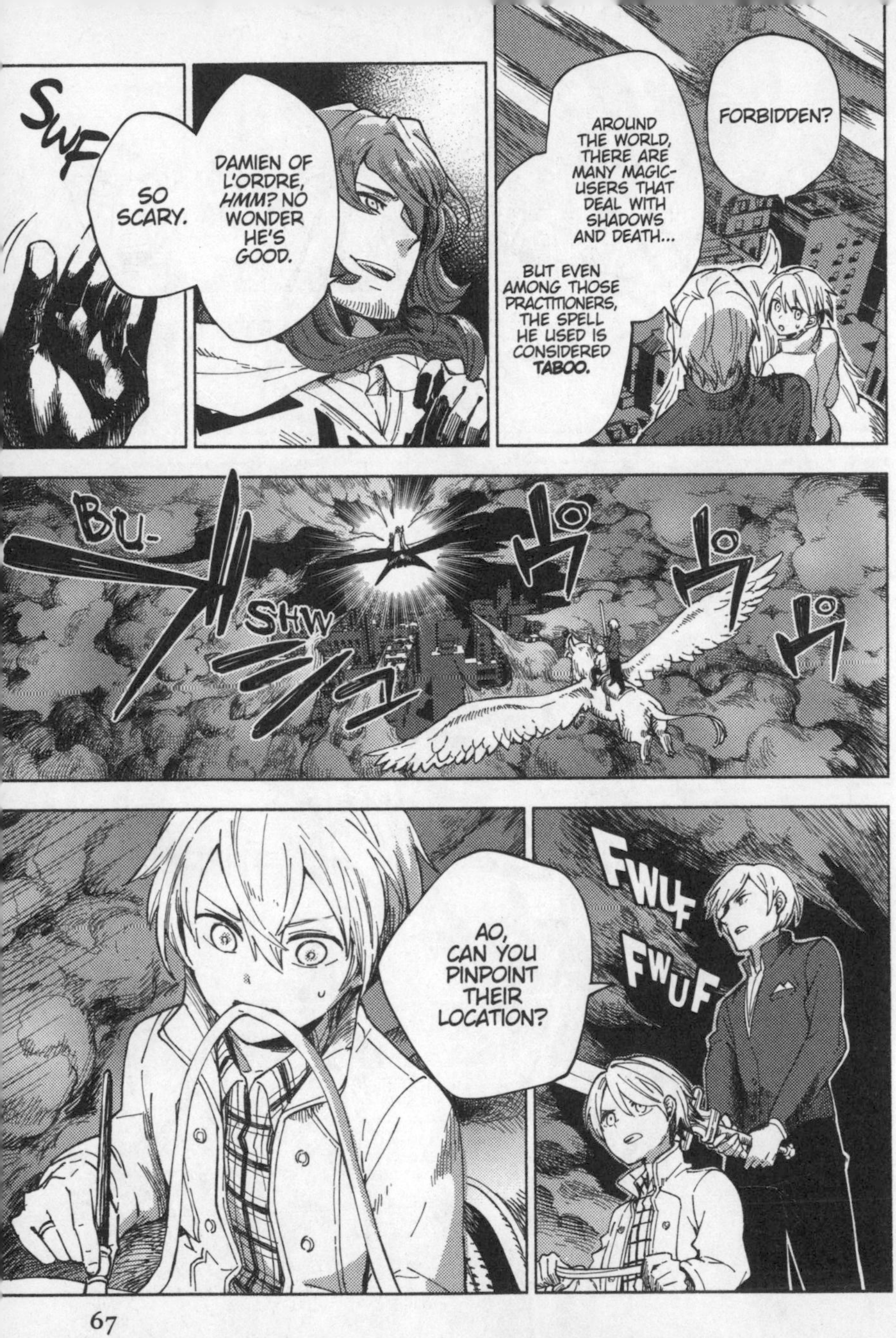
FORBIDDEN?
AROUND THE WORLD, THERE ARE MANY MAGIC-USERS THAT DEAL WITH SHADOWS AND DEATH...
BUT EVEN AMONG THOSE PRACTITIONERS, THE SPELL HE USED IS CONSIDERED **TABOO.**
DAMIEN OF L'ORDRE, *HMM?* NO WONDER HE'S GOOD.
SO SCARY.
SWF
BU-
SHW
FWUF
FWUF
AO, CAN YOU PINPOINT THEIR LOCATION?

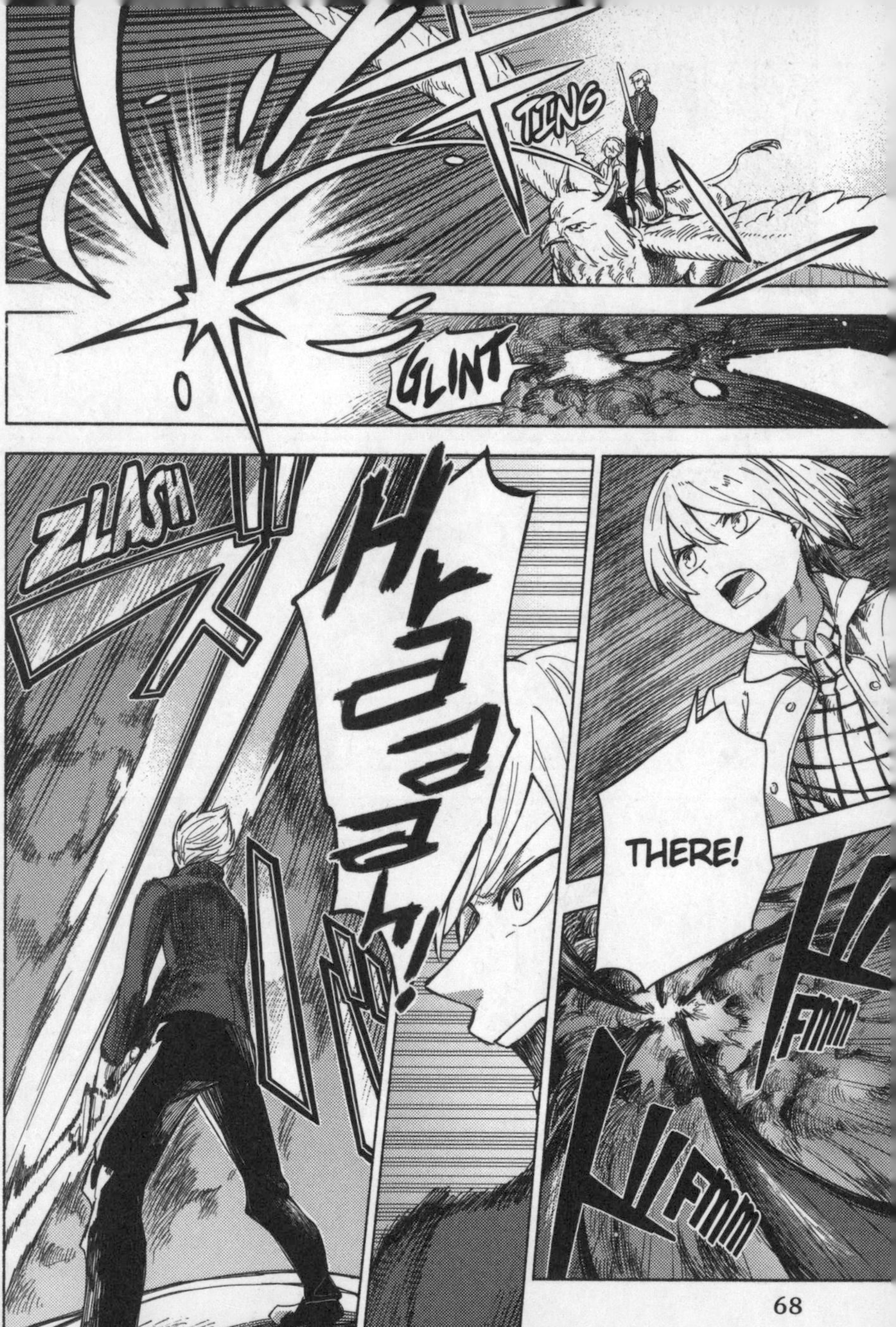
TIING
GLINT
THERE!
FMM
FMM
Hyaaaah!!
ZLASH

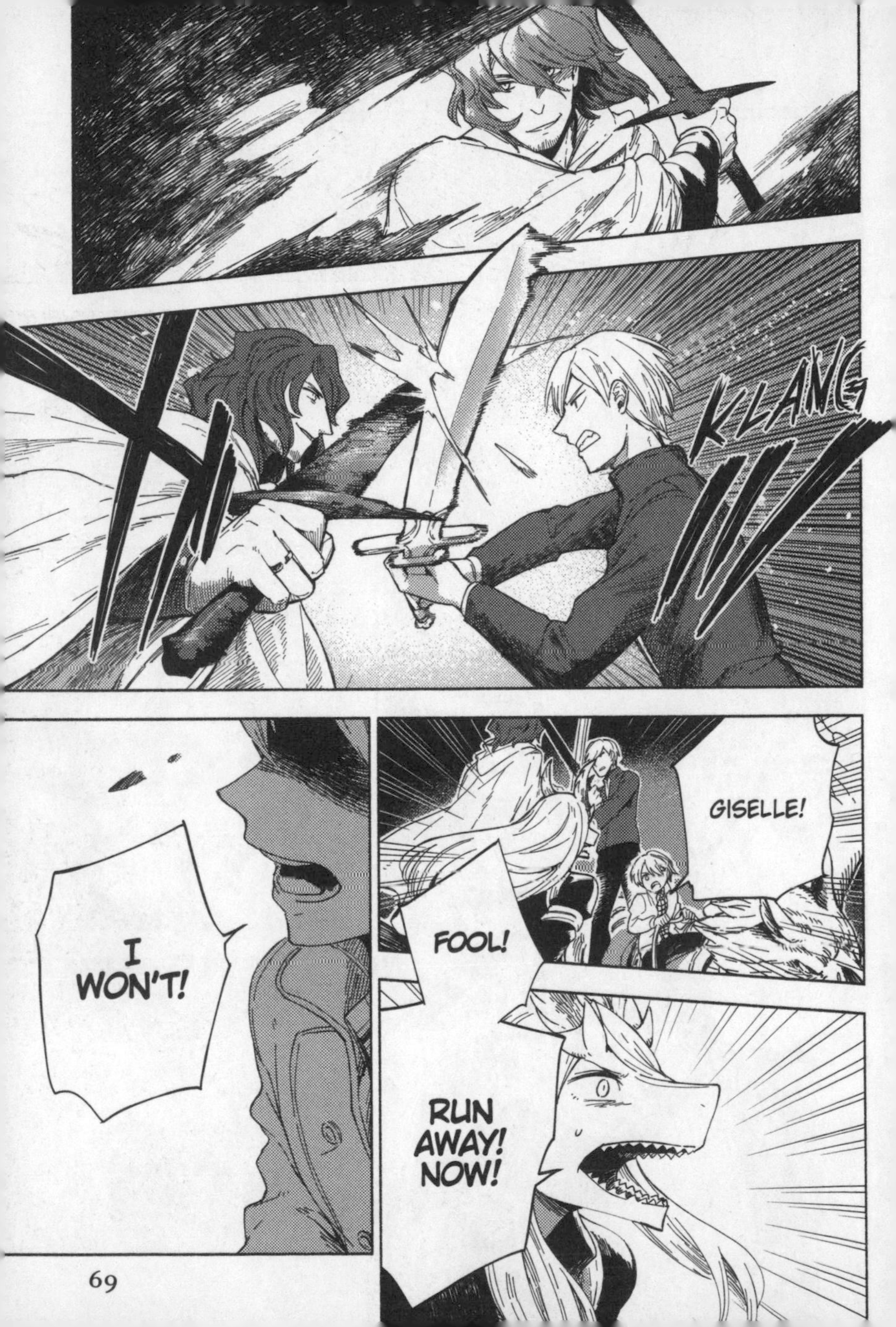
KLANG
GISELLE!
FOOL!
RUN AWAY! NOW!
I WON'T!

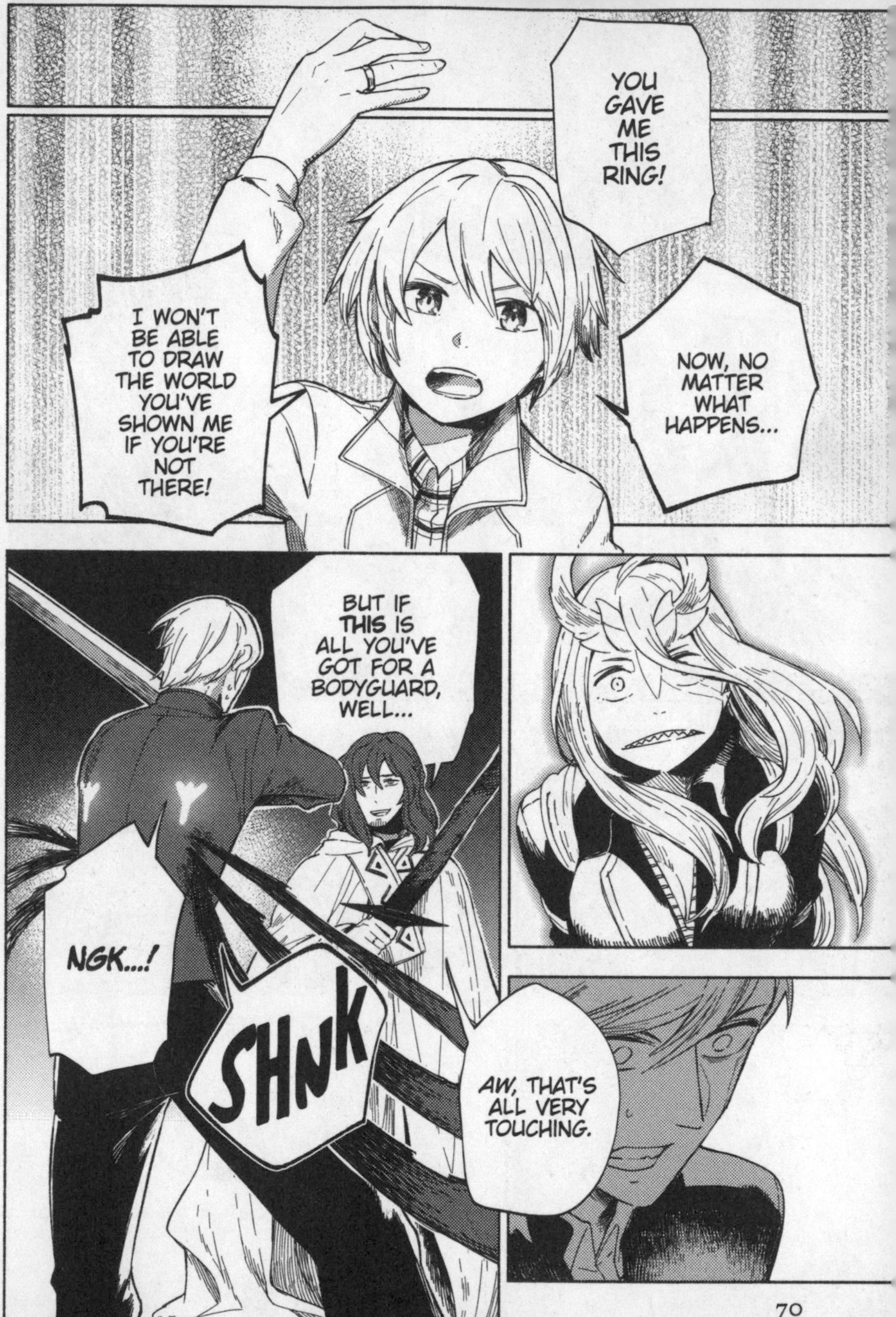

YOU GAVE ME THIS RING!
NOW, NO MATTER WHAT HAPPENS...
I WON'T BE ABLE TO DRAW THE WORLD YOU'VE SHOWN ME IF YOU'RE NOT THERE!
AW, THAT'S ALL VERY TOUCHING.
BUT IF THIS IS ALL YOU'VE GOT FOR A BODYGUARD, WELL...
NGK...!
SHNK

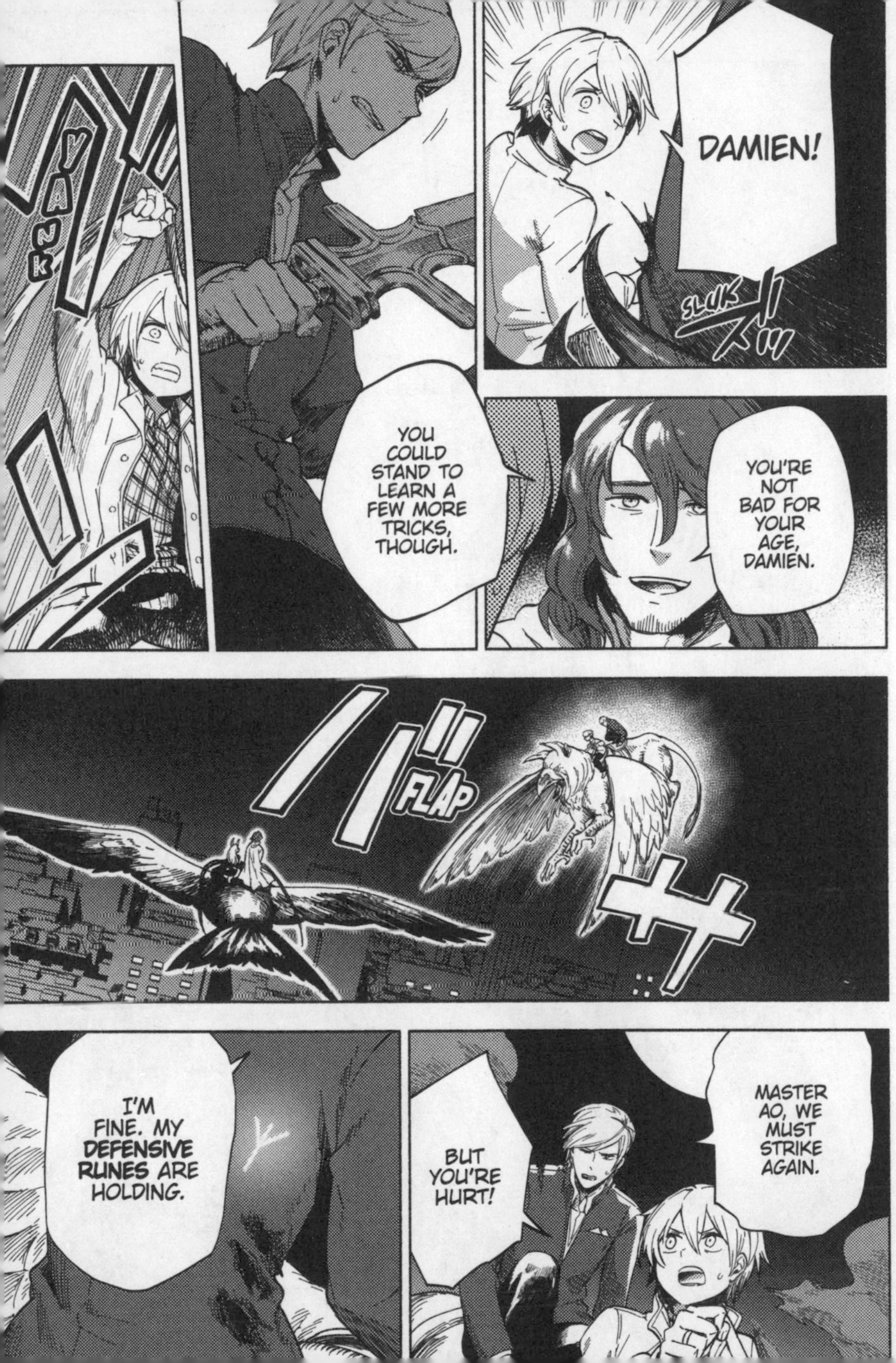
DAMIEN!
SLUK
YOU'RE NOT BAD FOR YOUR AGE, DAMIEN.
YOU COULD STAND TO LEARN A FEW MORE TRICKS, THOUGH.
YANK
FLAP
MASTER AO, WE MUST STRIKE AGAIN.
BUT YOU'RE HURT!
I'M FINE. MY DEFENSIVE RUNES ARE HOLDING.

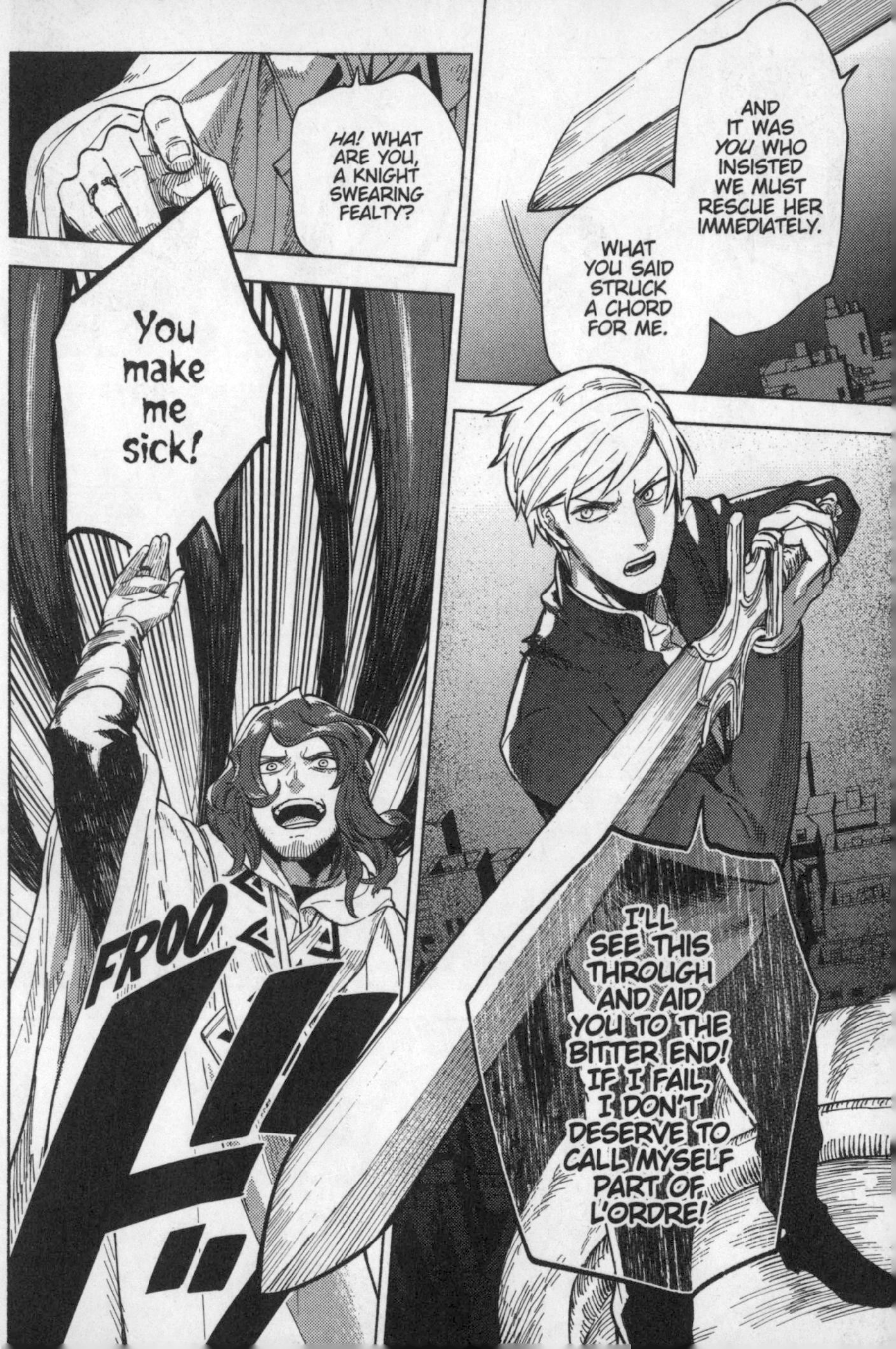
AND IT WAS *YOU* WHO INSISTED WE MUST RESCUE HER IMMEDIATELY.
WHAT YOU SAID STRUCK A CHORD FOR ME.
HA! WHAT ARE YOU, A KNIGHT SWEARING FEALTY?
I'LL SEE THIS THROUGH AND AID YOU TO THE BITTER END! IF I FAIL, I DON'T DESERVE TO CALL MYSELF PART OF L'ORDRE!
You make me sick!
FROOM!!

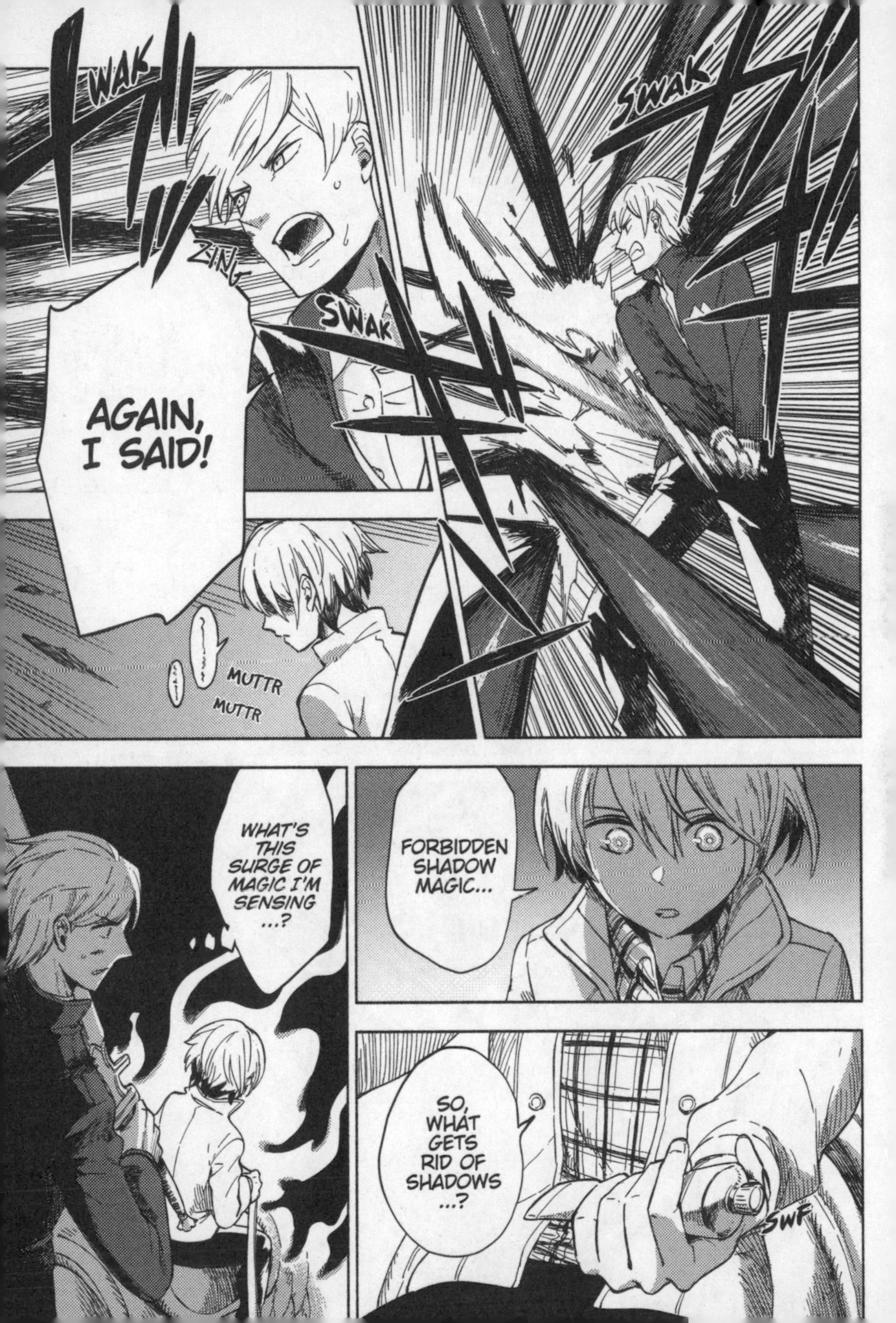
SWAK
SWAK
ZING
SWAK
AGAIN, I SAID!
MUTTR
MUTTR
FORBIDDEN SHADOW MAGIC...
SO, WHAT GETS RID OF SHADOWS ...?
SWF
WHAT'S THIS SURGE OF MAGIC I'M SENSING ...?
...

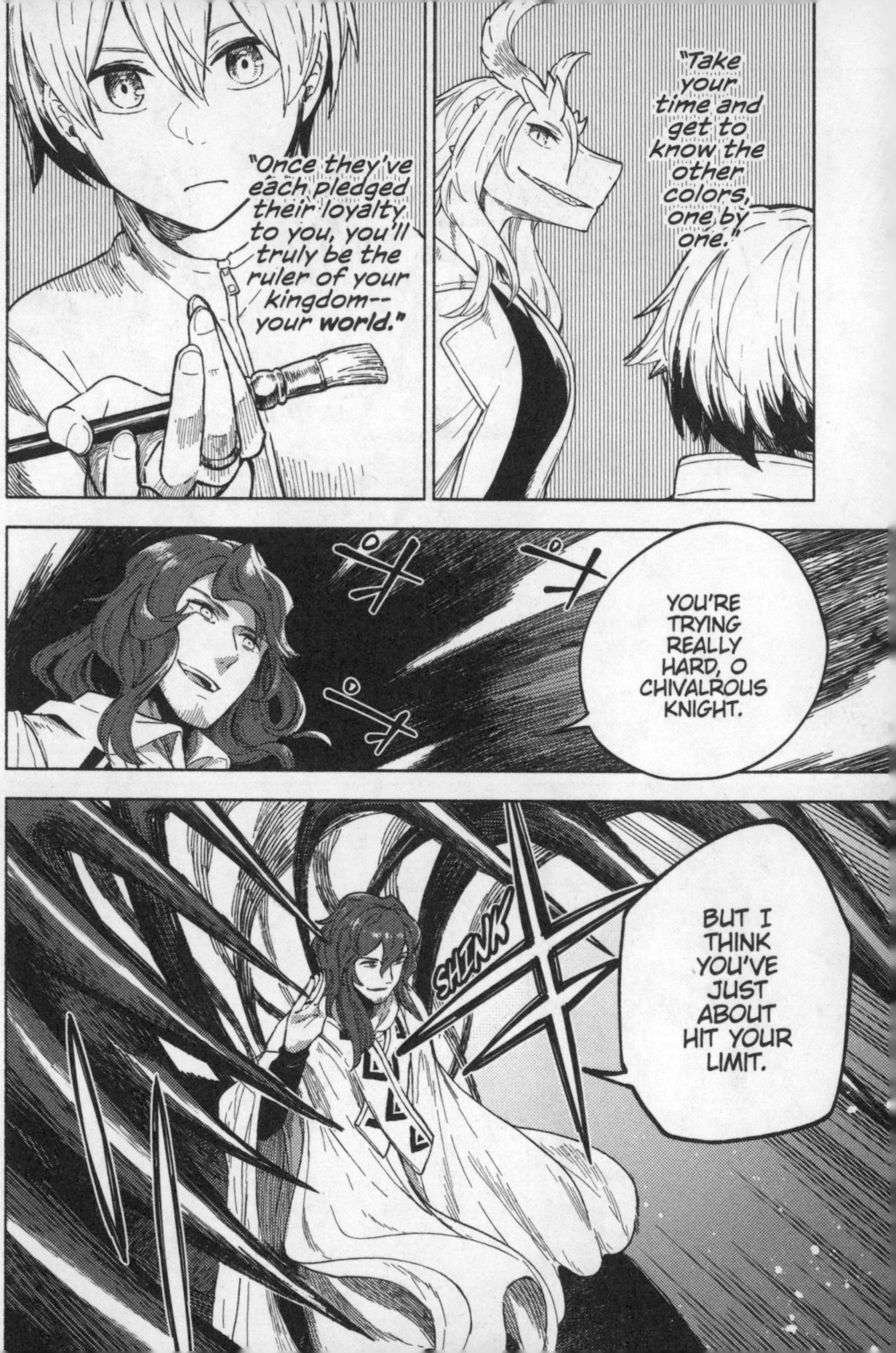
"Take your time and get to know the other colors, one by one."
"Once they've each pledged their loyalty to you, you'll truly be the ruler of your kingdom--your **world**."
YOU'RE TRYING REALLY HARD, O CHIVALROUS KNIGHT.
BUT I THINK YOU'VE JUST ABOUT HIT YOUR LIMIT.
SHINK

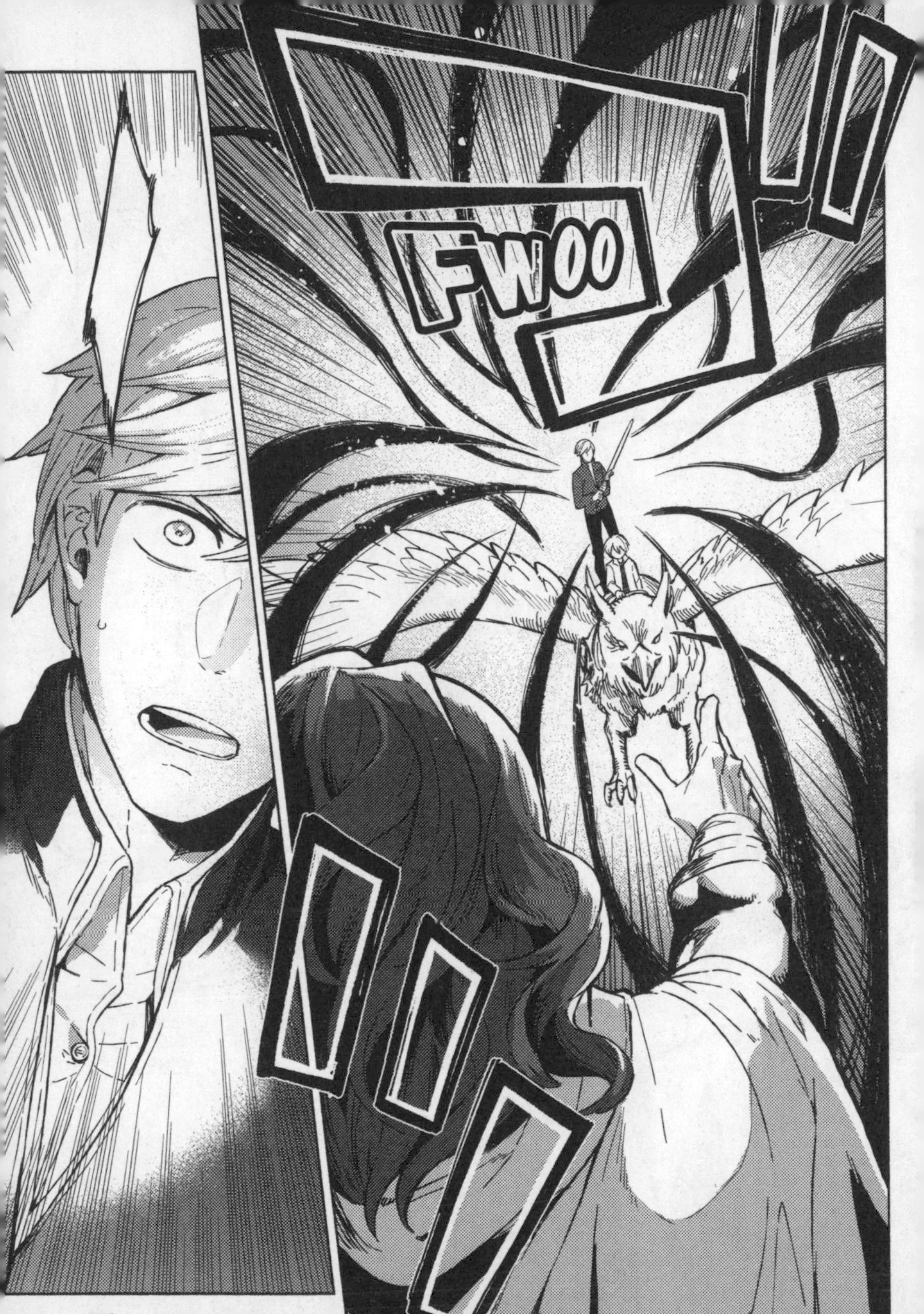
FWOO

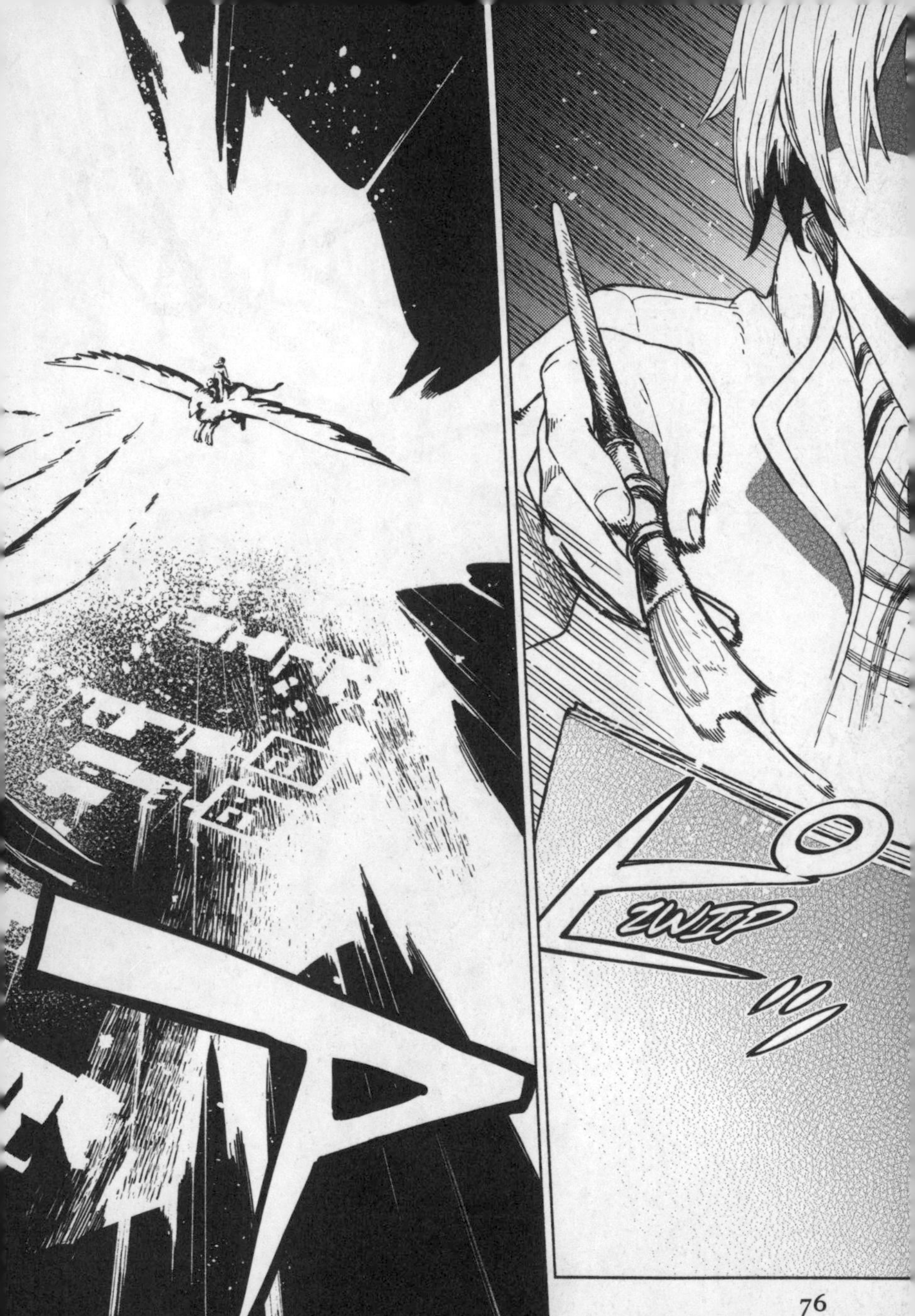
ZWIP

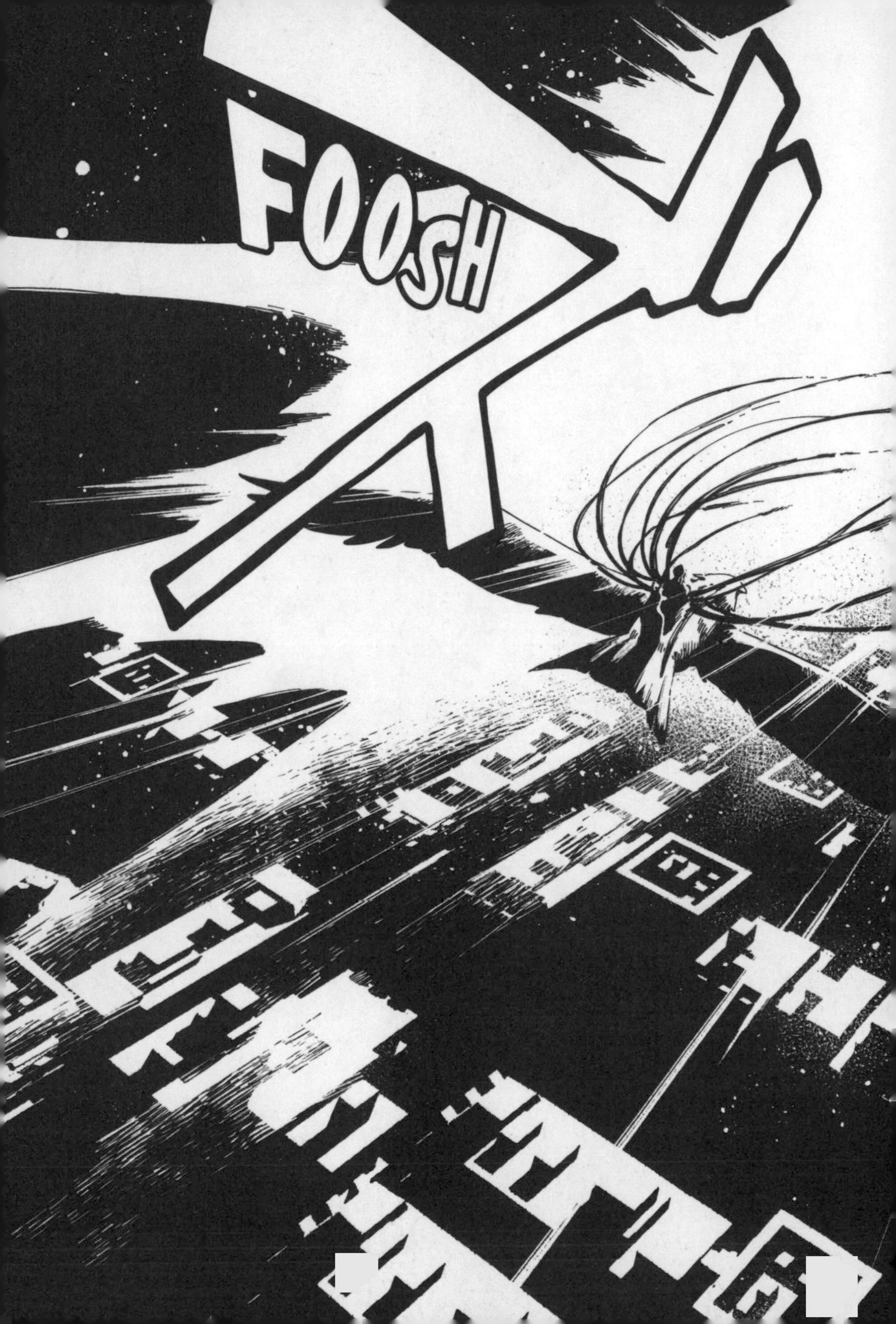
FOOSH

The Ancient
Magus' Bride
WIZARD's BLUE

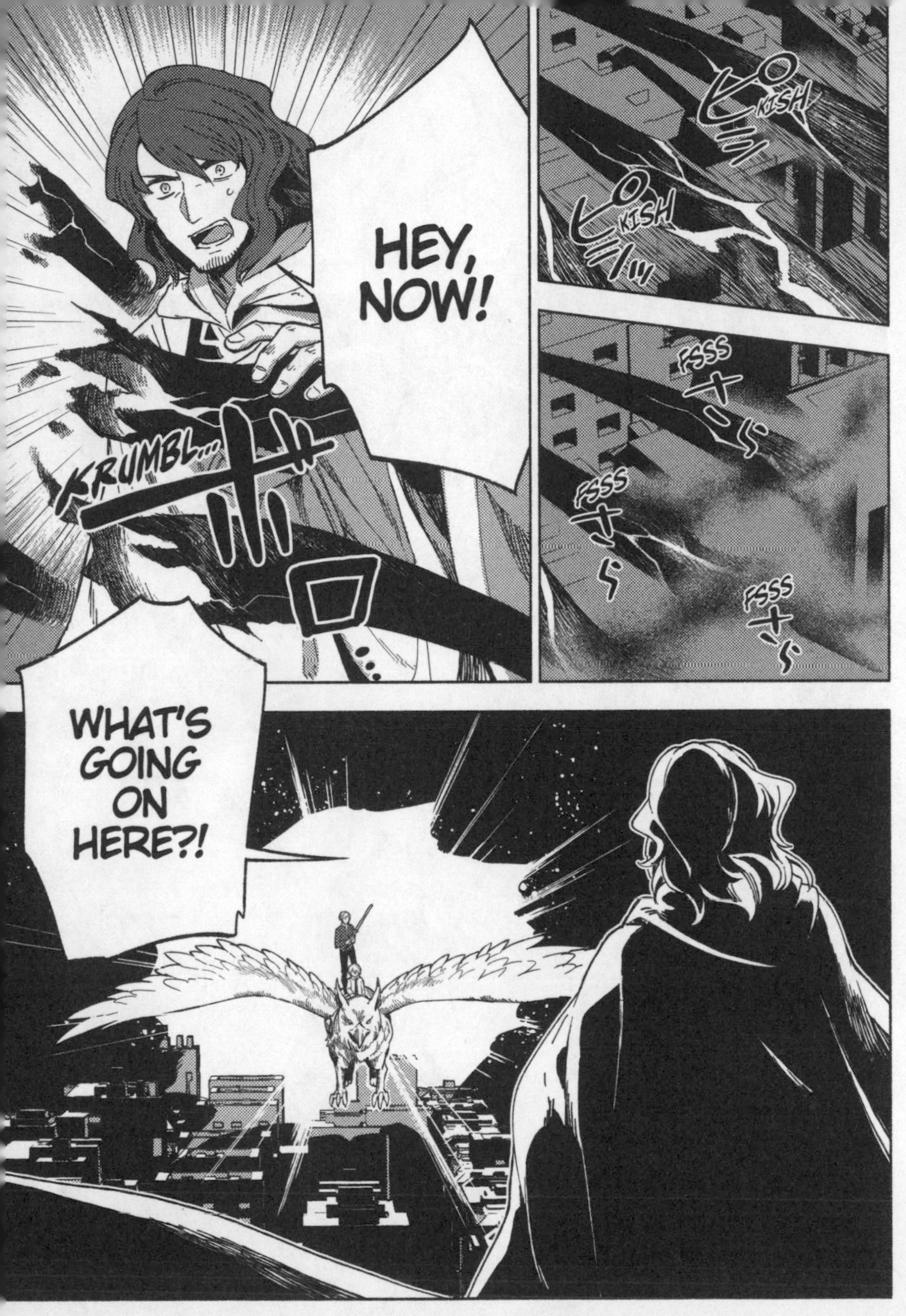
KISH
KISH
FSSS
FSSS
FSSS
HEY, NOW!
KRUMBL...
WHAT'S GOING ON HERE?!

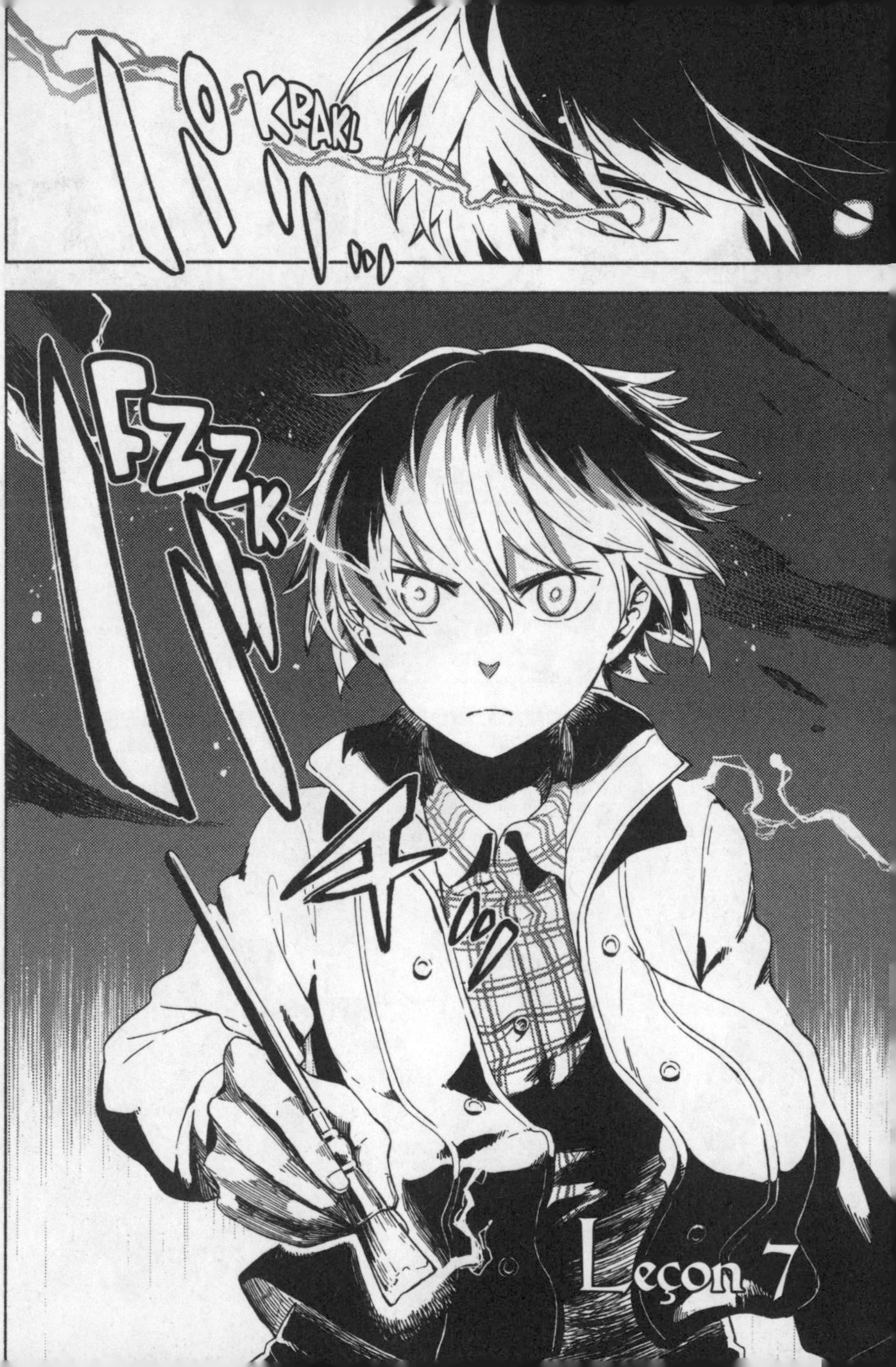
KRAKL
FZZK
Leçon 7

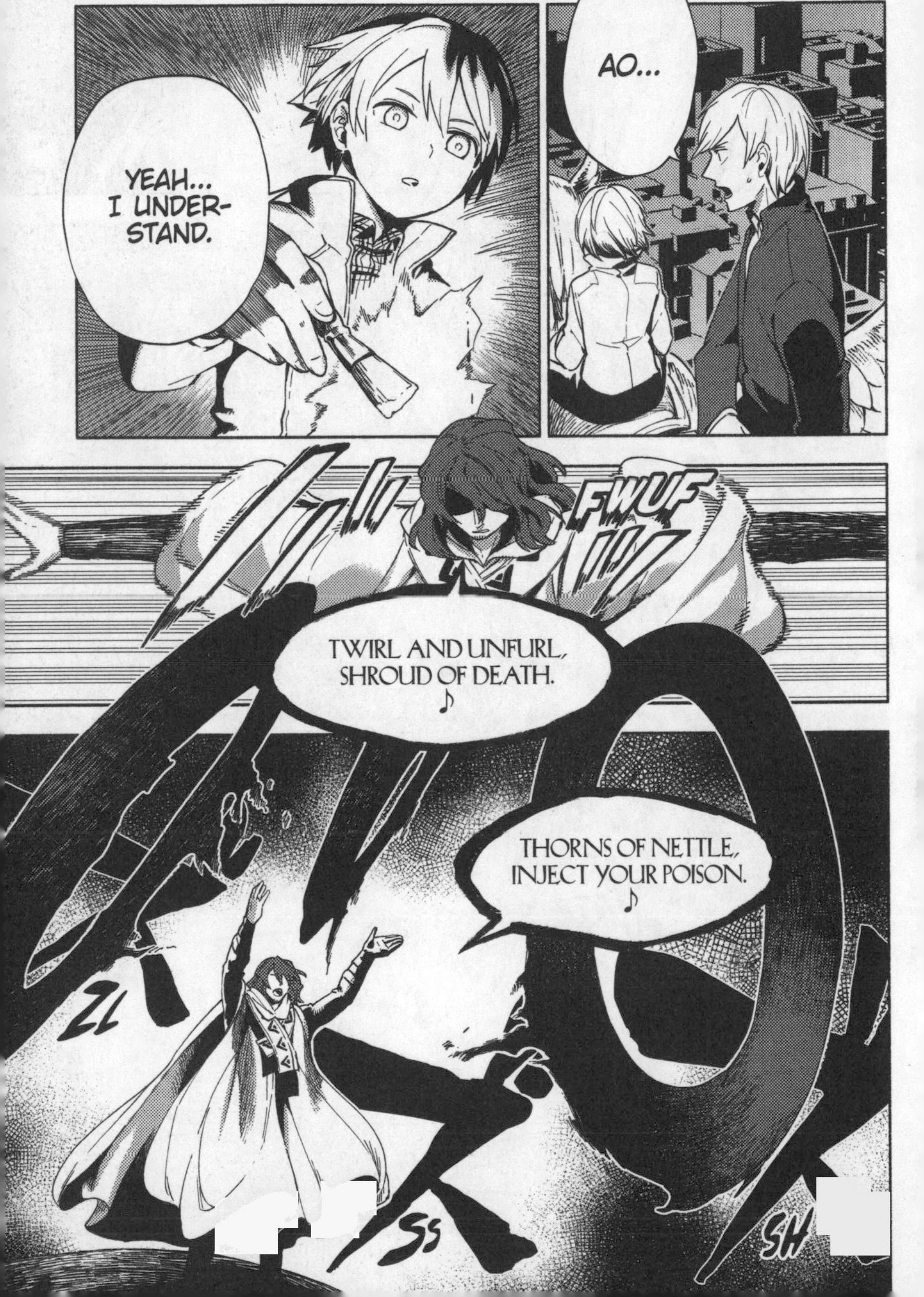
AO...
YEAH... I UNDER-STAND.
FWUF
TWIRL AND UNFURL, SHROUD OF DEATH. ♪
THORNS OF NETTLE, INJECT YOUR POISON. ♪
SH
SS

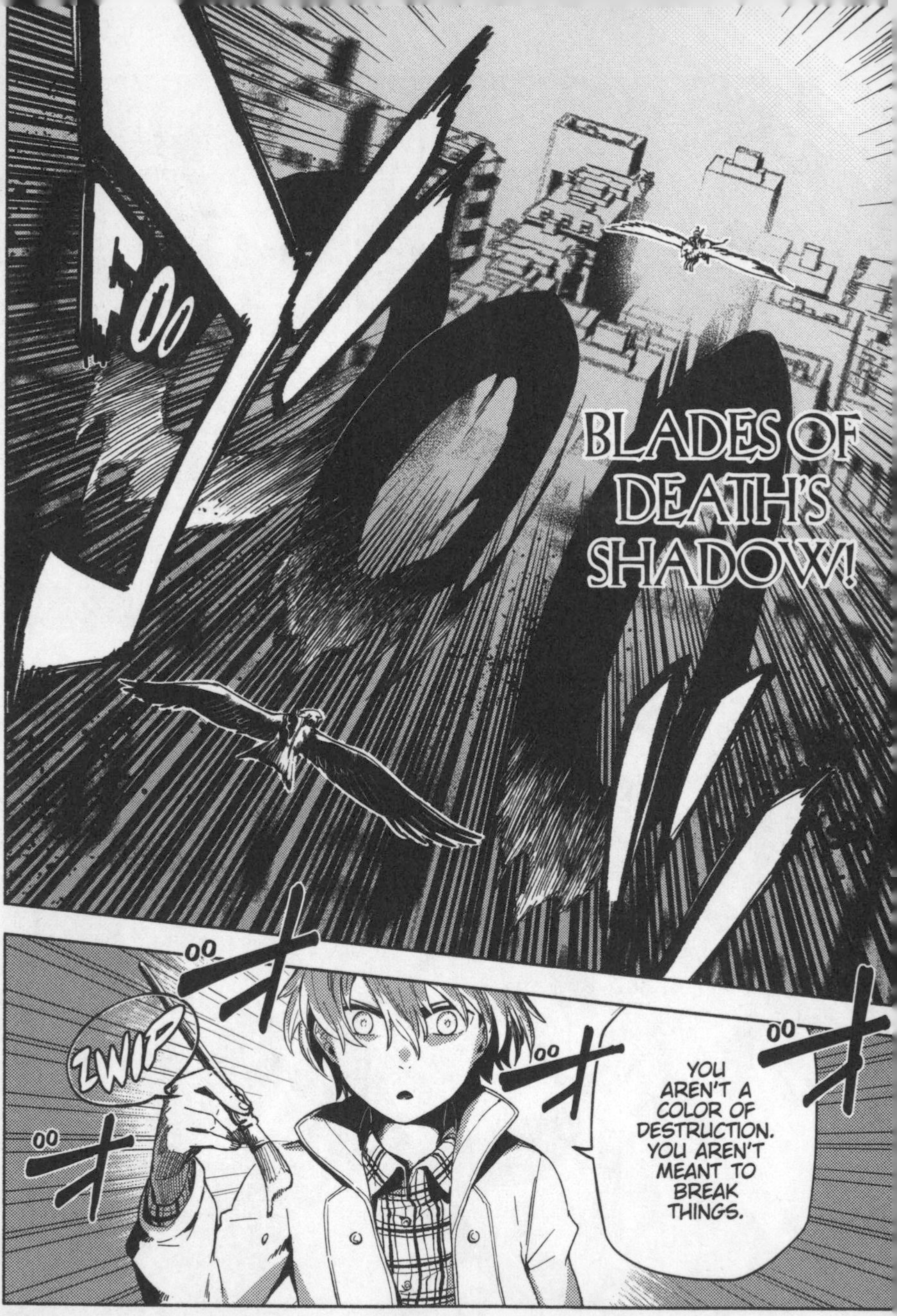
FOO
BLADES OF DEATH'S SHADOW!
YOU AREN'T A COLOR OF DESTRUCTION. YOU AREN'T MEANT TO BREAK THINGS.
ZWIP

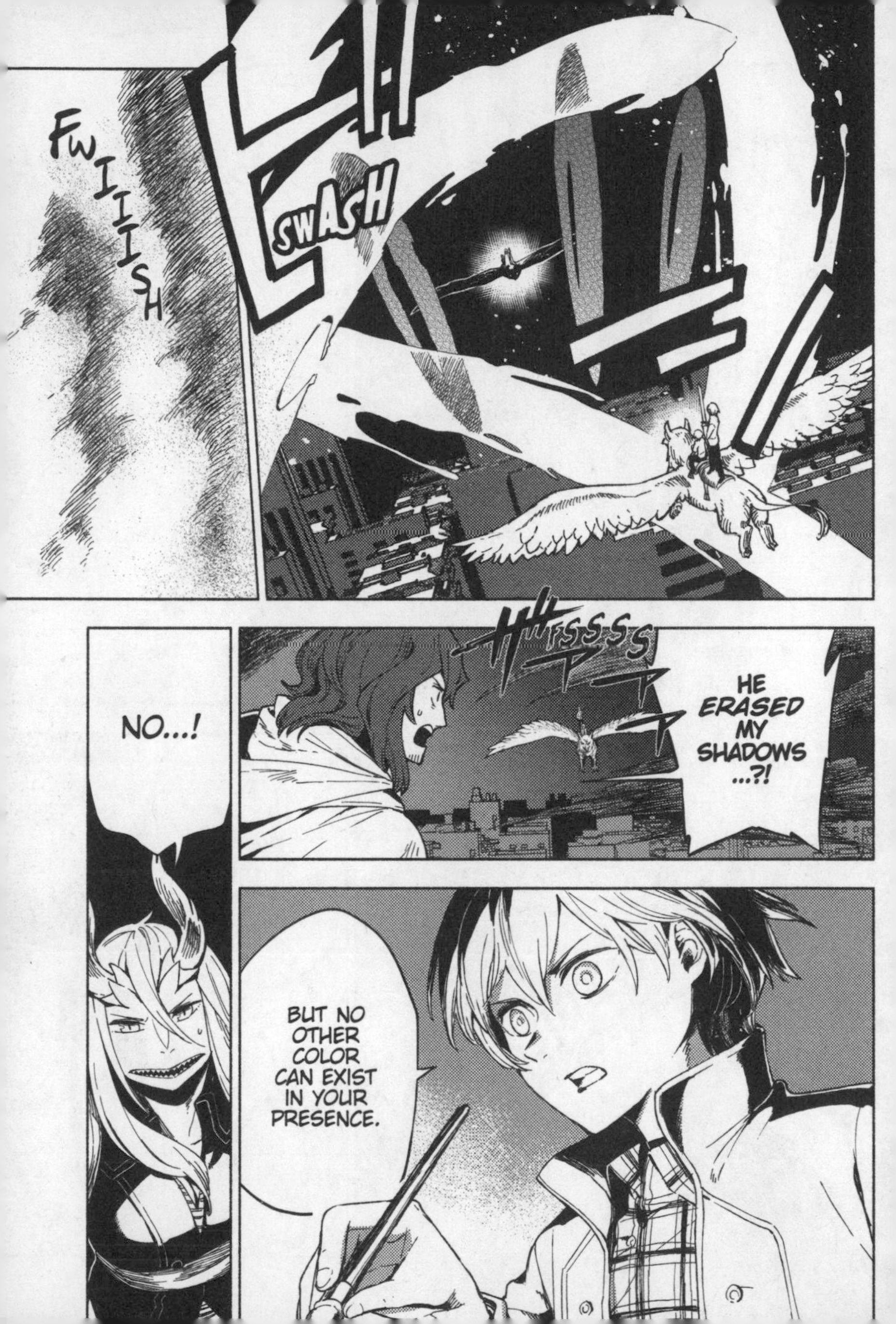
SWASH
FWIIISH
FSSSSS
HE ERASED MY SHADOWS ...?!
NO...!
BUT NO OTHER COLOR CAN EXIST IN YOUR PRESENCE.

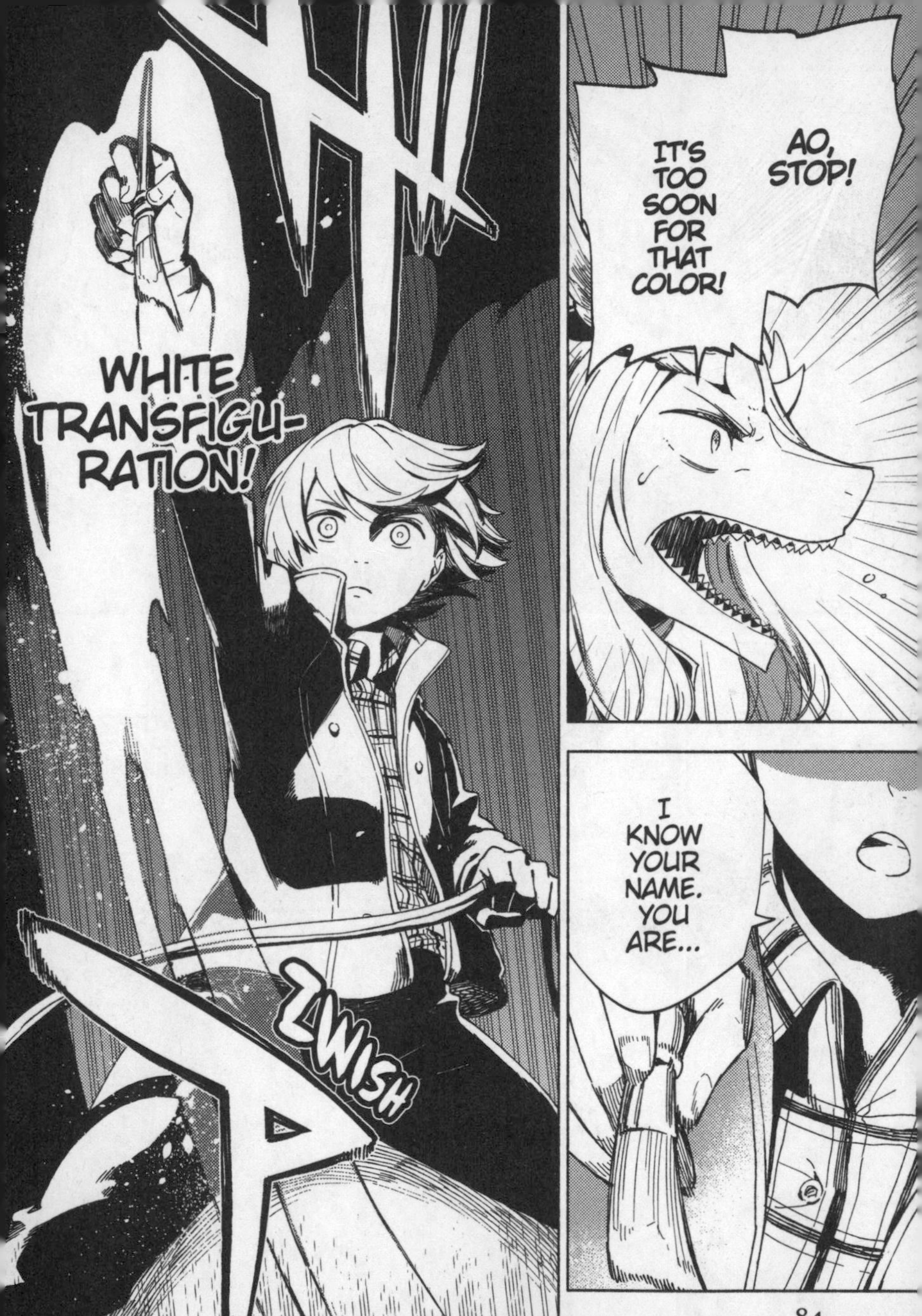
AO, STOP!
IT'S TOO SOON FOR THAT COLOR!
I KNOW YOUR NAME. YOU ARE...
WHITE TRANSFIGU-RATION!
ZWISH

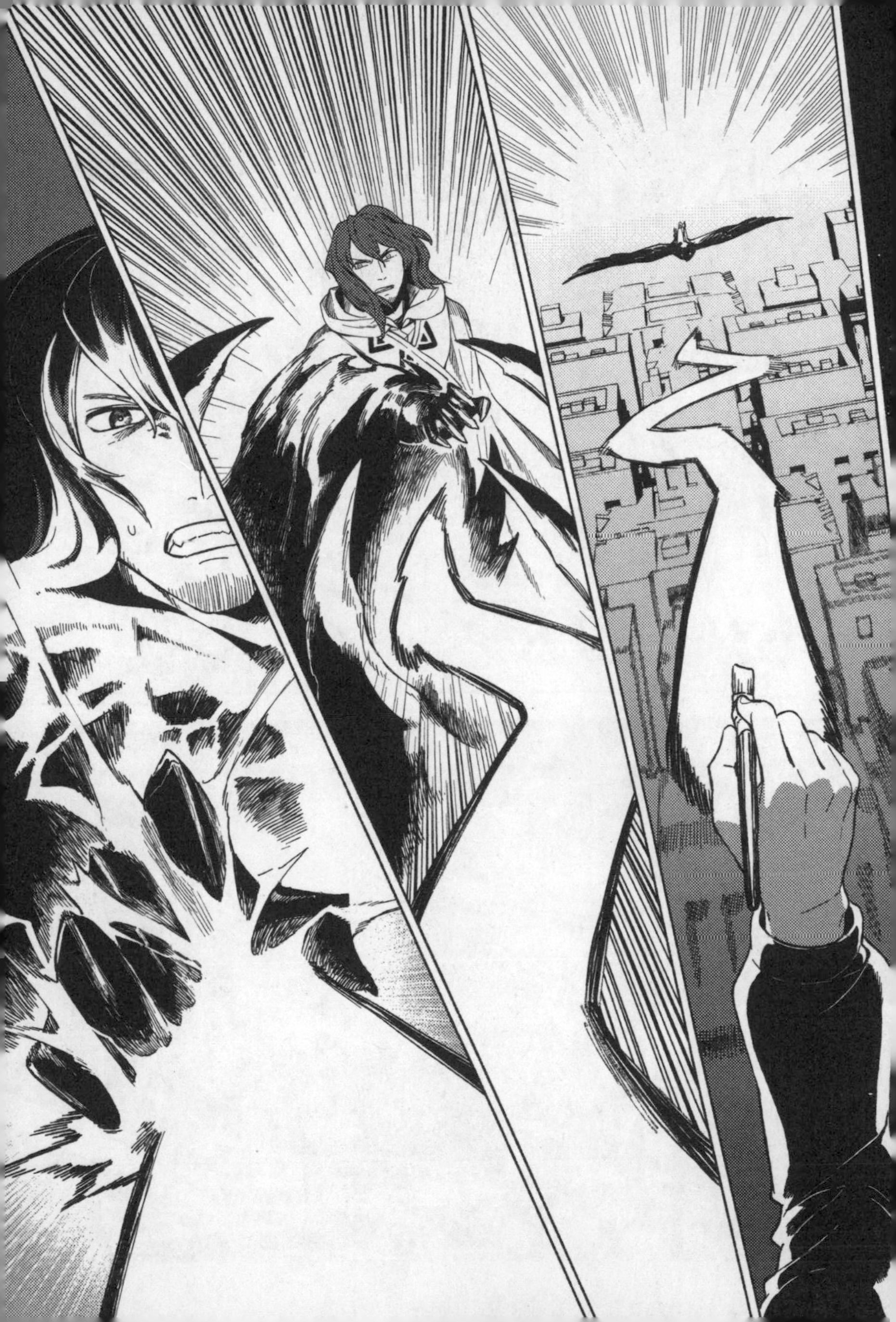

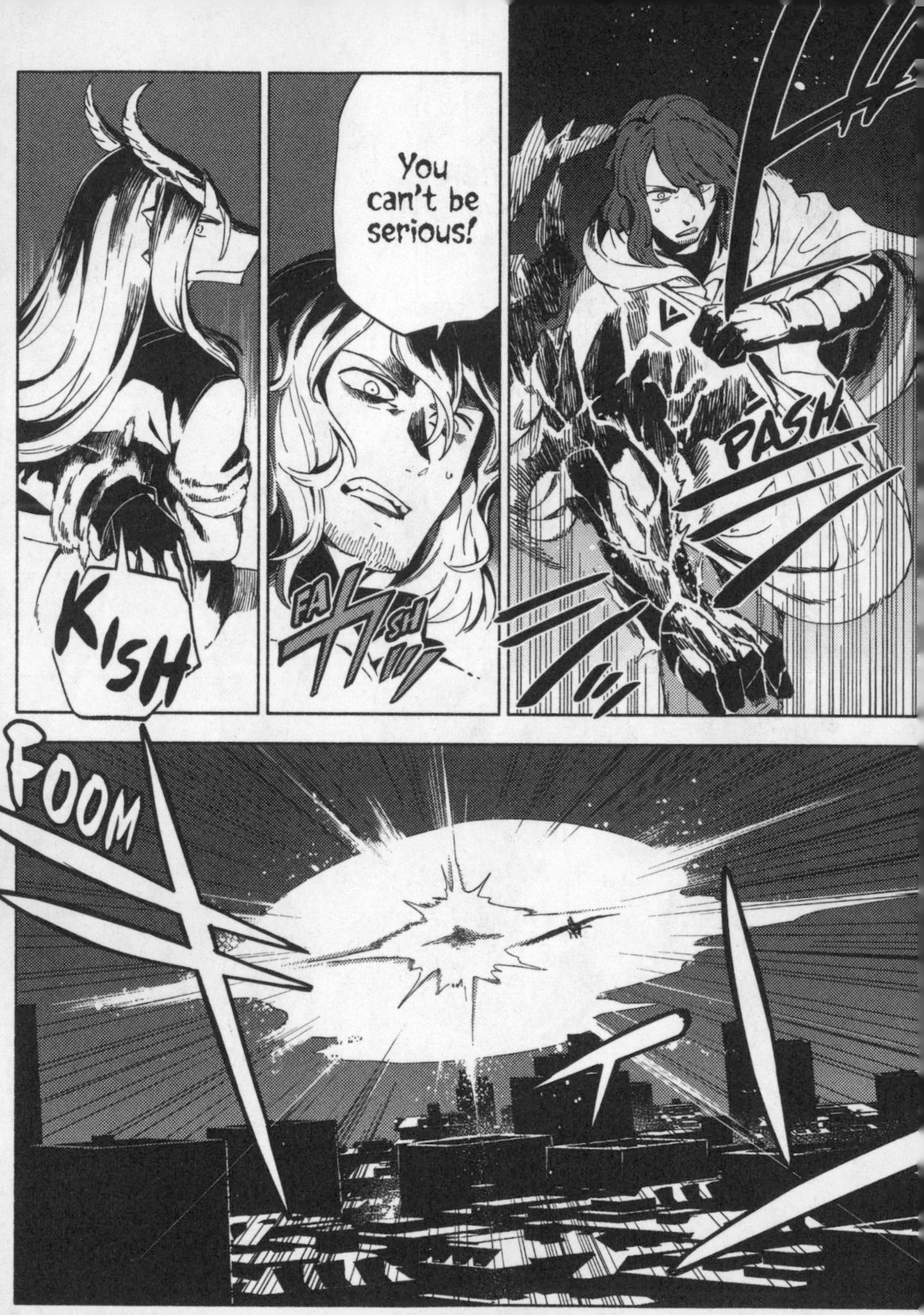
PASH
You can't be serious!
FASH
KISH
FOOM

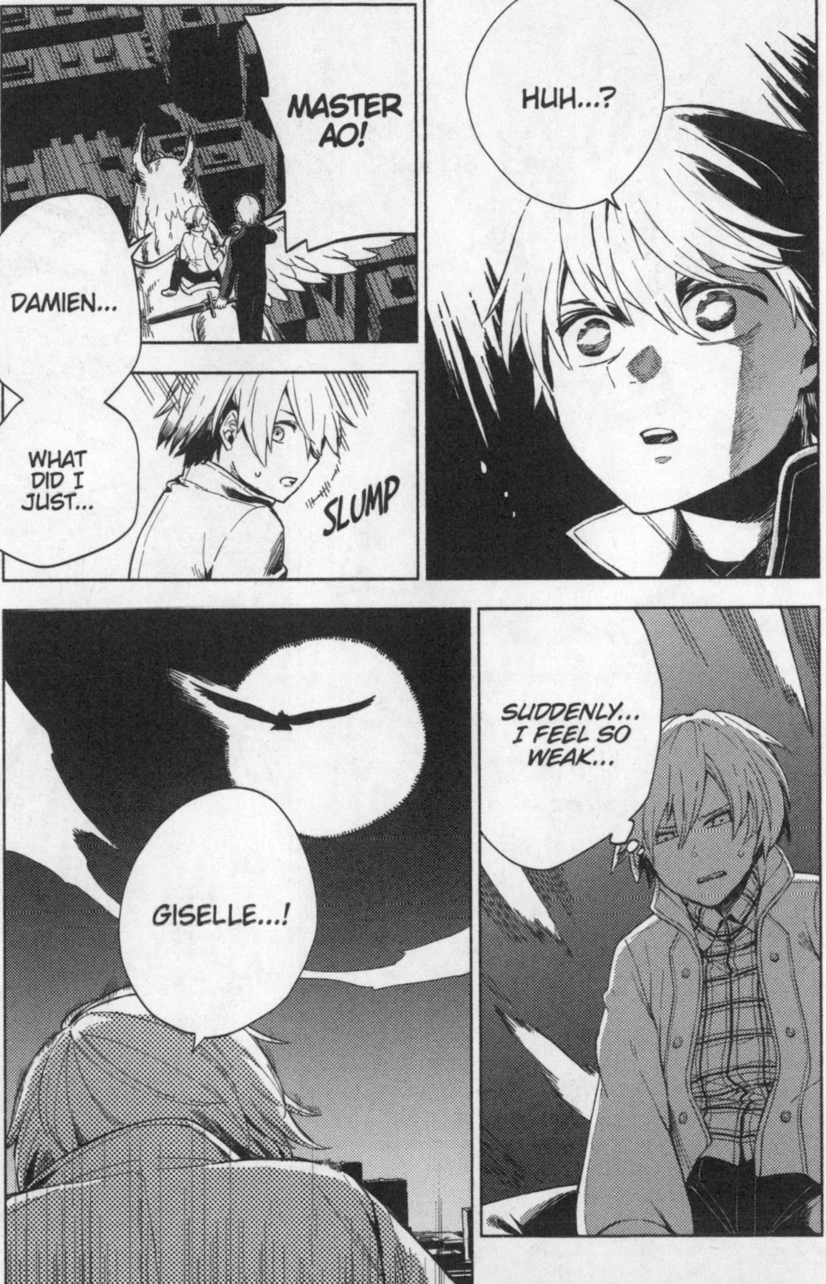
HUH...?
MASTER AO!
DAMIEN...
WHAT DID I JUST...
SLUMP
SUDDENLY... I FEEL SO WEAK...
GISELLE...!

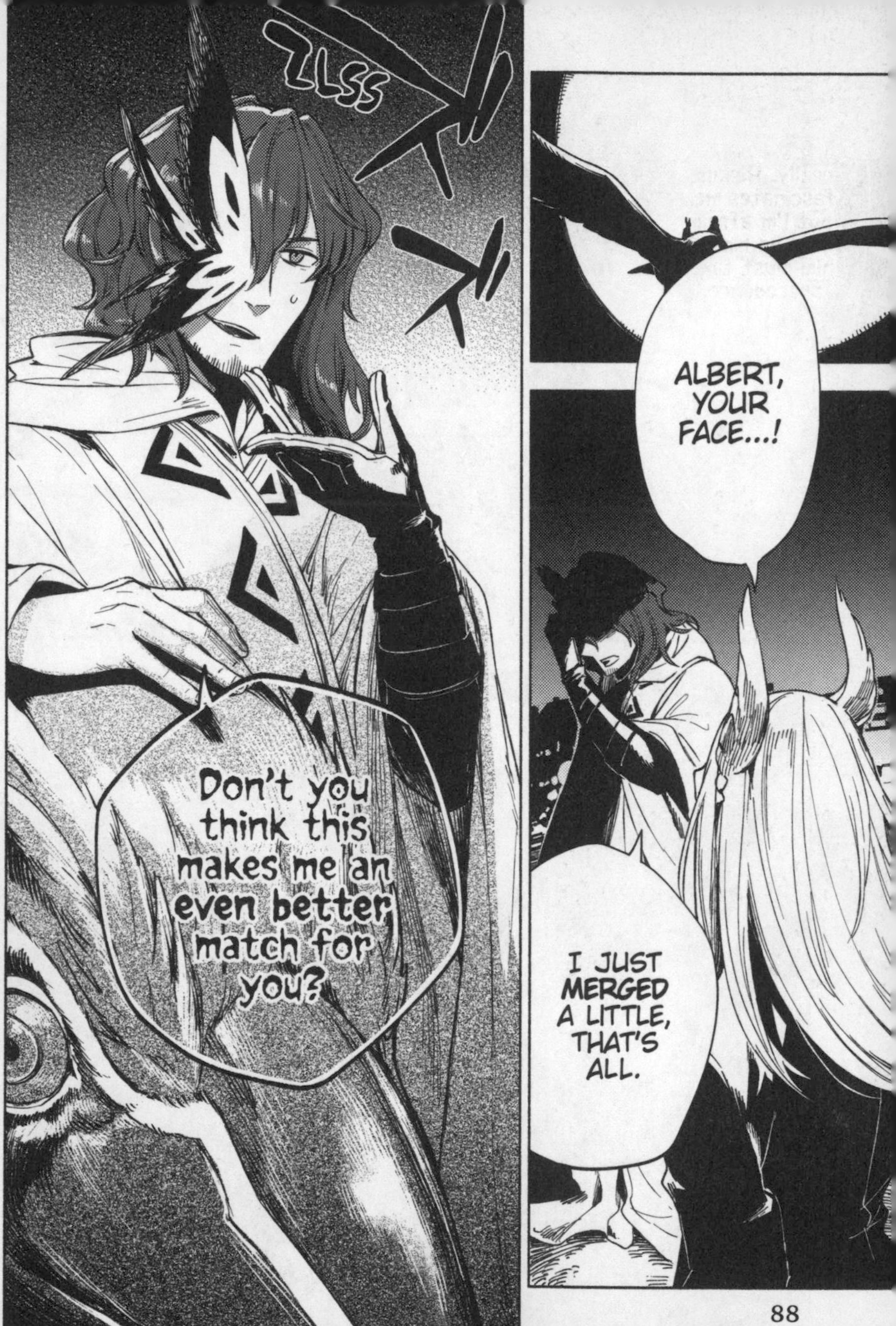
ALBERT, YOUR FACE...!
I JUST MERGED A LITTLE, THAT'S ALL.
ZLSS
Don't you think this makes me an even better match for you?

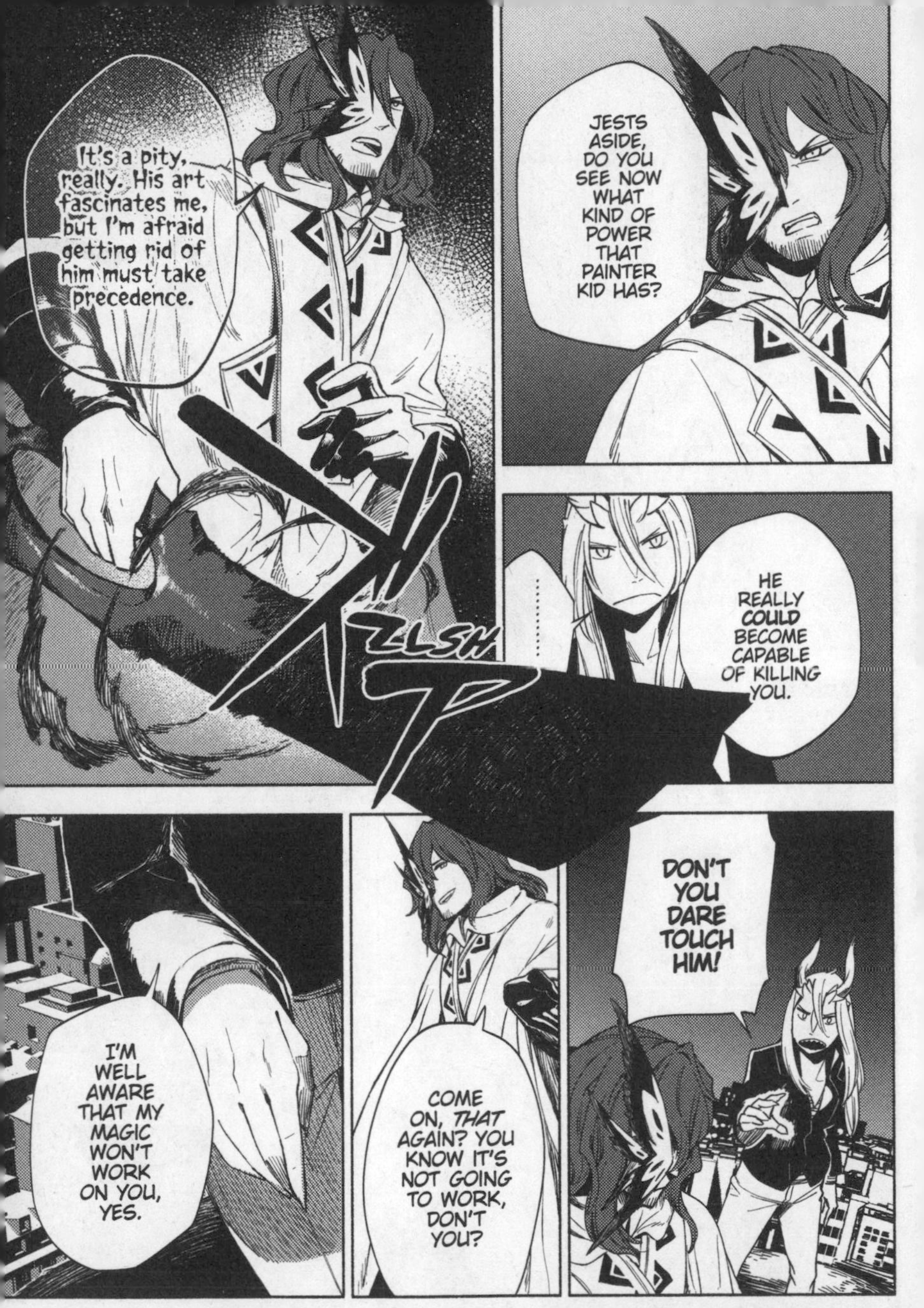
JESTS ASIDE, DO YOU SEE NOW WHAT KIND OF POWER THAT PAINTER KID HAS?
HE REALLY COULD BECOME CAPABLE OF KILLING YOU.
It's a pity, really. His art fascinates me, but I'm afraid getting rid of him must take precedence.
ZZLSH
DON'T YOU DARE TOUCH HIM!
COME ON, THAT AGAIN? YOU KNOW IT'S NOT GOING TO WORK, DON'T YOU?
I'M WELL AWARE THAT MY MAGIC WON'T WORK ON YOU, YES.

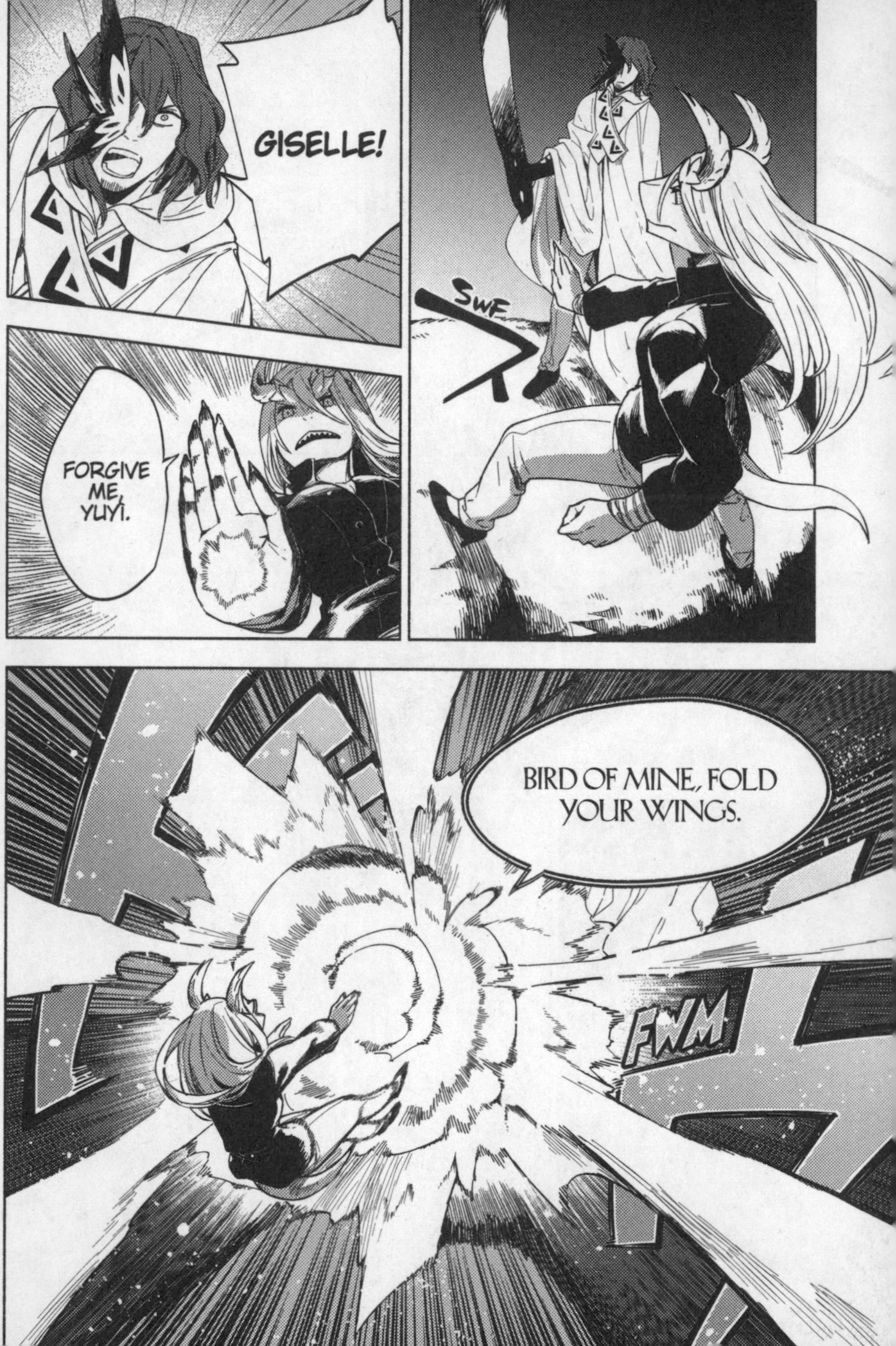
SWF
GISELLE!
FORGIVE ME, YUYI.
BIRD OF MINE, FOLD YOUR WINGS.
FWM

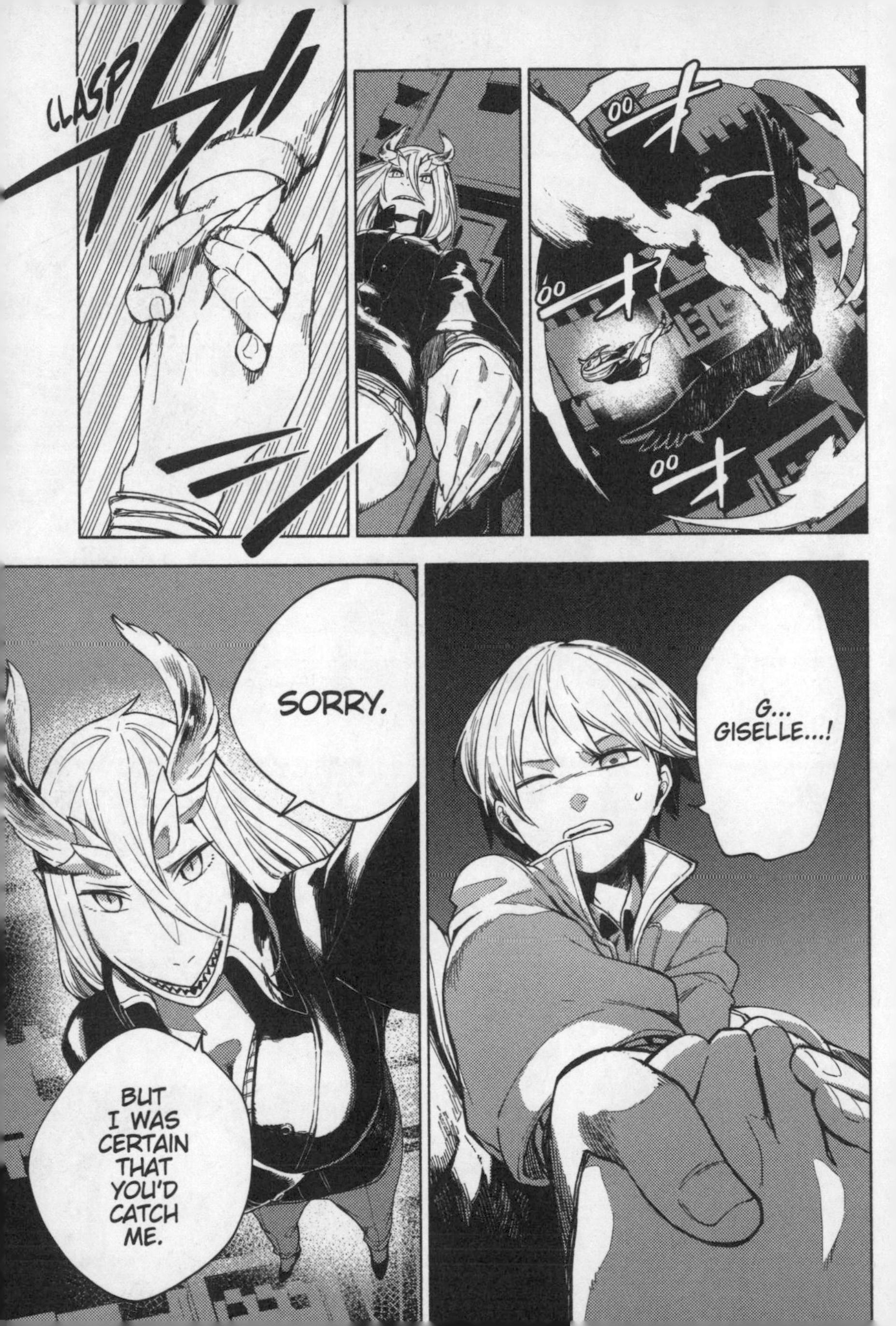
OO
OO
OO
CLASP
G... GISELLE...!
SORRY.
BUT I WAS CERTAIN THAT YOU'D CATCH ME.

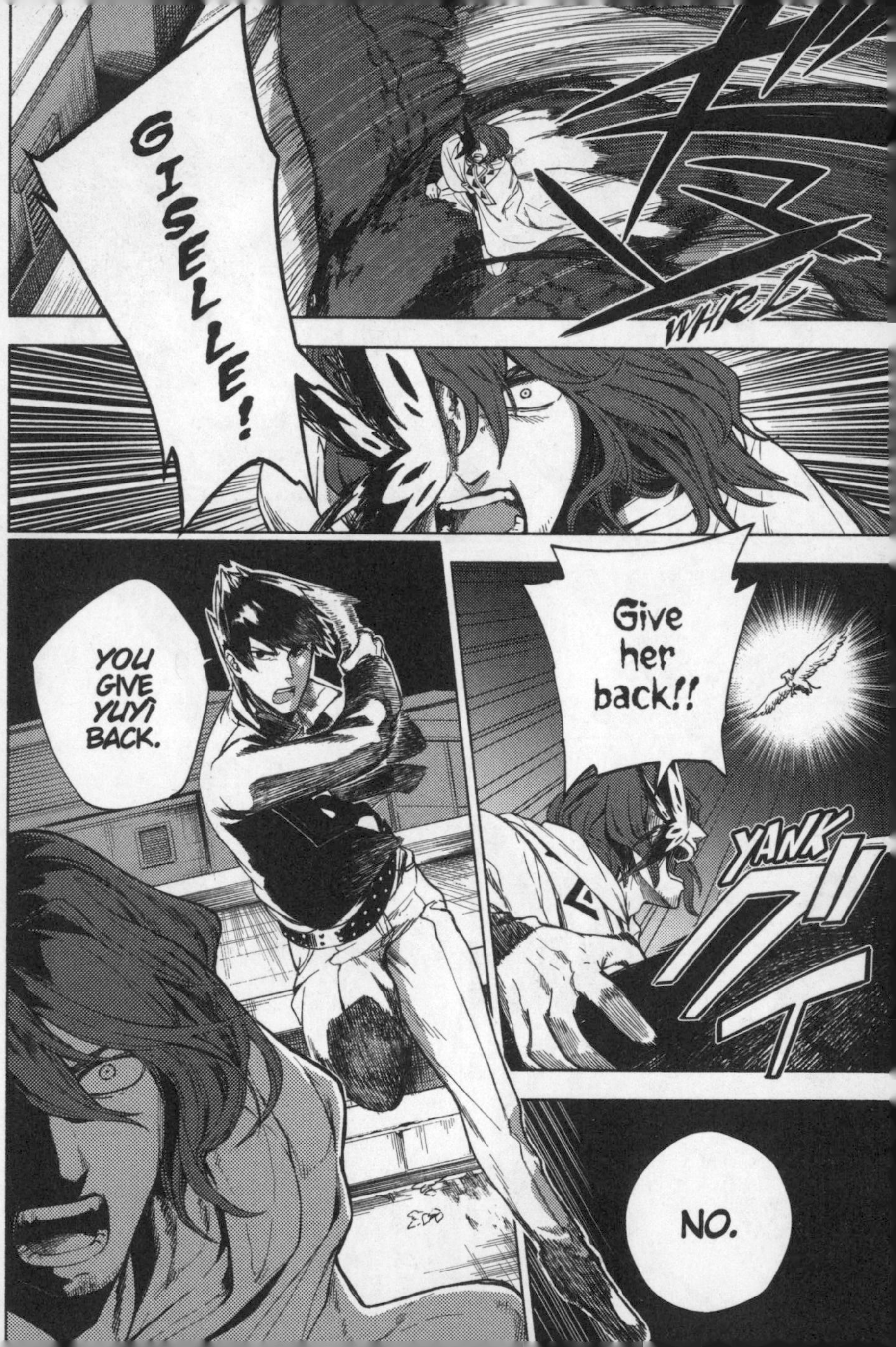
WHRL
GISELLE!!
Give her back!!
YANK
YOU GIVE YUYI BACK.
NO.

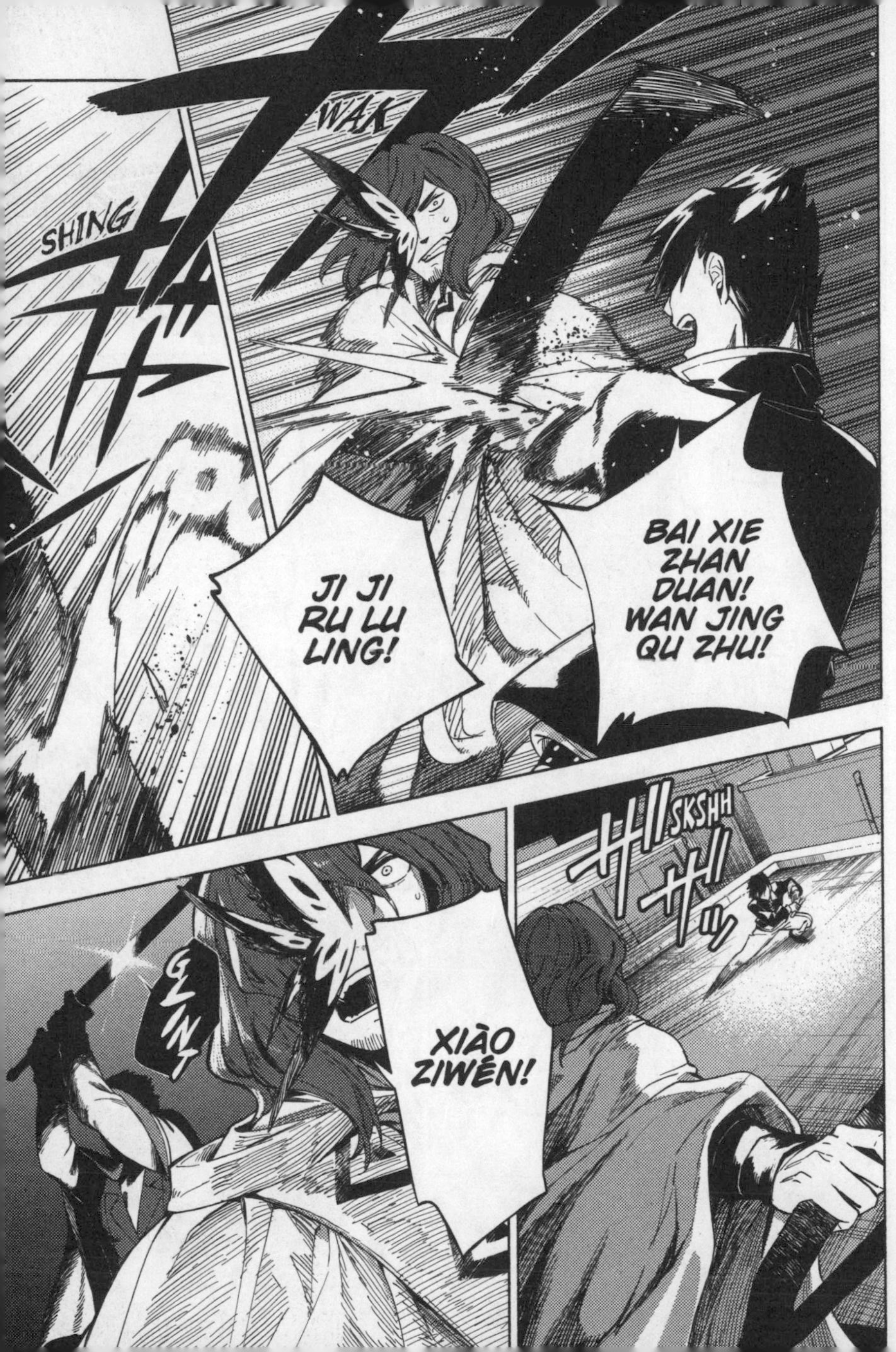
WAK
SHING
BAI XIE ZHAN DUAN! WAN JING QU ZHU!
JI JI RU LU LING!
SKSHH
GLINT
XIÀO ZIWÉN!

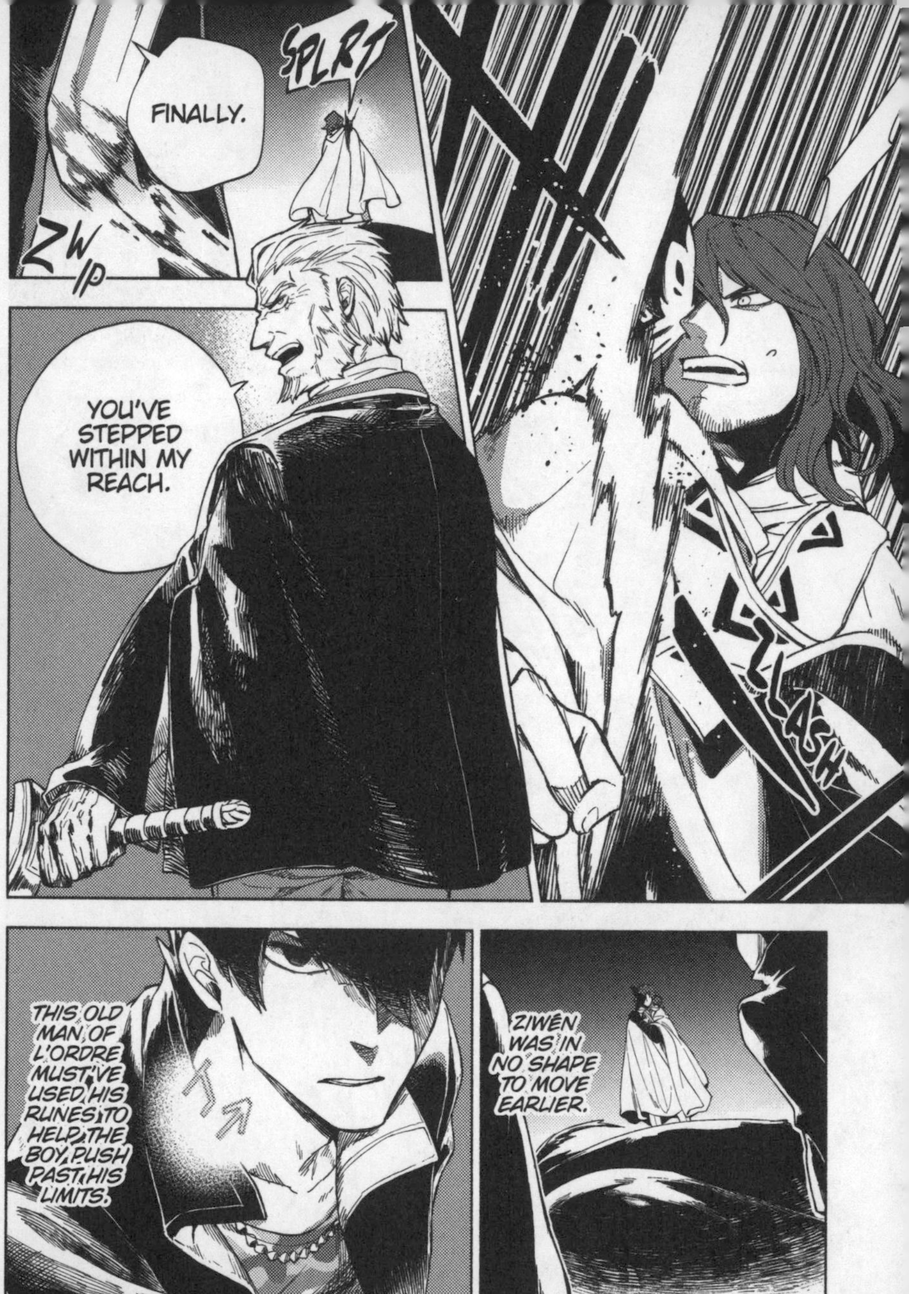
SLASH
SPLRT
FINALLY.
ZWIP
YOU'VE STEPPED WITHIN MY REACH.
ZIWEN WAS IN NO SHAPE TO MOVE EARLIER.
THIS OLD MAN OF L'ORDRE MUST'VE USED HIS RUNES TO HELP THE BOY PUSH PAST HIS LIMITS.

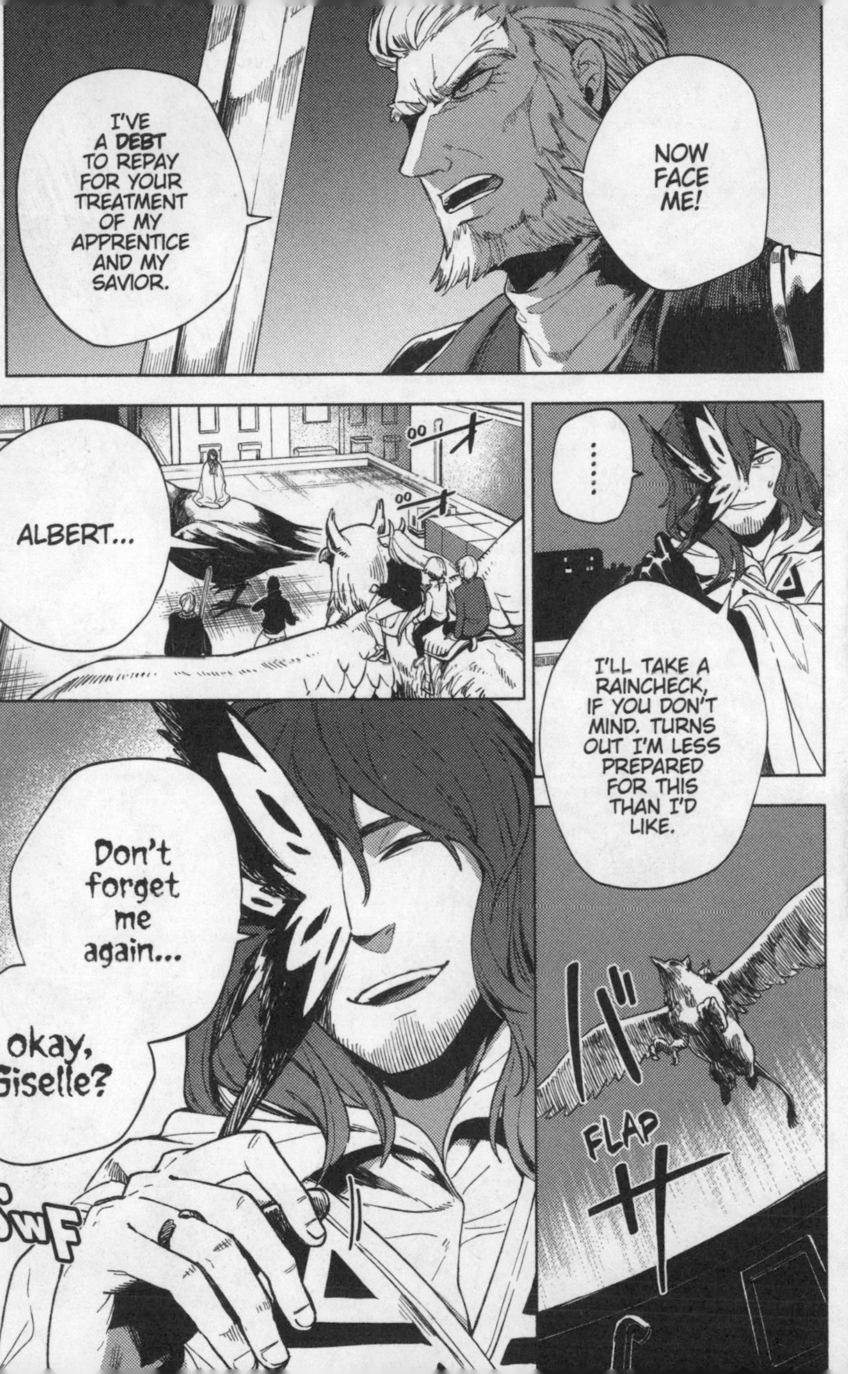
NOW FACE ME!
I'VE A DEBT TO REPAY FOR YOUR TREATMENT OF MY APPRENTICE AND MY SAVIOR.
......
I'LL TAKE A RAINCHECK, IF YOU DON'T MIND. TURNS OUT I'M LESS PREPARED FOR THIS THAN I'D LIKE.
ALBERT...
バ
FLAP
Don't forget me again...
okay, Giselle?
SWF

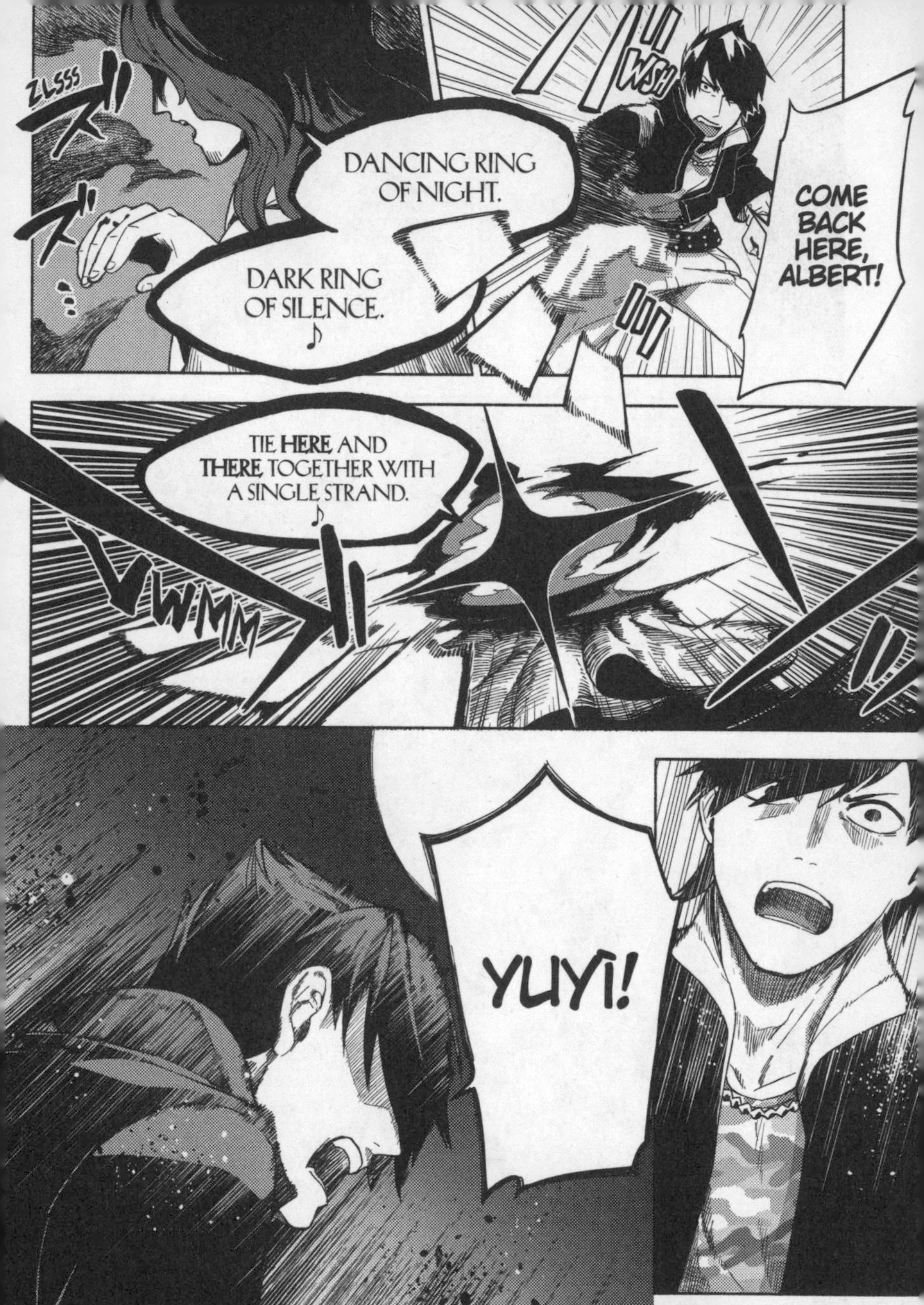
WSH
COME BACK HERE, ALBERT!
DANCING RING OF NIGHT.
DARK RING OF SILENCE. ♪
ZLSSS
TIE HERE AND THERE TOGETHER WITH A SINGLE STRAND. ♪
VWMM
YUYI!

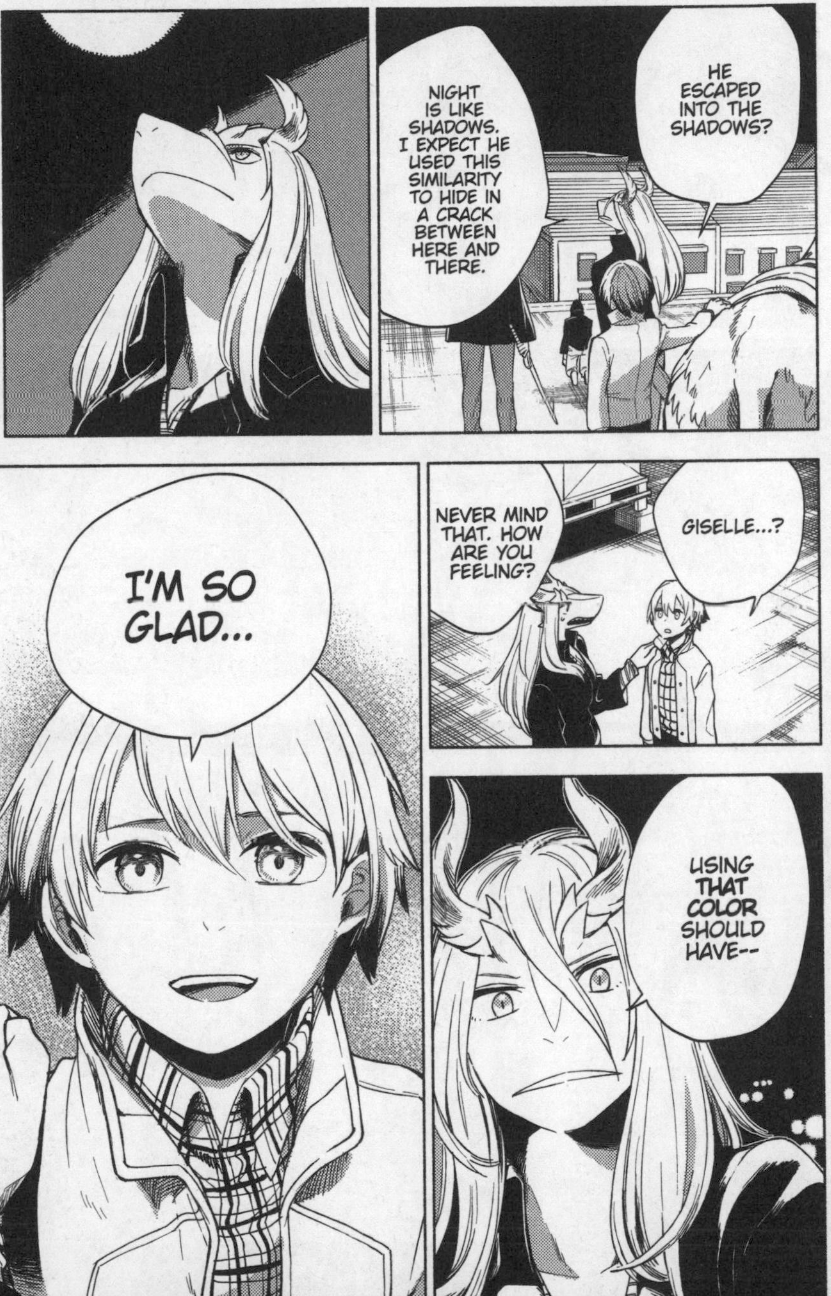
HE ESCAPED INTO THE SHADOWS?
NIGHT IS LIKE SHADOWS. I EXPECT HE USED THIS SIMILARITY TO HIDE IN A CRACK BETWEEN HERE AND THERE.
GISELLE...?
NEVER MIND THAT. HOW ARE YOU FEELING?
USING THAT COLOR SHOULD HAVE--
I'M SO GLAD...

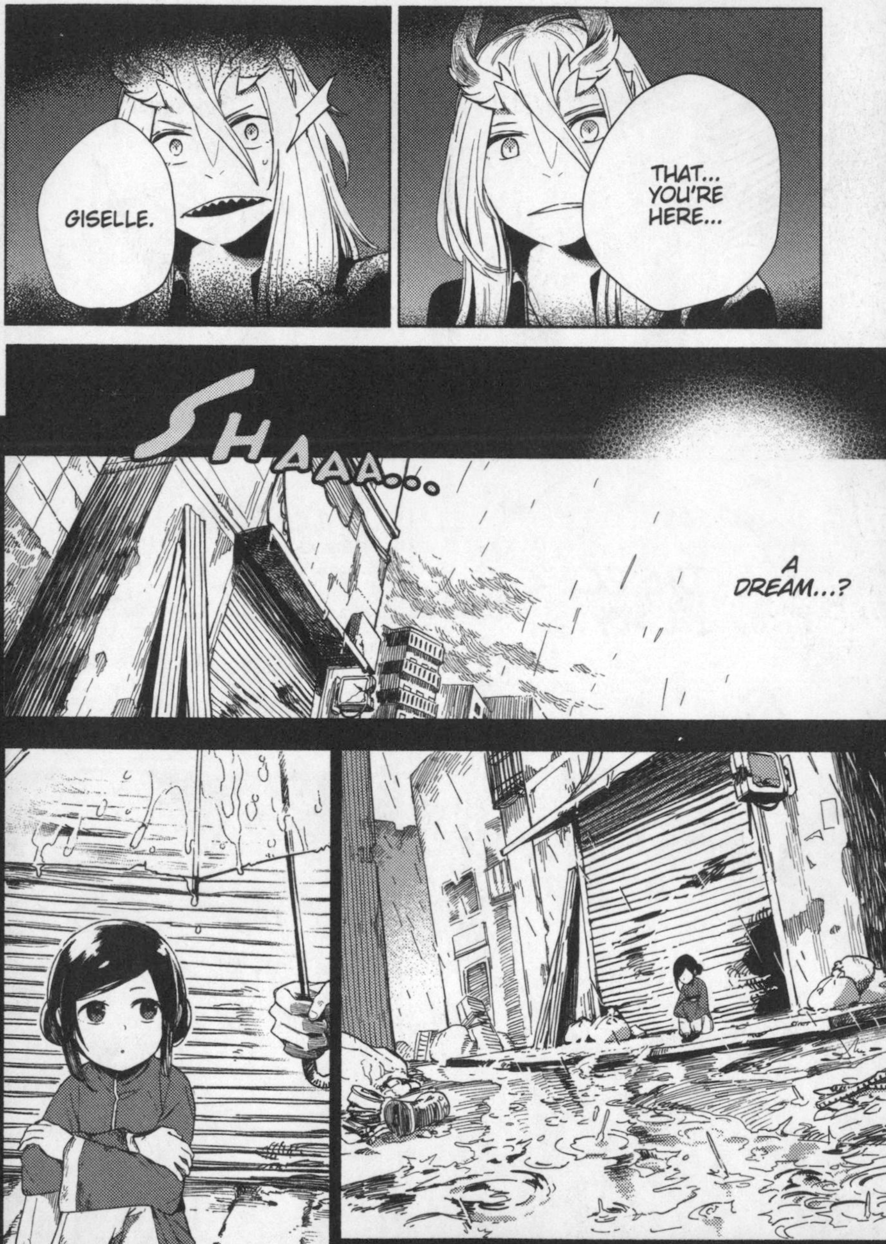
THAT... YOU'RE HERE...
GISELLE.
SHAAA...
A DREAM...?

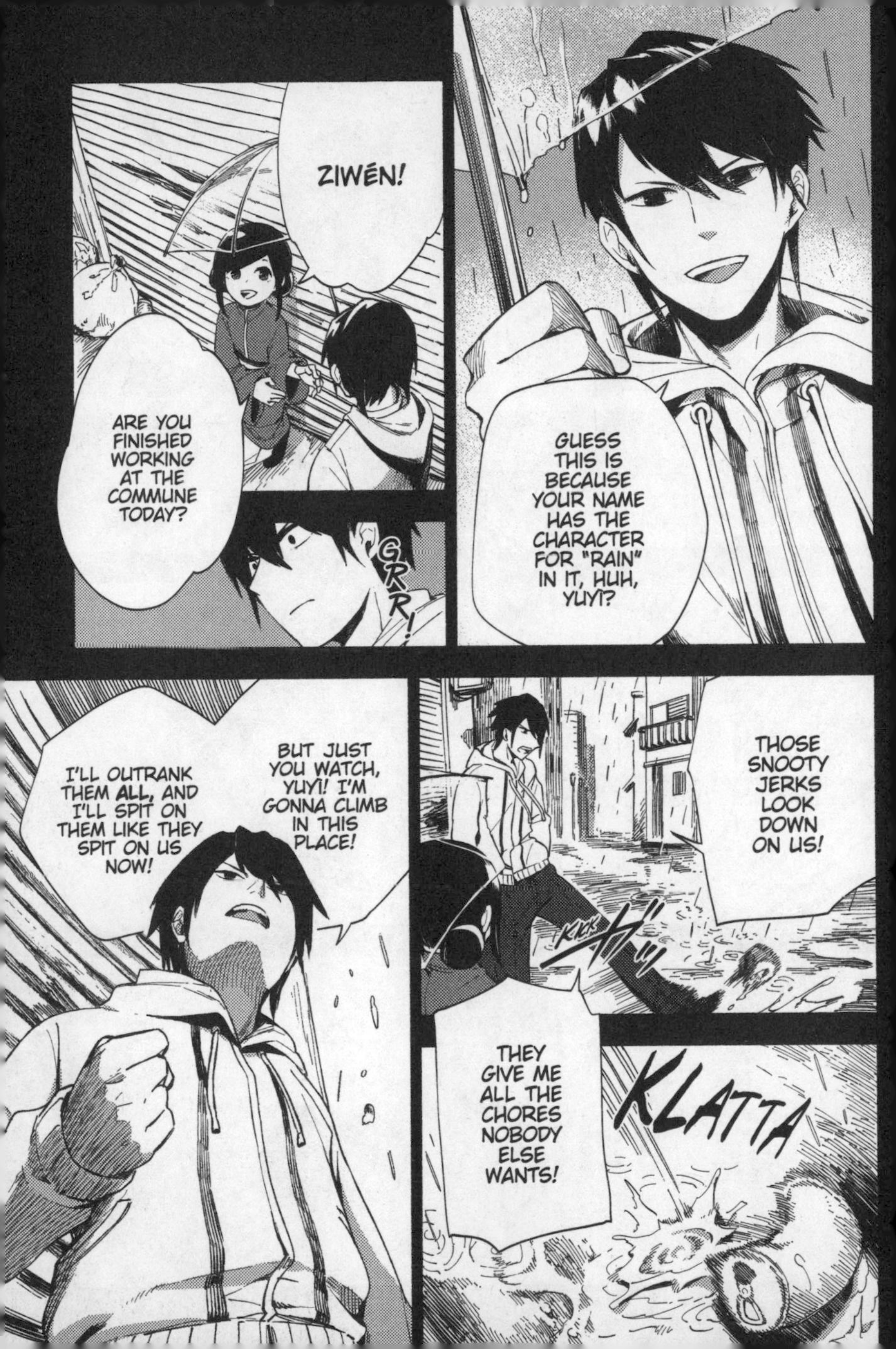
GUESS THIS IS BECAUSE YOUR NAME HAS THE CHARACTER FOR "RAIN" IN IT, HUH, YUYÍ?
ZIWÉN!
ARE YOU FINISHED WORKING AT THE COMMUNE TODAY?
GRR!
THOSE SNOOTY JERKS LOOK DOWN ON US!
KICK
THEY GIVE ME ALL THE CHORES NOBODY ELSE WANTS!
KLATTA
BUT JUST YOU WATCH, YUYÍ! I'M GONNA CLIMB IN THIS PLACE!
I'LL OUTRANK THEM ALL, AND I'LL SPIT ON THEM LIKE THEY SPIT ON US NOW!

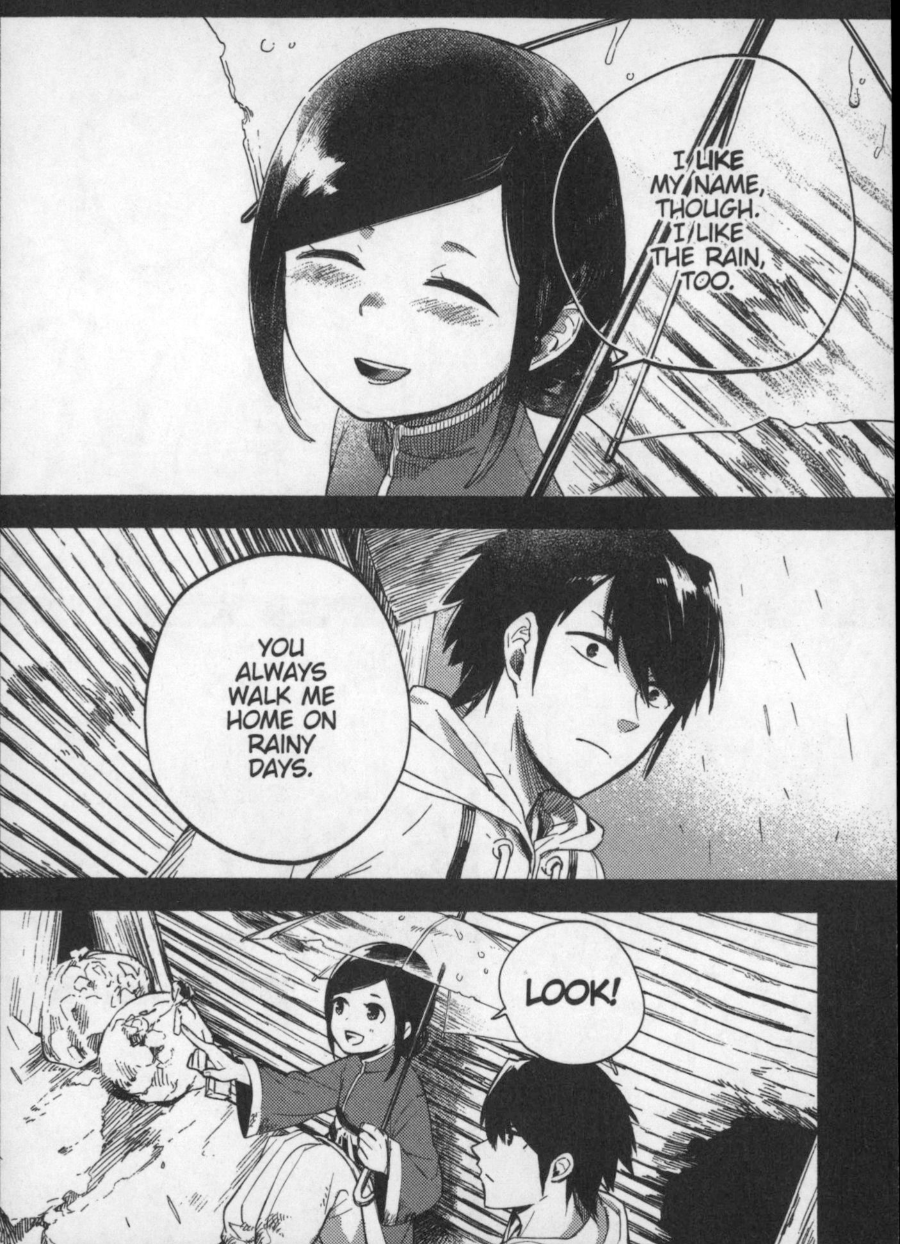
I LIKE MY NAME, THOUGH. I LIKE THE RAIN, TOO.
YOU ALWAYS WALK ME HOME ON RAINY DAYS.
LOOK!

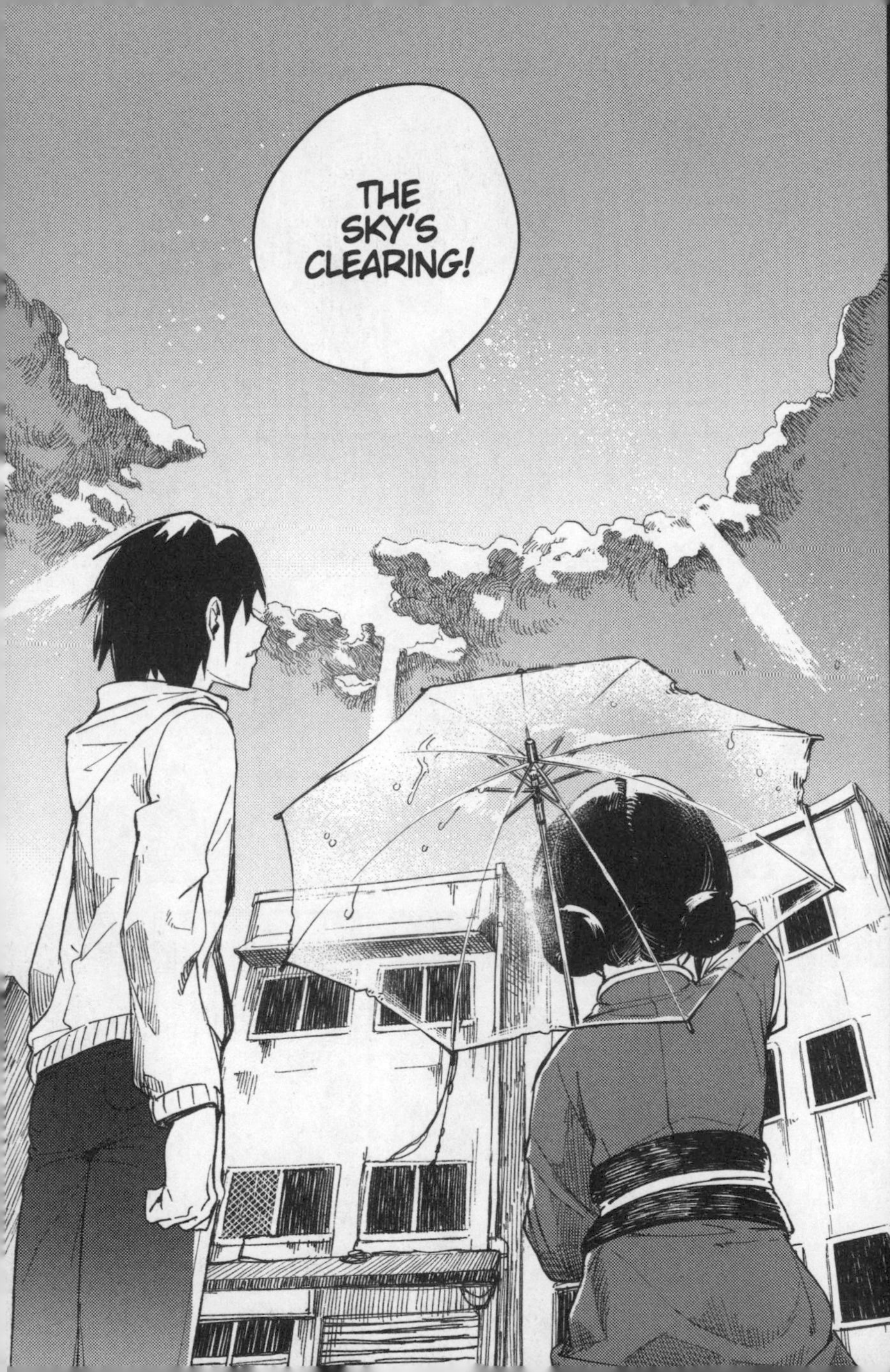
THE SKY'S CLEARING!

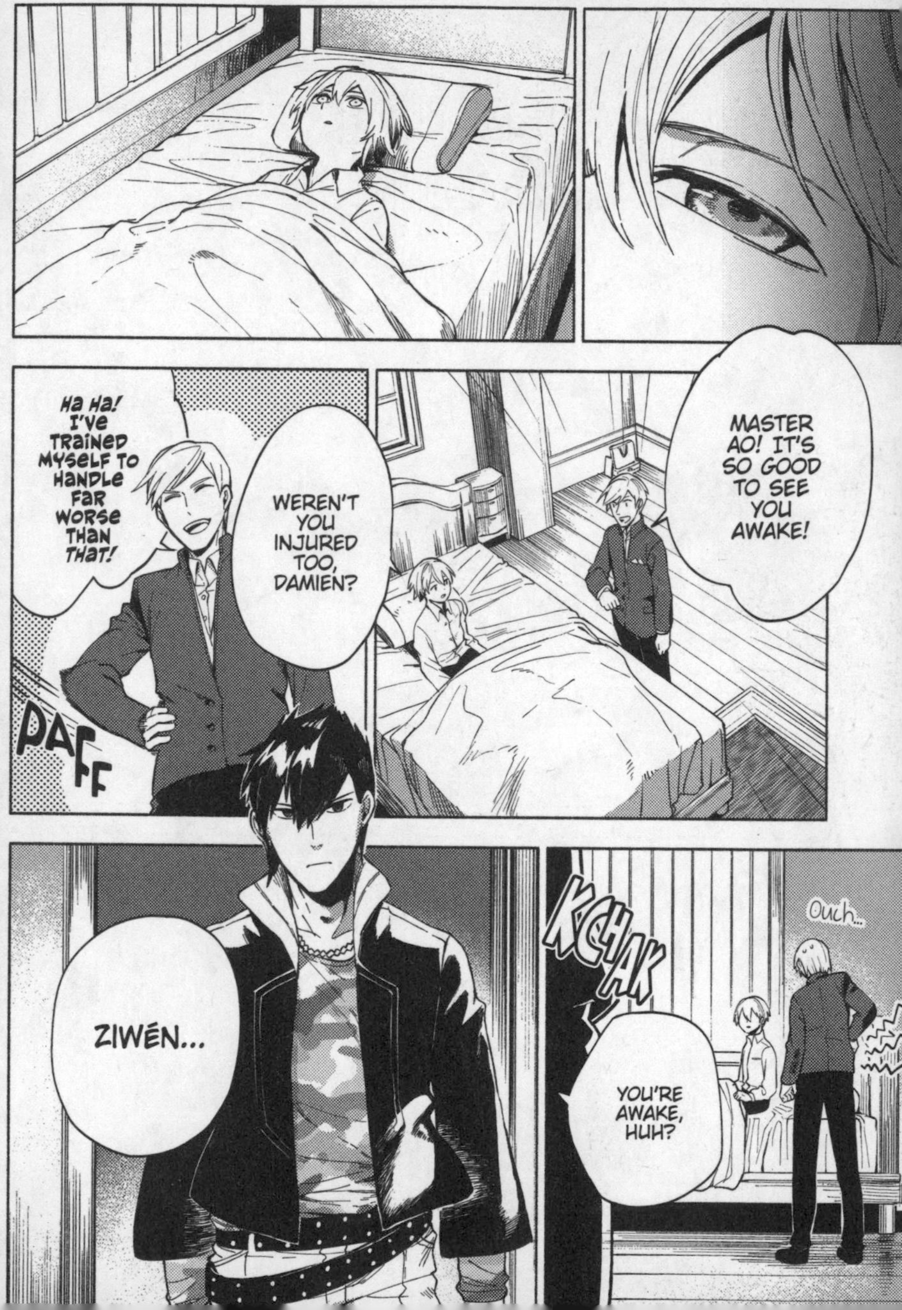
MASTER AO! IT'S SO GOOD TO SEE YOU AWAKE!
WEREN'T YOU INJURED TOO, DAMIEN?
Ha Ha! I've trained myself to handle far worse than that!
PAFF
KCHAK
Ouch...
YOU'RE AWAKE, HUH?
ZIWÉN...

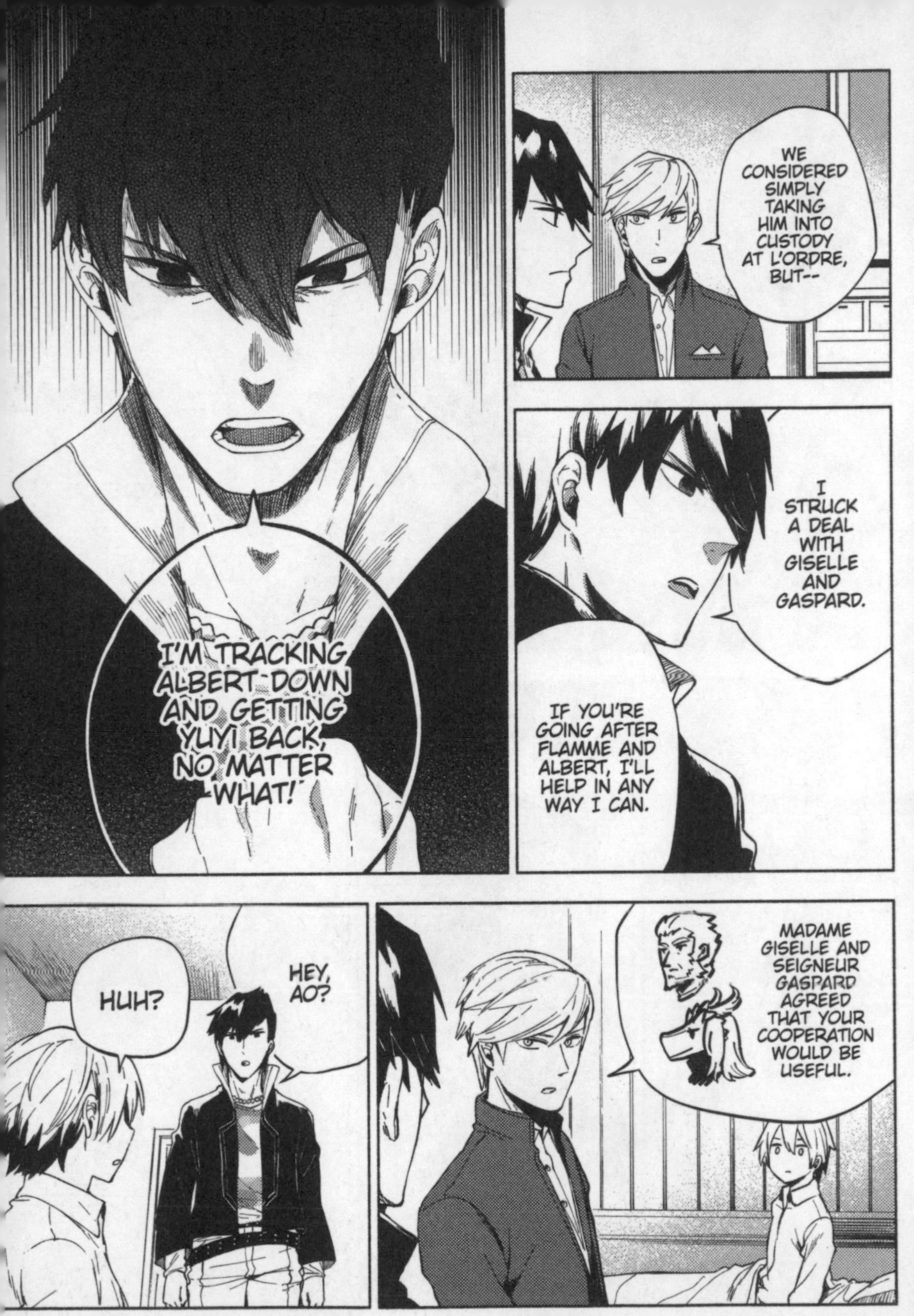
WE CONSIDERED SIMPLY TAKING HIM INTO CUSTODY AT L'ORDRE, BUT--
I STRUCK A DEAL WITH GISELLE AND GASPARD.
IF YOU'RE GOING AFTER FLAMME AND ALBERT, I'LL HELP IN ANY WAY I CAN.
I'M TRACKING ALBERT DOWN AND GETTING YUYI BACK, NO MATTER WHAT!
MADAME GISELLE AND SEIGNEUR GASPARD AGREED THAT YOUR COOPERATION WOULD BE USEFUL.
HEY, AO?
HUH?

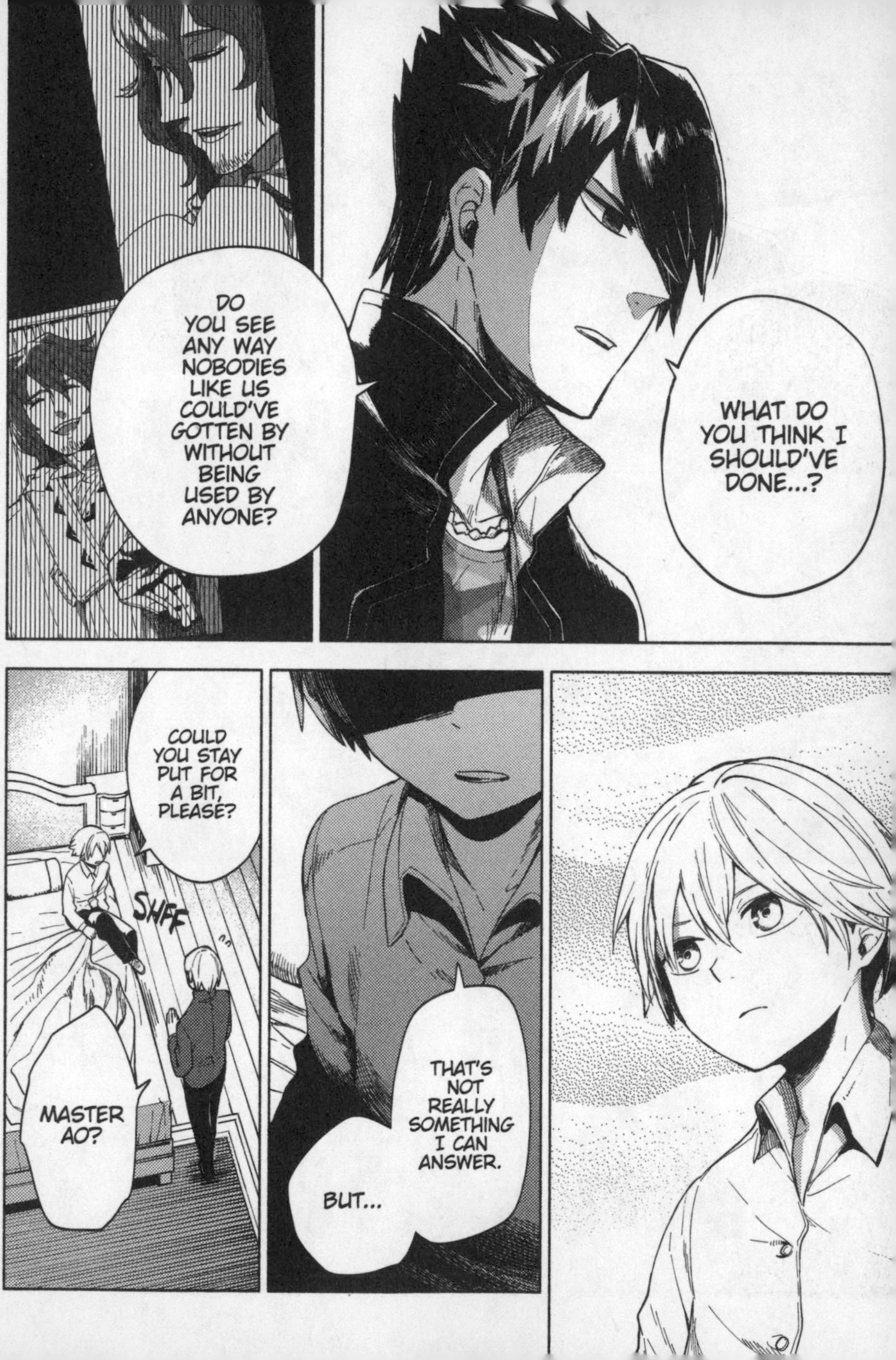
WHAT DO YOU THINK I SHOULD'VE DONE...?
DO YOU SEE ANY WAY NOBODIES LIKE US COULD'VE GOTTEN BY WITHOUT BEING USED BY ANYONE?
THAT'S NOT REALLY SOMETHING I CAN ANSWER.
BUT...
COULD YOU STAY PUT FOR A BIT, PLEASE?
SHFF
MASTER AO?

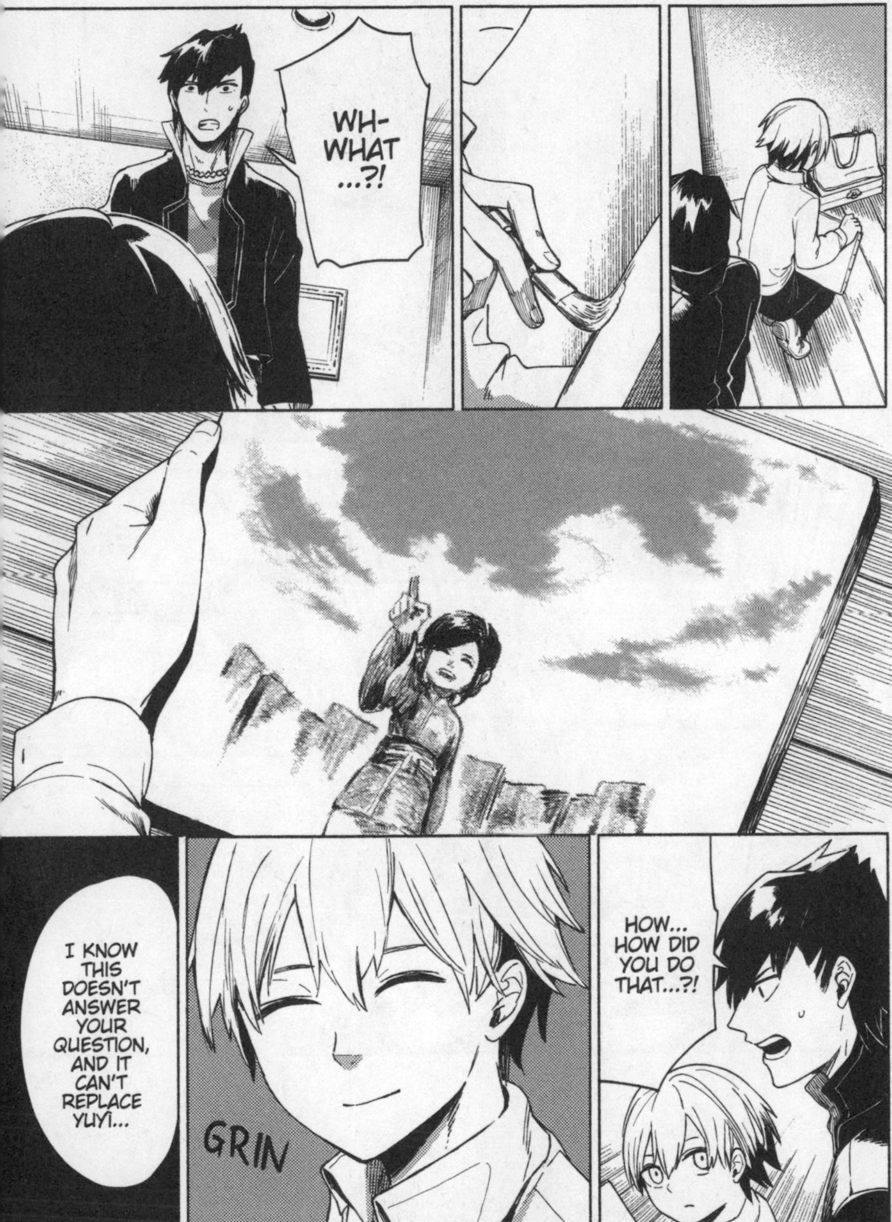
WH-WHAT ...?!
HOW... HOW DID YOU DO THAT...?!
GRIN
I KNOW THIS DOESN'T ANSWER YOUR QUESTION, AND IT CAN'T REPLACE YUYI...

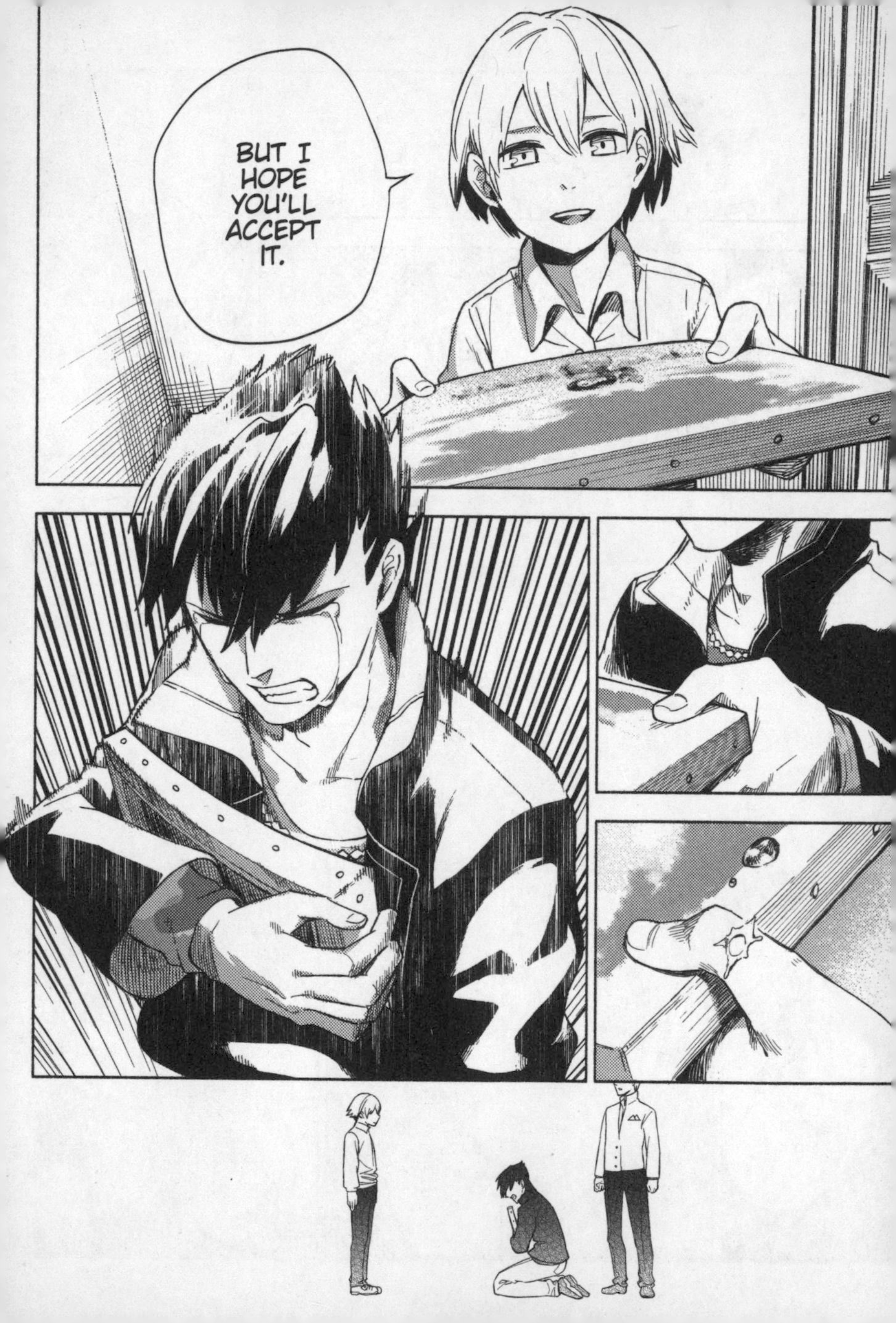
BUT I HOPE YOU'LL ACCEPT IT.

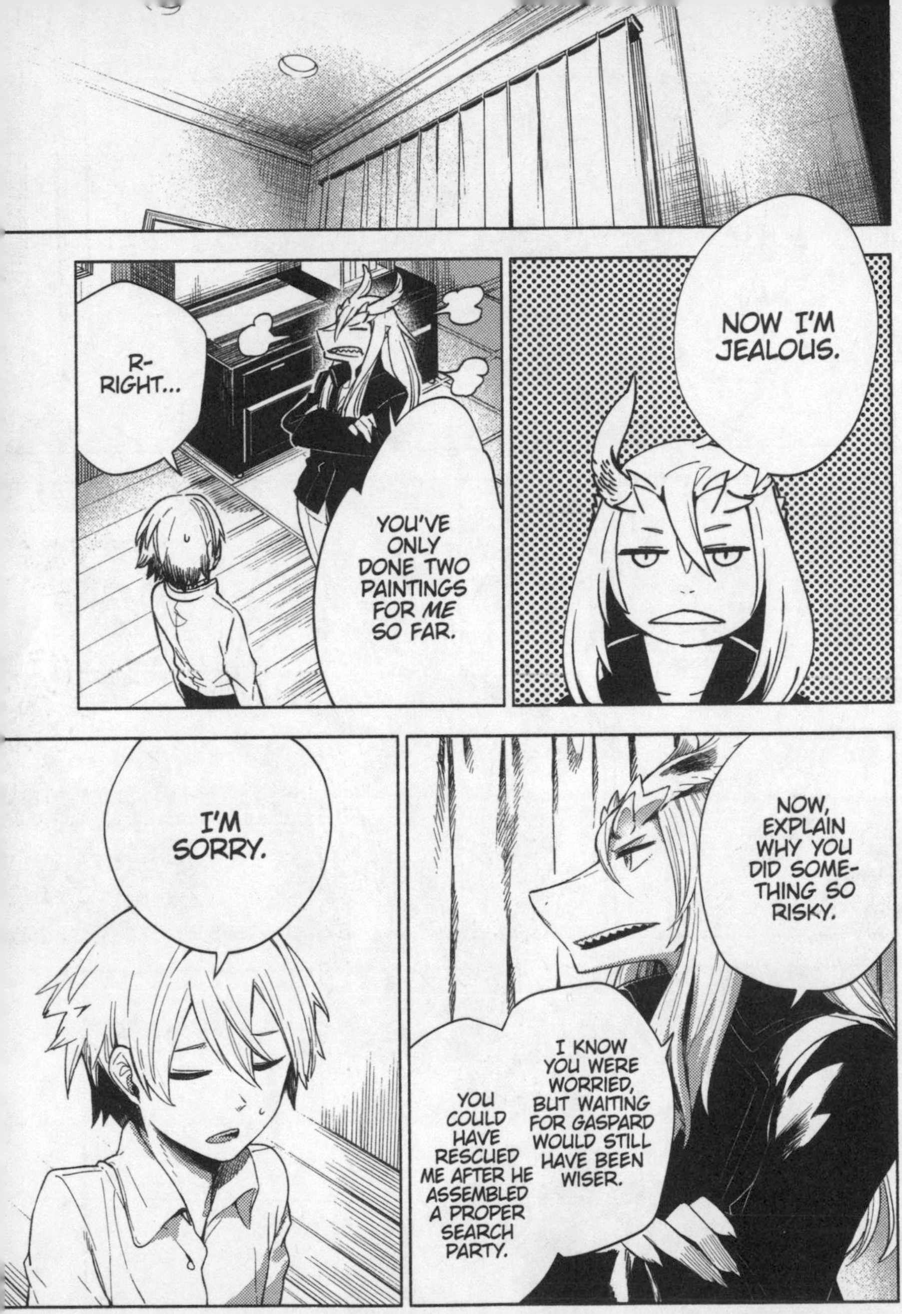
NOW I'M JEALOUS.
YOU'VE ONLY DONE TWO PAINTINGS FOR *ME* SO FAR.
R-RIGHT...
NOW, EXPLAIN WHY YOU DID SOME-THING SO RISKY.
I KNOW YOU WERE WORRIED, BUT WAITING FOR GASPARD WOULD STILL HAVE BEEN WISER.
YOU COULD HAVE RESCUED ME AFTER HE ASSEMBLED A PROPER SEARCH PARTY.
I'M SORRY.

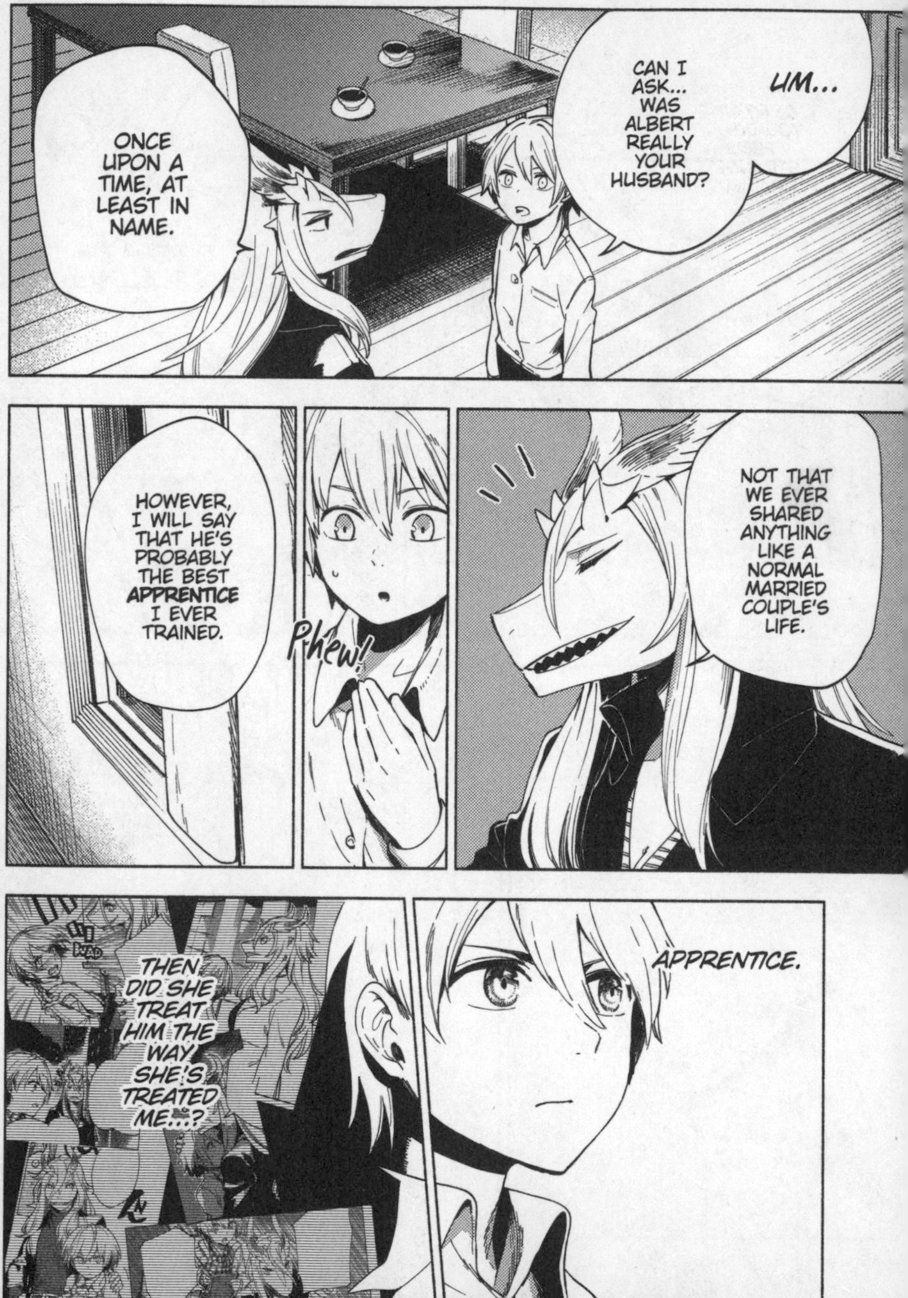
UM...
CAN I ASK... WAS ALBERT REALLY YOUR HUSBAND?
ONCE UPON A TIME, AT LEAST IN NAME.
NOT THAT WE EVER SHARED ANYTHING LIKE A NORMAL MARRIED COUPLE'S LIFE.
Phew!
HOWEVER, I WILL SAY THAT HE'S PROBABLY THE BEST **APPRENTICE** I EVER TRAINED.
APPRENTICE.
THEN DID SHE TREAT HIM THE WAY SHE'S TREATED ME...?

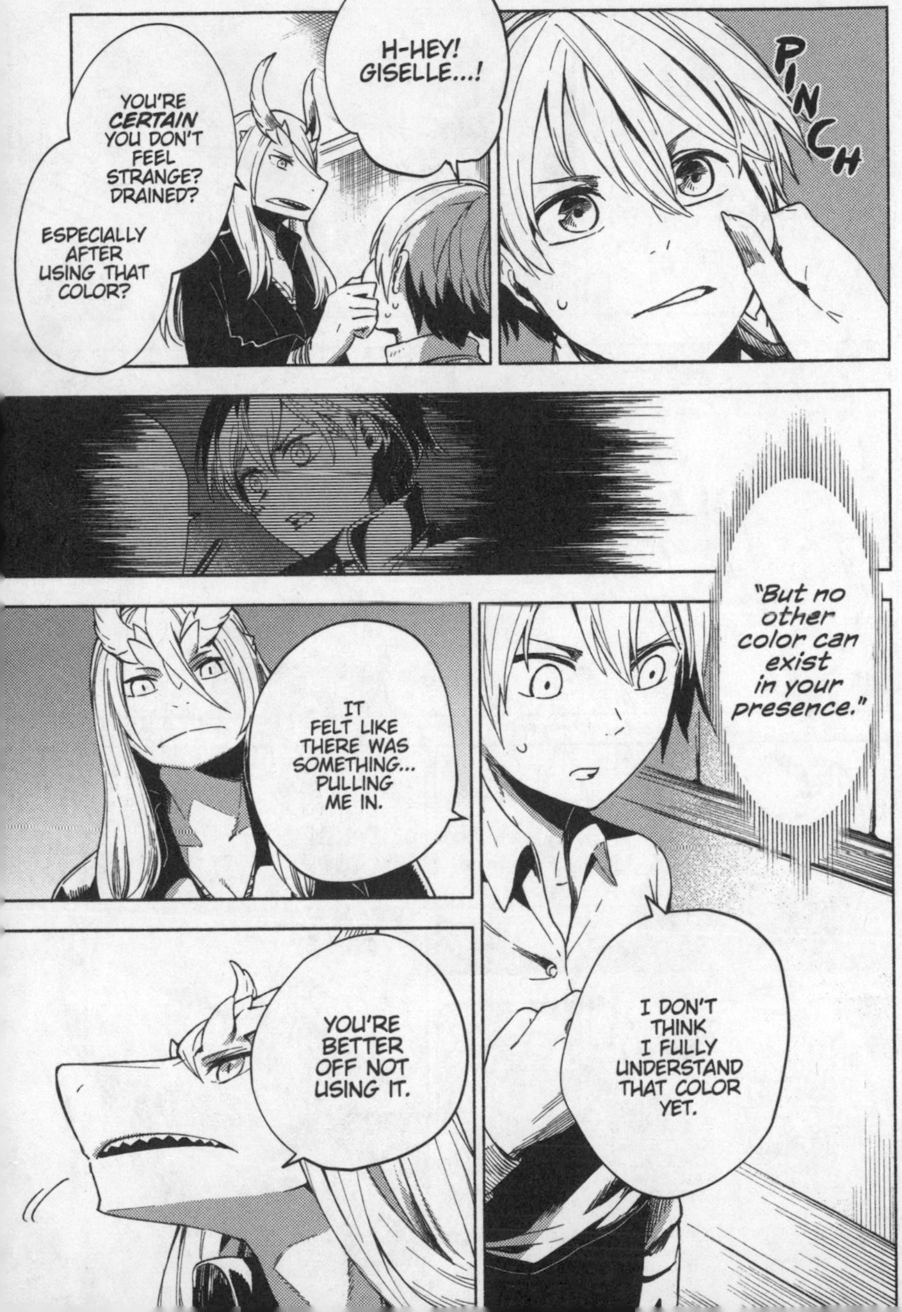
PINCH
H-HEY! GISELLE...!
YOU'RE *CERTAIN* YOU DON'T FEEL STRANGE? DRAINED?
ESPECIALLY AFTER USING THAT COLOR?
"But no other color can exist in your presence."
I DON'T THINK I FULLY UNDERSTAND THAT COLOR YET.
IT FELT LIKE THERE WAS SOMETHING... PULLING ME IN.
YOU'RE BETTER OFF NOT USING IT.

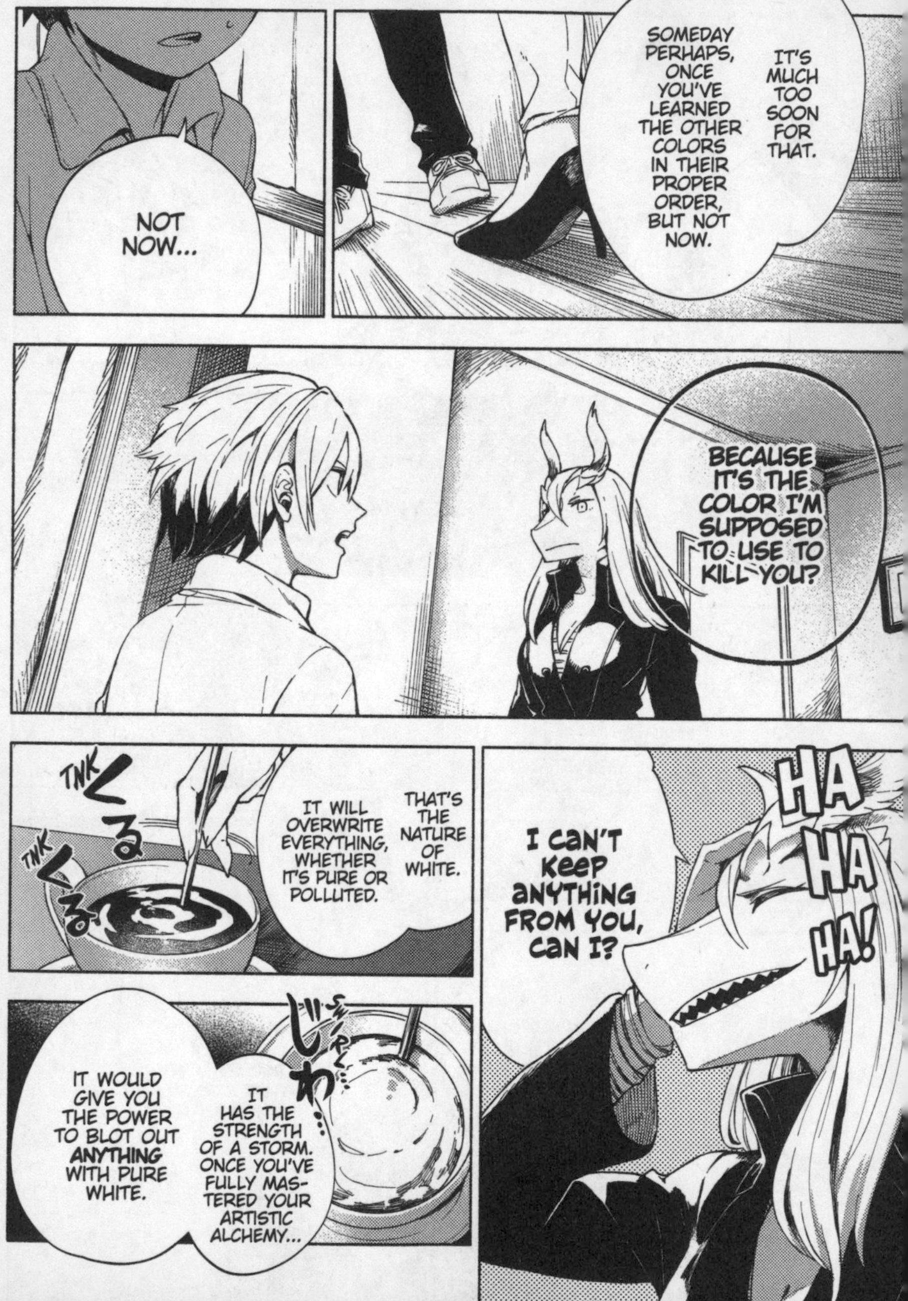
IT'S MUCH TOO SOON FOR THAT.
SOMEDAY PERHAPS, ONCE YOU'VE LEARNED THE OTHER COLORS IN THEIR PROPER ORDER, BUT NOT NOW.
NOT NOW...
BECAUSE IT'S THE COLOR I'M SUPPOSED TO USE TO KILL YOU?
HA HA HA!
I CAN'T KEEP ANYTHING FROM YOU, CAN I?
TNK くる
TNK くる
THAT'S THE NATURE OF WHITE.
IT WILL OVERWRITE EVERYTHING, WHETHER IT'S PURE OR POLLUTED.
じわ…
IT HAS THE STRENGTH OF A STORM. ONCE YOU'VE FULLY MAS-TERED YOUR ARTISTIC ALCHEMY...
IT WOULD GIVE YOU THE POWER TO BLOT OUT ANYTHING WITH PURE WHITE.

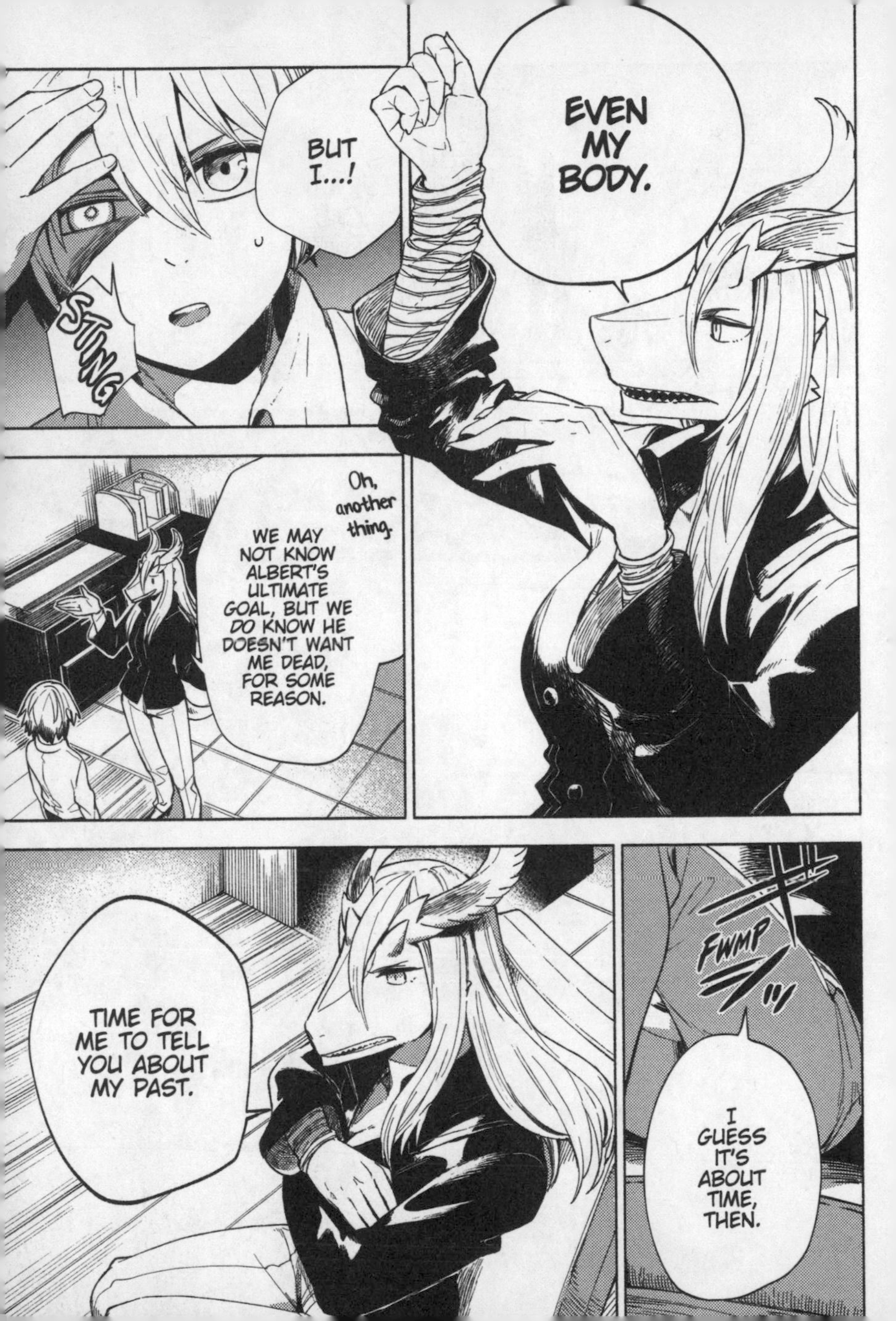
EVEN MY BODY.
BUT I...!
STING
Oh, another thing.
WE MAY NOT KNOW ALBERT'S ULTIMATE GOAL, BUT WE DO KNOW HE DOESN'T WANT ME DEAD, FOR SOME REASON.
FWMP
I GUESS IT'S ABOUT TIME, THEN.
TIME FOR ME TO TELL YOU ABOUT MY PAST.

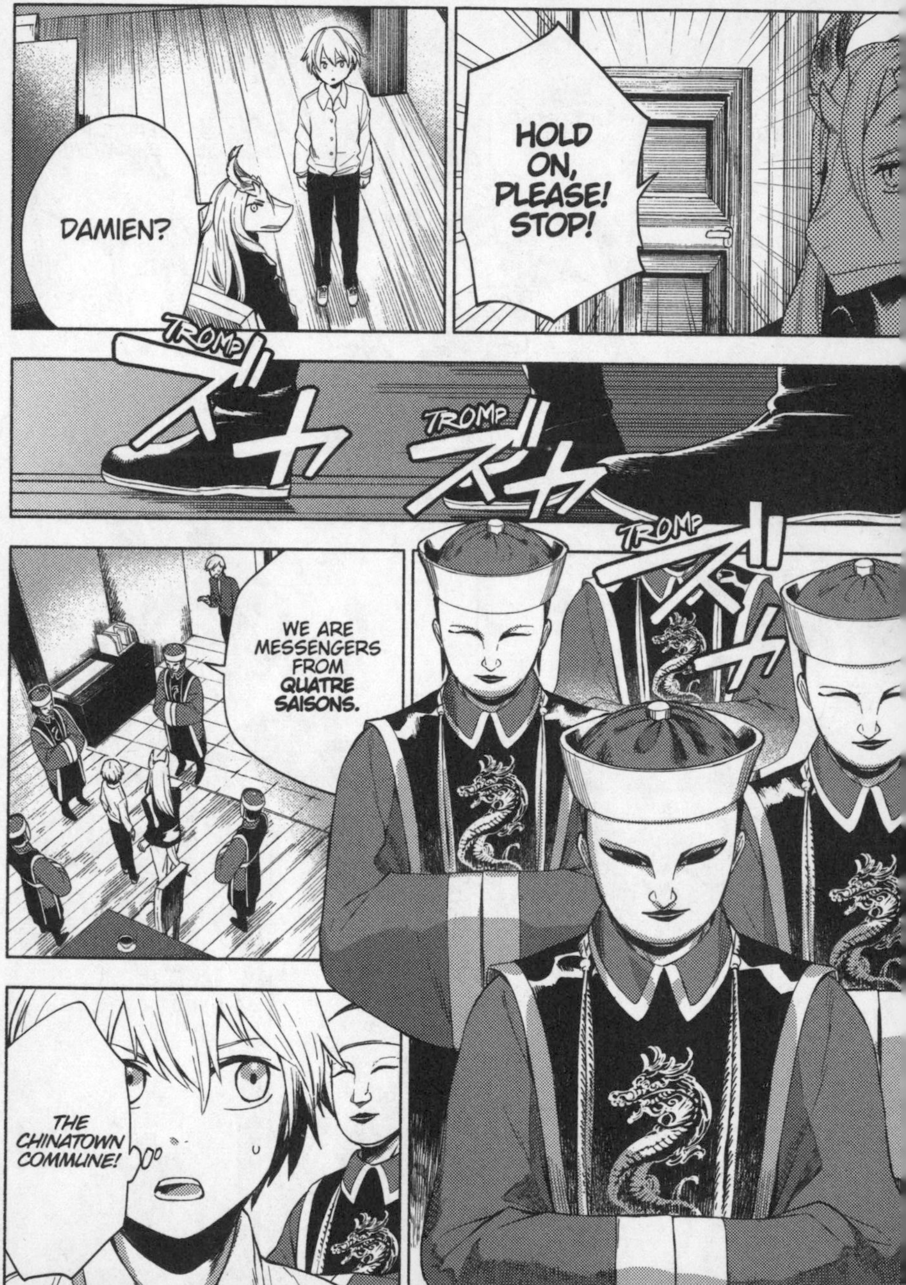
HOLD ON, PLEASE! STOP!
DAMIEN?
TROMP
TROMP
TROMP
WE ARE MESSENGERS FROM QUATRE SAISONS.
THE CHINATOWN COMMUNE!

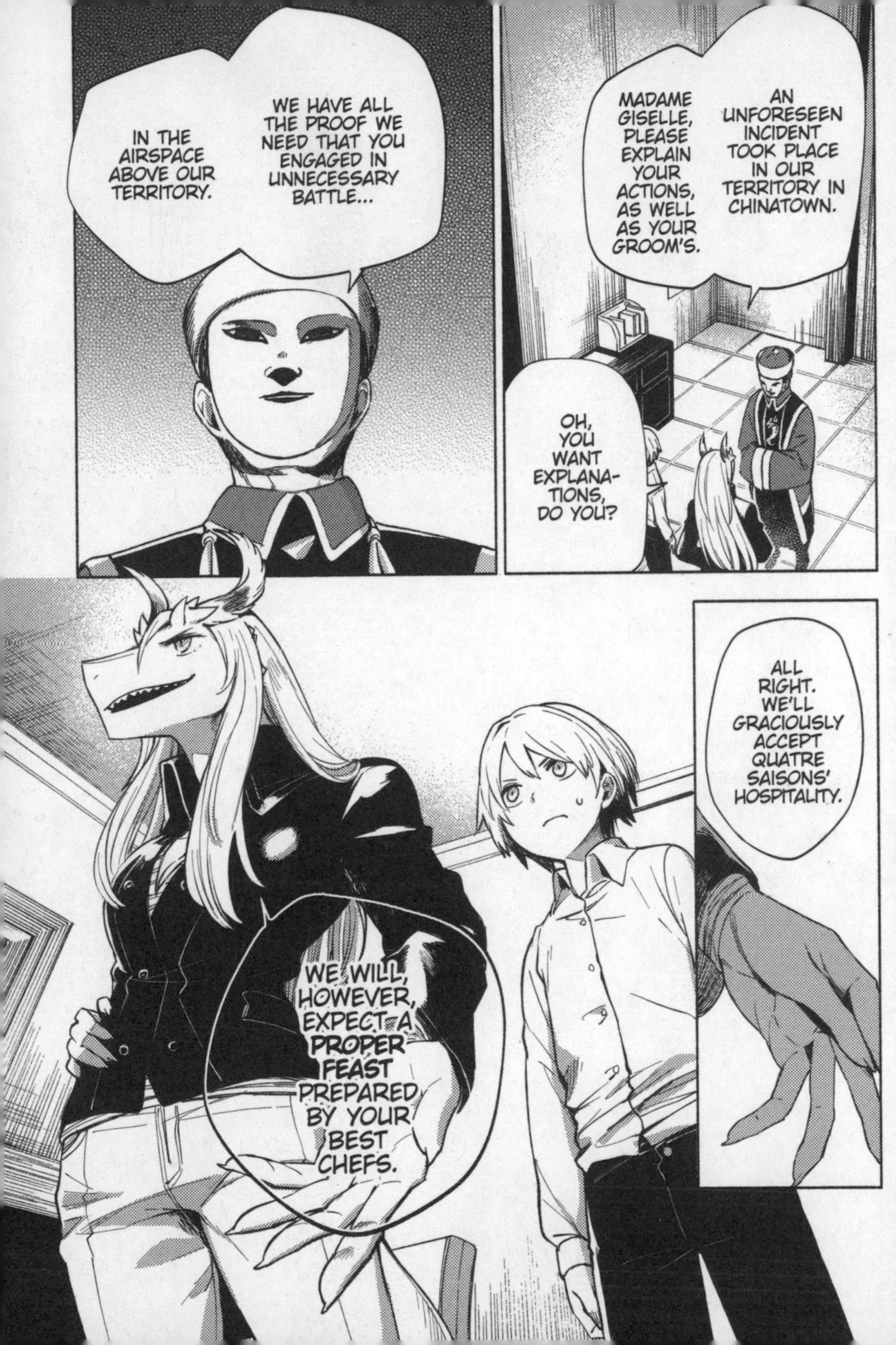
AN UNFORESEEN INCIDENT TOOK PLACE IN OUR TERRITORY IN CHINATOWN.
MADAME GISELLE, PLEASE EXPLAIN YOUR ACTIONS, AS WELL AS YOUR GROOM'S.
OH, YOU WANT EXPLANA-TIONS, DO YOU?
WE HAVE ALL THE PROOF WE NEED THAT YOU ENGAGED IN UNNECESSARY BATTLE...
IN THE AIRSPACE ABOVE OUR TERRITORY.
ALL RIGHT. WE'LL GRACIOUSLY ACCEPT QUATRE SAISONS' HOSPITALITY.
WE WILL, HOWEVER, EXPECT A PROPER FEAST PREPARED BY YOUR BEST CHEFS.

The Ancient Magus' Bride

WIZARD's BLUE

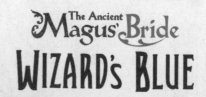

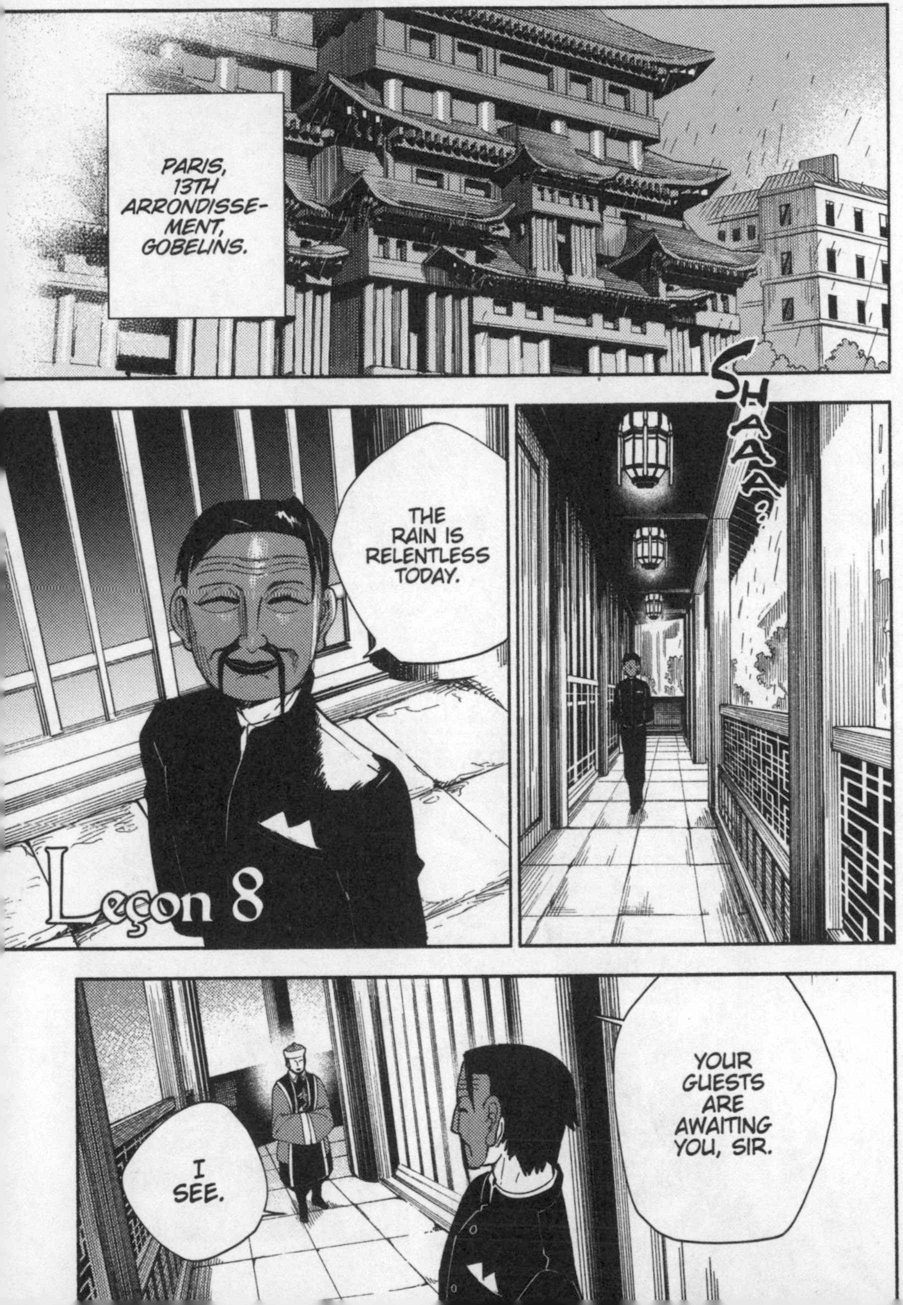
PARIS, 13TH ARRONDISSE-MENT, GOBELINS.
SHAAAA
THE RAIN IS RELENTLESS TODAY.
Leçon 8
YOUR GUESTS ARE AWAITING YOU, SIR.
I SEE.

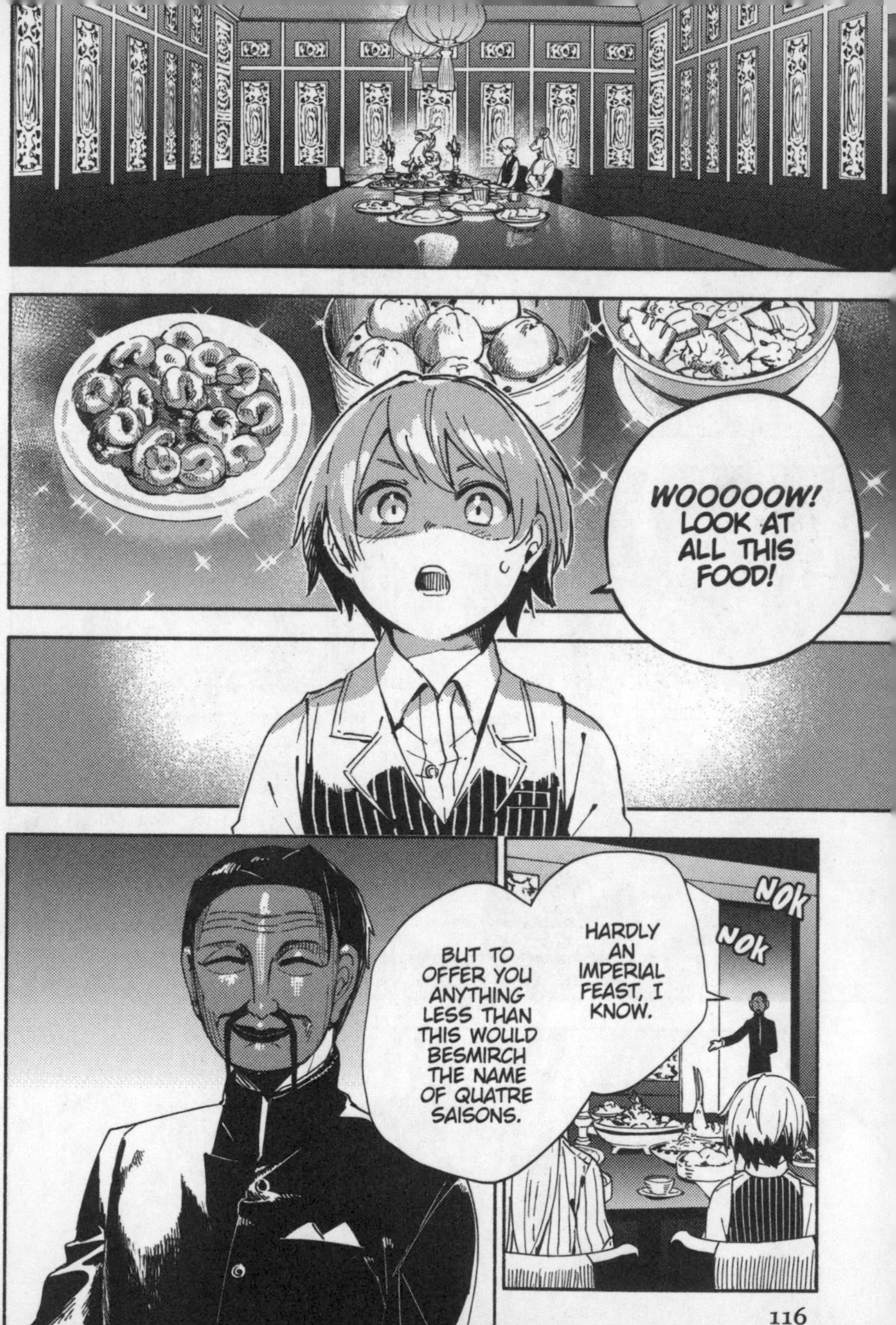
WOOOOOW! LOOK AT ALL THIS FOOD!
NOK
NOK
HARDLY AN IMPERIAL FEAST, I KNOW.
BUT TO OFFER YOU ANYTHING LESS THAN THIS WOULD BESMIRCH THE NAME OF QUATRE SAISONS.

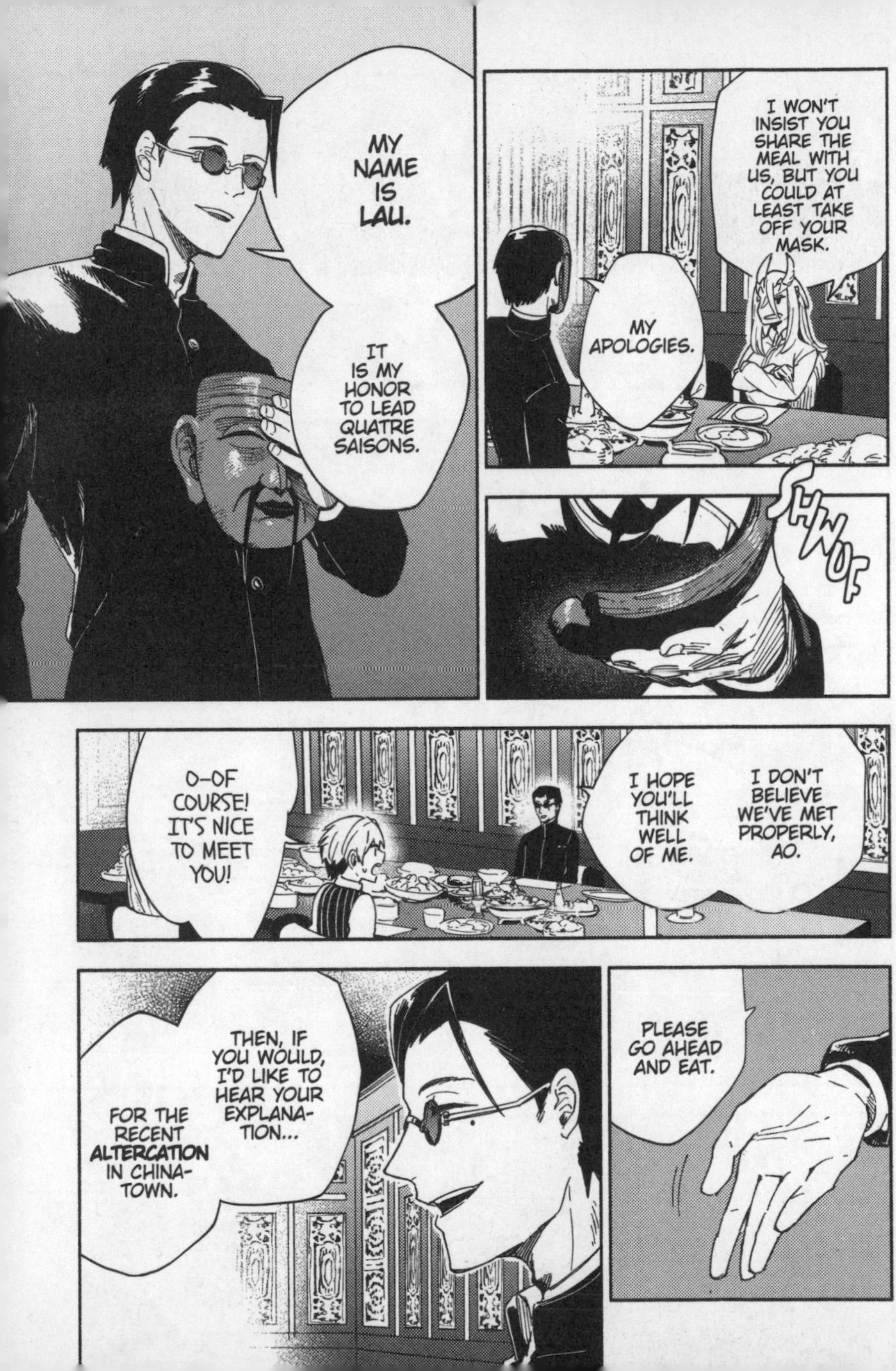
I WON'T INSIST YOU SHARE THE MEAL WITH US, BUT YOU COULD AT LEAST TAKE OFF YOUR MASK.
MY APOLOGIES.
SHWUF
MY NAME IS LAU.
IT IS MY HONOR TO LEAD QUATRE SAISONS.
I DON'T BELIEVE WE'VE MET PROPERLY, AO.
I HOPE YOU'LL THINK WELL OF ME.
O-OF COURSE! IT'S NICE TO MEET YOU!
PLEASE GO AHEAD AND EAT.
THEN, IF YOU WOULD, I'D LIKE TO HEAR YOUR EXPLANATION...
FOR THE RECENT ALTERCATION IN CHINATOWN.

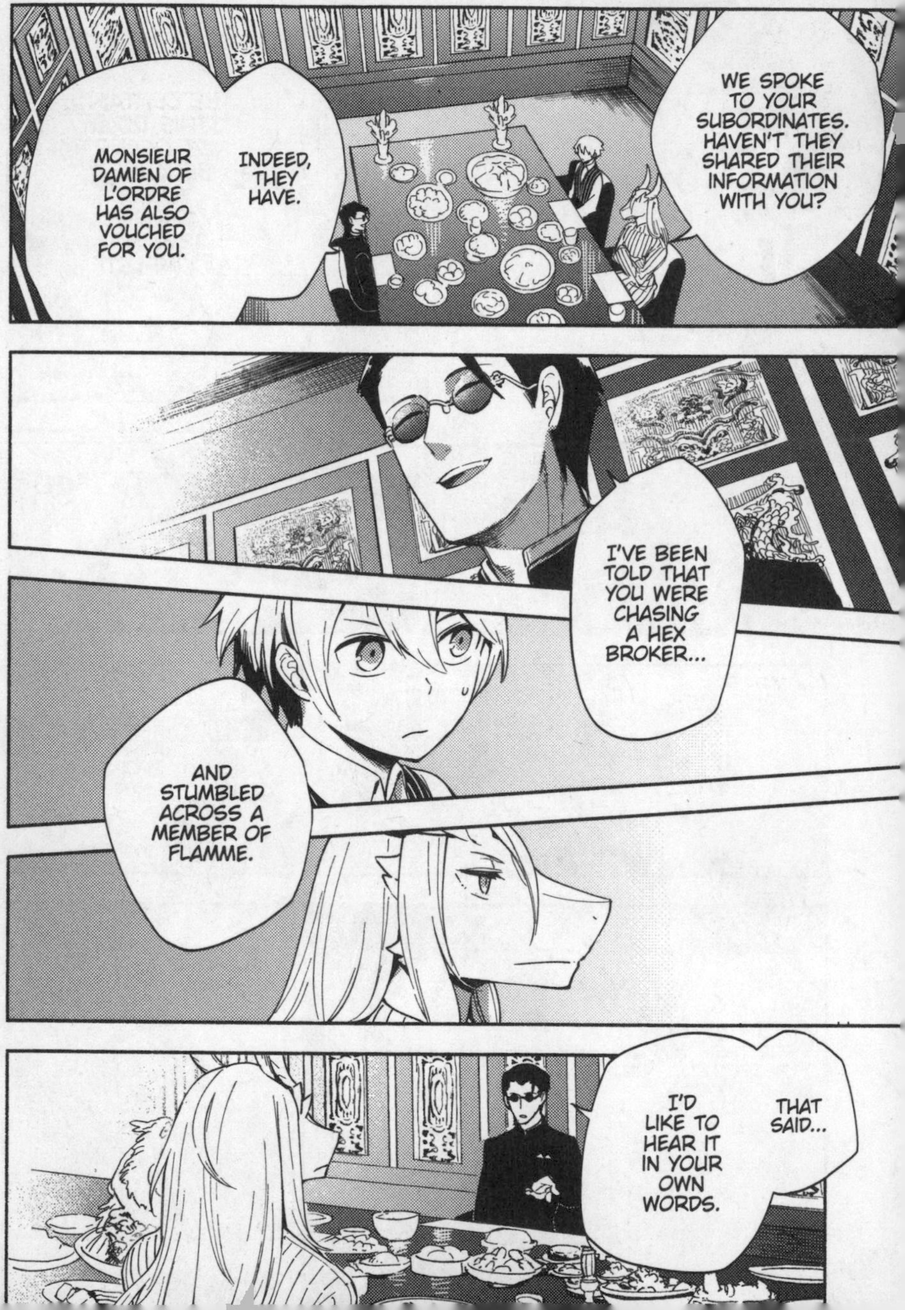
WE SPOKE TO YOUR SUBORDINATES. HAVEN'T THEY SHARED THEIR INFORMATION WITH YOU?
INDEED, THEY HAVE.
MONSIEUR DAMIEN OF L'ORDRE HAS ALSO VOUCHED FOR YOU.
I'VE BEEN TOLD THAT YOU WERE CHASING A HEX BROKER...
AND STUMBLED ACROSS A MEMBER OF FLAMME.
THAT SAID...
I'D LIKE TO HEAR IT IN YOUR OWN WORDS.

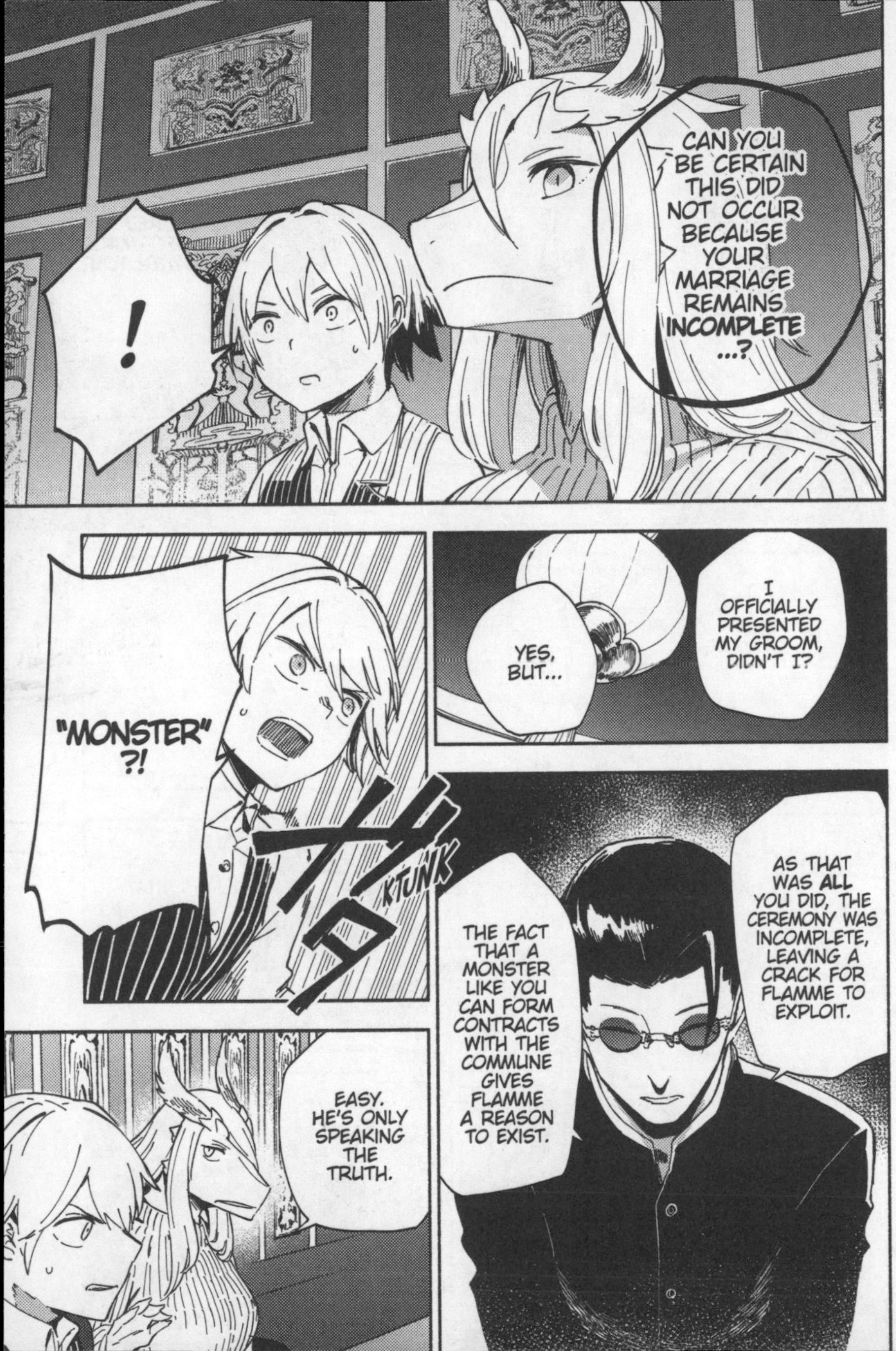

CAN YOU BE CERTAIN THIS DID NOT OCCUR BECAUSE YOUR MARRIAGE REMAINS INCOMPLETE ...?
!
I OFFICIALLY PRESENTED MY GROOM, DIDN'T I?
YES, BUT...
AS THAT WAS ALL YOU DID, THE CEREMONY WAS INCOMPLETE, LEAVING A CRACK FOR FLAMME TO EXPLOIT.
THE FACT THAT A MONSTER LIKE YOU CAN FORM CONTRACTS WITH THE COMMUNE GIVES FLAMME A REASON TO EXIST.
"MONSTER" ?!
KTUNK
EASY. HE'S ONLY SPEAKING THE TRUTH.

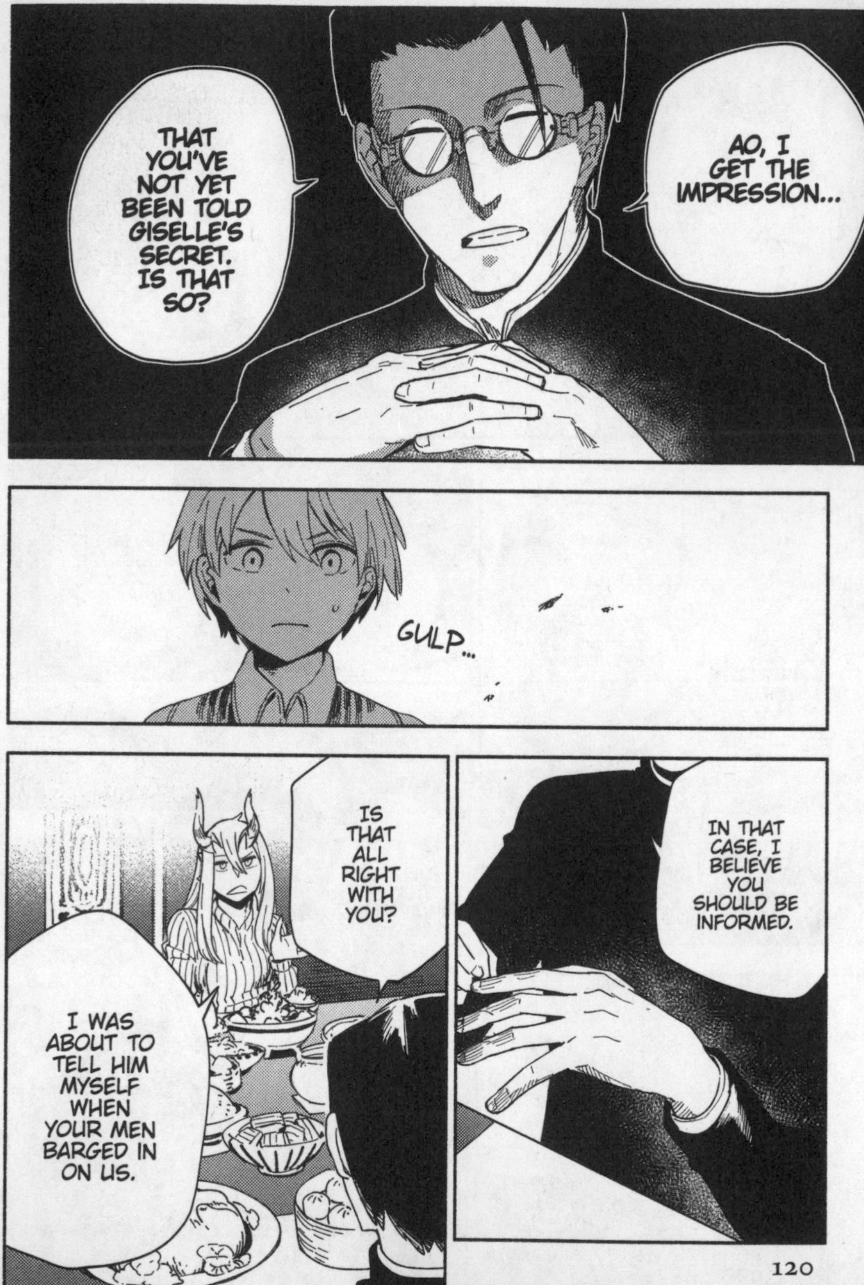
AO, I GET THE IMPRESSION...
THAT YOU'VE NOT YET BEEN TOLD GISELLE'S SECRET. IS THAT SO?
GULP...
IN THAT CASE, I BELIEVE YOU SHOULD BE INFORMED.
IS THAT ALL RIGHT WITH YOU?
I WAS ABOUT TO TELL HIM MYSELF WHEN YOUR MEN BARGED IN ON US.

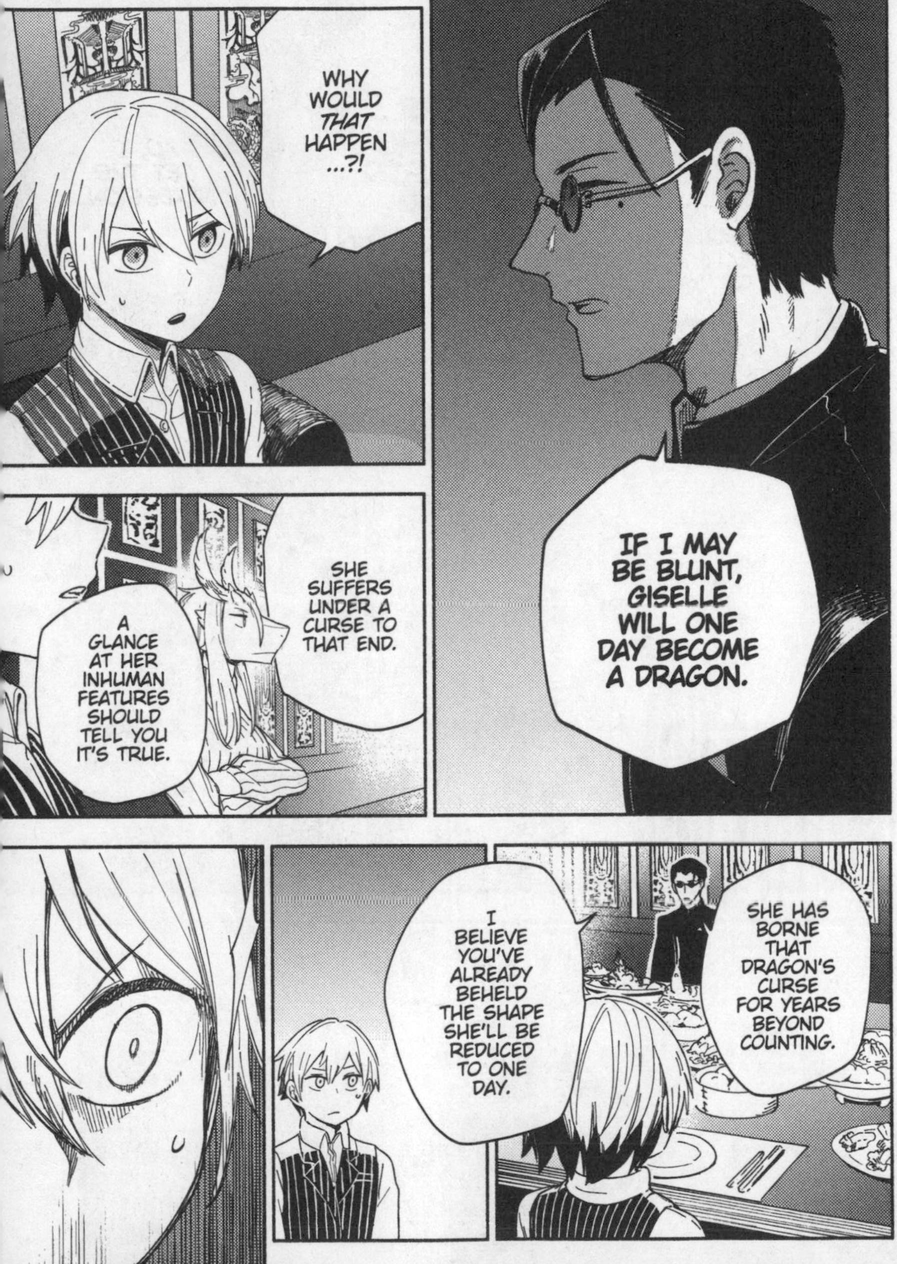
IF I MAY BE BLUNT, GISELLE WILL ONE DAY BECOME A DRAGON.
WHY WOULD *THAT* HAPPEN ...?!
SHE SUFFERS UNDER A CURSE TO THAT END.
A GLANCE AT HER INHUMAN FEATURES SHOULD TELL YOU IT'S TRUE.
SHE HAS BORNE THAT DRAGON'S CURSE FOR YEARS BEYOND COUNTING.
I BELIEVE YOU'VE ALREADY BEHELD THE SHAPE SHE'LL BE REDUCED TO ONE DAY.

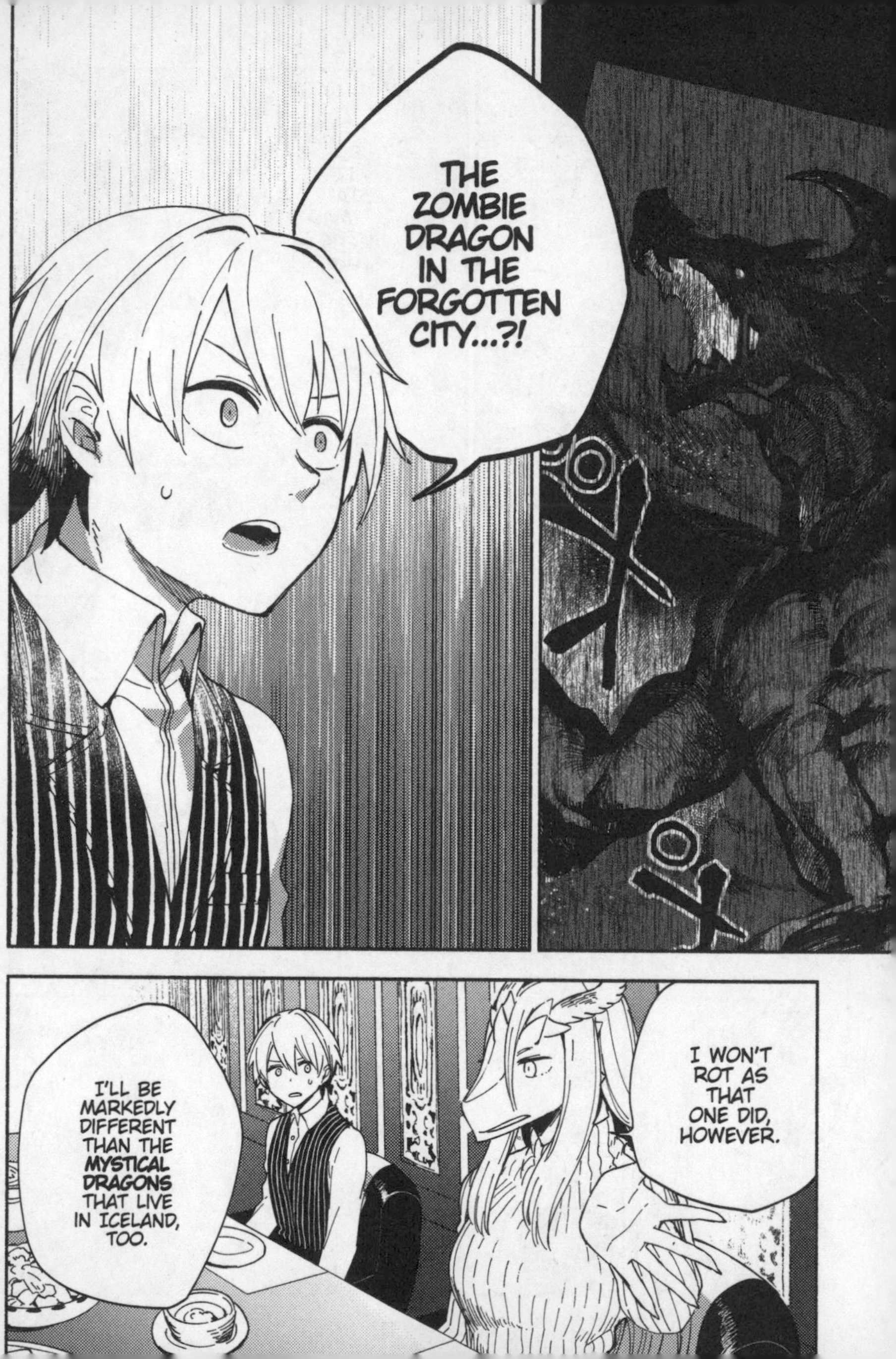
THE ZOMBIE DRAGON IN THE FORGOTTEN CITY...?!
I WON'T ROT AS THAT ONE DID, HOWEVER.
I'LL BE MARKEDLY DIFFERENT THAN THE MYSTICAL DRAGONS THAT LIVE IN ICELAND, TOO.

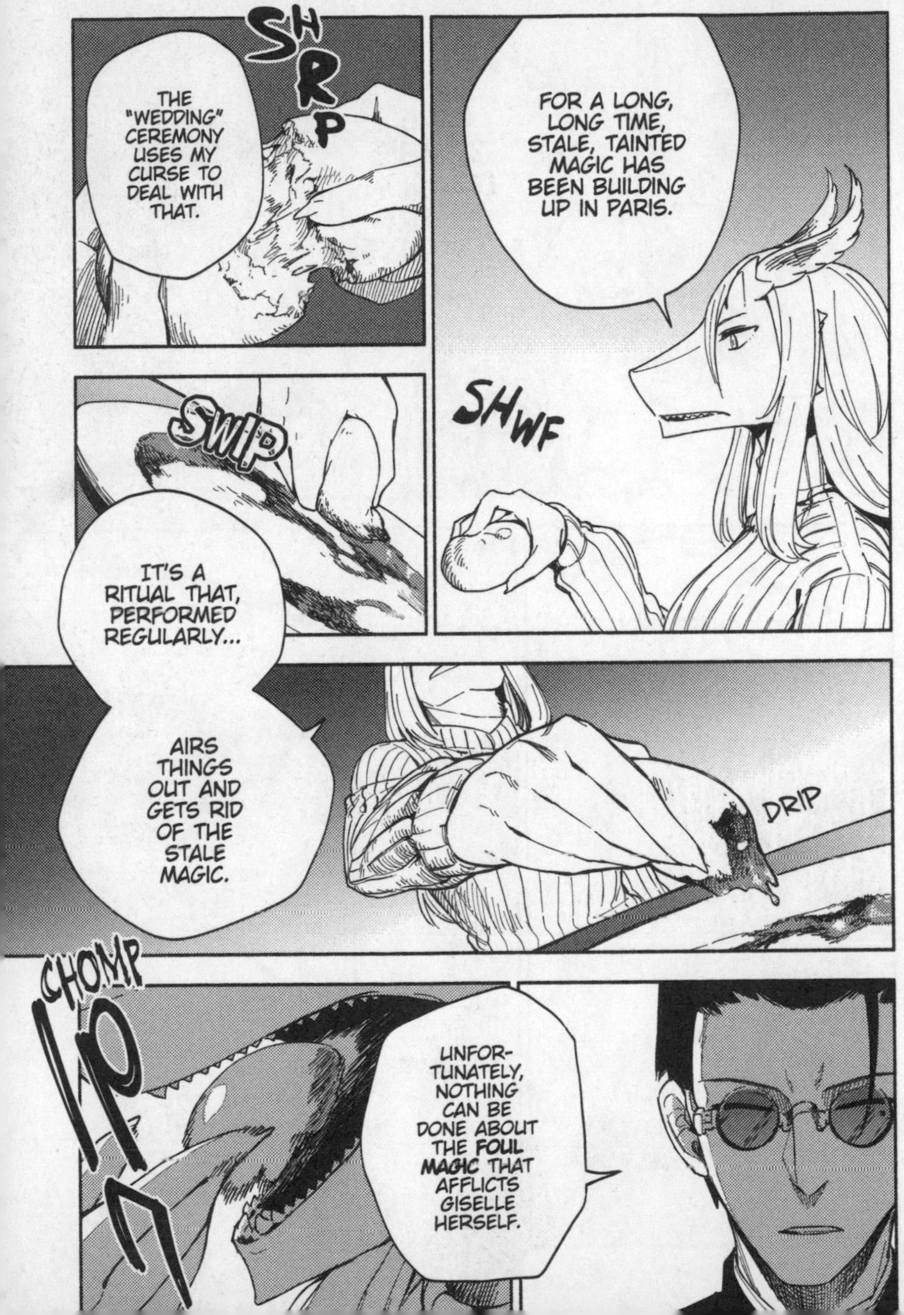
FOR A LONG, LONG TIME, STALE, TAINTED MAGIC HAS BEEN BUILDING UP IN PARIS.
SHWF
SHRP
THE "WEDDING" CEREMONY USES MY CURSE TO DEAL WITH THAT.
SWIP
IT'S A RITUAL THAT, PERFORMED REGULARLY...
AIRS THINGS OUT AND GETS RID OF THE STALE MAGIC.
DRIP
UNFORTUNATELY, NOTHING CAN BE DONE ABOUT THE **FOUL MAGIC** THAT AFFLICTS GISELLE HERSELF.
CHOMP

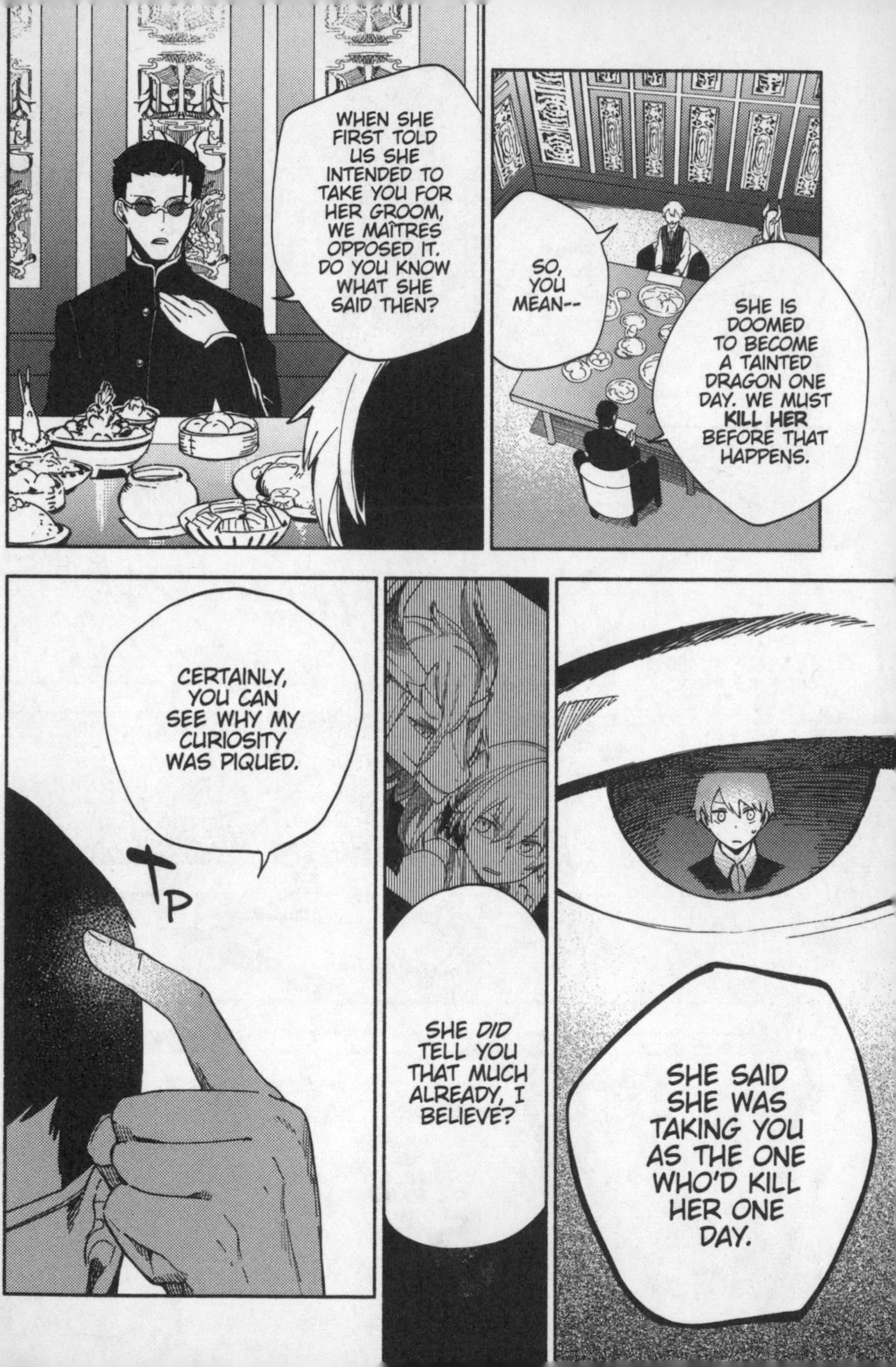
SO, YOU MEAN--
SHE IS DOOMED TO BECOME A TAINTED DRAGON ONE DAY. WE MUST **KILL HER** BEFORE THAT HAPPENS.
WHEN SHE FIRST TOLD US SHE INTENDED TO TAKE YOU FOR HER GROOM, WE MAÎTRES OPPOSED IT. DO YOU KNOW WHAT SHE SAID THEN?
SHE SAID SHE WAS TAKING YOU AS THE ONE WHO'D KILL HER ONE DAY.
SHE *DID* TELL YOU THAT MUCH ALREADY, I BELIEVE?
CERTAINLY, YOU CAN SEE WHY MY CURIOSITY WAS PIQUED.
TP

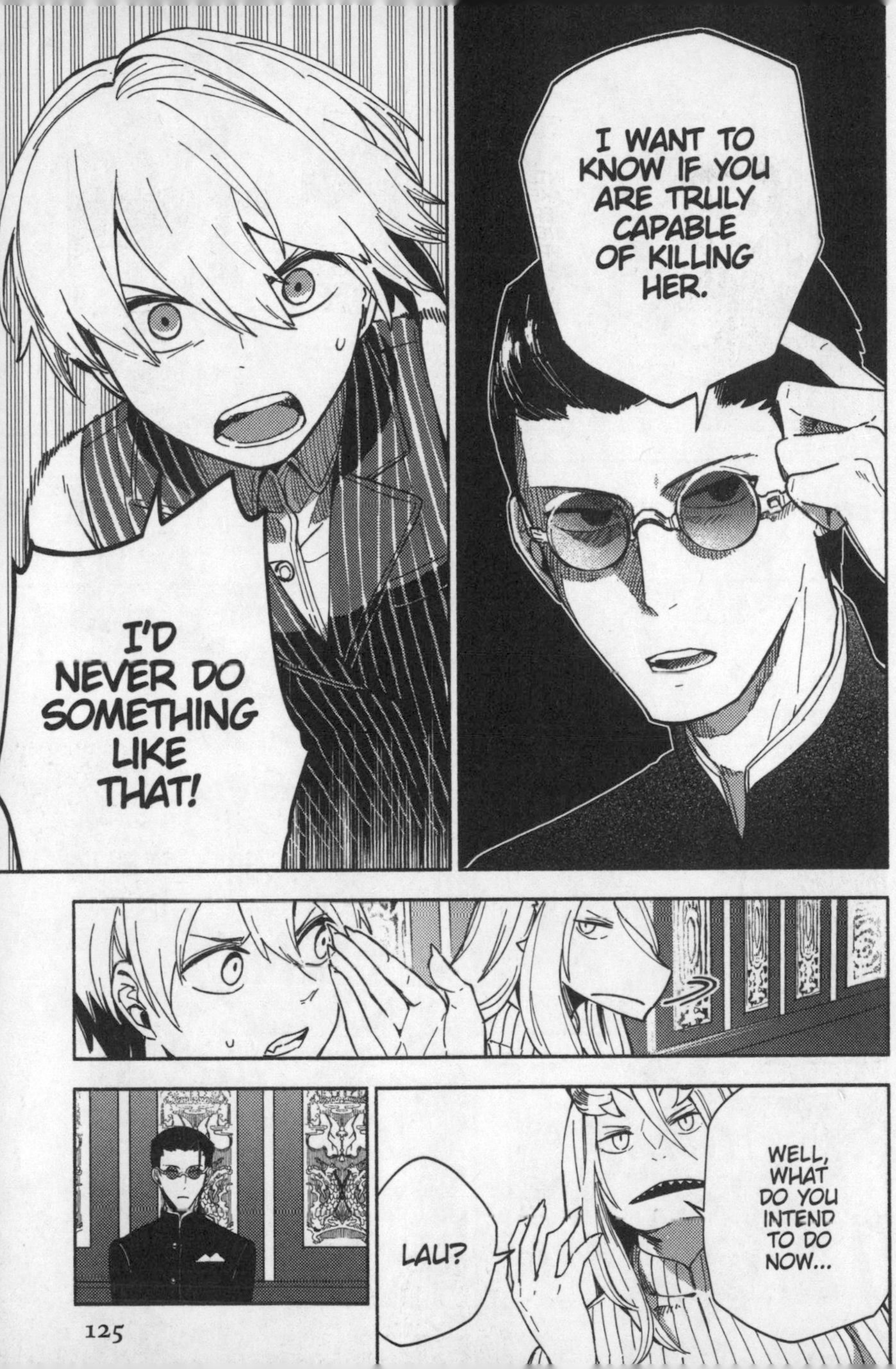
I WANT TO KNOW IF YOU ARE TRULY CAPABLE OF KILLING HER.
I'D NEVER DO SOMETHING LIKE THAT!
WELL, WHAT DO YOU INTEND TO DO NOW...
LAU?

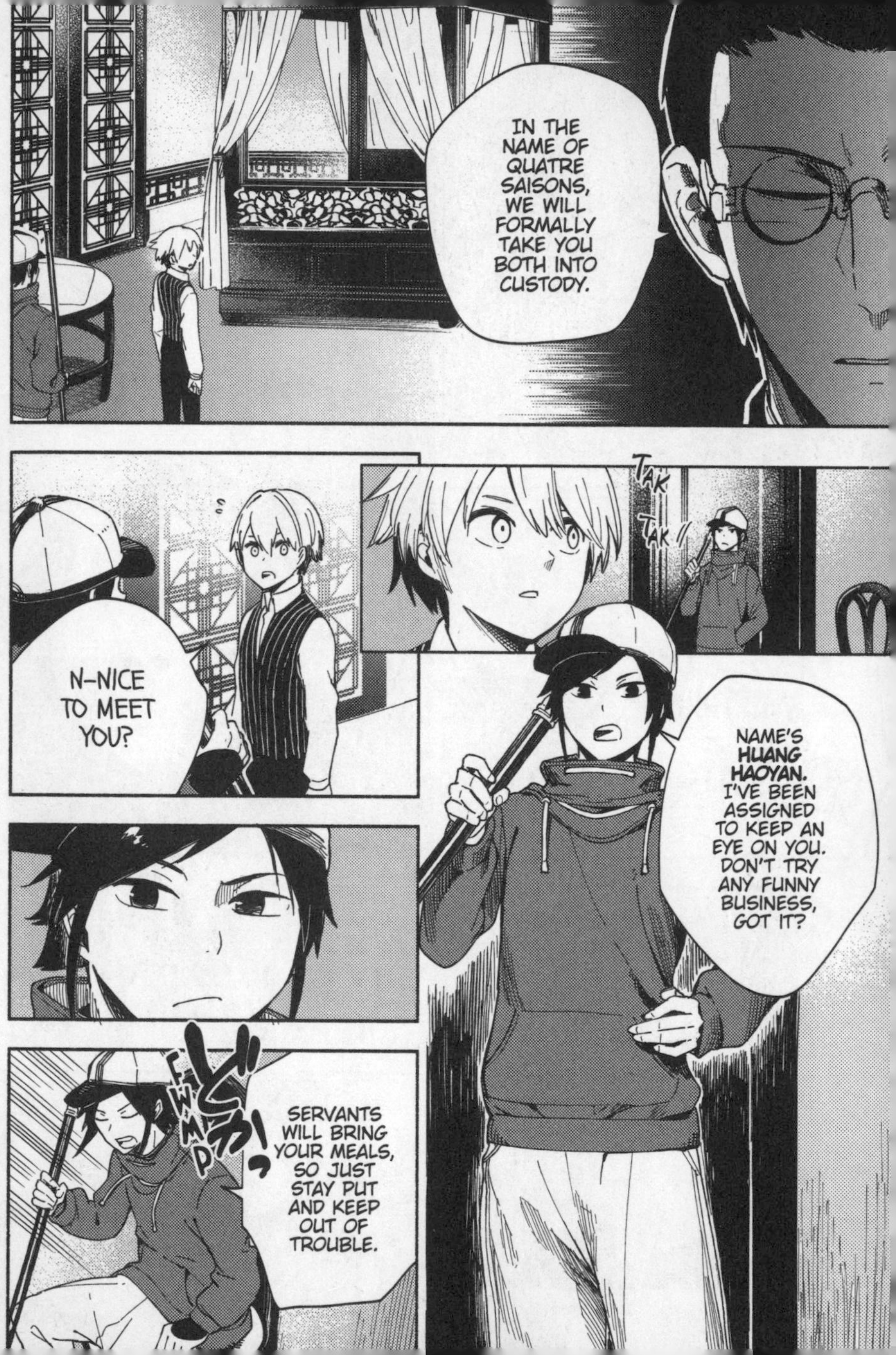
IN THE NAME OF QUATRE SAISONS, WE WILL FORMALLY TAKE YOU BOTH INTO CUSTODY.
TAK TAK
NAME'S **HUANG HAOYAN.** I'VE BEEN ASSIGNED TO KEEP AN EYE ON YOU. DON'T TRY ANY FUNNY BUSINESS, GOT IT?
N-NICE TO MEET YOU?
FWMP
SERVANTS WILL BRING YOUR MEALS, SO JUST STAY PUT AND KEEP OUT OF TROUBLE.

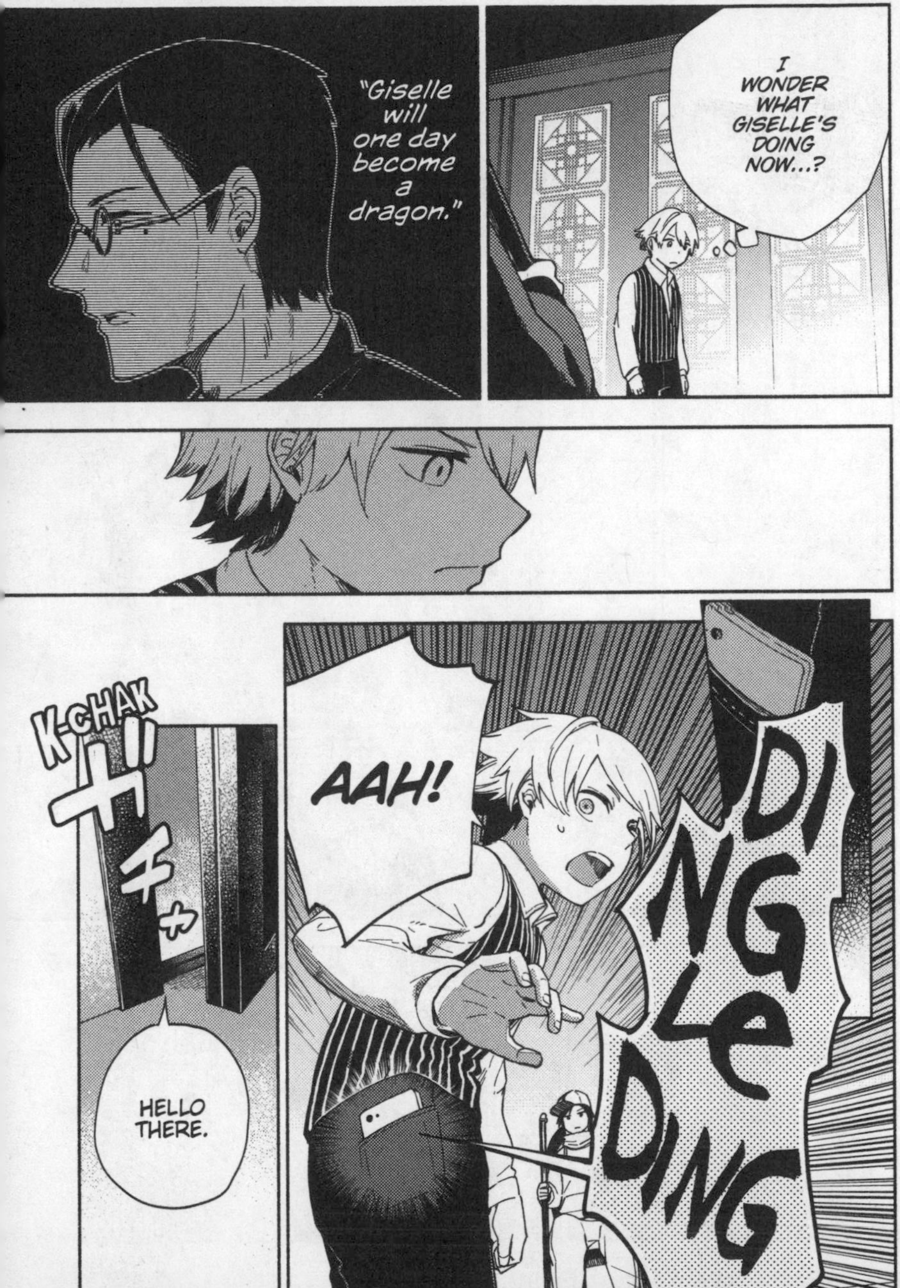

I WONDER WHAT GISELLE'S DOING NOW...?
"Giselle will one day become a dragon."
DINGLEDING
AAH!
K-CHAK
ガチャ
HELLO THERE.

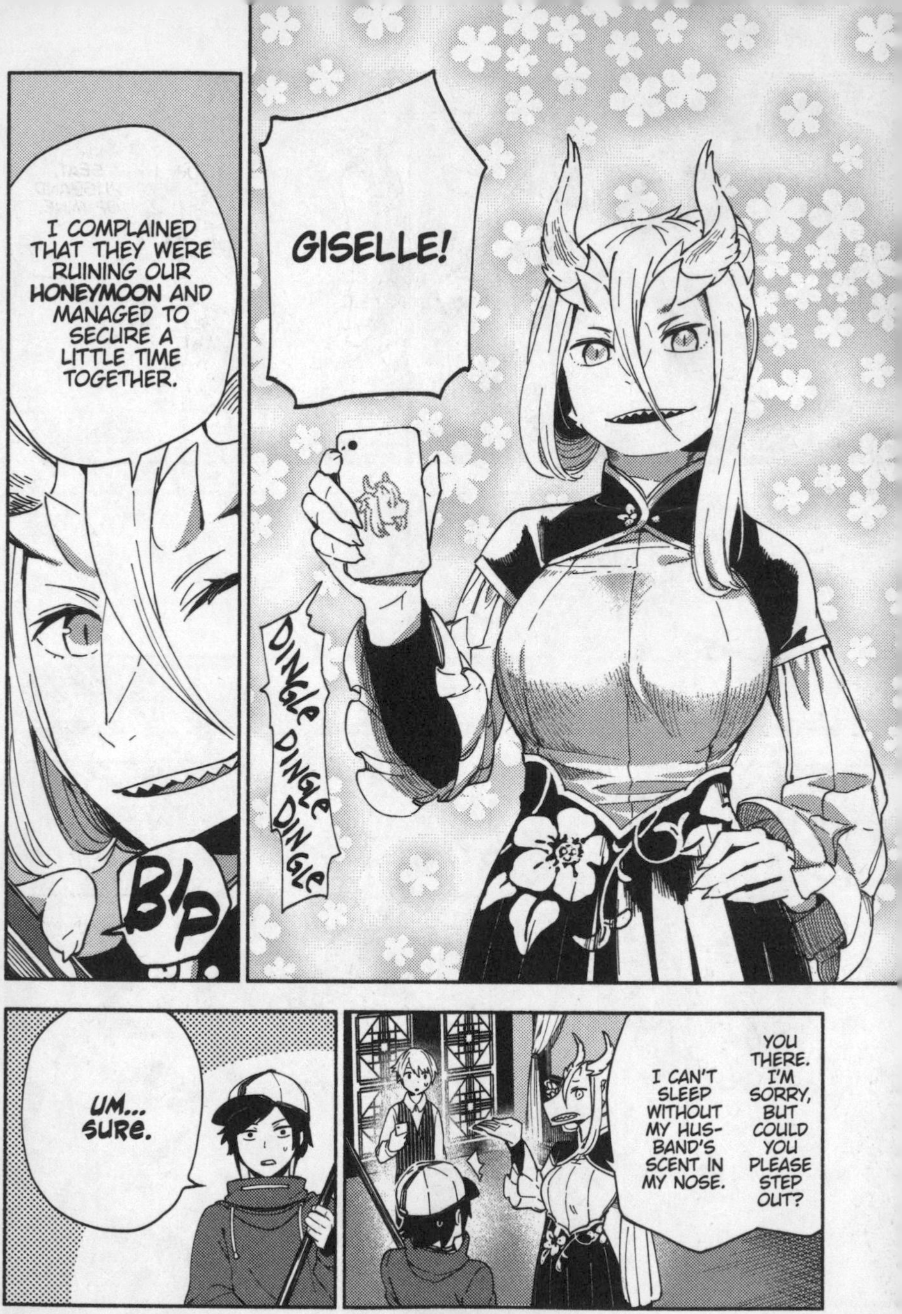
GISELLE!
DINGLE DINGLE DINGLE DINGLE
I COMPLAINED THAT THEY WERE RUINING OUR HONEYMOON AND MANAGED TO SECURE A LITTLE TIME TOGETHER.
BIP
YOU THERE. I'M SORRY, BUT COULD YOU PLEASE STEP OUT?
I CAN'T SLEEP WITHOUT MY HUS-BAND'S SCENT IN MY NOSE.
UM... SURE.

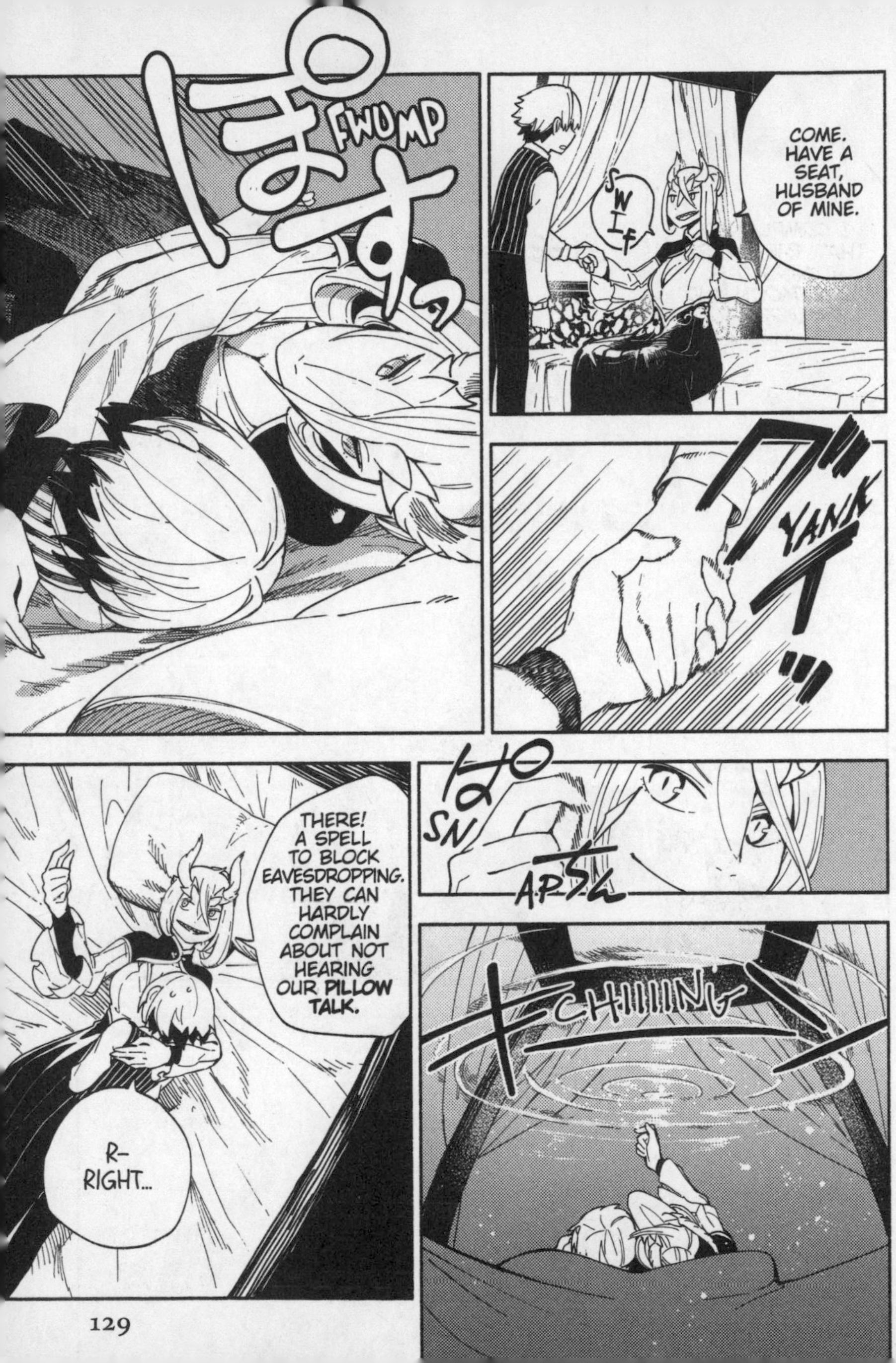
COME. HAVE A SEAT, HUSBAND OF MINE.
SWIF
YANK
FWUMP
SNAP
CHIIING
THERE! A SPELL TO BLOCK EAVESDROPPING. THEY CAN HARDLY COMPLAIN ABOUT NOT HEARING OUR PILLOW TALK.
R-RIGHT...

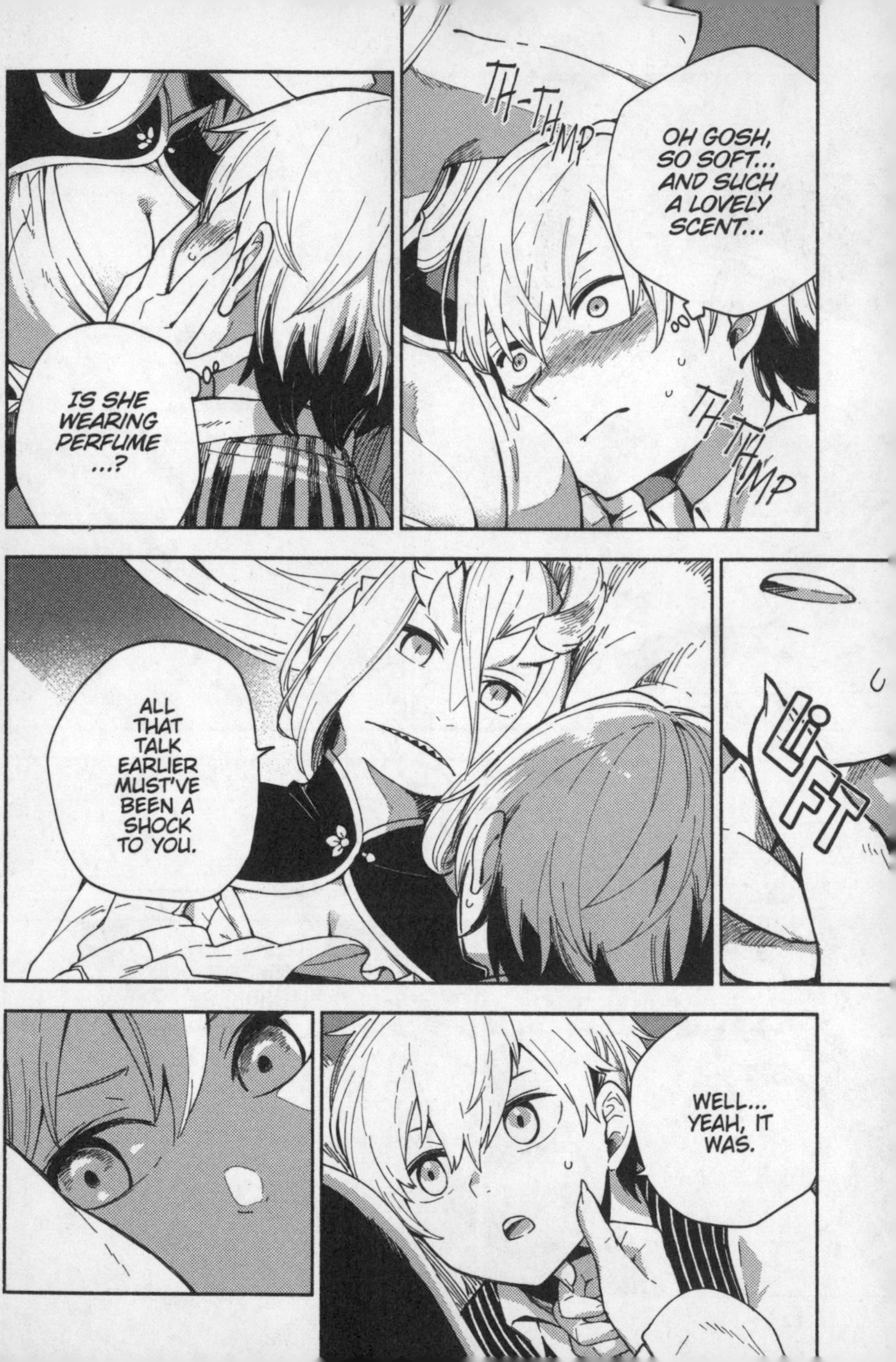
TH-THMP
OH GOSH, SO SOFT... AND SUCH A LOVELY SCENT...
TH-TH-THMP
IS SHE WEARING PERFUME ...?
LIFT
ALL THAT TALK EARLIER MUST'VE BEEN A SHOCK TO YOU.
WELL... YEAH, IT WAS.

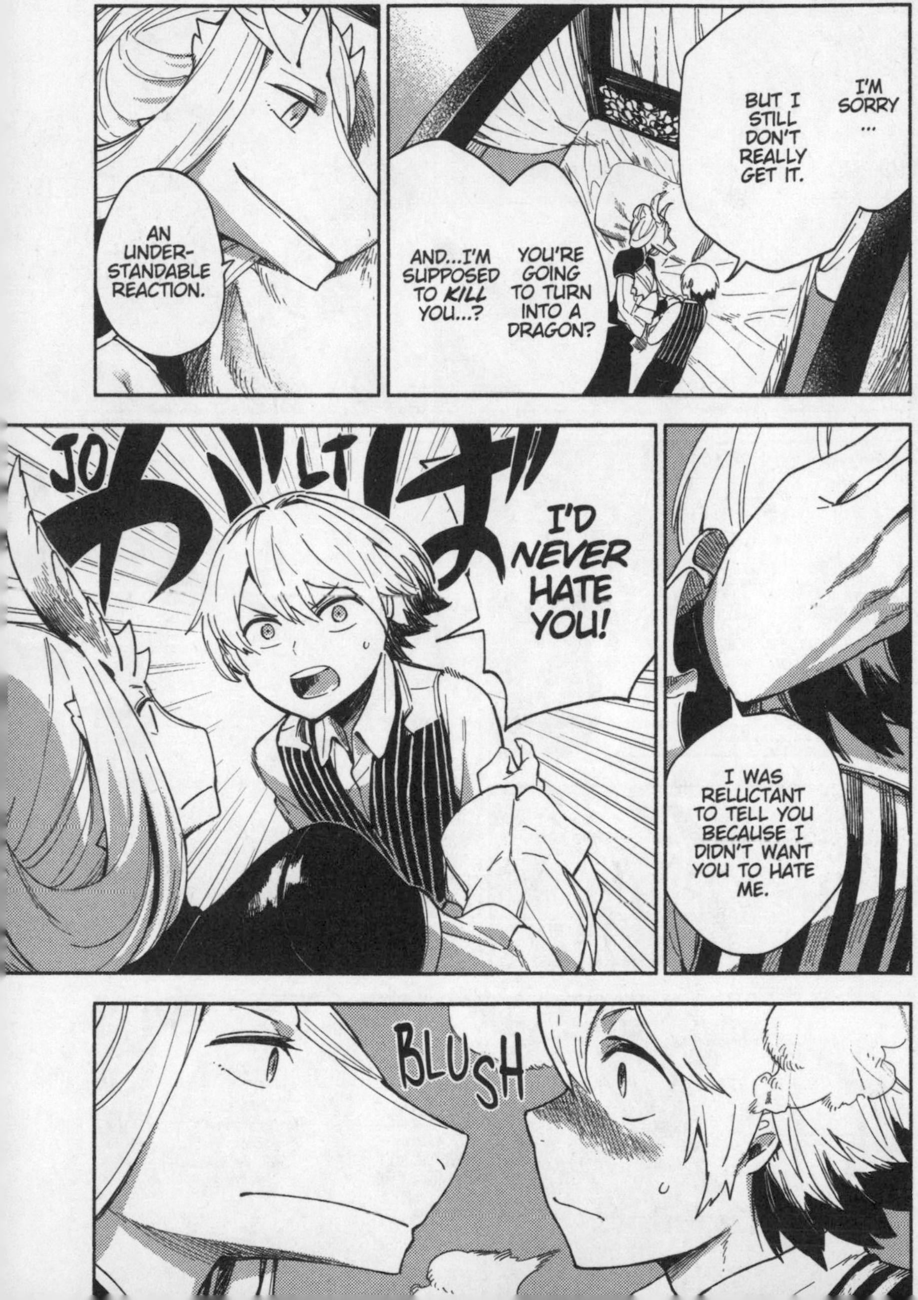
I'M SORRY ...
BUT I STILL DON'T REALLY GET IT.
YOU'RE GOING TO TURN INTO A DRAGON?
AND...I'M SUPPOSED TO *KILL* YOU...?
AN UNDER-STANDABLE REACTION.
I WAS RELUCTANT TO TELL YOU BECAUSE I DIDN'T WANT YOU TO HATE ME.
JOLT
I'D *NEVER* HATE YOU!
BLUSH

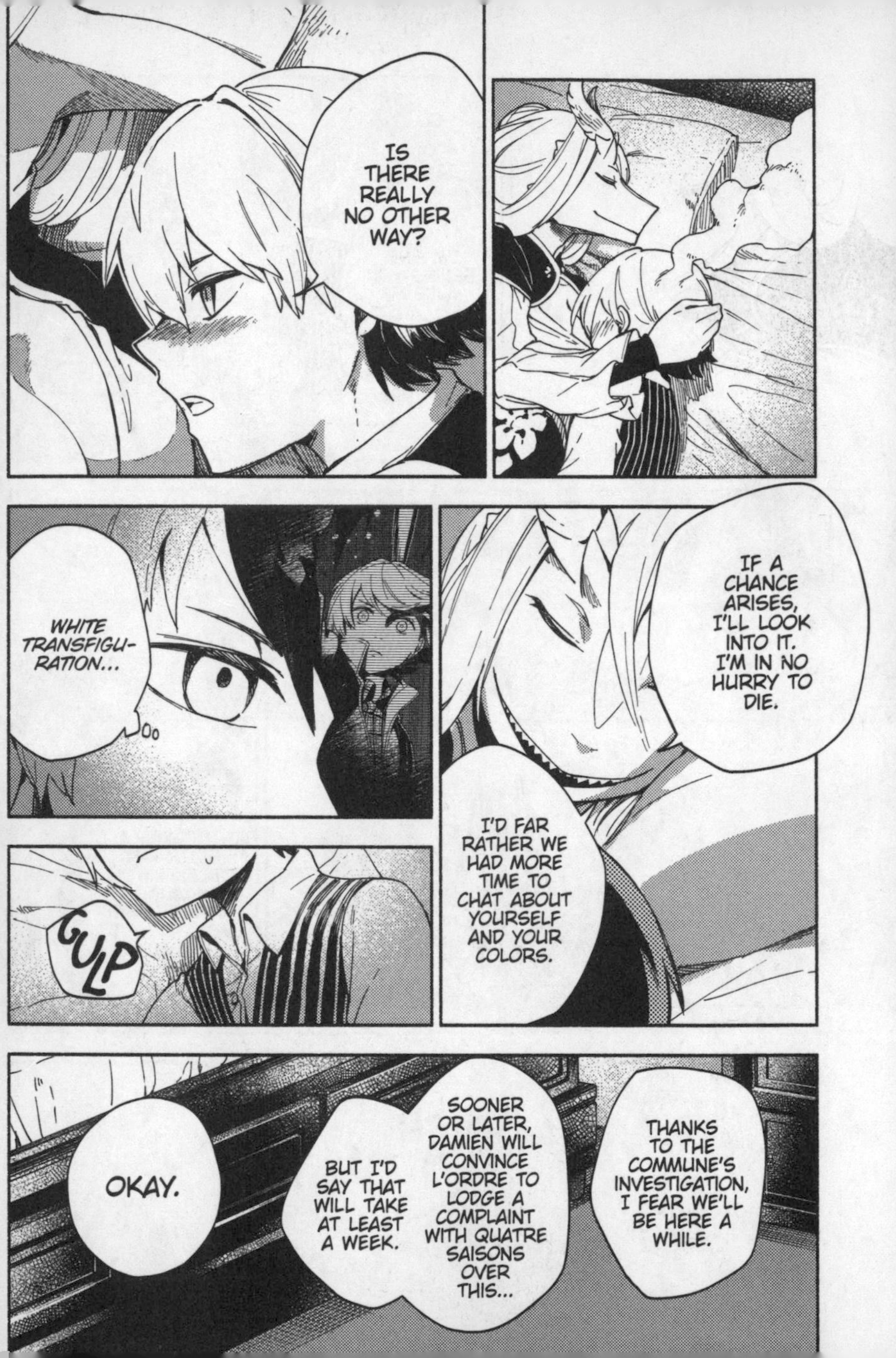
IS THERE REALLY NO OTHER WAY?
IF A CHANCE ARISES, I'LL LOOK INTO IT. I'M IN NO HURRY TO DIE.
I'D FAR RATHER WE HAD MORE TIME TO CHAT ABOUT YOURSELF AND YOUR COLORS.
WHITE TRANSFIGURATION...
GULP
THANKS TO THE COMMUNE'S INVESTIGATION, I FEAR WE'LL BE HERE A WHILE.
SOONER OR LATER, DAMIEN WILL CONVINCE L'ORDRE TO LODGE A COMPLAINT WITH QUATRE SAISONS OVER THIS...
BUT I'D SAY THAT WILL TAKE AT LEAST A WEEK.
OKAY.

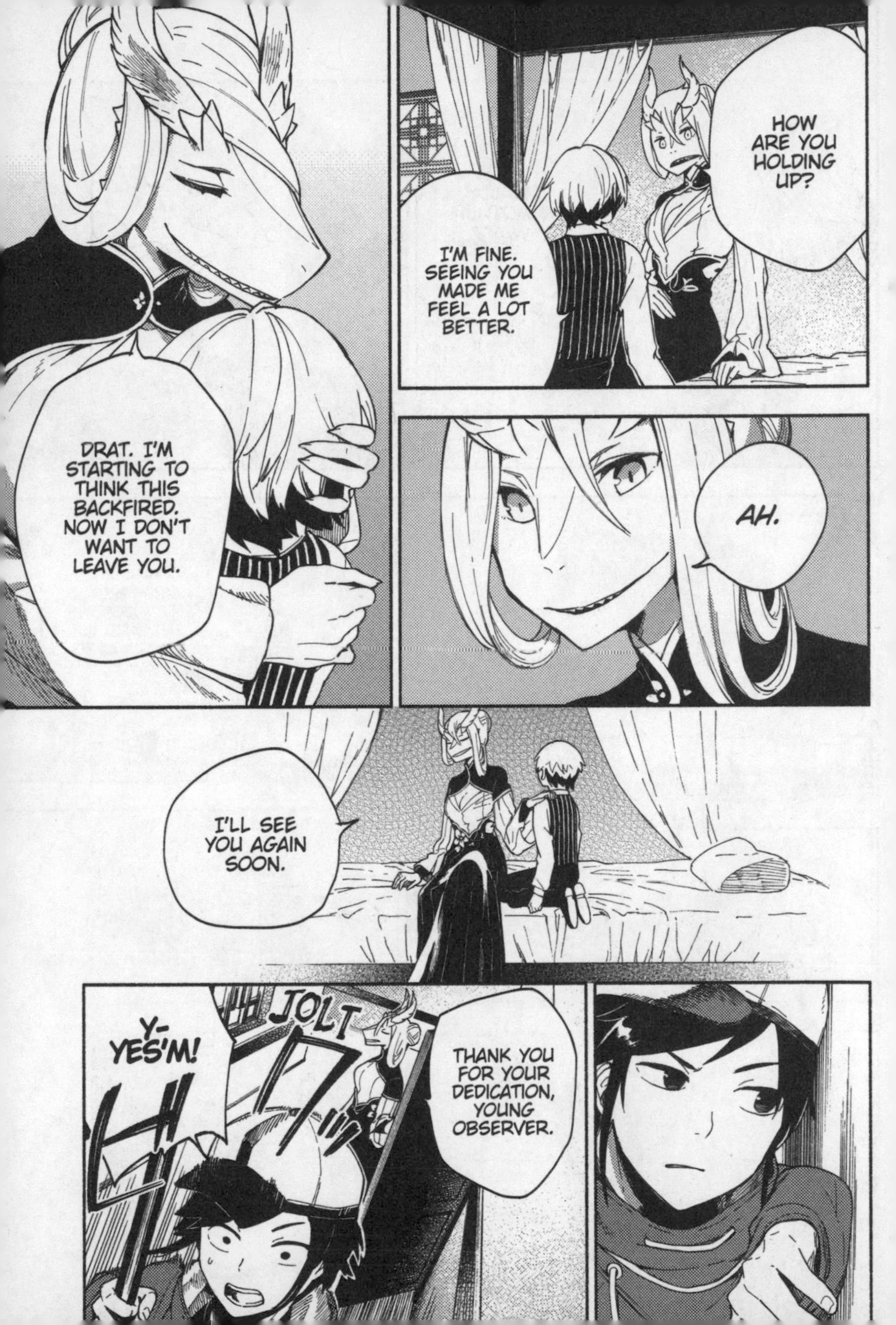
HOW ARE YOU HOLDING UP?
I'M FINE. SEEING YOU MADE ME FEEL A LOT BETTER.
AH.
DRAT. I'M STARTING TO THINK THIS BACKFIRED. NOW I DON'T WANT TO LEAVE YOU.
I'LL SEE YOU AGAIN SOON.
THANK YOU FOR YOUR DEDICATION, YOUNG OBSERVER.
JOLT
Y-YES'M!

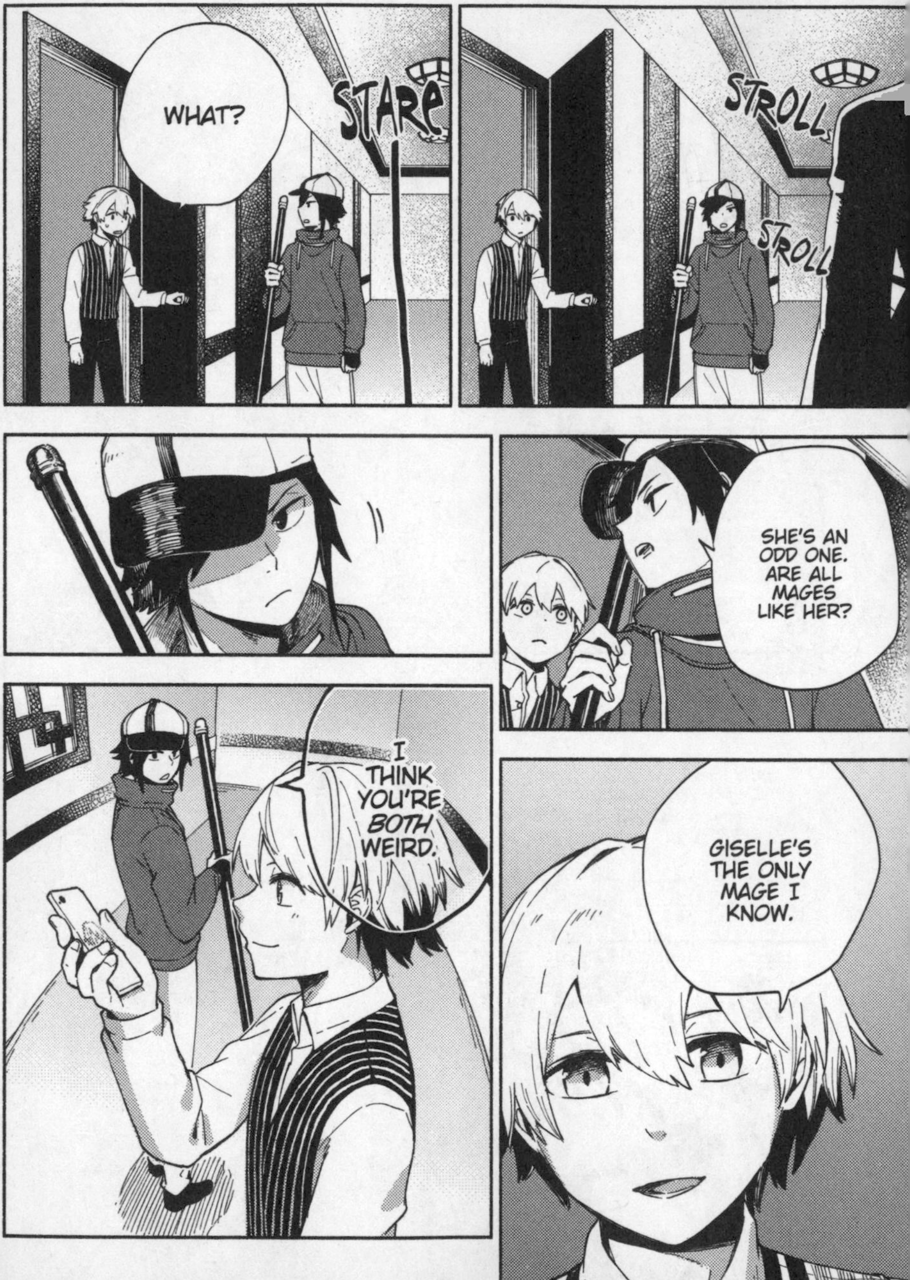
STROLL
STROLL
WHAT?
STARE
SHE'S AN ODD ONE. ARE ALL MAGES LIKE HER?
GISELLE'S THE ONLY MAGE I KNOW.
I THINK YOU'RE *BOTH* WEIRD.

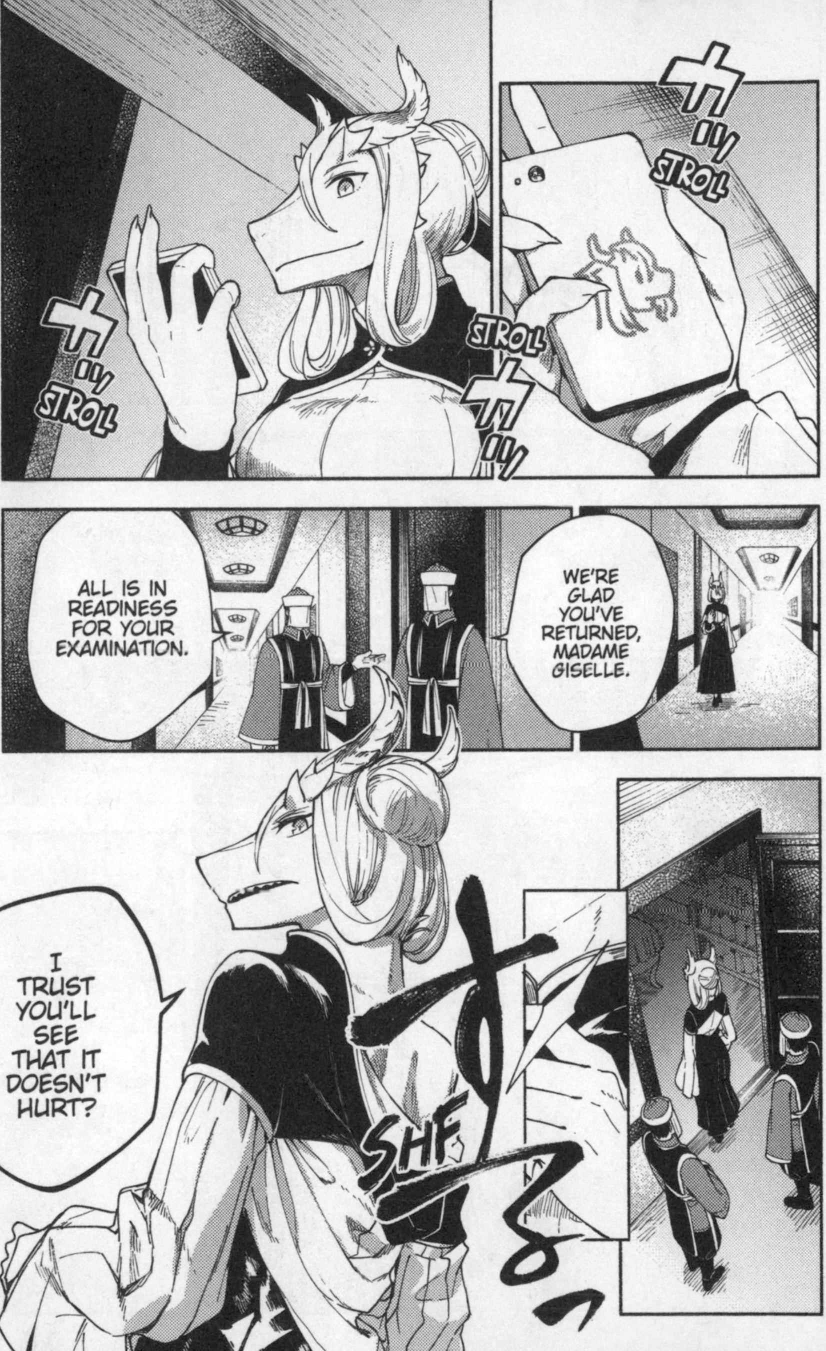
STROLL
STROLL
STROLL
WE'RE GLAD YOU'VE RETURNED, MADAME GISELLE.
ALL IS IN READINESS FOR YOUR EXAMINATION.
SHF
I TRUST YOU'LL SEE THAT IT DOESN'T HURT?

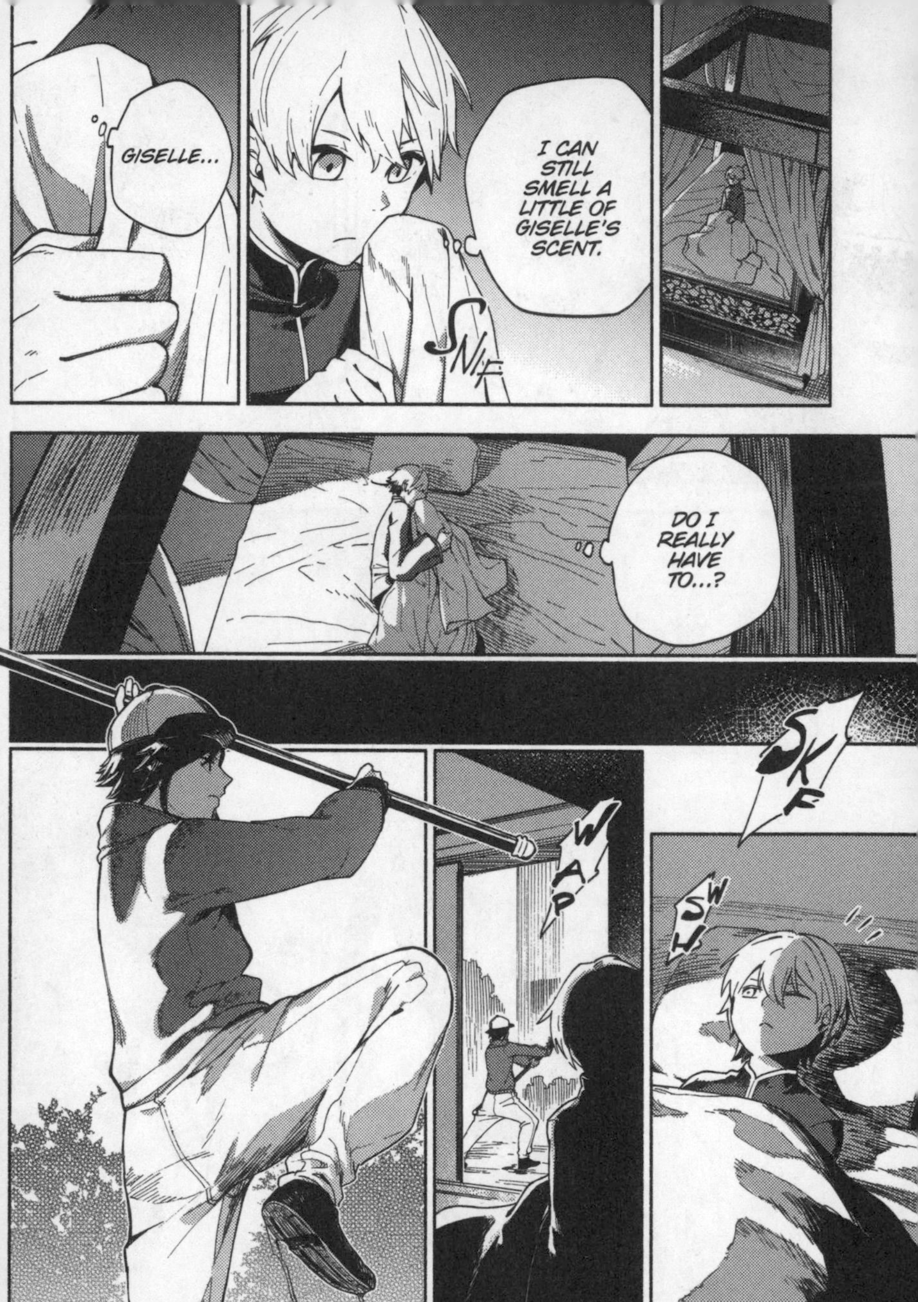
I CAN STILL SMELL A LITTLE OF GISELLE'S SCENT.
SNIF
GISELLE...
DO I REALLY HAVE TO...?
SKF
SWSH
WAP

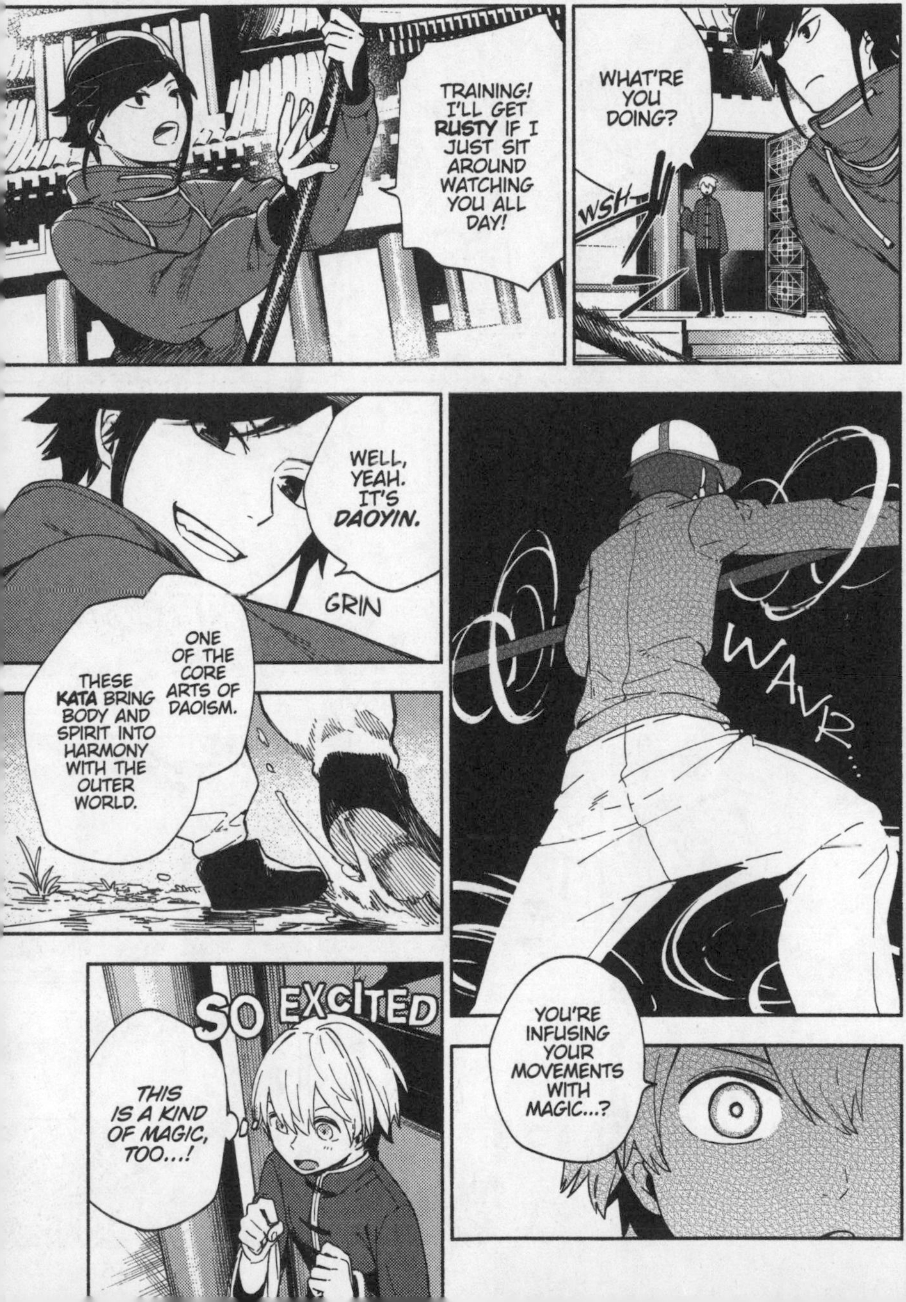
WHAT'RE YOU DOING?
WSH
TRAINING! I'LL GET RUSTY IF I JUST SIT AROUND WATCHING YOU ALL DAY!
WAVR...
YOU'RE INFUSING YOUR MOVEMENTS WITH MAGIC...?
WELL, YEAH. IT'S DAOYIN.
GRIN
ONE OF THE CORE ARTS OF DAOISM.
THESE KATA BRING BODY AND SPIRIT INTO HARMONY WITH THE OUTER WORLD.
SO EXCITED
THIS IS A KIND OF MAGIC, TOO...!

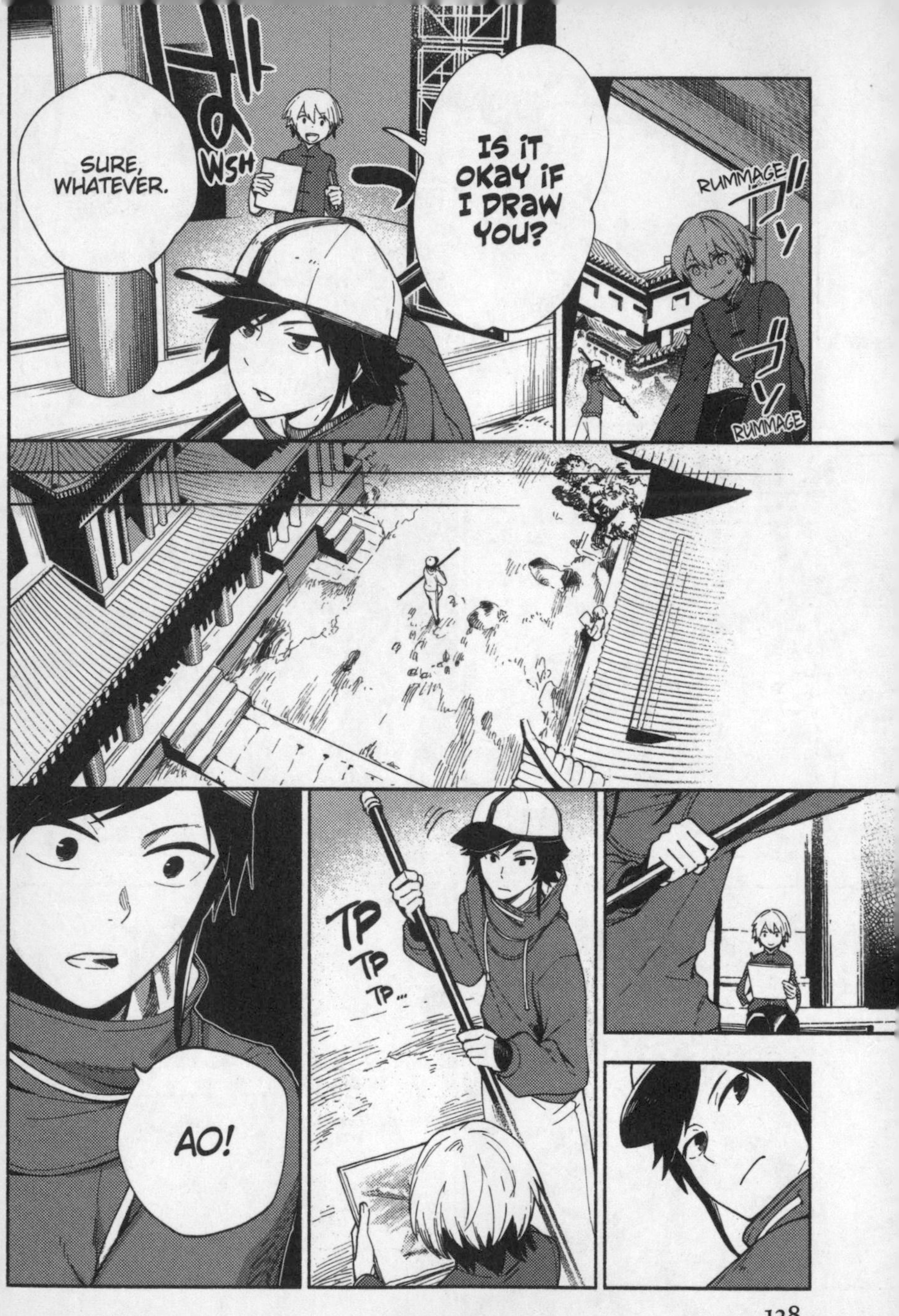
RUMMAGE
RUMMAGE
IS IT OKAY IF I DRAW YOU?
WSH
SURE, WHATEVER.
TP TP TP...
AO!

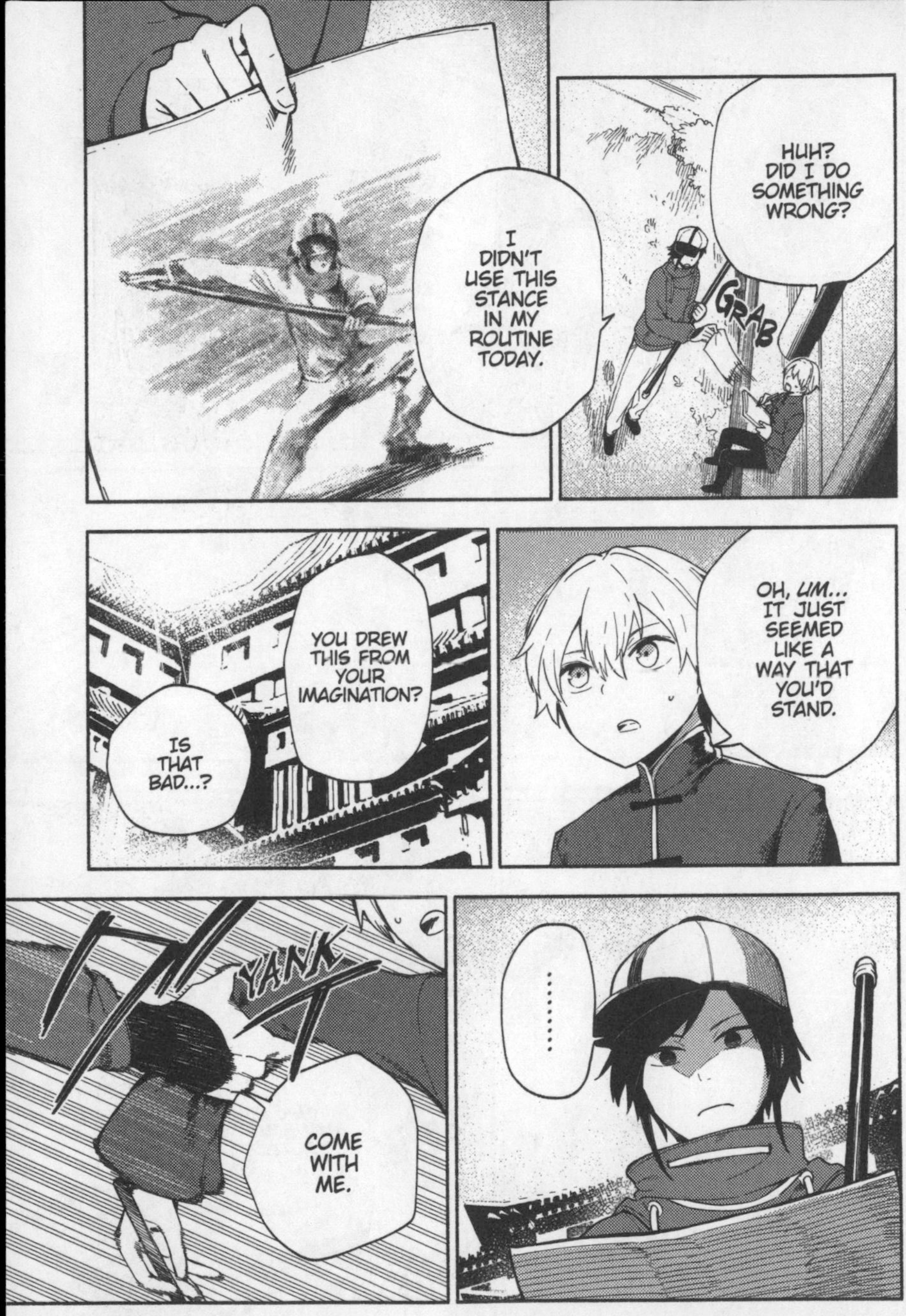
HUH? DID I DO SOMETHING WRONG?
GRAB
I DIDN'T USE THIS STANCE IN MY ROUTINE TODAY.
OH, UM... IT JUST SEEMED LIKE A WAY THAT YOU'D STAND.
YOU DREW THIS FROM YOUR IMAGINATION?
IS THAT BAD...?
......
YANK
COME WITH ME.

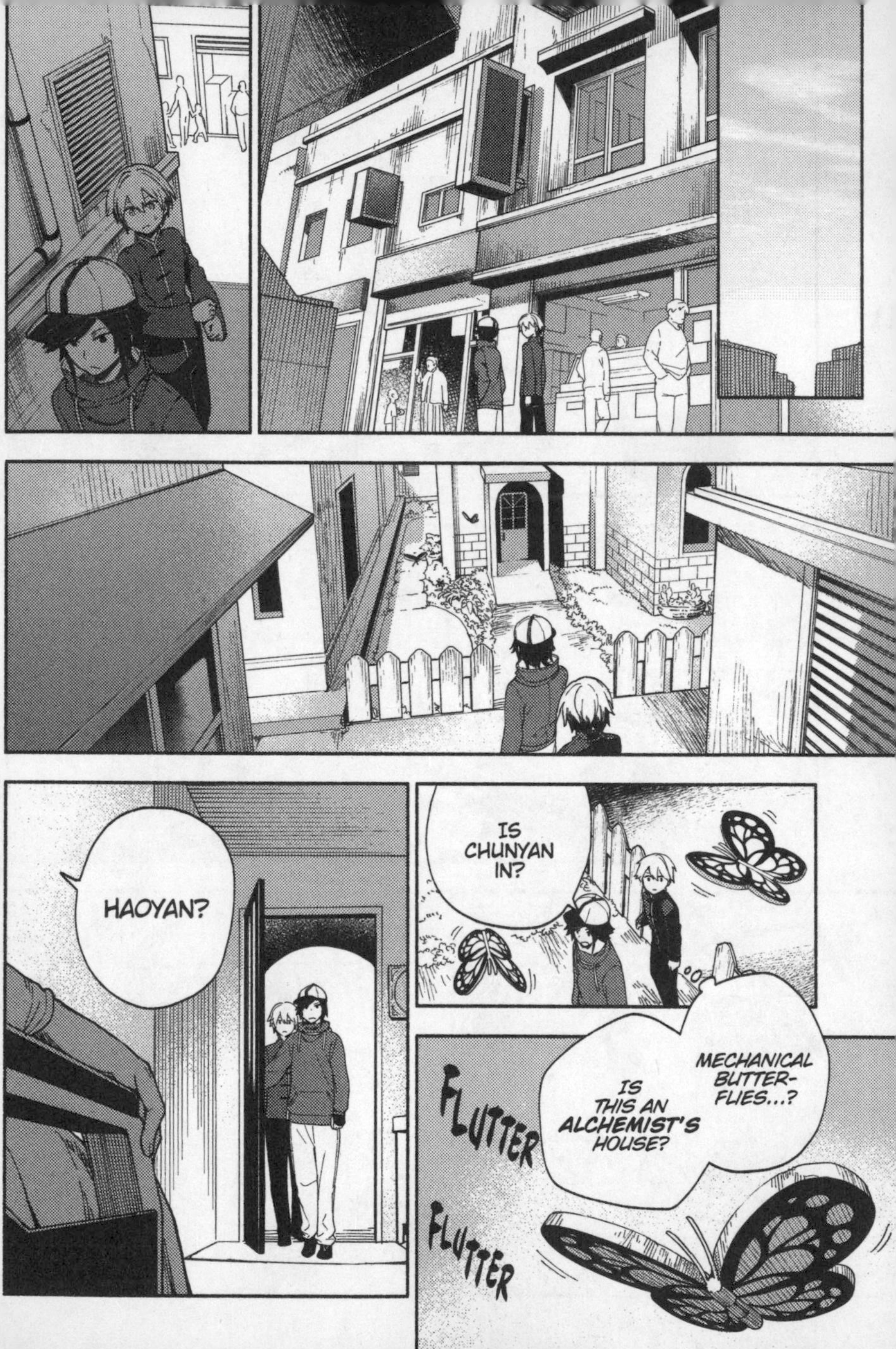
IS CHUNYAN IN?
MECHANICAL BUTTER-FLIES...?
IS THIS AN ALCHEMIST'S HOUSE?
FLUTTER
FLUTTER
HAOYAN?

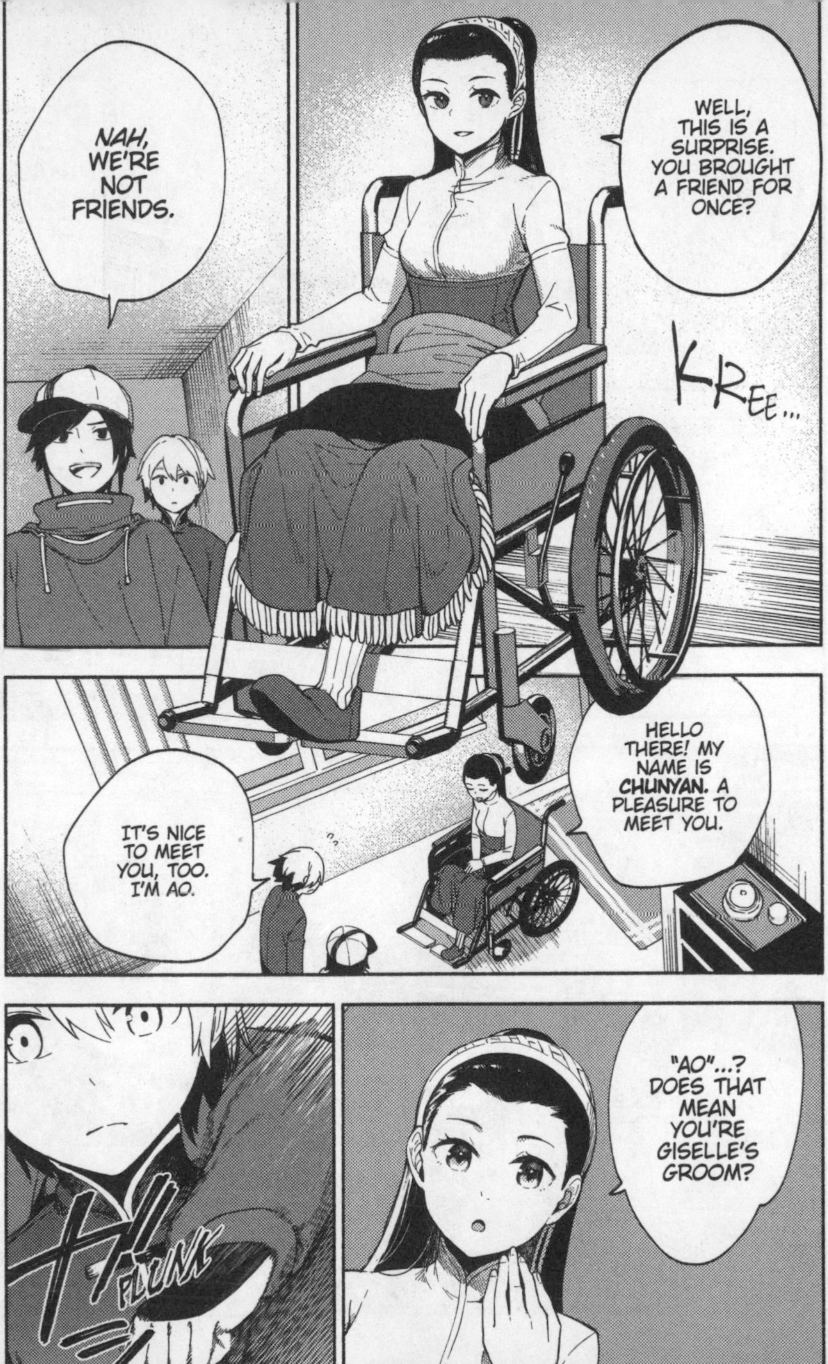
WELL, THIS IS A SURPRISE. YOU BROUGHT A FRIEND FOR ONCE?
KREE...
NAH, WE'RE NOT FRIENDS.
HELLO THERE! MY NAME IS CHUNYAN. A PLEASURE TO MEET YOU.
IT'S NICE TO MEET YOU, TOO. I'M AO.
"AO"...? DOES THAT MEAN YOU'RE GISELLE'S GROOM?
FLUNK

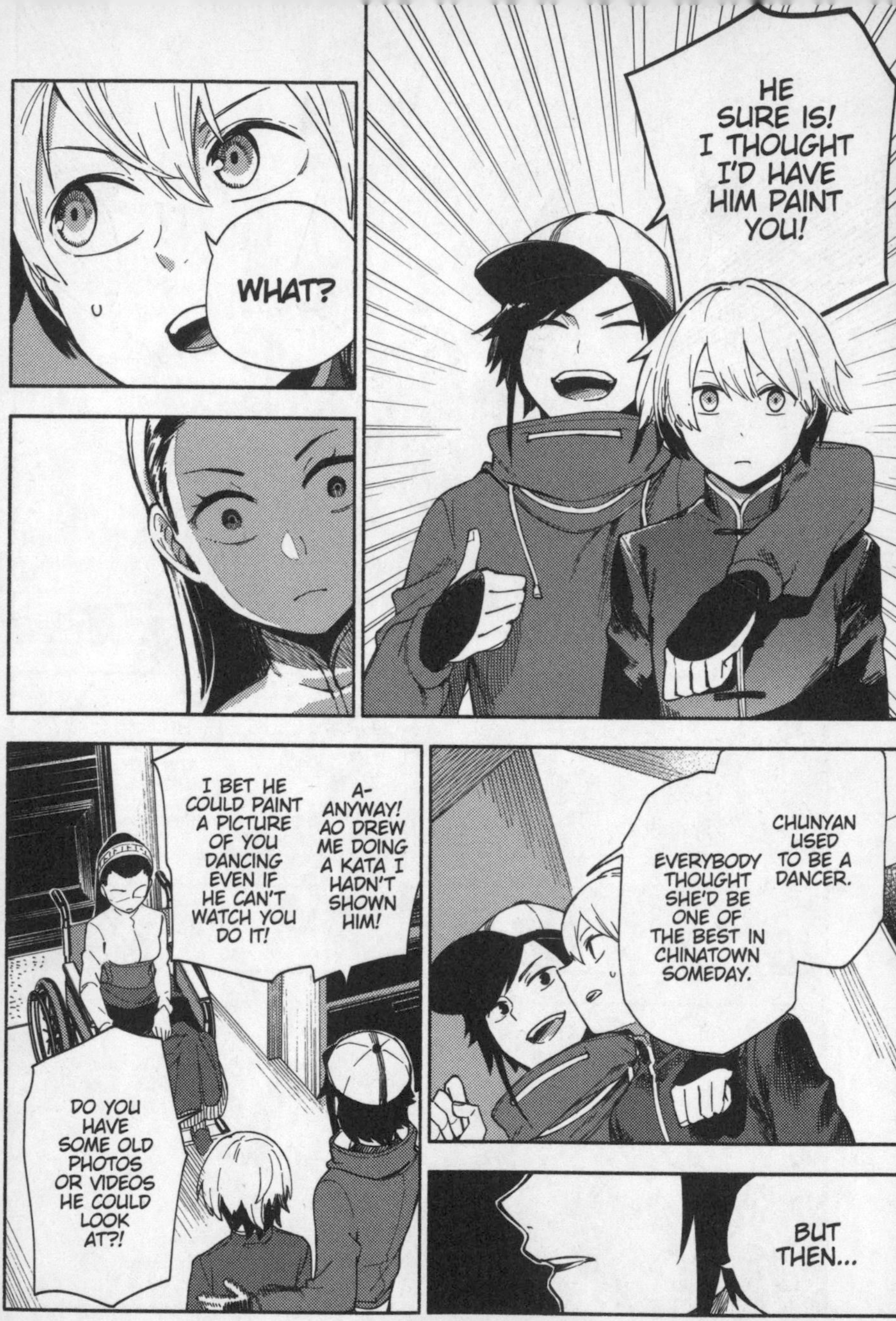
HE SURE IS! I THOUGHT I'D HAVE HIM PAINT YOU!
WHAT?
CHUNYAN USED TO BE A DANCER.
EVERYBODY THOUGHT SHE'D BE ONE OF THE BEST IN CHINATOWN SOMEDAY.
BUT THEN...
A-ANYWAY! AO DREW ME DOING A KATA I HADN'T SHOWN HIM!
I BET HE COULD PAINT A PICTURE OF YOU DANCING EVEN IF HE CAN'T WATCH YOU DO IT!
DO YOU HAVE SOME OLD PHOTOS OR VIDEOS HE COULD LOOK AT?!

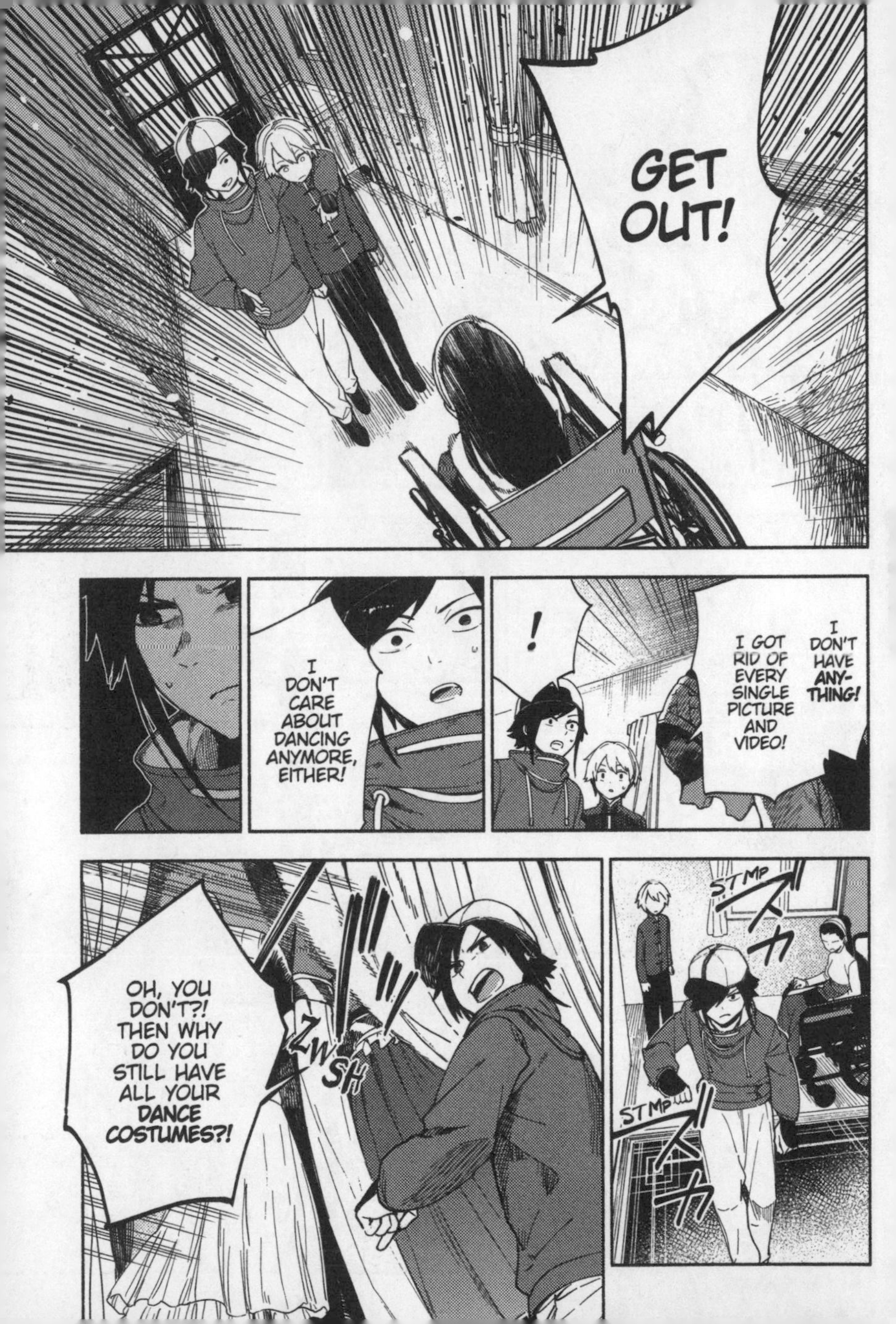
GET OUT!
I DON'T HAVE ANY-THING!
I GOT RID OF EVERY SINGLE PICTURE AND VIDEO!
!
I DON'T CARE ABOUT DANCING ANYMORE, EITHER!
STMP
STMP
OH, YOU DON'T?! THEN WHY DO YOU STILL HAVE ALL YOUR DANCE COSTUMES?!
ZWSH

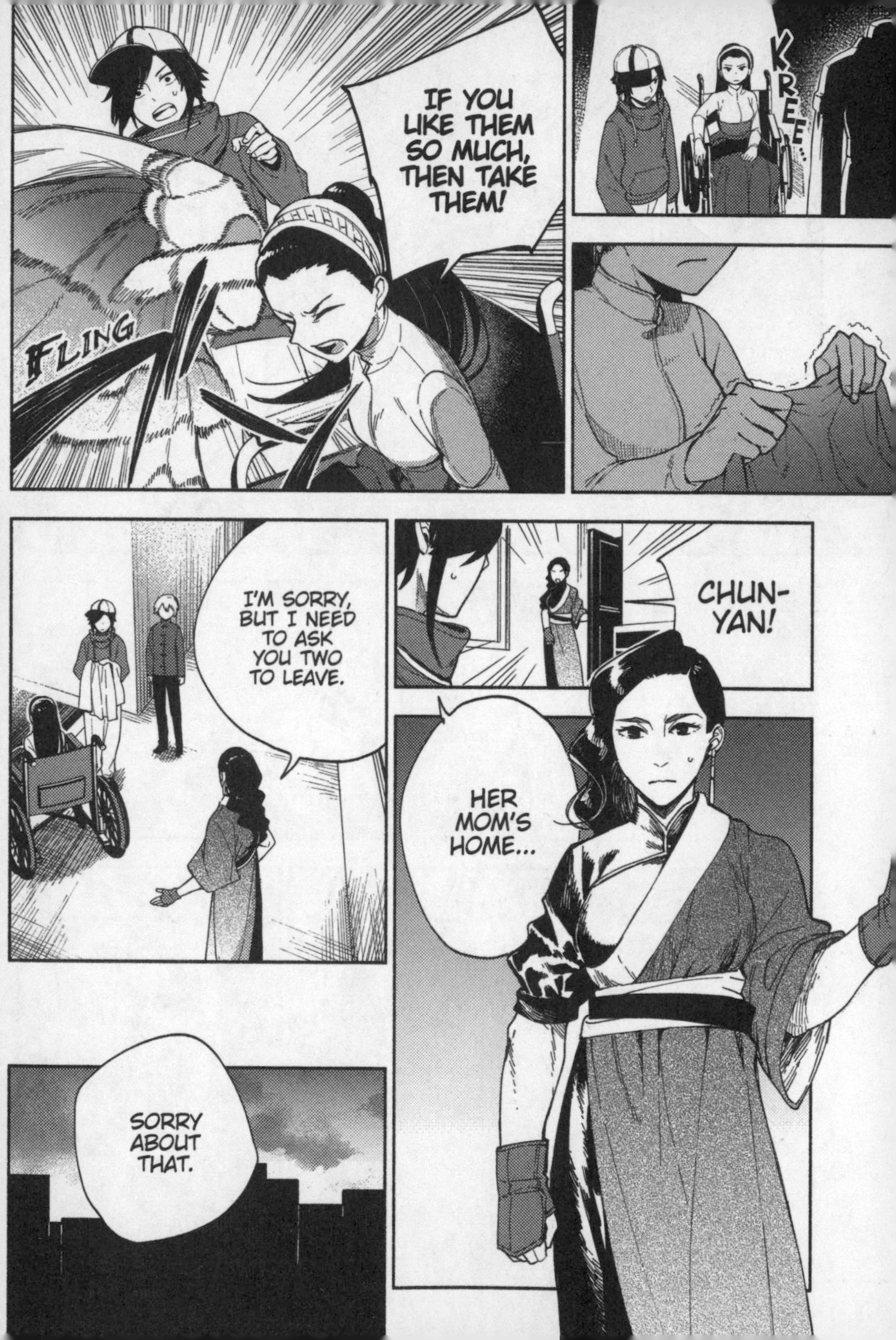
KREE...
IF YOU LIKE THEM SO MUCH, THEN TAKE THEM!
FLING
CHUN-YAN!
HER MOM'S HOME...
I'M SORRY, BUT I NEED TO ASK YOU TWO TO LEAVE.
SORRY ABOUT THAT.

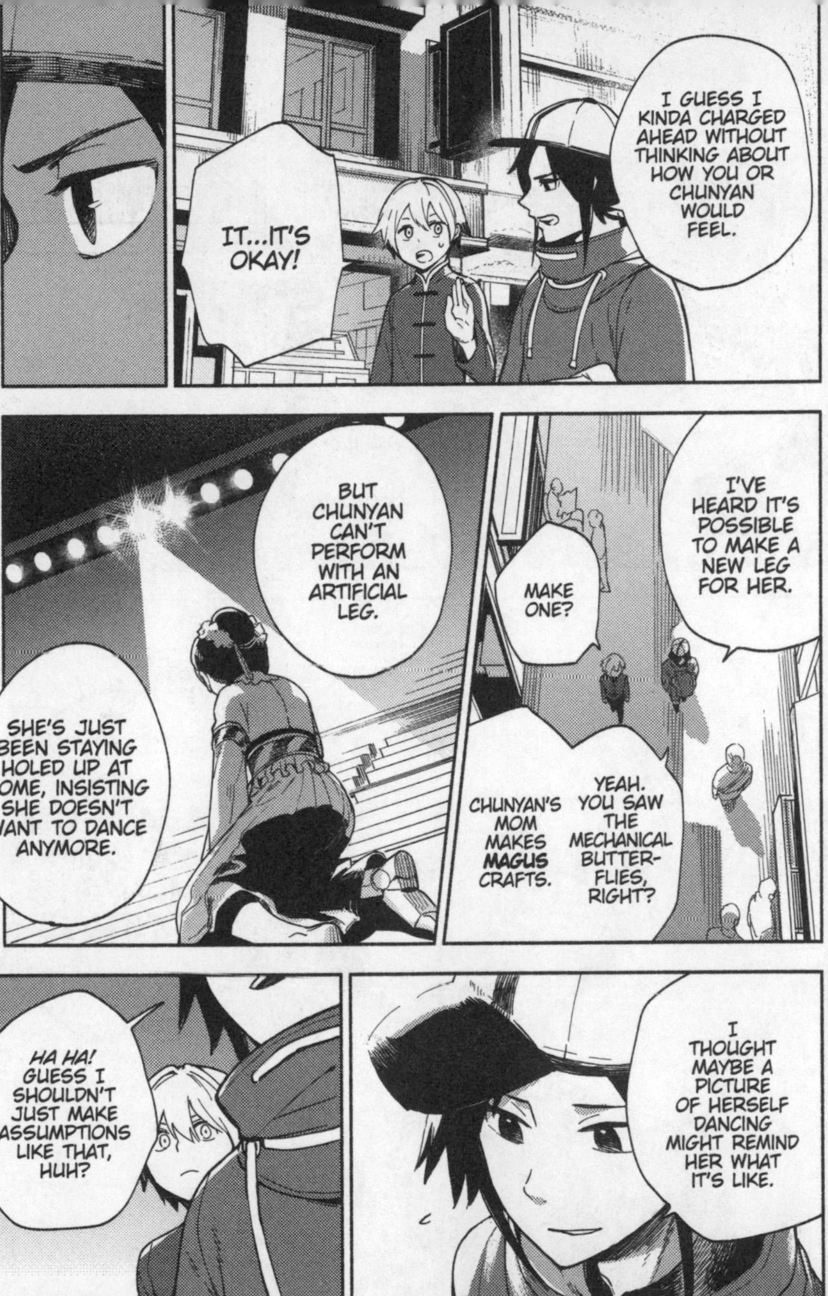

I GUESS I KINDA CHARGED AHEAD WITHOUT THINKING ABOUT HOW YOU OR CHUNYAN WOULD FEEL.
IT...IT'S OKAY!
I'VE HEARD IT'S POSSIBLE TO MAKE A NEW LEG FOR HER.
MAKE ONE?
YEAH. YOU SAW THE MECHANICAL BUTTER-FLIES, RIGHT?
CHUNYAN'S MOM MAKES **MAGUS** CRAFTS.
BUT CHUNYAN CAN'T PERFORM WITH AN ARTIFICIAL LEG.
SHE'S JUST BEEN STAYING HOLED UP AT HOME, INSISTING SHE DOESN'T WANT TO DANCE ANYMORE.
I THOUGHT MAYBE A PICTURE OF HERSELF DANCING MIGHT REMIND HER WHAT IT'S LIKE.
HA HA! GUESS I SHOULDN'T JUST MAKE ASSUMPTIONS LIKE THAT, HUH?

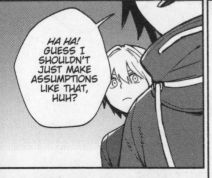

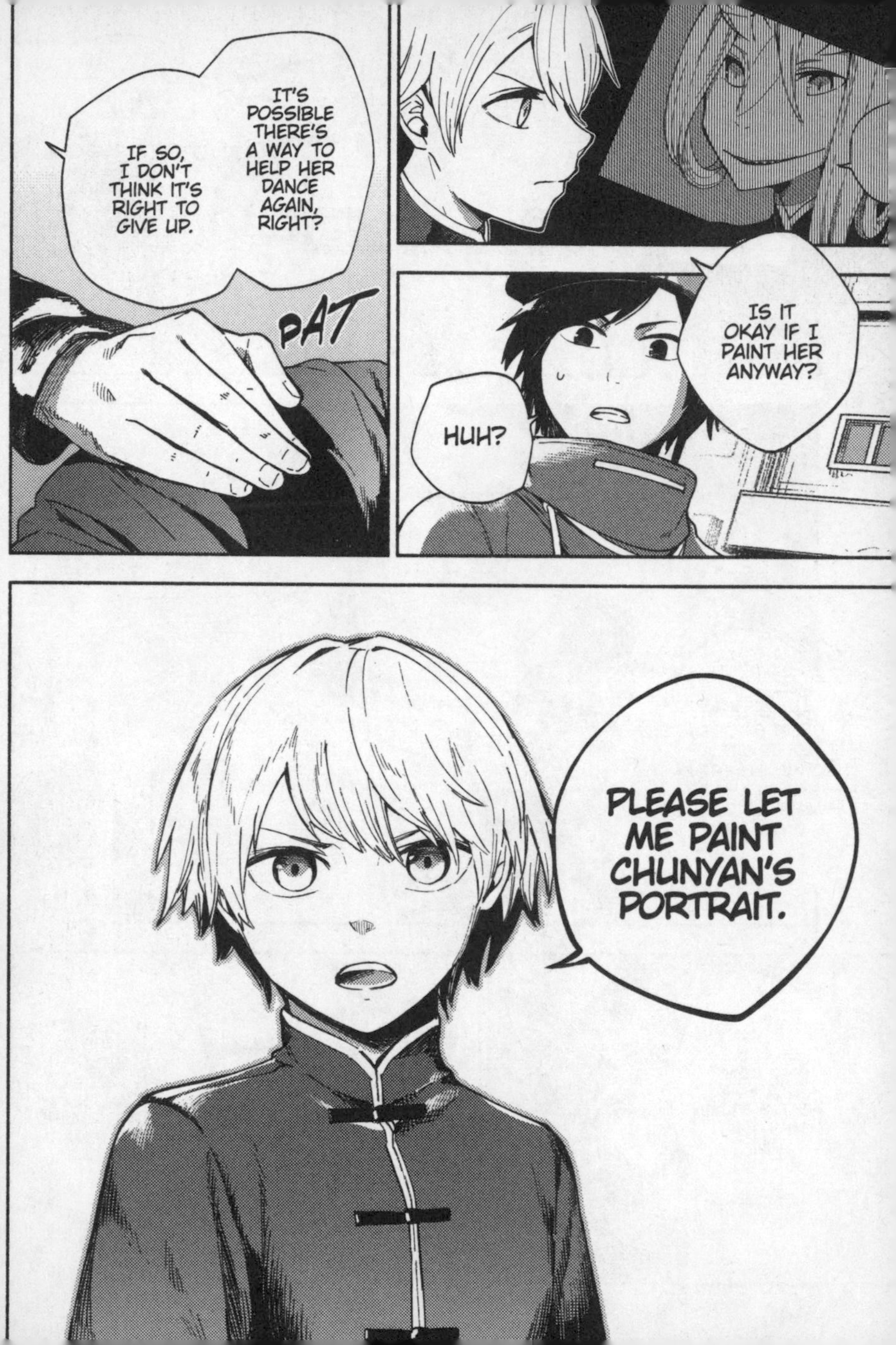
IS IT OKAY IF I PAINT HER ANYWAY?
HUH?
IT'S POSSIBLE THERE'S A WAY TO HELP HER DANCE AGAIN, RIGHT?
IF SO, I DON'T THINK IT'S RIGHT TO GIVE UP.
PAT
PLEASE LET ME PAINT CHUNYAN'S PORTRAIT.

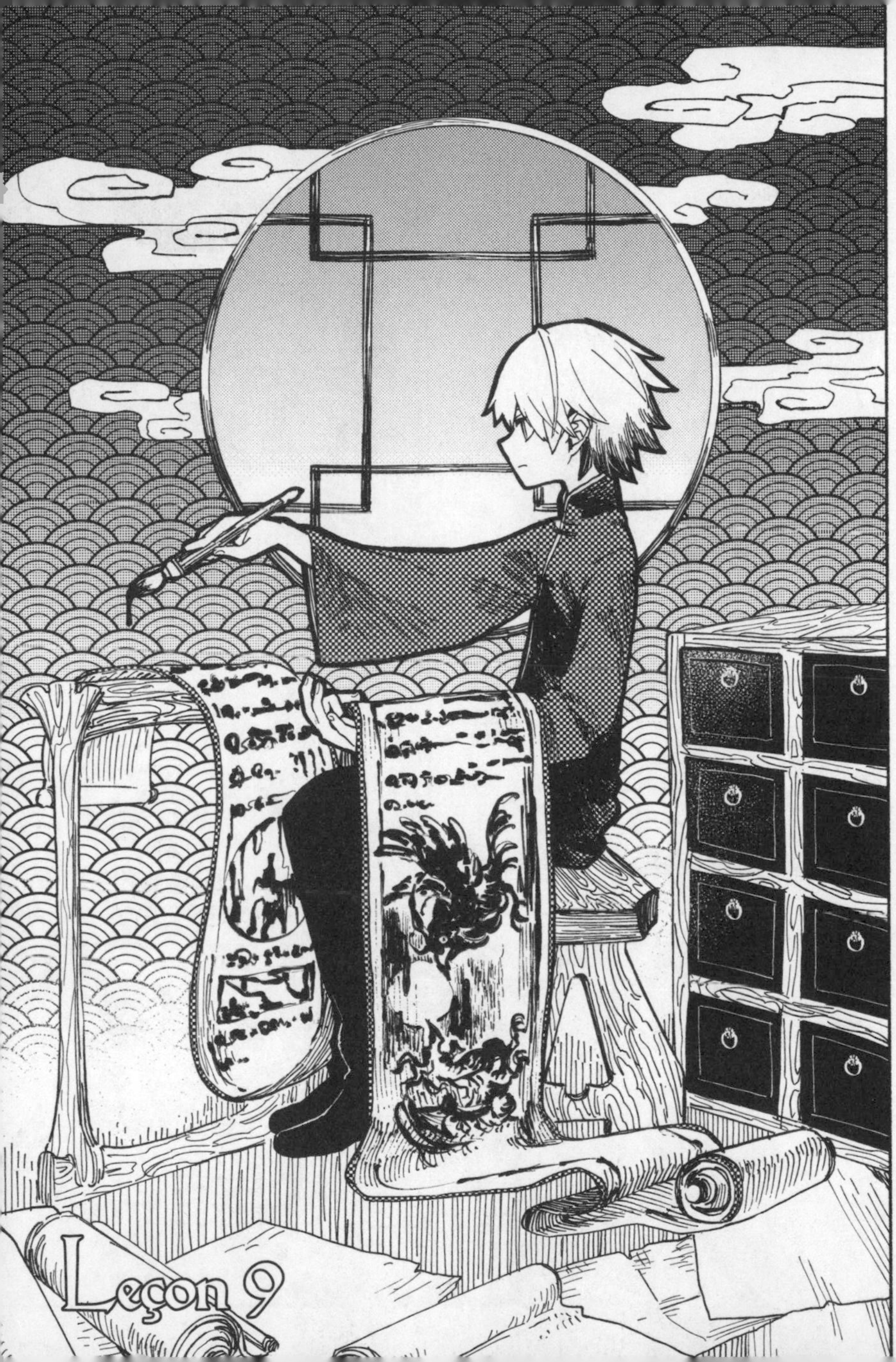
Leçon 9

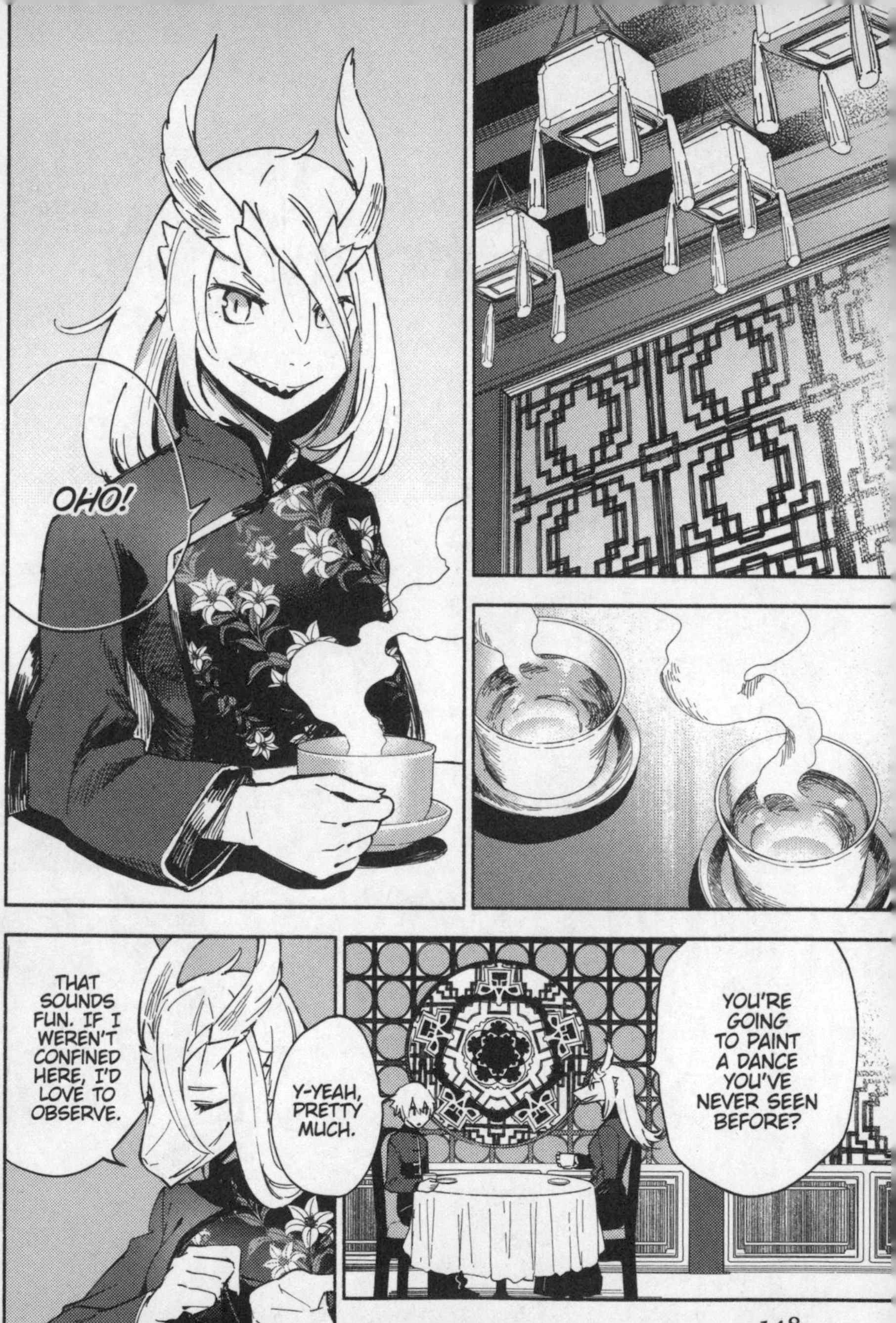
OHO!
YOU'RE GOING TO PAINT A DANCE YOU'VE NEVER SEEN BEFORE?
Y-YEAH, PRETTY MUCH.
THAT SOUNDS FUN. IF I WEREN'T CONFINED HERE, I'D LOVE TO OBSERVE.

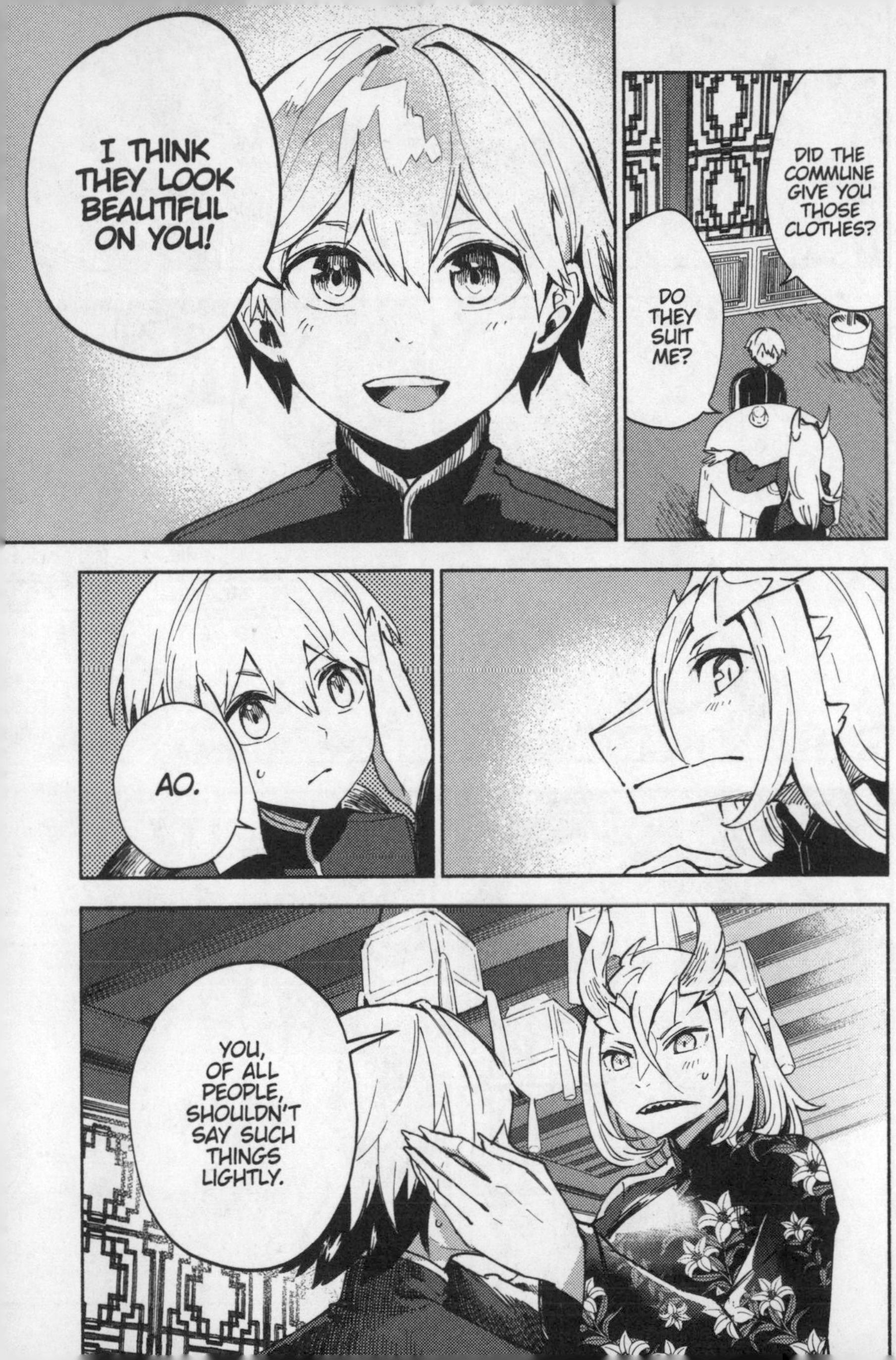
DID THE COMMUNE GIVE YOU THOSE CLOTHES?
DO THEY SUIT ME?
I THINK THEY LOOK BEAUTIFUL ON YOU!
AO.
YOU, OF ALL PEOPLE, SHOULDN'T SAY SUCH THINGS LIGHTLY.

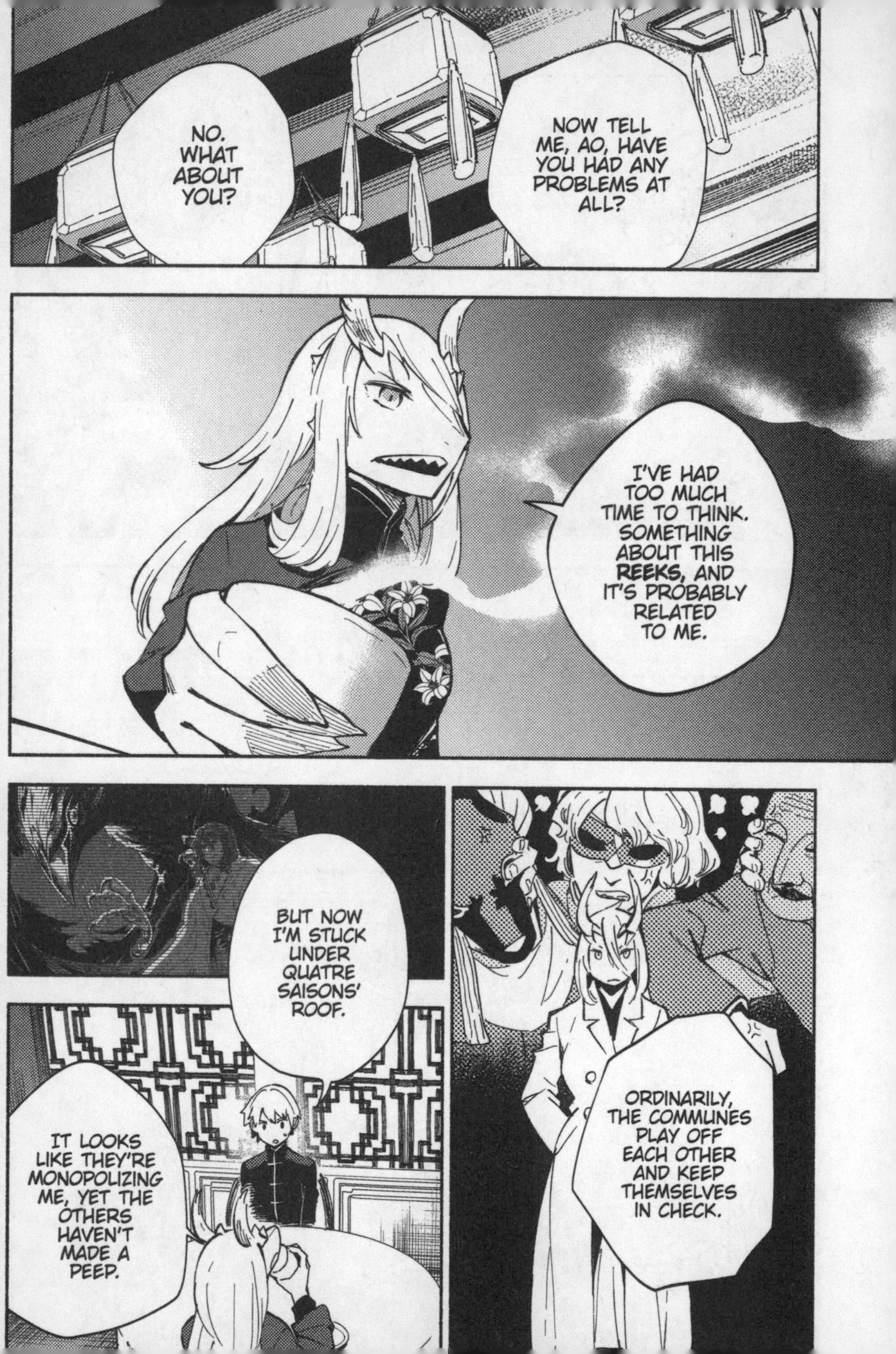
NOW TELL ME, AO, HAVE YOU HAD ANY PROBLEMS AT ALL?
NO. WHAT ABOUT YOU?
I'VE HAD TOO MUCH TIME TO THINK. SOMETHING ABOUT THIS **REEKS**, AND IT'S PROBABLY RELATED TO ME.
ORDINARILY, THE COMMUNES PLAY OFF EACH OTHER AND KEEP THEMSELVES IN CHECK.
BUT NOW I'M STUCK UNDER QUATRE SAISONS' ROOF.
IT LOOKS LIKE THEY'RE MONOPOLIZING ME, YET THE OTHERS HAVEN'T MADE A PEEP.

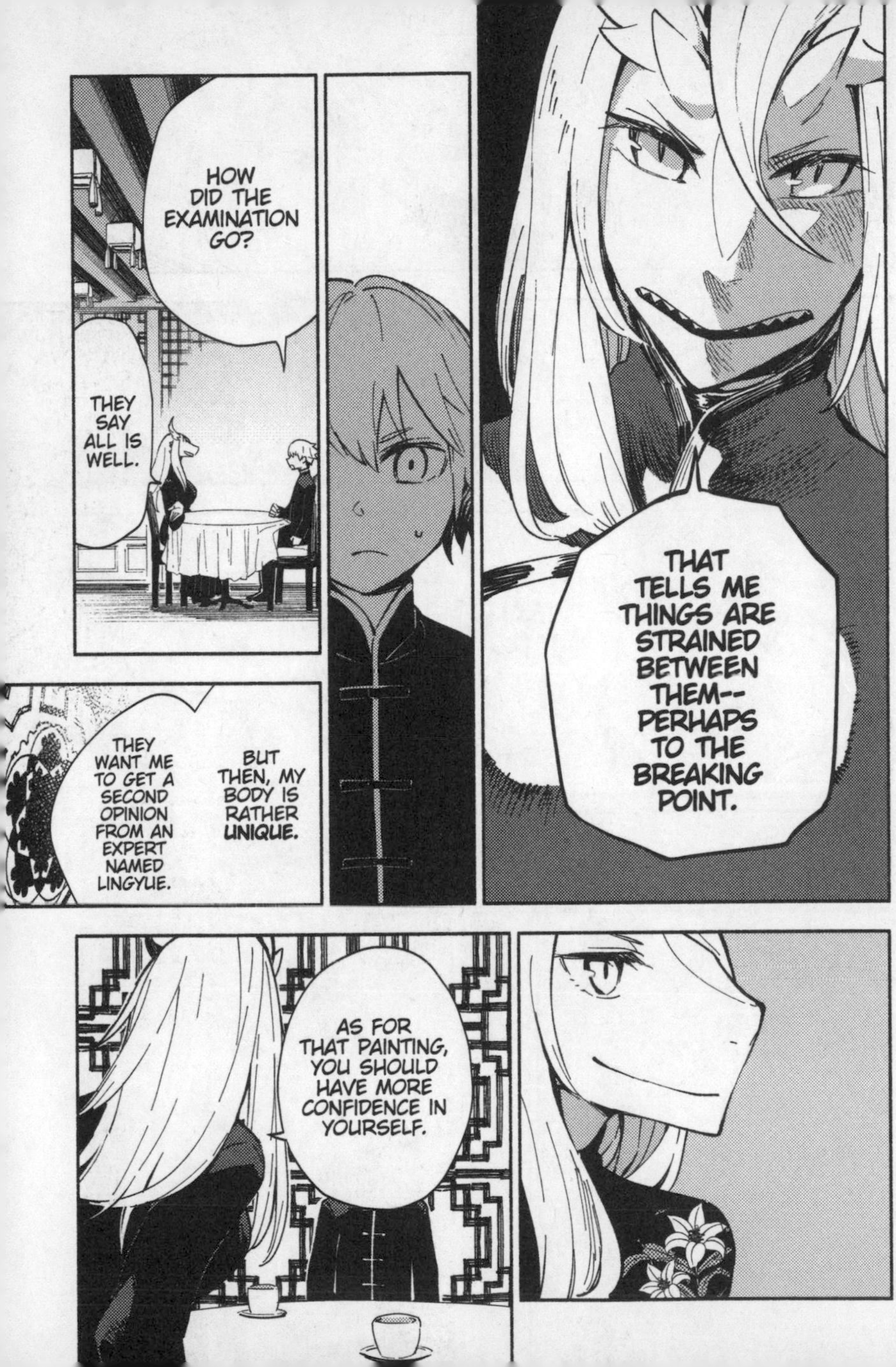
THAT TELLS ME THINGS ARE STRAINED BETWEEN THEM-- PERHAPS TO THE BREAKING POINT.
HOW DID THE EXAMINATION GO?
THEY SAY ALL IS WELL.
THEY WANT ME TO GET A SECOND OPINION FROM AN EXPERT NAMED LINGYUE.
BUT THEN, MY BODY IS RATHER **UNIQUE**.
AS FOR THAT PAINTING, YOU SHOULD HAVE MORE CONFIDENCE IN YOURSELF.

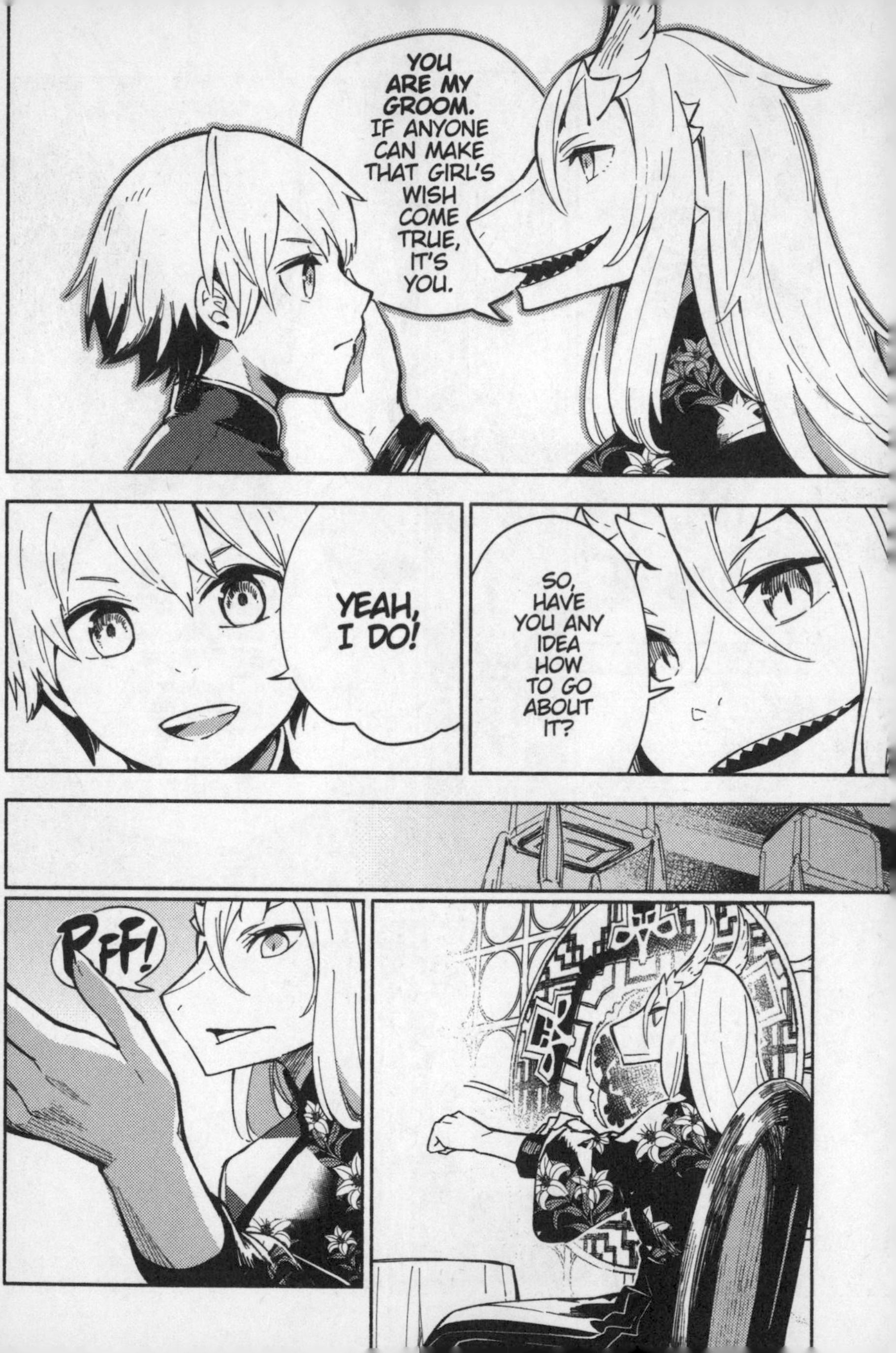
YOU ARE MY GROOM. IF ANYONE CAN MAKE THAT GIRL'S WISH COME TRUE, IT'S YOU.
SO, HAVE YOU ANY IDEA HOW TO GO ABOUT IT?
YEAH, I DO!
PFF!

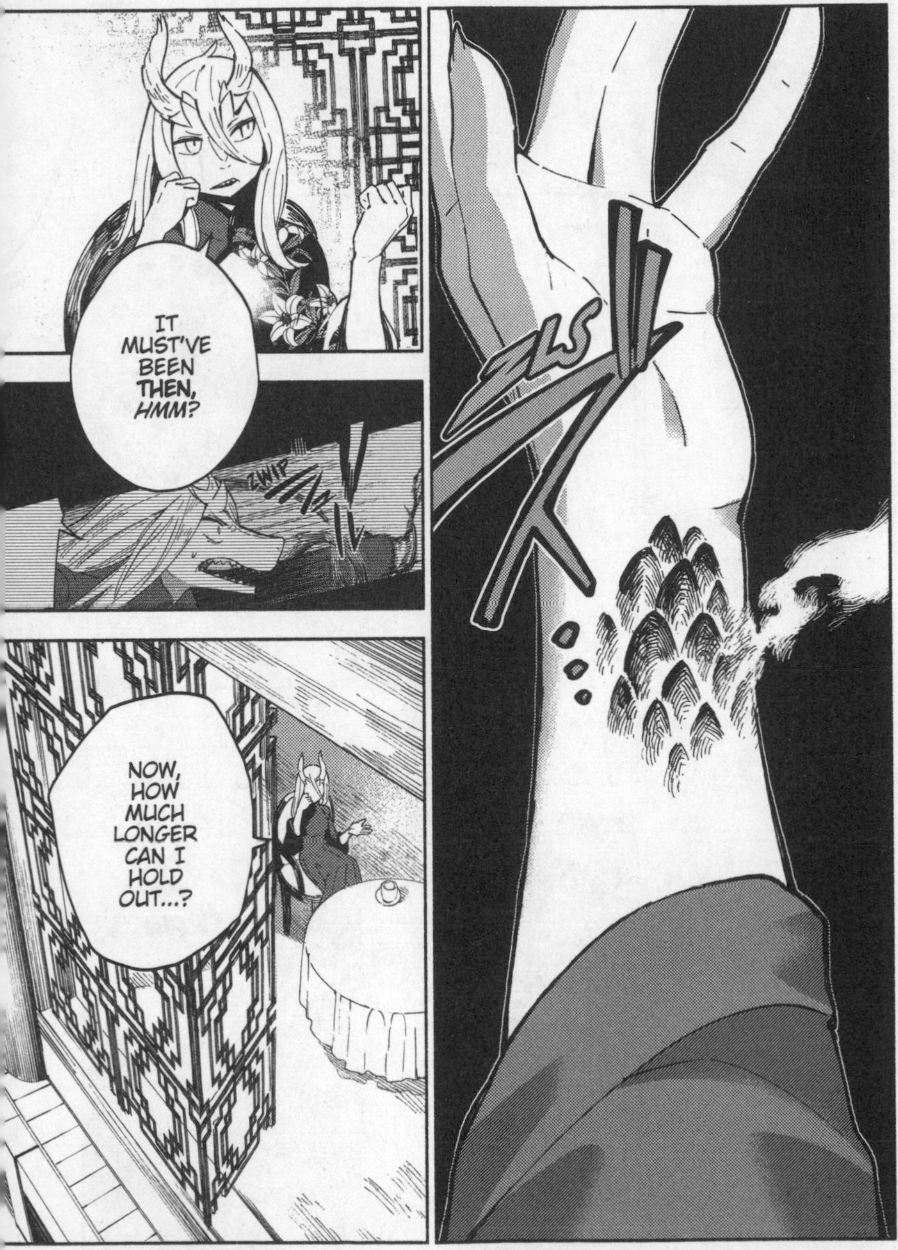
ZLS
IT MUST'VE BEEN THEN, *HMM?*
ZWIP
NOW, HOW MUCH LONGER CAN I HOLD OUT...?

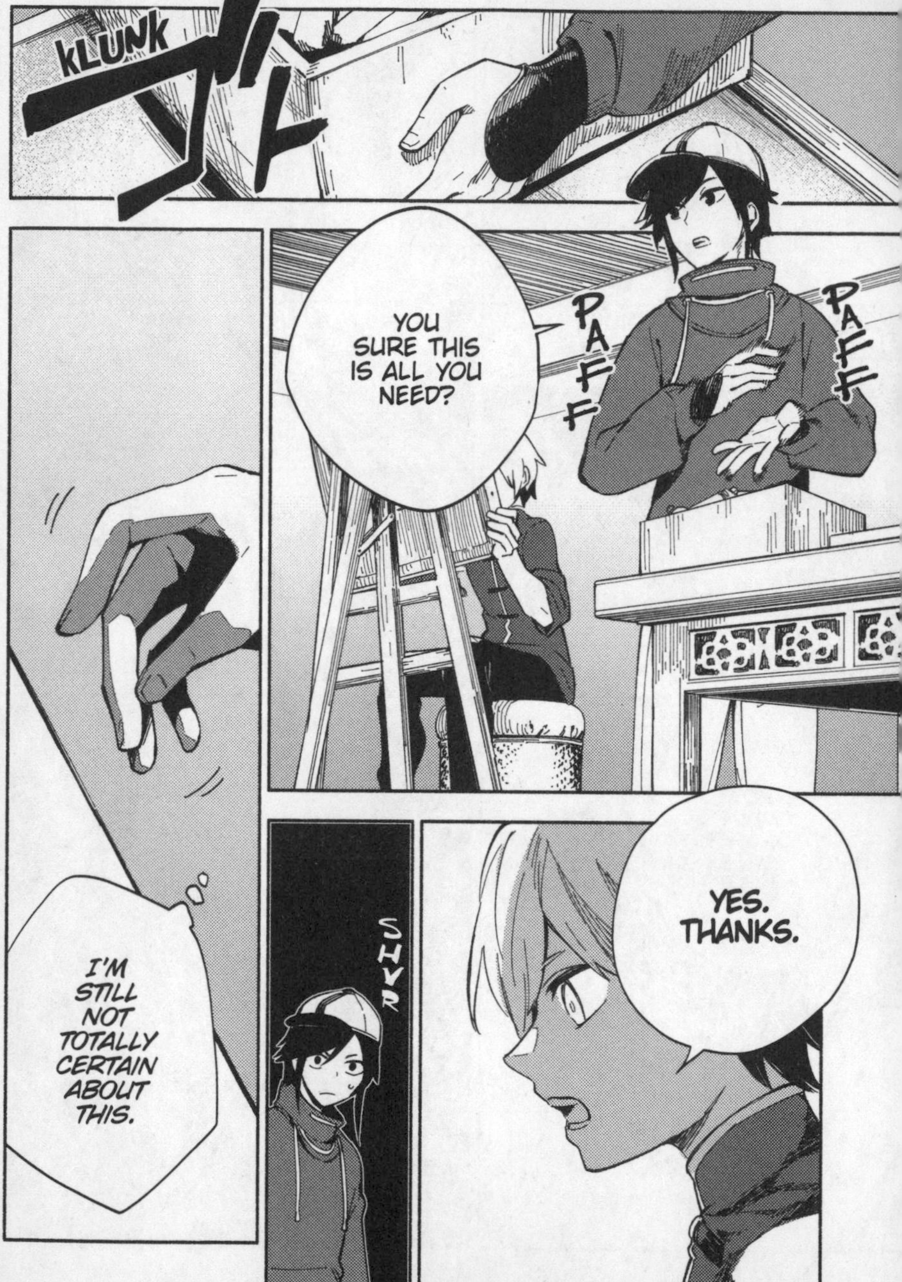
KLUNK
PAFF
PAFF
YOU SURE THIS IS ALL YOU NEED?
YES. THANKS.
SHVR
I'M STILL NOT TOTALLY CERTAIN ABOUT THIS.

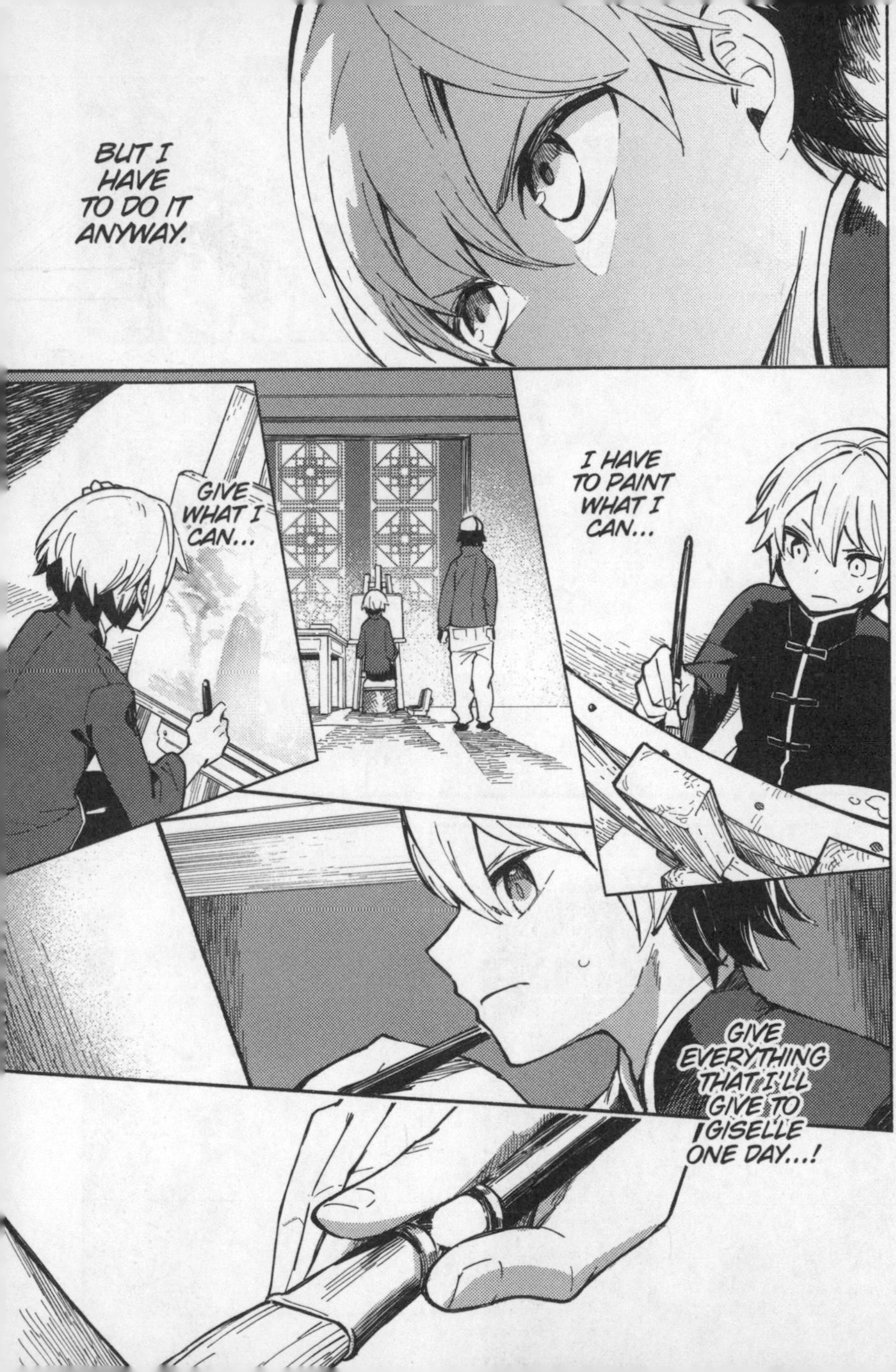
BUT I HAVE TO DO IT ANYWAY.
I HAVE TO PAINT WHAT I CAN...
GIVE WHAT I CAN...
GIVE EVERYTHING THAT I'LL GIVE TO GISELLE ONE DAY...!

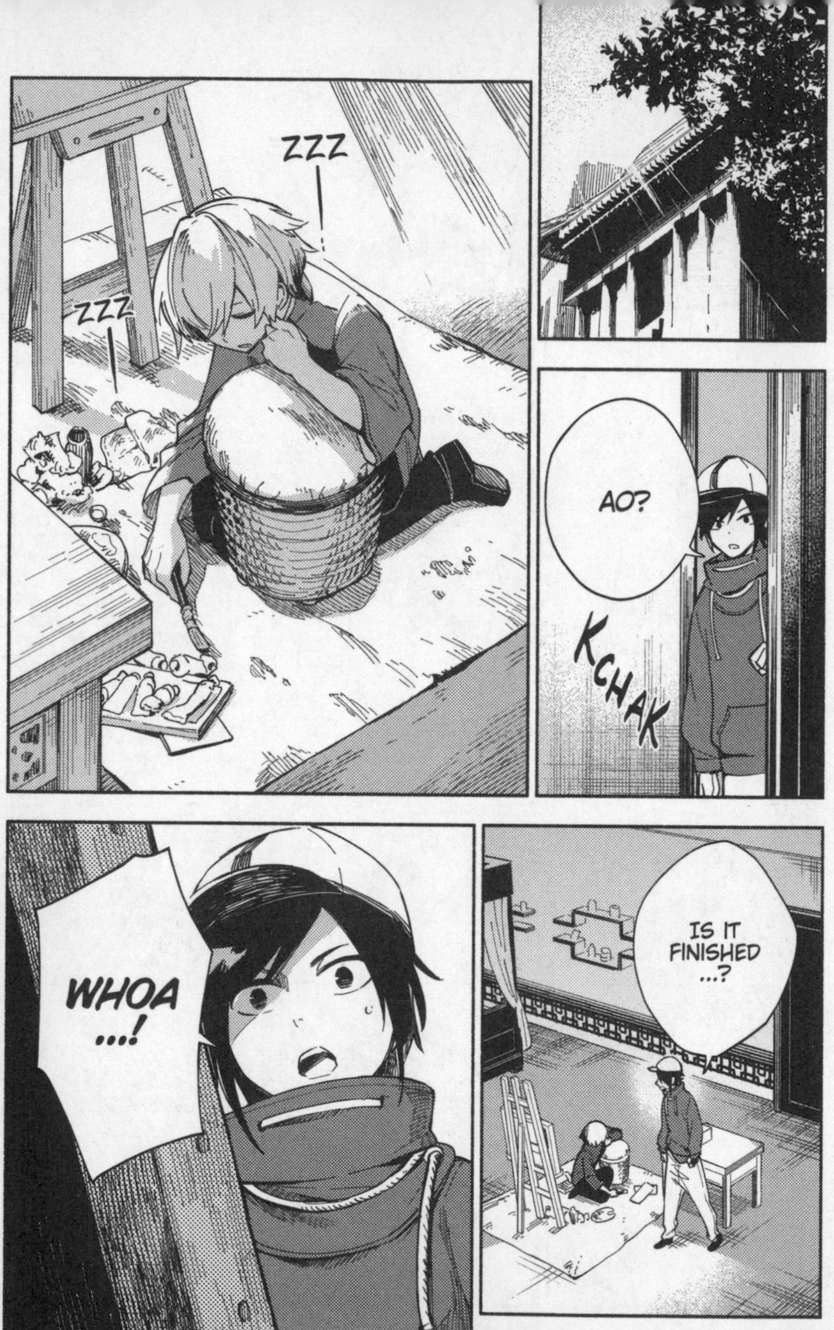
AO?
KCHAK
ZZZ
ZZZ
IS IT FINISHED ...?
WHOA ...!

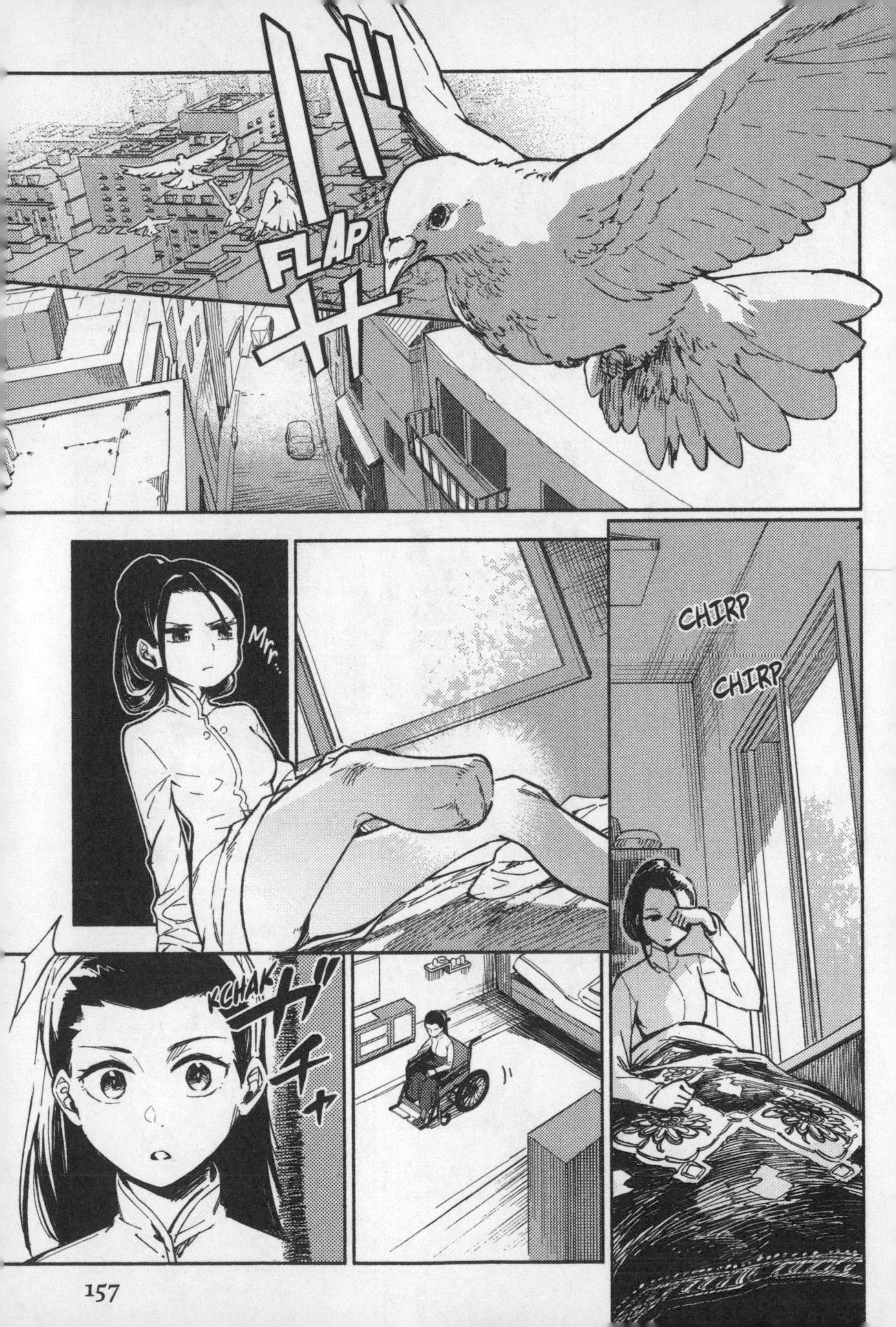
FLAP
CHIRP
CHIRP
Mrr...
KCHAK
ガチャ

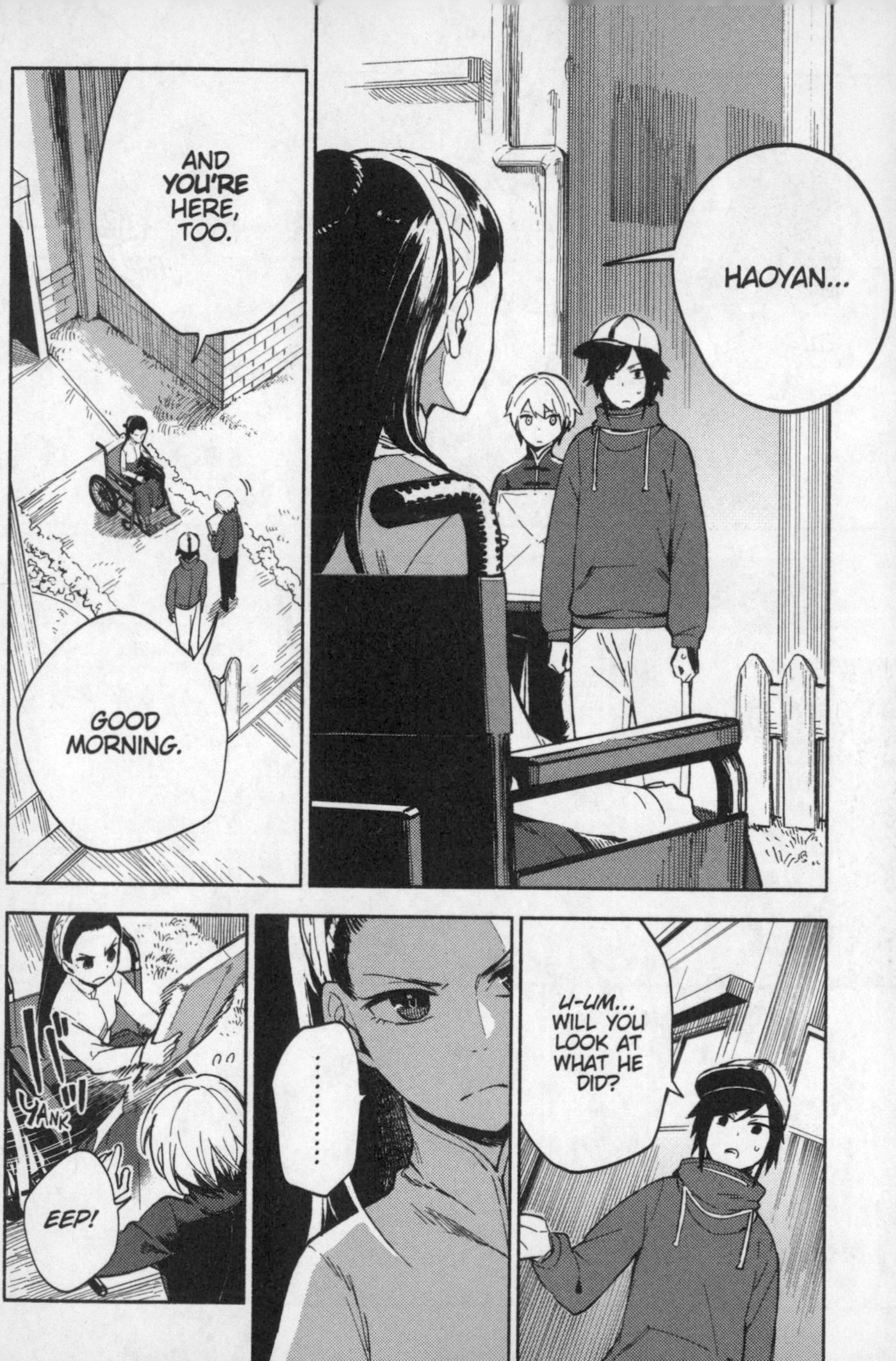
HAOYAN...
AND YOU'RE HERE, TOO.
GOOD MORNING.
U-UM... WILL YOU LOOK AT WHAT HE DID?
......
YANK
EEP!

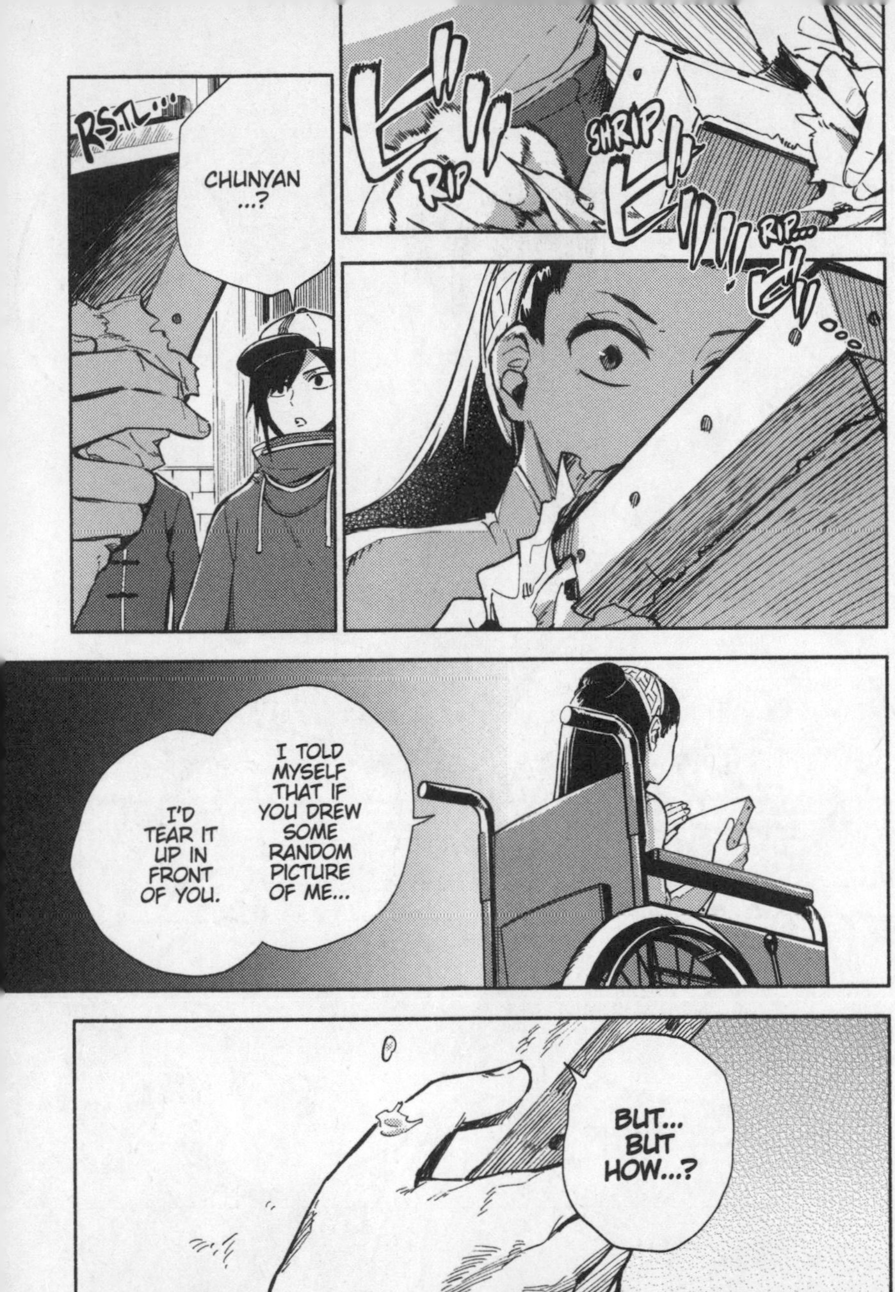
RIP
SHRIP
RIP...
RS.T.L...
CHUNYAN ...?
I TOLD MYSELF THAT IF YOU DREW SOME RANDOM PICTURE OF ME...
I'D TEAR IT UP IN FRONT OF YOU.
BUT... BUT HOW...?

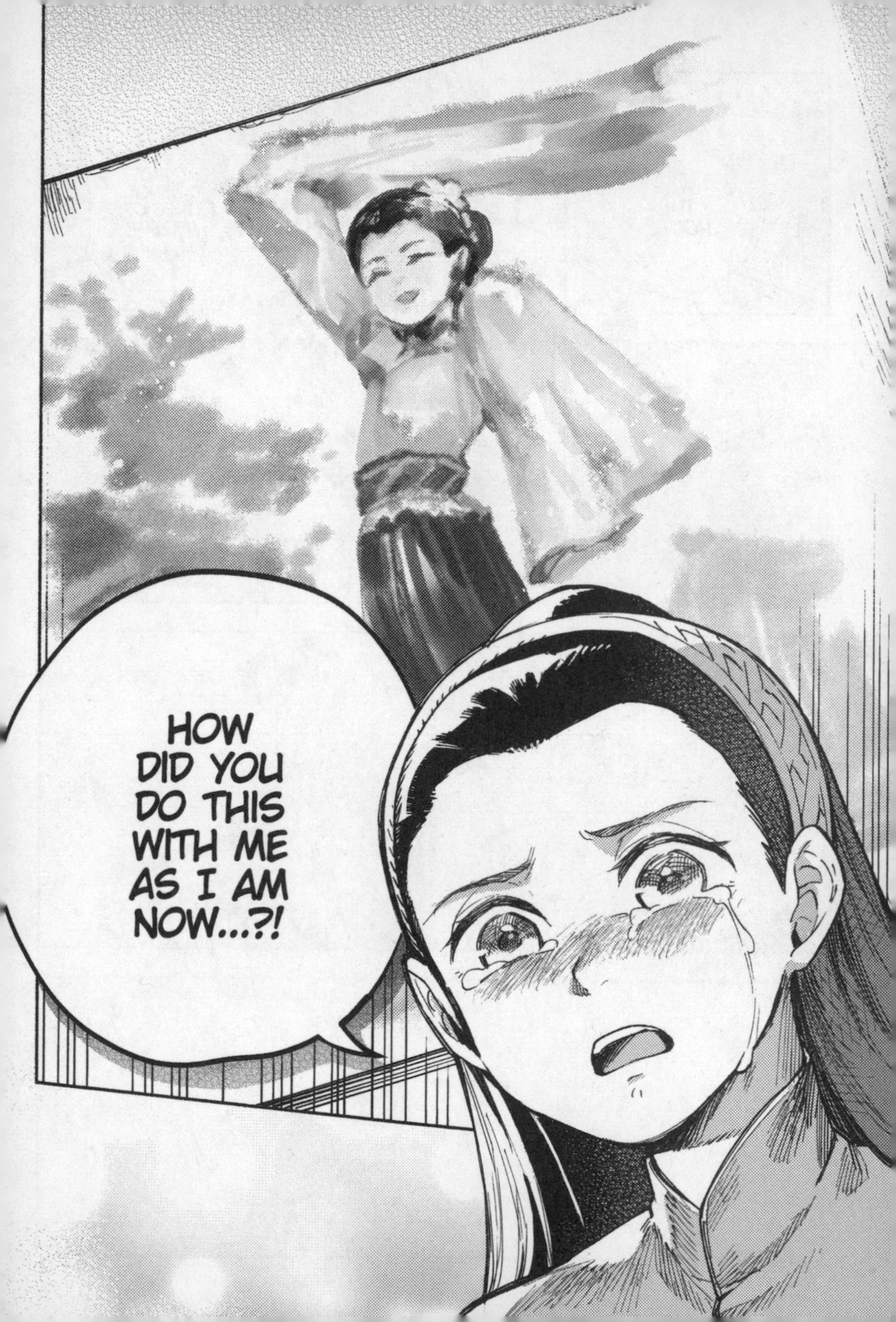
HOW DID YOU DO THIS WITH ME AS I AM NOW...?!

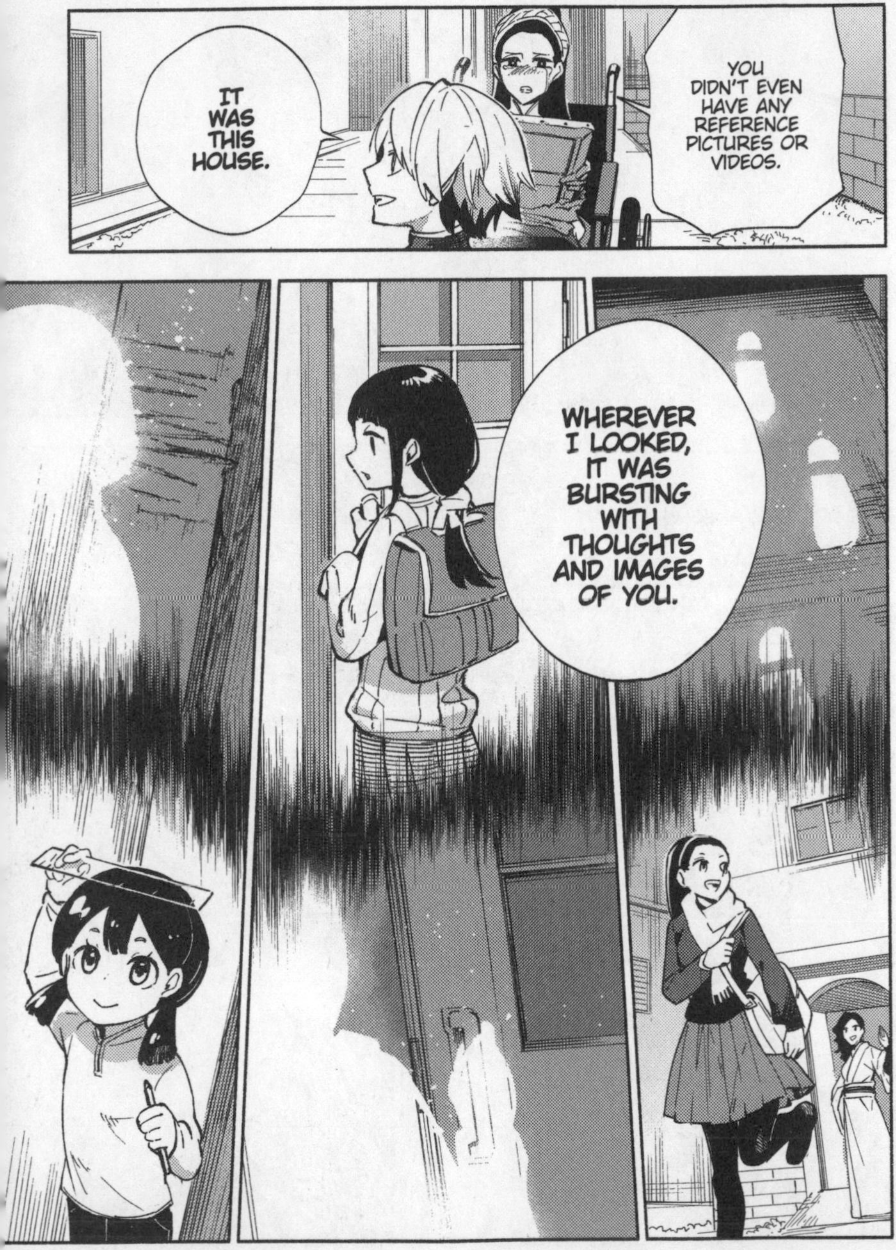
YOU DIDN'T EVEN HAVE ANY REFERENCE PICTURES OR VIDEOS.
IT WAS THIS HOUSE.
WHEREVER I LOOKED, IT WAS BURSTING WITH THOUGHTS AND IMAGES OF YOU.

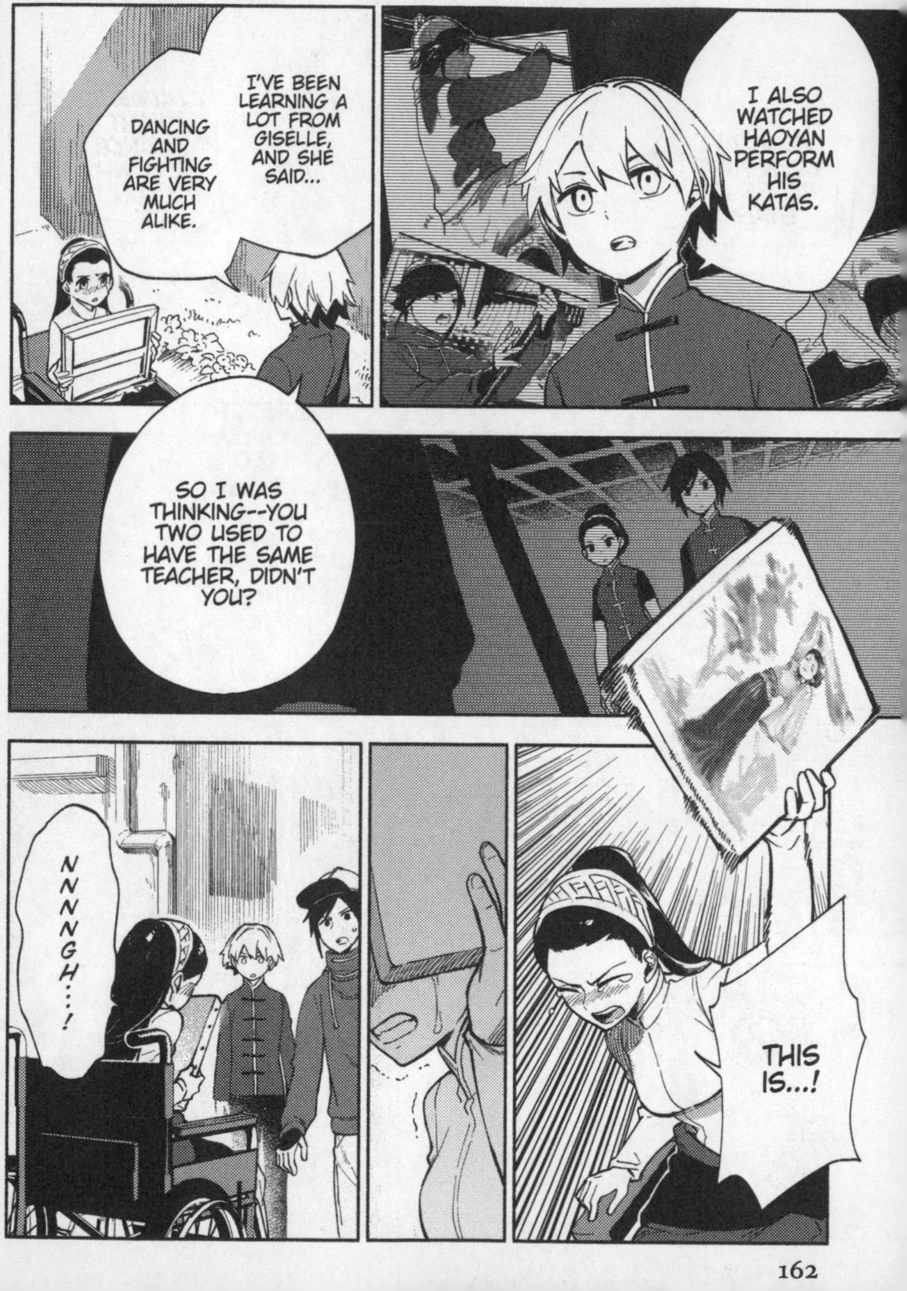
I ALSO WATCHED HAOYAN PERFORM HIS KATAS.
I'VE BEEN LEARNING A LOT FROM GISELLE, AND SHE SAID...
DANCING AND FIGHTING ARE VERY MUCH ALIKE.
SO I WAS THINKING--YOU TWO USED TO HAVE THE SAME TEACHER, DIDN'T YOU?
THIS IS...!
NNNNGH...!

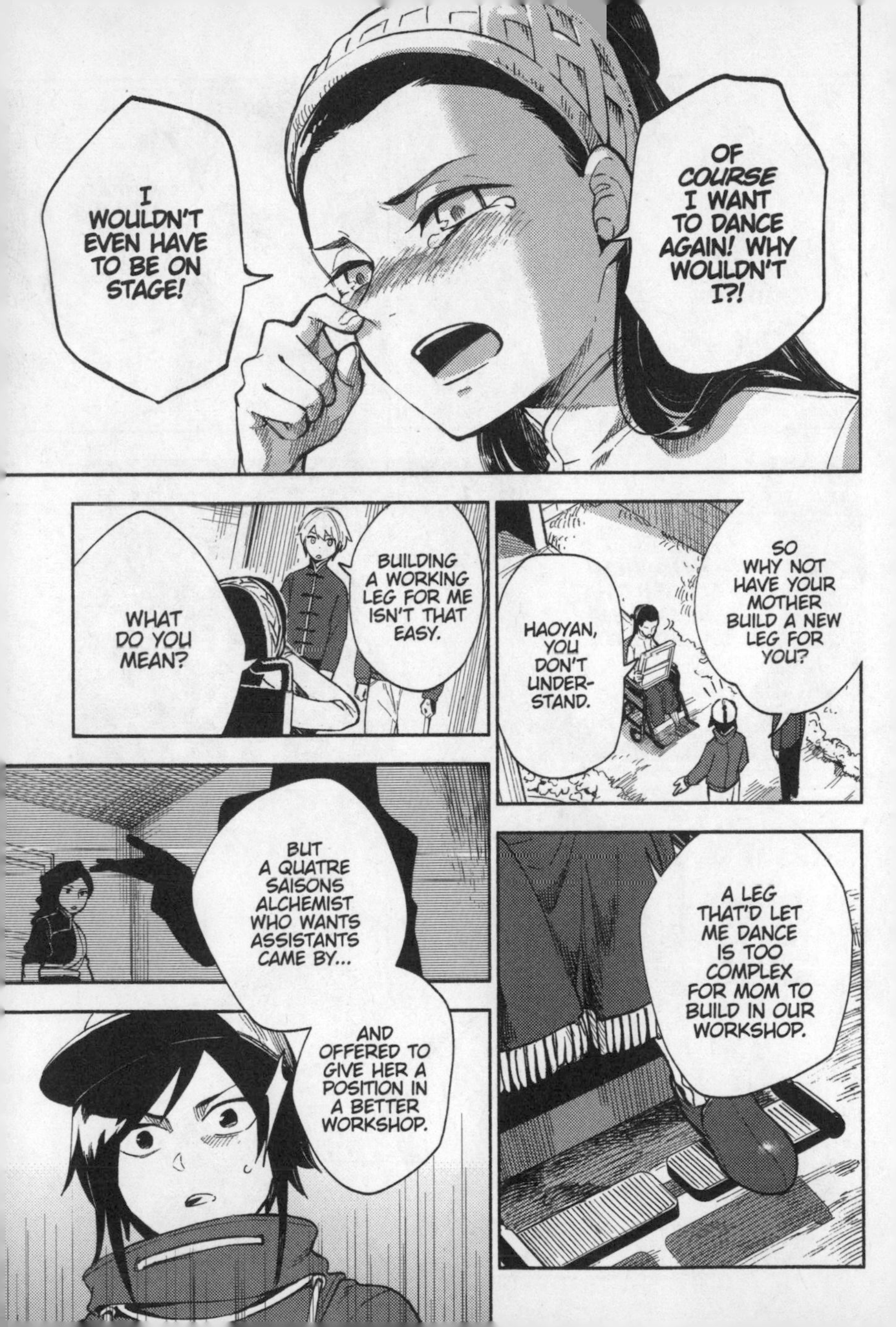
OF COURSE I WANT TO DANCE AGAIN! WHY WOULDN'T I?!
I WOULDN'T EVEN HAVE TO BE ON STAGE!
SO WHY NOT HAVE YOUR MOTHER BUILD A NEW LEG FOR YOU?
HAOYAN, YOU DON'T UNDER-STAND.
BUILDING A WORKING LEG FOR ME ISN'T THAT EASY.
WHAT DO YOU MEAN?
A LEG THAT'D LET ME DANCE IS TOO COMPLEX FOR MOM TO BUILD IN OUR WORKSHOP.
BUT A QUATRE SAISONS ALCHEMIST WHO WANTS ASSISTANTS CAME BY...
AND OFFERED TO GIVE HER A POSITION IN A BETTER WORKSHOP.

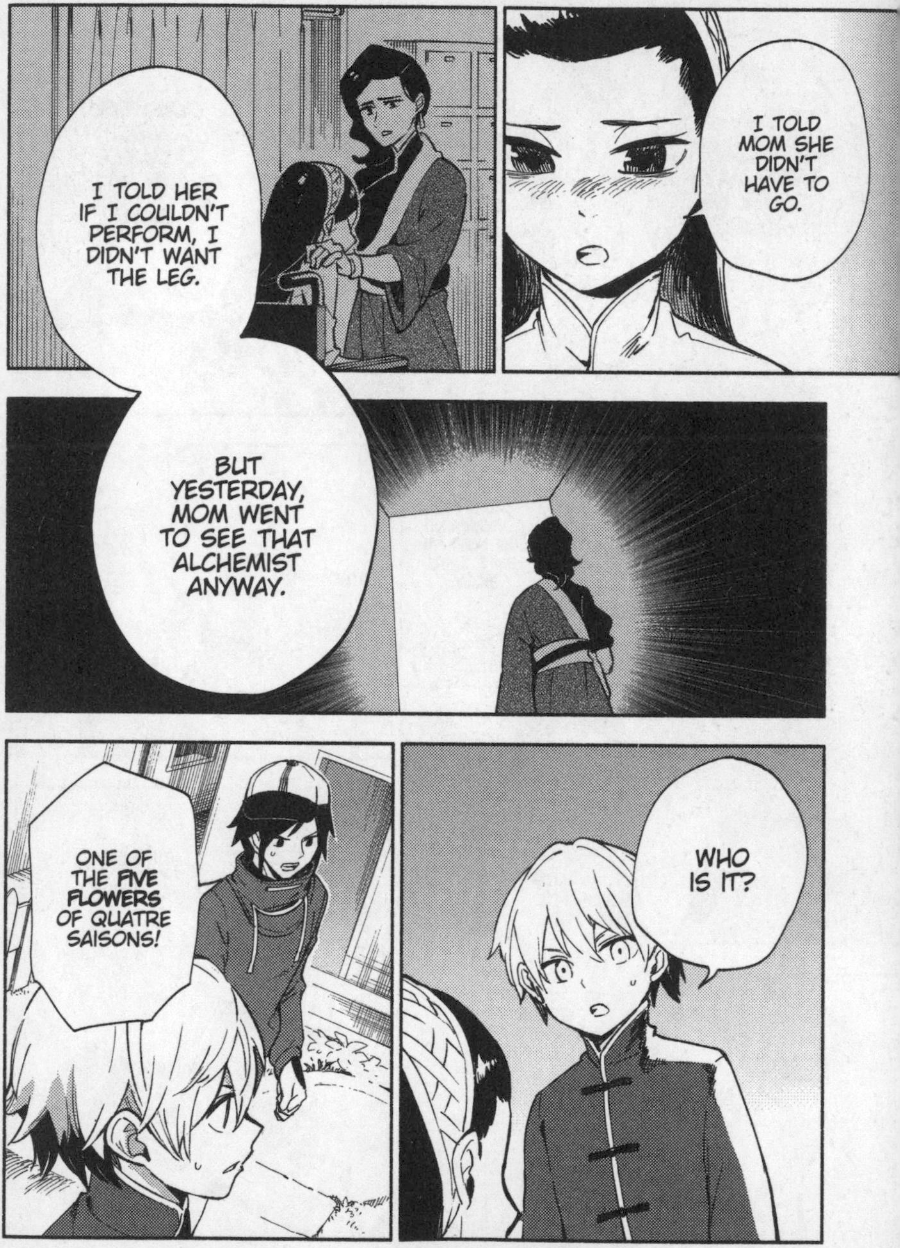
I TOLD MOM SHE DIDN'T HAVE TO GO.
I TOLD HER IF I COULDN'T PERFORM, I DIDN'T WANT THE LEG.
BUT YESTERDAY, MOM WENT TO SEE THAT ALCHEMIST ANYWAY.
WHO IS IT?
ONE OF THE **FIVE FLOWERS** OF QUATRE SAISONS!

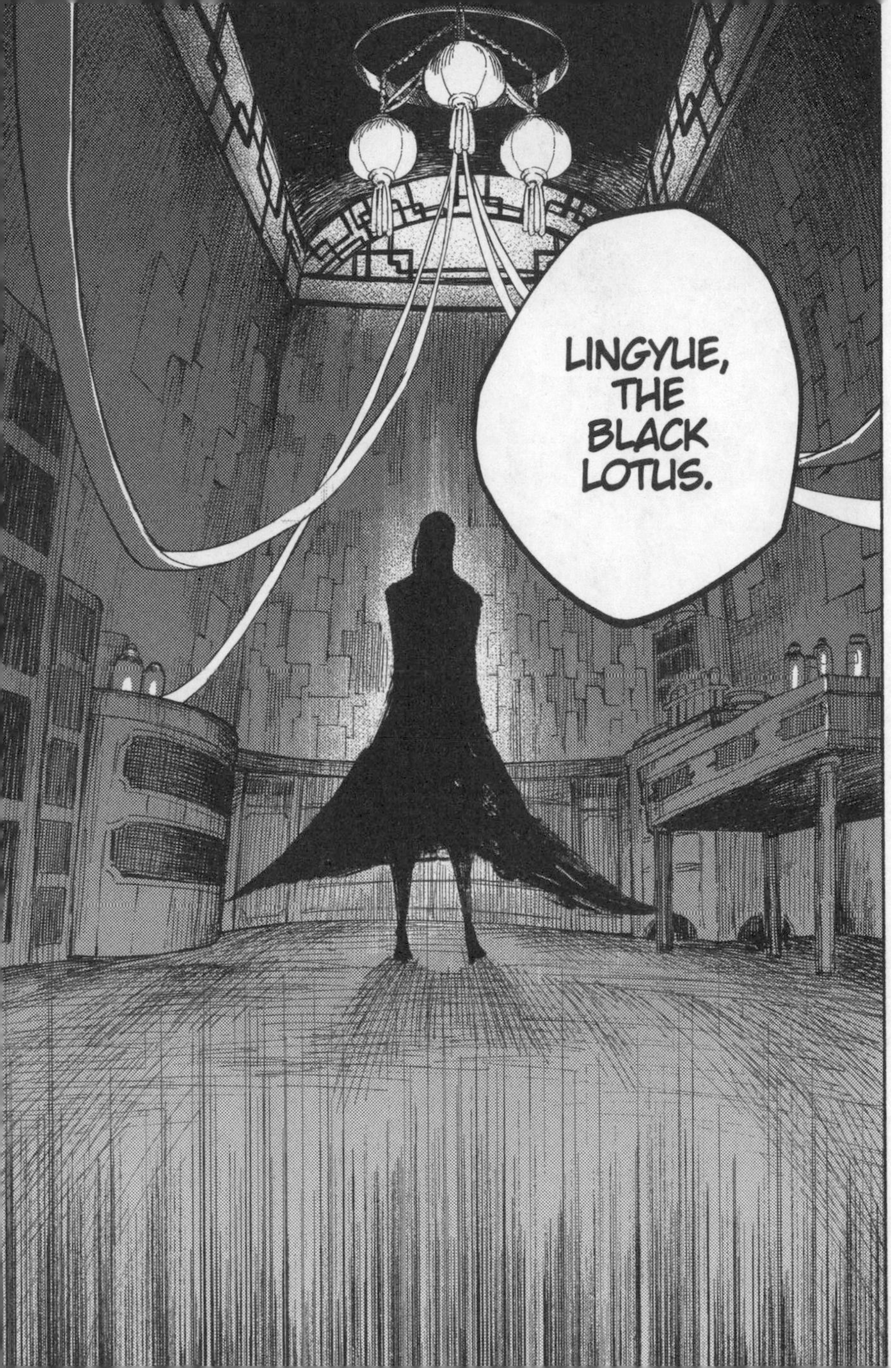
LINGYUE, THE BLACK LOTUS.

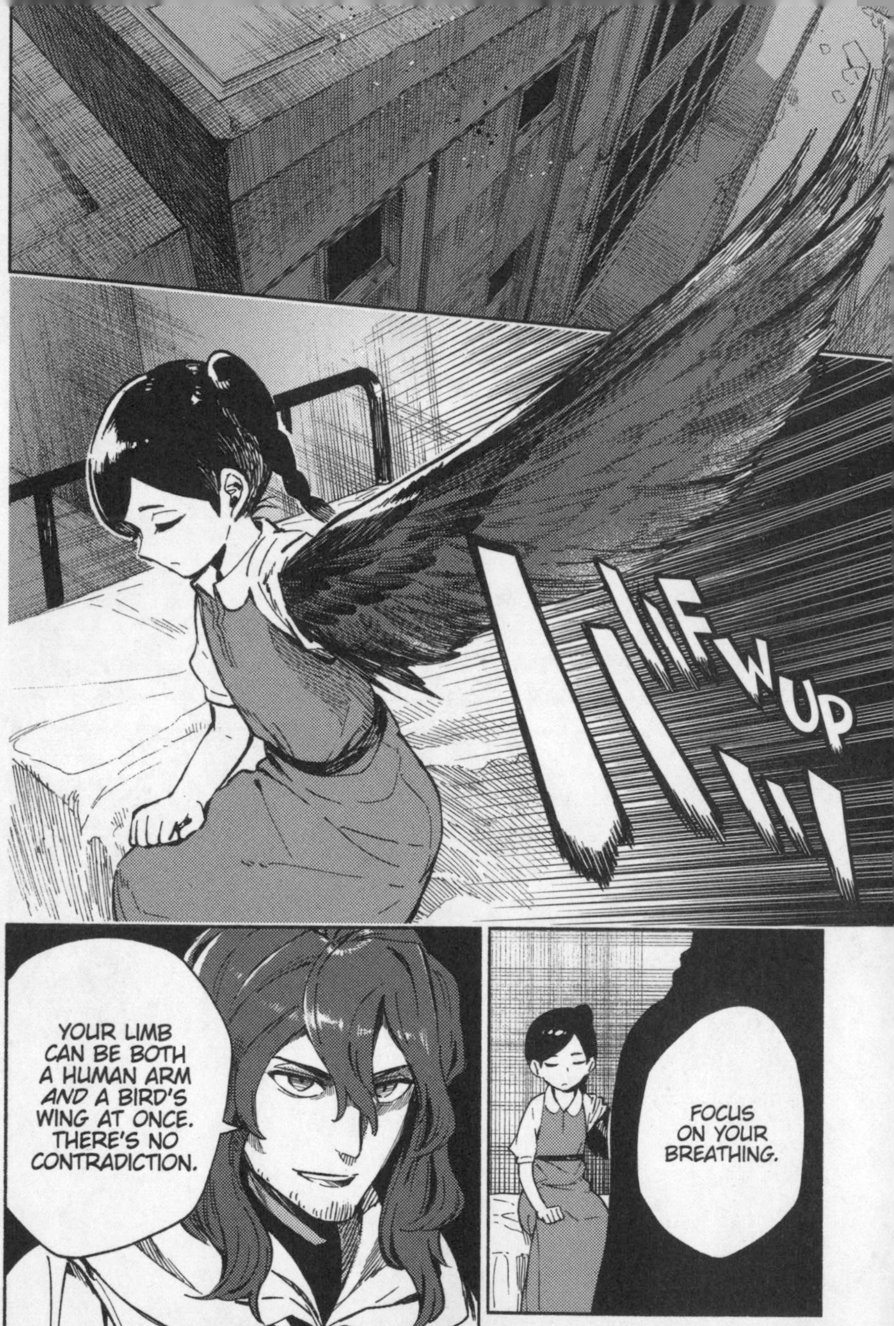
FWUP
FOCUS ON YOUR BREATHING.
YOUR LIMB CAN BE BOTH A HUMAN ARM AND A BIRD'S WING AT ONCE. THERE'S NO CONTRADICTION.

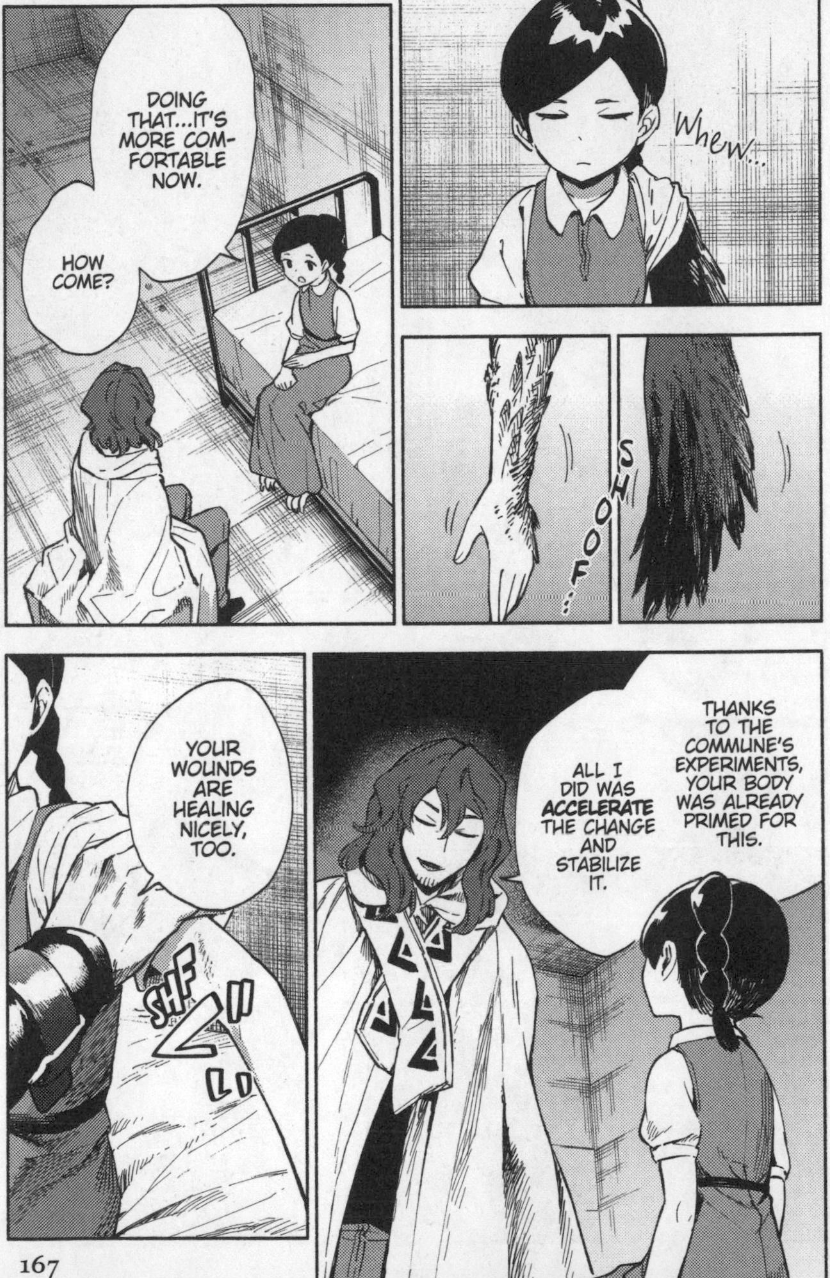
Whew...
SHOOF...
DOING THAT...IT'S MORE COM-FORTABLE NOW.
HOW COME?
THANKS TO THE COMMUNE'S EXPERIMENTS, YOUR BODY WAS ALREADY PRIMED FOR THIS.
ALL I DID WAS **ACCELERATE** THE CHANGE AND STABILIZE IT.
YOUR WOUNDS ARE HEALING NICELY, TOO.
SHF

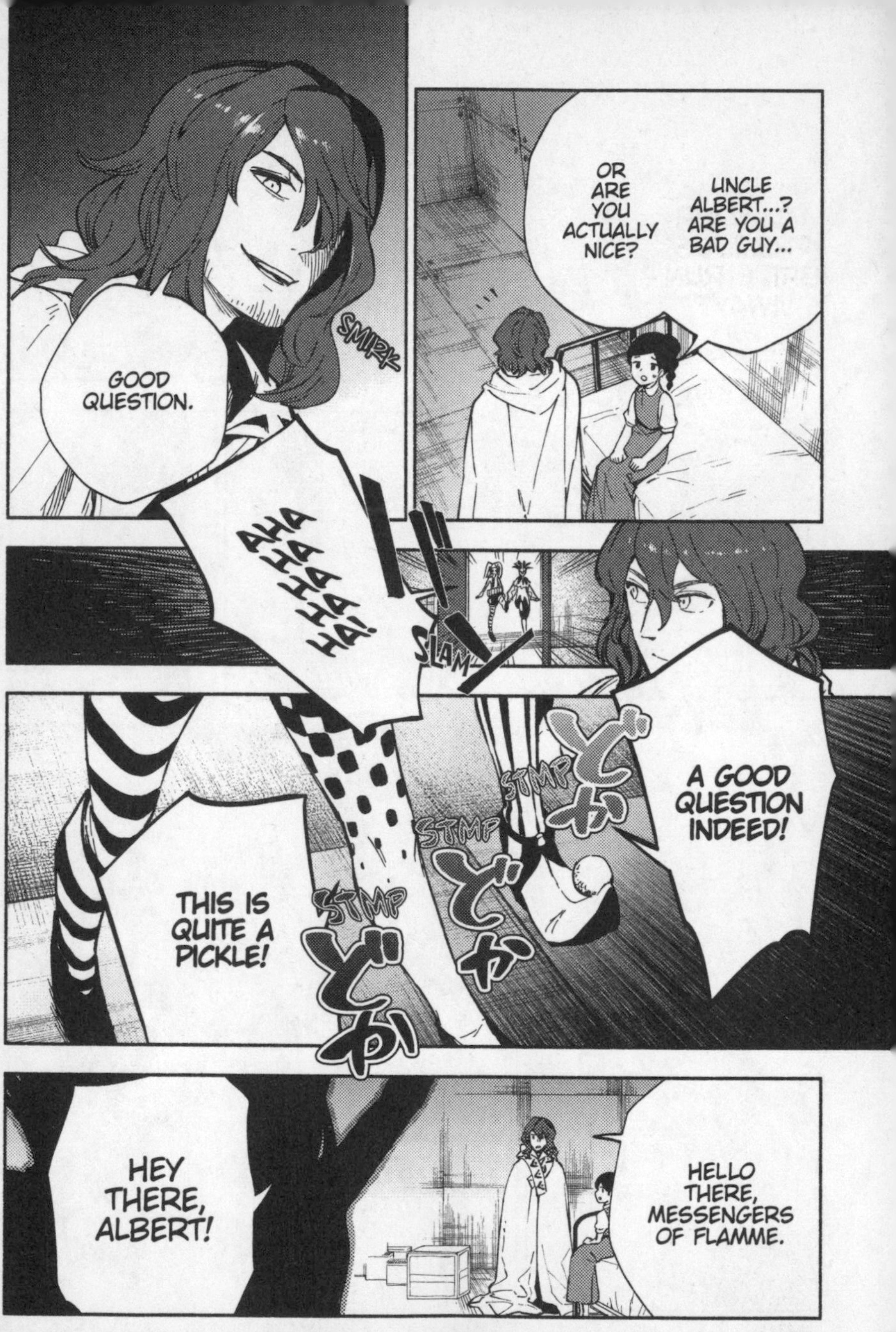
UNCLE ALBERT...? ARE YOU A BAD GUY...
OR ARE YOU ACTUALLY NICE?
SMIRK
GOOD QUESTION.
AHAHAHAHA!
SLAM
A GOOD QUESTION INDEED!
STMP
どか
STMP
どか
THIS IS QUITE A PICKLE!
STMP
どか
HELLO THERE, MESSENGERS OF FLAMME.
HEY THERE, ALBERT!

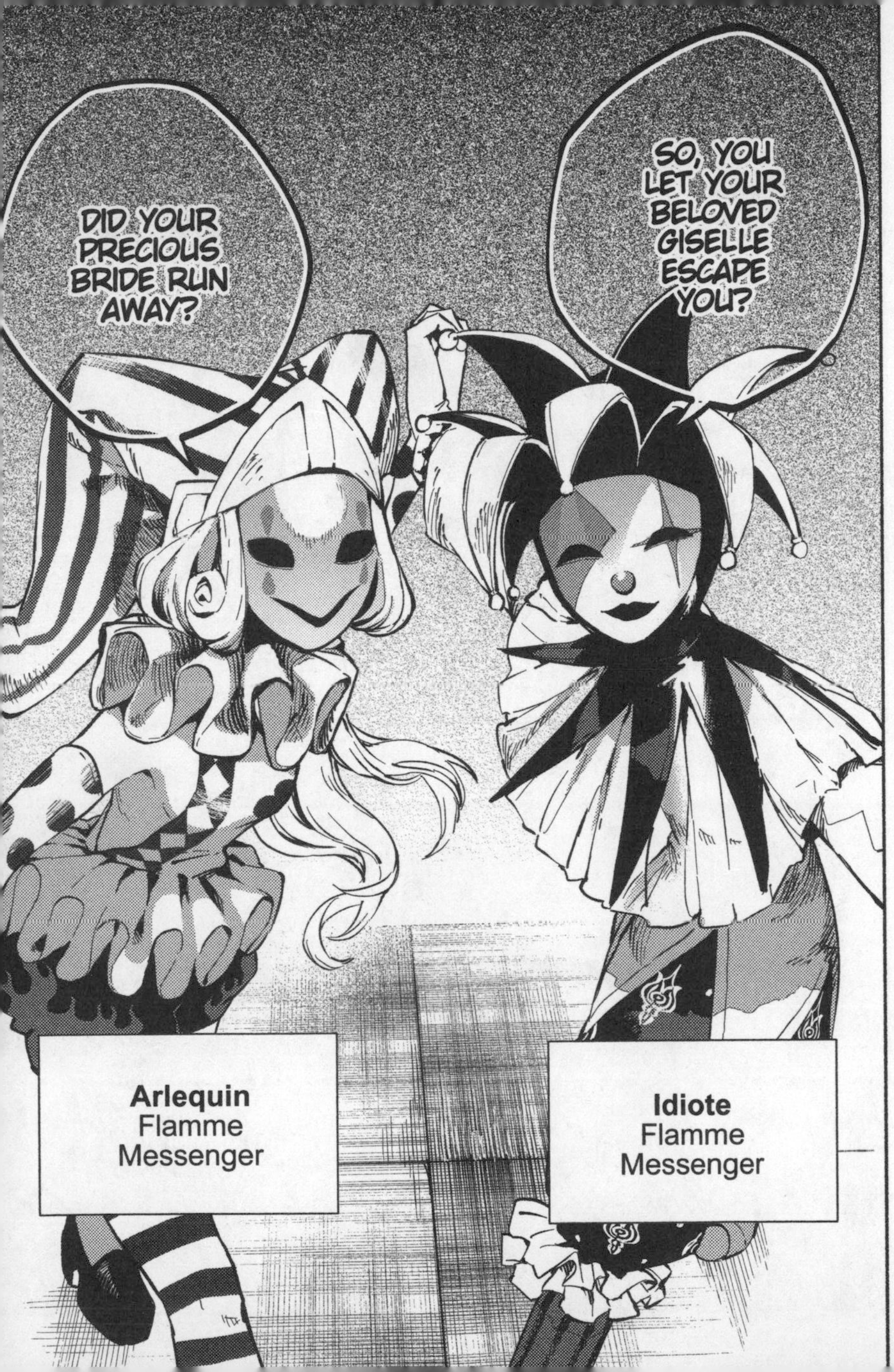
SO, YOU LET YOUR BELOVED GISELLE ESCAPE YOU?
DID YOUR PRECIOUS BRIDE RUN AWAY?
Idiote Flamme Messenger
Arlequin Flamme Messenger

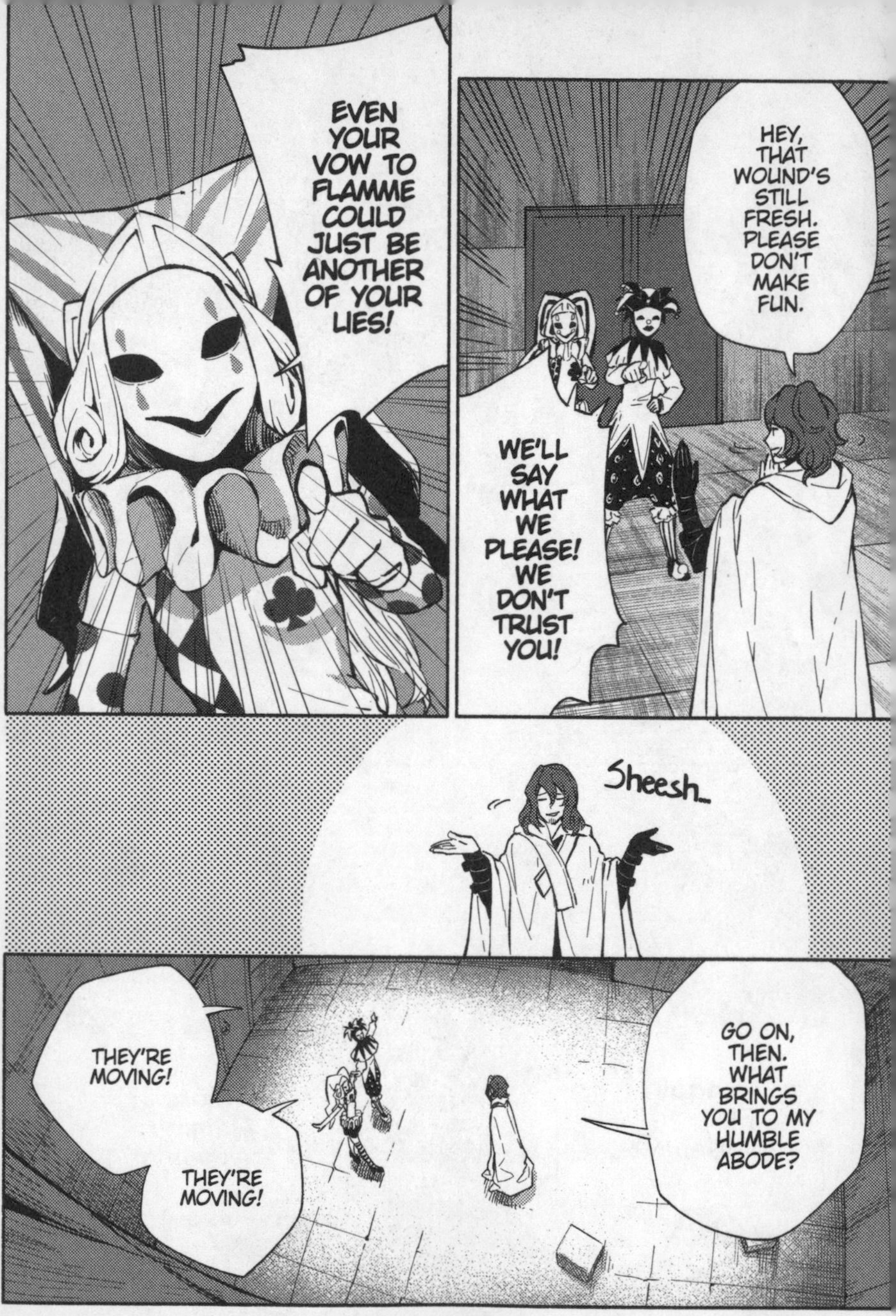
HEY, THAT WOUND'S STILL FRESH. PLEASE DON'T MAKE FUN.
WE'LL SAY WHAT WE PLEASE! WE DON'T TRUST YOU!
EVEN YOUR VOW TO FLAMME COULD JUST BE ANOTHER OF YOUR LIES!
Sheesh...
GO ON, THEN. WHAT BRINGS YOU TO MY HUMBLE ABODE?
THEY'RE MOVING!
THEY'RE MOVING!

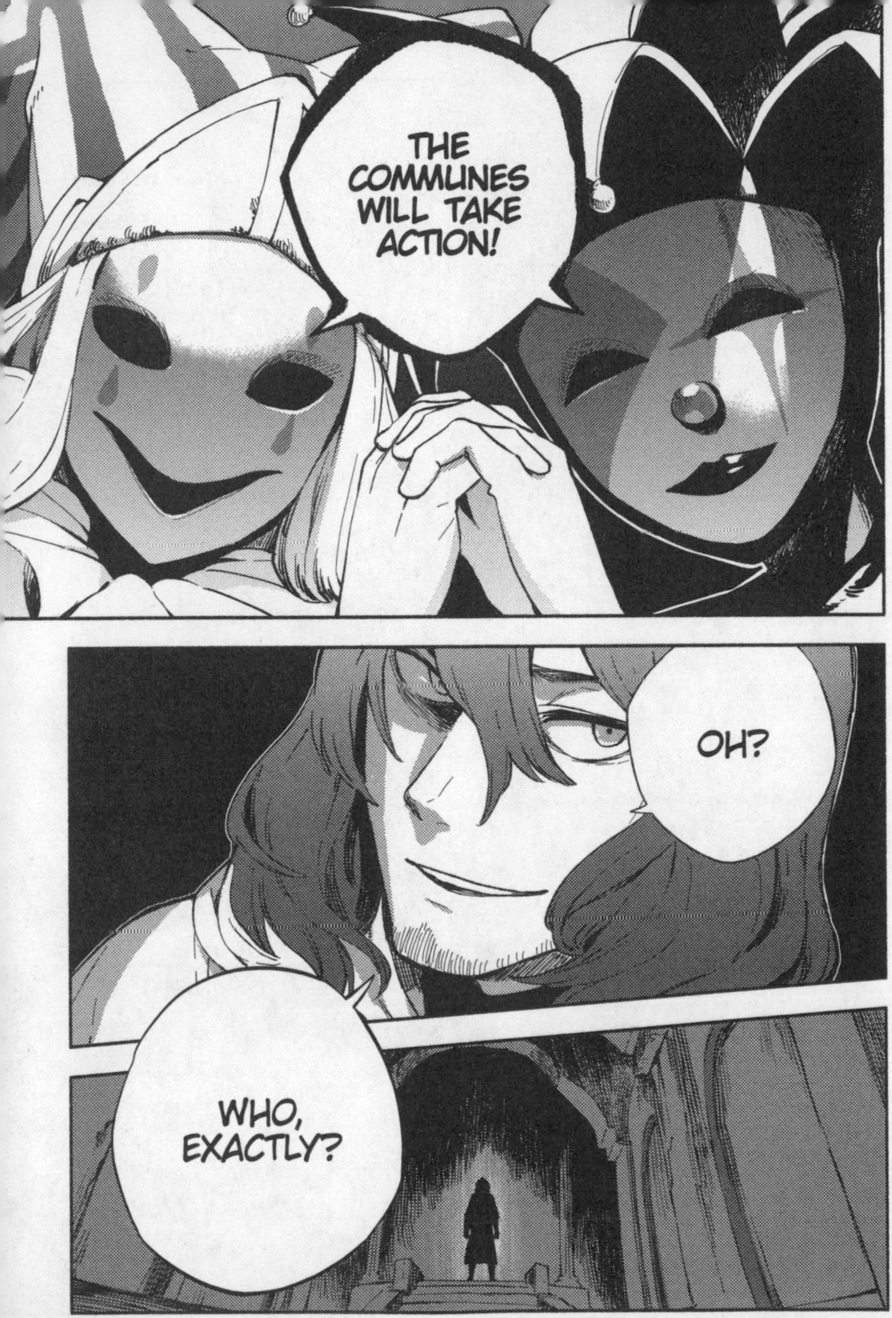
THE COMMUNES WILL TAKE ACTION!
OH?
WHO, EXACTLY?

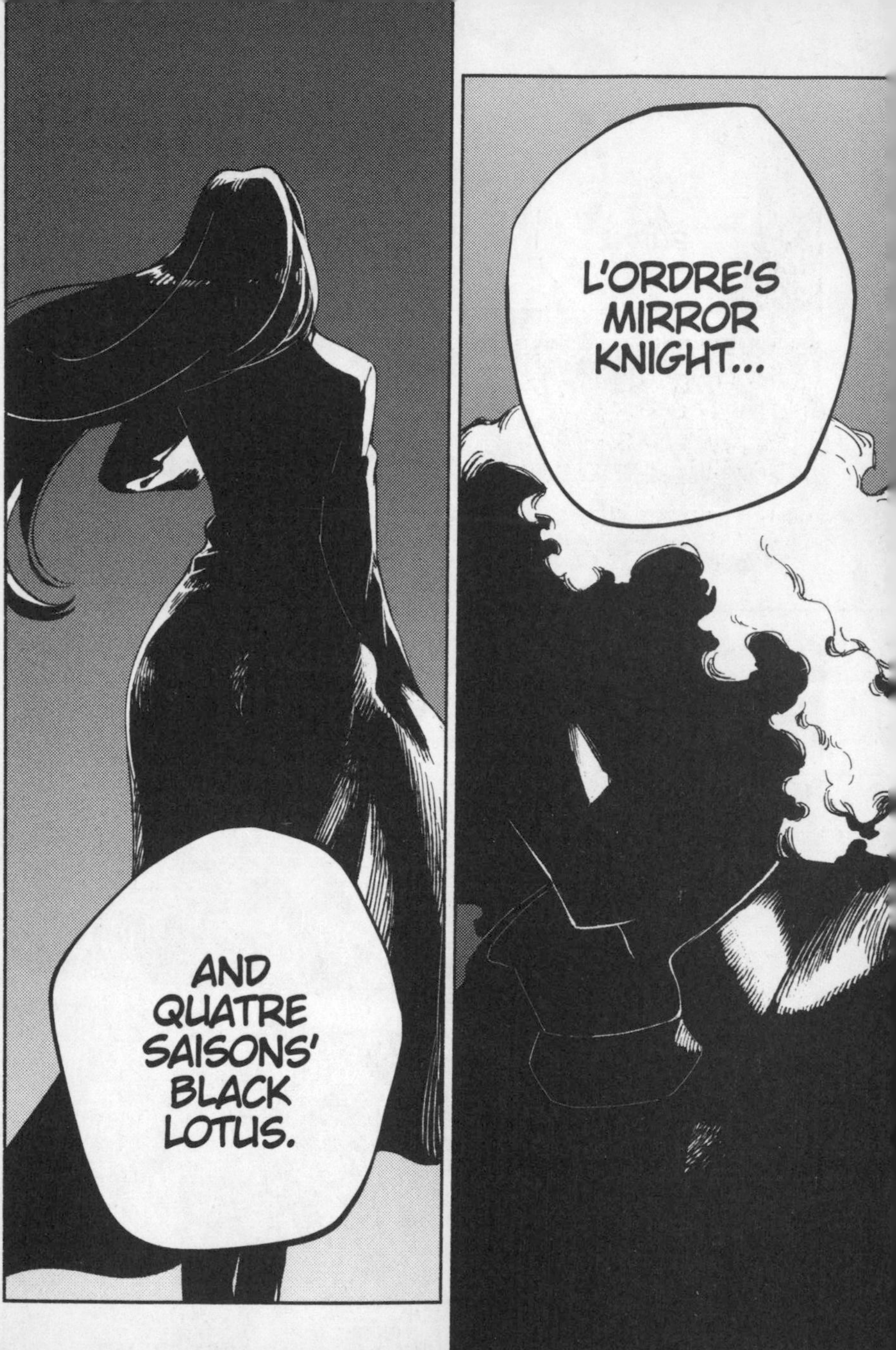
L'ORDRE'S MIRROR KNIGHT...
AND QUATRE SAISONS' BLACK LOTUS.

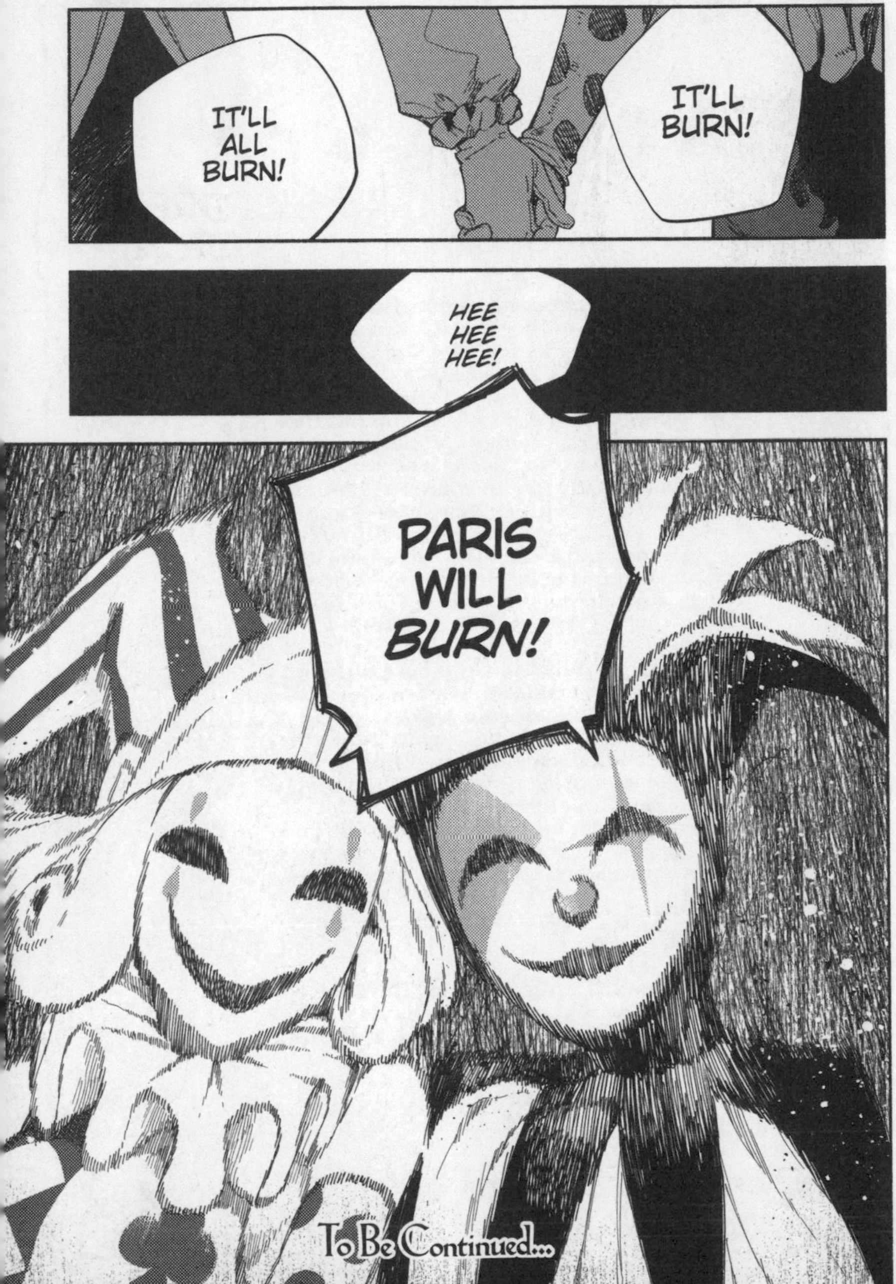
IT'LL BURN!
IT'LL ALL BURN!
HEE HEE HEE!
PARIS WILL BURN!
To Be Continued...

Wizard's Blue

Afterword

Hi! I'm Makoto Sanda, the writer.
Thank you very much for picking up
Volume 2, which begins the Chinatown
Arc. Paris is so incredibly diverse that
it was hard to choose which of its many
different areas to focus on, but this
volume centers primarily on
Chinatown. Giselle's secrets are
slowly starting to come to light, and
Ao is learning new secrets and
mastering more colors through
meeting alchemists and enduring
harrowing battles. If you come to
love Ao and his world even a little,
I'll be greatly honored.

Finally, I'd like to say a big thank-you to
Kore Yamazaki-san, both for permitting
me to add new colors to the world of
The Ancient Magus' Bride and for her
detailed supervision of this work.
I'm sure my scripts ask for too much,
but I'm eternally grateful to Isuo
Tsukumo-san for bringing them vibrantly to
life. And, last but not least, I am forever
grateful to my readers. Thank you.

I hope to see you again next time.

Penned while watching the delayed
release of the stage production of *The
Case Files of Lord El-Melloi II: Adra
Castle Separation*

三田 誠
Sanda Makoto

Understanding Tsukumo in Six Panels or Less! Computer Battles Arc

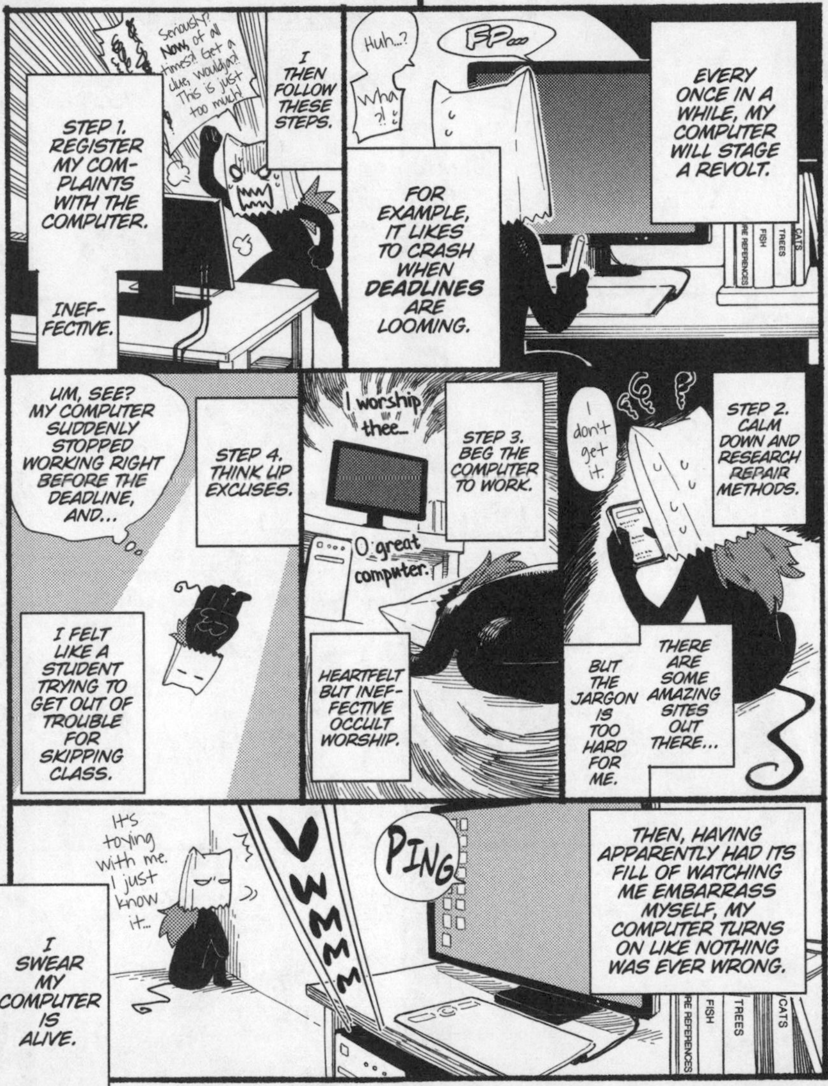
EVERY ONCE IN A WHILE, MY COMPUTER WILL STAGE A REVOLT.
FP...
Huh...?
Wha?!
FOR EXAMPLE, IT LIKES TO CRASH WHEN DEADLINES ARE LOOMING.
I THEN FOLLOW THESE STEPS.
Seriously?! Now, of all times?! Get a clue, wouldja?! This is just too much!
STEP 1. REGISTER MY COMPLAINTS WITH THE COMPUTER.
INEFFECTIVE.
STEP 2. CALM DOWN AND RESEARCH REPAIR METHODS.
I don't get it.
THERE ARE SOME AMAZING SITES OUT THERE...
BUT THE JARGON IS TOO HARD FOR ME.
STEP 3. BEG THE COMPUTER TO WORK.
I worship thee...
O great computer.
HEARTFELT BUT INEFFECTIVE OCCULT WORSHIP.
STEP 4. THINK UP EXCUSES.
UM, SEE? MY COMPUTER SUDDENLY STOPPED WORKING RIGHT BEFORE THE DEADLINE, AND...
I FELT LIKE A STUDENT TRYING TO GET OUT OF TROUBLE FOR SKIPPING CLASS.
THEN, HAVING APPARENTLY HAD ITS FILL OF WATCHING ME EMBARRASS MYSELF, MY COMPUTER TURNS ON LIKE NOTHING WAS EVER WRONG.
PING
VWMMM
It's toying with me. I just know it...
I SWEAR MY COMPUTER IS ALIVE.

Thank you very much for purchasing Volume 2!

Bonus Four-Panel Manga (Part 2)

Because You Won't Notice

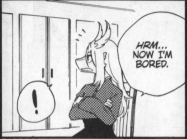

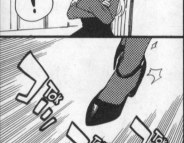

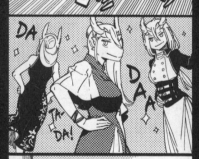

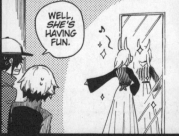

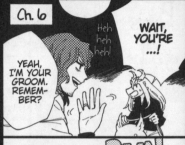

WAIT, YOU'RE ...!
Heh heh heh!
Ch. 6
YEAH, I'M YOUR GROOM. REMEMBER?
DUN
I HAVE PROOF!
Pages from your personal diary. Private photos.
To punish you for not noticing me, I'll post these online...
for the whole world to see.
WAK
SCUM!
Gyaaaaa!
BIFF
DIE!!
YOU'RE A BLIGHT ON MODERN SOCIETY!!
PER-VERT!!
And show me those pictures later!!

Time on my Hands

HRM... NOW I'M BORED.
!
TOK
TOK
TOK
DA
DAA
TA-DA!
WELL, SHE'S HAVING FUN.

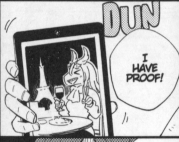

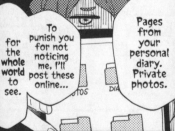

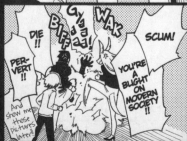

Will Paris really burn?

Delve deeper into *The Ancient Magus' Bride* universe with *Wizard's Blue's* fresh take on the relationship between the human and the inhuman!

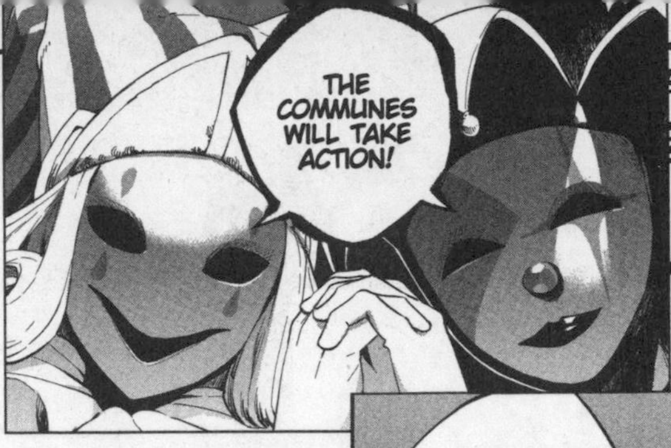
THE COMMUNES WILL TAKE ACTION!

While the communes squabble amongst themselves over Giselle, the rebel group Flamme begins making moves in the shadows.

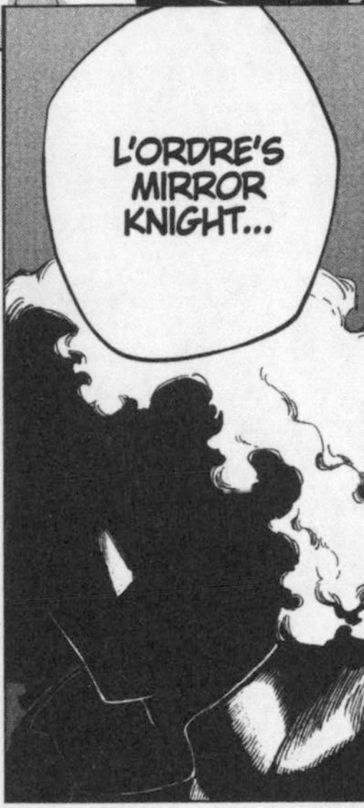
L'ORDRE'S MIRROR KNIGHT...

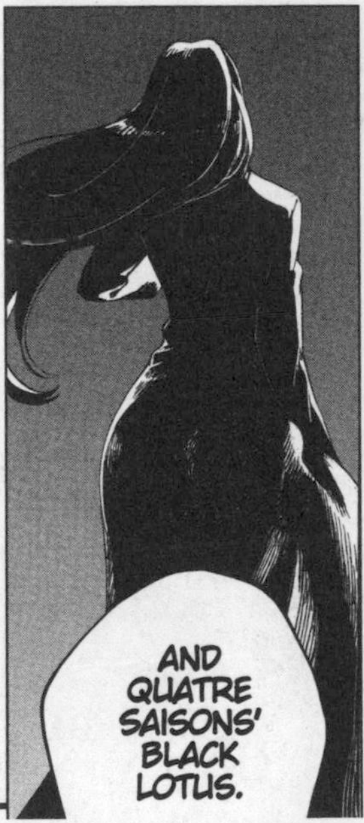
AND QUATRE SAISONS' BLACK LOTUS.

Giselle and Ao... They care deeply for each other, but their lives are guided by a great fate--whether they desire it or not.

The Ancient Magus' Bride: Wizard's Blue

VOLUME 3 COMING SOON

SEVEN SEAS ENTERTAINMENT PRESENTS

The Ancient Magus' Bride
WIZARD'S BLUE
VOLUME 2

story: MAKOTO SANDA art: ISUO TSUKUMO script supervisor: KORE YAMAZAKI

TRANSLATION
Adrienne Beck

ADAPTATION
Ysabet Reinhardt MacFarlane

LETTERING AND RETOUCH
Carolina Hernández Mendoza

COVER DESIGN
Nicky Lim
(LOGO) Kris Aubin

PROOFREADER
Dawn Davis
Janet Houck

EDITOR
Shanti Whitesides

PREPRESS TECHNICIAN
Rhiannon Rasmussen-Silverstein

PRODUCTION MANAGER
Lissa Pattillo

MANAGING EDITOR
Julie Davis

ASSOCIATE PUBLISHER
Adam Arnold

PUBLISHER
Jason DeAngelis

Originally published in Japan in 2020 by MAG Garden Corporation, TOKYO.
English translation rights arranged through TOHAN CORPORATION, Tokyo.

Seven Seas press and purchase enquiries can be sent to Marketing Manager Lianne Sentar at press@gomanga.com. Information regarding the distribution and purchase of digital editions is available from Digital Manager CK Russell at digital@gomanga.com.

ISBN: 978-1-64505-986-8

Printed in Canada

First Printing: February 2021

10 9 8 7 6 5 4 3 2 1

FOLLOW US ONLINE: *www.sevenseasentertainment.com*

READING DIRECTIONS

This book reads from ***right to left***, Japanese style. If this is your first time reading manga, you start reading from the top right panel on each page and take it from there. If you get lost, just follow the numbered diagram here. It may seem backwards at first, but you'll get the hang of it! Have fun!!

1
2
3
4
5
6
7
8
9

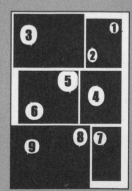